Politics & Power Three

Routledge & Kegan Paul

London, Boston and Henley

First published in 1981
by Routledge & Kegan Paul Ltd
39 Store Street
London WC1E 7DD,
9 Park Street
Boston, Mass. 02108, USA and
Broadway House
Newtown Road
Henley-on-Thames
Oxon RG9 1EN

Printed in Great Britain by
Thomson Litho Ltd
East Kilbride, Scotland

*Books for review should be sent to Geoff Roberts,
3a Southend Lane, London SE6*

ISBN 0 7100 0830 9

WITHDRAWN

Politics & Power Three

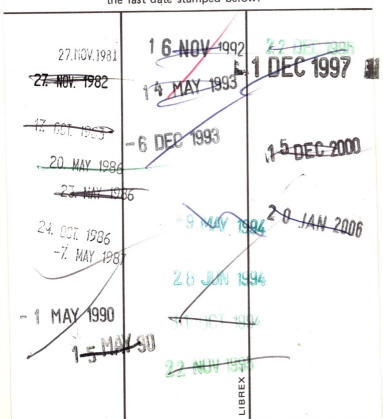

Contents

Editorials

This issue of P&P contains a number of articles on the general themes of personal and sexual politics. These begin with editorials written by women and men on the board who have been meeting separately to discuss these questions over a period of several months. We would like to encourage further debate upon these themes and welcome any contributions.

Amongst other articles we include a letter received from a group of socialists in Ireland. We publish this because it raises serious questions. However, it does not represent any editorial position of P&P. We hope in the future to publish a number of longer articles on Ireland.

Women's editorial

What would a feminist practice be on the Editorial Board of *Politics & Power*?

Given that the board is comprised of feminists and men, that question is one that we have to ask of ourselves as feminists; but it is also a question that we ask of the men. It is a question produced by our critique of the board's practice and the journal's current function. It is a question. But the asking of it is a criticism.

How does the board function; what does the journal express; are feminist questions successfully asked and answered?

What should a 'feminist practice' on the board be? For us, if nothing else, it should be that feminism is enabled to bring to this alliance of disparate socialists and socialist feminists the political priorities, practices and problems of the Women's Liberation Movement. The board should be an exemplar of collaboration between men and women - an explicit and self-aware cooperation between socialism and feminism in the crucial processes of the Left's renewal out of the chaos of its recent decline.

But more: could we imagine that, for once in British politics, such an enterprise would't subordinate:
women as persons
feminism as politics
patriarchy as a problem ?
The answer to all those questions, after the first round, is negative.

Even the most innocent of our readers and ourselves will notice that patriarchy as a problem hardly features in the journal. Feminism as a politics has not been fully embraced by the *Politcs & Power* collective - in terms of what is expressed either in our editorial commitment and priorities, or in the collective's routine practice. Even in *Politics & Power Three*, which has as a theme 'Issues in Sexual Politics', an understanding of feminism is notably absent. We were horrified, for example, that, although Paul Hirst's article (in this volume) raises some extremely important issues, it seems to have been written in a vacuum, without any contact with the ongoing debate taking place within feminism about the family, and in isolation from the situation of men and women in and out of families in society at large.

For some of the women, as persons, the journal has been an excrutiating experience. For others, no better or worse than any other journal. That, necessarily, constitutes failure.

In terms of the journal's contents, we as feminists didn't see our role as incrementally adding to the body of published material this or that article about women. We didn't want to pirate material that should support the feminist publications already around - Spare Rib, Red Rag, Feminist Review, Scarlet Women, m/f etc. This of course has created a problem which only the board as a whole can deal with. We didn't want to mirror the dominant practice, which is: "Why don't we have a piece on this or that, and is X or Y willing to deliver it ?' - for the feminist media have first claim on us. Rather, our input was towards engaging in precisely the dialogue between feminism and socialism that made us cooperate in the project in the first place.

We wanted *Politics & Power* to be *in* that dialogue, taking responsibility for it, giving expression to it, generating it. Since it is a journal, we wanted that dialogue created in debate in the pages of *Politics & Power*. We wanted the material contained to bear witness to that dialogue. In the simplest language, we felt that we should have been able to learn from each other.

If there was no dialogue in the journal, then there was no basis for the alliance between the men and women who produced it, which means that there was no alliance, which means that feminism was defeated - or at best subordinated. Attempts are being made in other areas of political activity to initiate such a dialogue. The most well-known example is probably the conference organised in Leeds last year around 'Beyond the Fragments'. But within the collective production process of a journal, we hoped to progress beyond the over-emphasis on the crisis of the Left as organisational, to be solved through organisational change, which we detected in 'Beyond the Fragments'.

We were in the journal as socialist feminists; we are only too aware that we are women. For us, engagement in such a project was conditional. It was contingent on the journal's practical commitment to feminism's concerns and on feminism being able to express itself. For us, then, our participation was neither unselfconscious nor was it given. We suspect that, until recently, the men's existence AS MEN was unselfconscious.

For many months now, in addition to full board meetings, the men and women on the editorial board have been meeting as autonomous groups. We considered this a radical and positive departure in the field of mixed participation in a project such as this, and welcomed it as such. However, the full implications of such a new practice have not, we feel, been brought back to the full editorial board. There seems to be political resistance to the wider implications of feminism: democratisation of institutions, hierarchies and production processes - including the institutions in which we work such as universities, and the P&P project itself; a commitment to personal change, and the necessity of feminist priorities for a socialist perspective; a concern for a new relationship between intellectuals and society; and a challenge to old and received ideas about the site of 'real' politics and political change.

A second question for the board as a whole, which will clarify the meaning of the first question we asked, is: what has *Politics & Power* to offer the Women's Liberation Movement, and in terms of feminism what does the journal offer to the men of the Left? So far, very little.

We thought initially that the positions expressed in editorial number One could form the basis of an alliance between feminists and socialists. In particular, the critical attitude of that editorial statement towards traditional Left positions on economic policies, the EEC, and the State, seemed to be a perspective whose relationship with feminism might be mutually beneficial. We thought that the situation might have arisen in which socialist men were ready to accept feminist perspectives, to learn from the experience of feminists' autonomy, and to take their lead from the dynamism of the Women's Liberation Movement. We were neither ignorant nor naive about the difficulties of working as feminists within mixed groups. But we were, and remain, convinced that the crisis faced by British socialism and the Left in general demands new forms of political alliances and perspectives, in which the experiences and aims of the Women's Liberation Movement have a crucial role to play.

However, during the increasingly frustrating experience of the journal, we have realised that a critique of existing Left priorities and practices does not necessarily lead to a positive commitment to new forms of political behaviour and the awareness of new sites of struggle for which we had been hoping. Increasingly, we as feminists have found ourselves moving in ever-diminishing circles towards deadlock, rather than expanding into new areas of alliance and exploration. In particular, we have felt that to raise political issues was immediately to be constructed as a disruptive element interrupting the efficient process of the journal's production.

This process has not been a valuable experience for our own development as feminists either. We would be the first to admit that we have not felt able to discuss freely problems, dilemmas and differences within feminism itself, nor have we developed our own feminist thinking in constructive ways, as a result of our experience on the board of *Politics & Power*. Rather, we have retreated into a position of defensive solidarity in the face of an apparent refusal to take what we were saying seriously.

It is not accidental that it has consistently been the feminists on the editorial board who have been raising serious questions both about the 'internal' practices and about the 'external' impact of the journal. The experiences and analysis of the Women's Liberation movement have led us to investigate critically any enterprise which fails to acknowledge the close relationship between knowledge and power. A commitment to reaching a wider audience, not organised into the political constituencies of various Left groups, should inevitably lead to an examination of the form and language in which that is carried out. An awareness that the current crisis of the Left in part stems from its failure to develop policies that in any way address people's real, everyday needs implies an undertaking to explore and respond to those needs in an accessible form. The traditional forms of Left politics and organisation just will not do - as the Women's Liberation Movement in other countries, too, has not been slow to point out. The very crisis of British society is challenging those forms. If the Left as a whole does not adequately take account of that challenge, it is bound to remain ineffective.

We have come to the conclusion that despite our raising a series of issues about feminism and about a new approach to politics, and despite initiating a series of debates which forced the men on the board to begin to think about their existence as *men*, we have remained subordinate and we have failed politically. Why? Because in order to affect the working of the journal we would have had to develop *our* version of what such a project should do to be of use to feminists and to the socialist movement. While the men themselves had to undertake their personal development, we, as women, should have intervened to lead politically, to carry the project onto a new terrain. To be successful politically, to work together with socialist men, feminists have to formulate a new political programme for both women and men. *We* have to draw out the implications of feminism for socialist politics. We have to create a concrete basis for dialogue. We can't wait for the men. Women must lead. This is the demanding but necessary condition for feminists to work with socialist men.

Politics & Power has travelled some distance in what must inevitably be a long process towards accomplishing the aims expressed in its first editorial. We do not wish to diminish the difficulty of that process. But as feminists we feel that the conditions that would lead to a positive answer to the questions we are posing would be a dialogue, expressing in the journal political debate and priorities that can't be found elsewhere, and a productive rleationship between men and women that would reassure us that we're not wasting our time. And as feminists we feel that our

existence on such a board is impossible without the fulfillment of
such conditions. They are not fulfilled at present on the *Politics
& Power* editorial board, or in the journal known as *Politics & Power*.

Fran Bennett
Beatrix Campbell
Rosalind Coward
Anne Showstack Sassoon
Carole Snee

*Carole Snee resigned from the Editorial Board in summer 1980.
The other signatories resigned as this edition was going to press
in January 1981.
Diana Adlam disagrees with the contents of this editorial and
remains a member of the Editorial Board.*

Men's editorial

Over the past decade the women's movement has been one of the most
innovative and dynamic forces in British politics. Although feminism's intellectual and political roots go back many years, a more
coherent intervention by the women's movement developed around 1968.
Since then it has been involved in major legislative changes, made a
significant and often decisive impact in the field of culture and
organised grass roots activities right across the country. It is not
too much to say that these events have decisively shifted the terms
in which a progressive politics can be thought in the 1980s.
    What are the terms of that shift? And what are its implications
for political thought and analysis, and for the content and forms of
political struggle? In its initial editorial statement, P&P asserted
its commitment to the development of socialist feminist politics, but
the way it did so was marked by a predominant left response to feminism. That is, feminism was listed amongst a number of 'new political
forces' that have 'challenged and revitalised' socialism, thus
implicitly allowing the location and assessment of feminist analyses,
demands and forms of organisation to be undertaken *from the perspective of socialism*. This approach tends to produce a politics in which
feminism becomes an instrument for the reconstruction of socialism.
Feminism becomes important not because of its specific objectives and
analyses, but because it is functional for some other conception of
politics. Perhaps because it offers a critique of the left. Perhaps
because it breaks down the barriers within women's minds which prevent
them from being involved in the socialist movement. Perhaps because
it encourages women to enter the workforce and realise their common
interests with the rest of the (male) working class.
    This response is inadequate. Serious consideration of the range
of questions posed by feminism requires rethinking some of our most
cherished prejudices about socialist politics and socialism itself.
Indeed, the scope and importance of these questions is such that it
is by no means clear that a progressive politics which takes these
questions seriously can unproblematically treat socialism as the
organising principle of its strategies and objectives.

Examining the relationship between feminism and socialism is fundamental to the process of rethinking politics which informs the project
of P&P. This editorial, written by the men on the editorial board,
represents only one part of the beginning of this rethinking.

Why an editorial on socialism and feminism written by the men?
Many men who have experienced the encounters between feminism and
socialism over the last decade would argue that radical changes have
resulted both in public politics and in personal relations. At the
public level, many of the demands of the women's movement have become
an accepted part of political debate and programmes in the Labour
Party, the Communist Party and most other left groups. At the personal
level, encounters with feminist women have, for many of us, opened the
possibility of new kinds of personal relations with both men and women.
Yet, despite these apparently positive changes, feminists who are also
socialists are, with good reason, deeply suspicious of the response
of the organised left in general, and male socialists in particular,
to the problems and issues raised by feminism. On the board of P&P,
the men have consistently been challenged by the women to think
through and make explicit what we mean by 'taking feminism seriously'.
There have been real and significant changes, but if we do want to
'take feminism seriously' we have to identify and analyse their
shortcomings and the areas where there has been no change, specify
the problems as far as we can, and start doing something about them.

Too often, socialist men have avoided the difficulties raised by
paying lip service, by apparently accepting the demands of feminists
while actually evading the radical challenge which feminist principles
make to traditional conceptions of politics. Too often also, the
difficulties have been avoided by using deft and ambiguous formulations which disguise more than they reveal and which fudge the real
political problems involved. While finding compromises is a necessary part of any politics of alliances and strategic links, and while
it is the condition for any possible unity among the diverse positions
represented on the board of P&P, compromises become obstacles when
they inhibit confronting and thinking through crucial political questions and differences. This editorial is part of the response of the
men on the board of P&P to the challenge of feminism, and to the
specific challenge made to us by the women on the board. It begins
from our recognition that, if the issues raised by feminism are
crucial, and we believe them to be so, the responsibility for dealing
with them cannot be conveniently devolved by men onto women.

In the course of this editorial we make various criticisms of the
characteristic responses of the left to feminism. But we should make
it clear at the outset that, in discussing these responses, we are
speaking as much of positions which have characterised our own responses as of those of others. Making explicit the assumptions and
weaknesses of such positions has been and is, for us, a crucial
stage in transforming them, beginning to clarify the problems, tensions, contradictions and possibilities in the relations of feminism
and socialism, and beginning to develop strategic objectives around
them.

Feminism and the labour movement

When the women's movement accuses the left of not taking feminism
seriously, part of what is at stake is a series of responses which
purport to have assimilated the feminist challenge, but end up by
leaving the business of left politics more or less unchanged. Overt
adherence to the view that women's liberation is a marginal or petty
bourgeois concern, or can be deferred until 'after the revolution',
is rare today, although representatives of such views can still be
found. But the various positions adopted within the main body of the
labour movement and the organised left are only slightly more adequate.
    The first response is to assert, pretty directly, that the women's
movement is politically wet behind the ears, naive, ignorant of the
cold hard realities of political life. To learn these realities is
to recognise the labour movement as the natural home of all progressive tendencies, but a home which has its own rules and regulations
which women must accept like everyone else: it is about time they
started learning. The labour movement is broad and complex, it has
a long and bitter history of political struggle to achieve the benefits which women, like everyone else, now enjoy; to contribute to the
furtherance of that struggle women must enter and learn to swim like
everyone else. You won't change the movement from the outside, and
once inside you will have to learn that women are just one item
amongst many on the political agenda, somewhere between energy and
the environment. The inadequacy of this response is clear: politically, theoretically and strategically it seems blissfully ignorant of
the range, depth and implications of the challenges which have been
posed to such a politics, not merely by women but by the many semi-
autonomous political movements of blacks, gays, environmentalists and
others over the past decade. A politics where an ossified tradition
justifies the administration and policing of acceptable struggles and
their relative priorities has little claim to be progressive.
    Over recent years this response has been somewhat displaced by
another which may appear more virtuous, and which we can term a
'politics of adoption'. It arises in a number of distinct versions.
The first, perhaps, characterises current movements within the Labour
Party and other left groups. What is adopted are specific objectives
which have been prioritised by and in feminist politics, objectives
which intersect with many of the left's traditional concerns. Thus,
after much political struggle by women, qualified support has been
given to objectives concerning equal pay, conditions of employment,
civil rights and abortion. In some cases this support has been
translated into legislative or organisational reality. The gains
here have been real ones, accompanied by significant changes in the
labour movement's ideology and political priorities. But they represent a shift in left politics only in respect of a limited set of the
questions raised by feminism. Much of the women's movement has been
critical of such activities because of their tendency to reduce
feminism to questions of rights and equality with men, neglecting
the fundamental challenge to the form and conception of politics itself. Faced with this criticism, the response of many male socialists, and many women too, has been blank incomprehension, active
hostility or mute embarrassment, frequently bolstered by arguments

about the realities of politics to which we have already referred.
What is it, it is often asked, that women want which always seems to
be in excess of what is delivered?

A different version of the politics of adoption offers solidarity
and support for the women's movement. To the extent that feminist
demands flow from an experience of oppression which is specific to
women, which men can never themselves experience and to which they
actively contribute, all they can do is listen, agree and support.
Thus male socialists can support women's struggles for the same reason
that they support the struggles of all oppressed people, and feminism
is linked to socialism through the general category of oppression.
This kind of male solidarity with feminism seems to offer a new version of an old problem facing white middle class male intellectuals:
the fact that the objects of their political concern have always been
external and other - the poor, the black, the colonised, exploited and
physically or spiritually crushed in some inaccessible combination.

Such adoptive support and the morality which underpins it may be
denied, parodied or dismissed, but there is no doubt that it has
formed a potent even if deeply ambiguous force propelling much of the
most dedicated left-wing activism. It is no exaggeration to say that
without it socialist parties and groups of all types would not exist
in their current form. However, despite its mobilising function and
utility with respect to certain questions, such a politics of adoptive
support is fundamentally unable to come to terms with the challenges
posed to socialist politics by feminism.

Firstly, in identifying with oppression it is usually possible to
appropriate some element of that oppression: some degree of class
oppression (teachers as productive workers), some kind of material
deprivation (inequalities of income), or some loss of political liberty
could be found to demonstrate the links between the oppressed and
those supporting them. But when the argument is posed as men's
solidarity with women's oppression, this option is clearly not open
- to the extent that *women* are oppressed, men must stand firmly on
the other side of that divide. Where adoptive politics attempted to
resolve this problem on the basis of guilt or humility, it failed.
Any attempt to deny it through the assertion that men and women are
equally oppressed by sexism has led, in our view, to an equally
fruitless impasse.

But more important than this, the purpose of the solidarity traditionally shown to the oppressed has always been to remove that oppression, to eliminate poverty and toil, to decolonise and liberate. And
thus our privilege could be set up as a marker for future attainment
of all. However, with feminism, it is clear that such a position
founders upon the fact that it is not equalisation with the state of
masculinity which is at stake at all. Neither does the women's movement want, or need, men to speak on women's behalf.

It is by no means adequate for men, or for socialists, to be
simply 'on the side of women', supporting them in *their* struggles,
as if they were, in some sense, related to but distinct from *our*
struggles. For to take the challenge of feminism seriously it is
not sufficient for men to adopt a humble, dependent or subservient
posture towards it, or merely to support or express solidarity with it.
To take such a stance is to negate that challenge at the very moment

when one appears to be accepting it. The politics of feminism and of
socialism cannot merely be grafted on to one another, for feminism
both greatly increases and fundamentally transforms the range of
objectives and principles on the agenda of contemporary left politics,
and restructures their political priority and strategic importance.

THE WOMEN'S MOVEMENT AND PROBLEMS OF POLITICAL ORGANISATION

One of the central aspects of feminism's critique of the left concerns
the question of political organisation itself. This critique ranges
from the hierarchical structure and bureaucratisation of left parties
and institutions, through the ways of organising meetings and campaigns, to the ways in which individuals conduct themselves within
such activities. Now critiques of authoritarian, bureaucratic and
hierarchical forms of politics are not specific to feminism, but they
are raised today in their most urgent and coherent form by the women's
movement. And, as we will discuss in a later section, much of the
women's movement would give this political critique a particular theoretical foundation, arguing that these undesirable aspects of the
left's political practice derive from its domination by men, its
organisational form being an expression of aspects of masculinity.
Leaving the issues raised here to one side for the present, however,
it is possible to sketch out two important points raised by this
critique for the conduct of politics.
     The first concerns the organisation of meetings, discussions and
other aspects of political work including, most pressing for us in
our immediate practice, the production of journals. It is probably
true that, as a consequence of the critiques of the women's movement,
most left political groupings pay *some* attention to these questions.
On P&P some effort is made to reach decisions only after collective
discussions, the board is as non-hierarchical as possible, special
responsibilities are allocated on a rotating basis, and so forth.
And forms of conduct are encouraged at meetings which allow all
present to participate as fully as possible. But on P&P, and in
other forms of organisation, a series of oppositions tends to get
set up - democracy vs. efficiency, politics vs. production, special-
isation vs. generalisation of tasks, collective work vs. individual
initiative - most of us could probably prolong this list on the basis
of our own political activities. The difficulty with discussion of
these questions is that commitment to non-authoritarianism as a
principle is frequently only gestural, and the simple oppositions
reveal that we haven't really got very far in thinking through precisely what the political implications of different organisational
forms are. What are the conditions necessary for collective decision
making in specialised areas? What are the situations in which division of labour is essential, and how can undesirable political
consequences be dealt with? How can decisions be made in collectiv-
ities where the notion of direct democracy without the intervention
of representation is a practical impossibility?
     These and many other questions not only face us in our everyday
political practice, but are also crucial for considering the forms of
social organisation which, as socialists, we seek - organisation of

enterprises and workers' control, management of the national economy, legislative and executive arrangements, issues of democracy in the field of welfare and the allocation of provisions such as health care. We have to go beyond our simple oppositions and our slogans of ending the divisions between mental and manual labour or between decision and execution. Serious consideration of these questions is central to a progressive politics. It is the women's movement which has placed these issues firmly on the political agenda and initiated the most advanced discussion of them to date; the notion of a politics of adoption is quite inadequate to conceive of our relationship to it. A pressing question is to explore the implications of the feminist critique, as expressed in *Beyond the Fragments*, derived from the experience of small participatory groups for the possible transformations that can be envisaged and struggled for in large-scale national organisations and institutions.

The second point concerns a different aspect of political organisation and focusses on the question of 'the party'. The party is perhaps the central programmatic idea organising left political thought for the past sixty years - the unified political organisation representing in politics the unity of the interests of the oppressed against the unity of the state and power of the bourgeoisie. In recent years the desirability of this ideal object has become rather less convincing. Serious doubts have been cast upon its supposed virtues not only by the weakness of its theoretical foundations and by our historical experience, but also by challenges to this supposed unity within the field of politics. We face a great diversity of political struggles which is not amenable to a programmatic logic that demands their political identification with a single organisation. Nobody doubts the need for coordinating political struggles and strategies, and there is a clear need for party forms of political organisation to contest in the parliamentary field. But it is essential that we thoroughly rethink this notion of the party and consider again the variety of levels and forms of political practice and the variety of forms of organisation necessary to contest them. The women's movement has been foremost among the forces which should have caused us to undertake this rethinking.

The urgency of this pressure from the women's movement is linked to (though it is not dependent upon) the experience of women and others of the response to them by traditional left organisations. They have been regarded as potential recruiting grounds, or as merely supporting actors in a global political drama, called upon to subordinate the reality of their demands to a political programme which decrees that the interests and priorities of all the oppressed are congruent with one another. We reject these conceptions of politics, theoretically, politically and strategically. This is not to ignore the problems of contestation in parliamentary and electoral politics, nor to advocate some form of syndicalism, nor merely to defer the moment when a new and better version of the party may coalesce out of the fragments of political struggle into a single act of unity. It is to say that political struggles are genuinely diverse and require different kinds of organisation and activity, and that there are no automatic reasons why the objectives of all progressive forces should be commensurate with each other. It is to raise as urgent

political problems the questions of political organisation, of coordination and articulation of struggles, of the links and dependencies
no less than the tensions between struggles in different arenas.

Realising this means that if we want to pose the question of relations between political forces, we must look to the specificity of
movements, their struggles, principles and objectives. The precondition for a discussion of relations between feminism and the left is
a discussion of the intervention made by feminism into left conceptions of politics and objectives.

The politics of the personal

Many of feminism's concerns have been currency on the left for over
a century. But modern feminism has effected a qualitative shift in
the nature and significance of these concerns. It denies that its
objectives can be met by extending to women as a category the traditional socialist concerns with human rights and social inequalities.
A critique of the left and a positive articulation of alternatives
has become condensed into perhaps the most potent slogan of feminist
ideology - the personal is political.

It is this central question of the political construction of
personal existence which feminists accuse socialists of continually
repressing. Over several decades, socialist politics have largely
neglected a range of questions now prioritised by feminism concerning
personal life, sexual relations, habits and norms of conduct, household and conjugal arrangements, values and emotions (although these
do have an accepted place in other, non-socialist, political ideologies). Feminism insists that these are not sacrosanct issues of
private concern, but that they are socially constructed, entail
definite relations of power, and are possible and necessary objects
of political struggle and change.

Many feminists would go beyond just prioritising these issues and
argue that these personal relations have a general form, of oppressing women, and are organised in a general system of patriarchy. The
concept of patriarchy is currently being debated in the women's movement, and elsewhere, and we do not intend to enter that debate here.
But without prejudging that question, it is clear that taking these
issues seriously raises an important challenge to current left conceptions and political priorities.

Mainstream left politics may treat these issues as marginal, but
the unmistakeable fact is that our 'private' and 'personal' lives,
and indeed our very conception of what is 'personal', are constructed
and traversed by directly political interventions made over a long
period. Relations between men and women, sexual practice and other
modes of personal conduct, conjugal and family relations, the rearing
of children - all these and others have been the object of political
interventions for at least two hundred years by a variety of intellectual, political and social forces, often reactionary ones. These
interventions have been designed to produce certain effects in the
personal sphere, with a view to maximising wealth, maintaining the
good order and health of the population and minimising social dis-
content. For socialists who recognise these processes, a politics

of adoptive support is inadequate as a response to feminism's assertion of the necessity and possibility of transforming them.

These questions are not subsidiary or residual, items to be tacked
onto the end of the socialist agenda, leaving the order of business
essentially unchanged. In the field of the personal we do not
experience what are simply the effects of a power whose determinants
lie solely in the system of production, effects whose transformation
is therefore conditional upon and to be secured by economic transformation. Relations of power in the personal field have their own
conditions and consequences. They are, indeed, centrally involved
in the formation and maintenance of present forms of economic organisation. But also they constitute a crucial political arena in their
own right.

However, the slogan that 'the personal is political' takes us
beyond this criticism of left conceptions of what is properly 'political'. For to pose the question as we just have and to leave it
there is to leave the notion of politics virtually unscathed. 'The
politics of the personal' would still equate 'the political' with the
actions and strategies of organised social forces, while 'the personal'
would be the object of those forces' attention. Accordingly, new
political priorities would arise around the transformation of the
content and forms of administration, regulation, funding and so on.
Such issues are important, but the feminist intervention seeks to
extend and transform the concept of politics in a more basic sense.

The sphere of the personal - ways of living, style, behaviour,
personal interaction, sexual relations, language and gesture - is
seen by feminism *directly* as a political field. It is not *made*
political by the intervention of 'outside' forces; it *is* political.
A number of things are implied if the personal is political in this
sense. Firstly, if politics involves power relations and efforts to
maintain or transform them, it therefore includes the details of relations between individuals - since they directly involve relations of
power they are thus an appropriate object of political struggle.
Secondly, these relations are not natural, essential or eternal but
are socially and historically variable, and are thus also possible
objects of political transformation. Thirdly, this process of transformation cannot be pursued through more or less distant policies and
political tactics; the process must begin at the times and in the
field to which it is addressed - at the level of behaviour and
personal life itself. Thus, the politics of the personal, the
struggle to reform behaviour in a wide sense, constitutes an appropriate, possible and immediate political task.

Following these implications through, however, confronts further
difficulties and further necessities for change in our conception of
politics. It is a widespread experience that men have a deep-seated
reluctance truly to discuss and explore this complex of issues,
especially those which most sharply refer to personal conduct, and
it seems to be especially hard for men to discuss them with other
men. For while it is crucial to see how social and political forces
have intervened into the personal, if the personal field is seen
directly as a political field we must also consider our own place
in personal relations of power. The point is that designating the
personal sphere directly as a political field means confronting the

contradictions and relations of power involved in our relations with
other people. This is a difficult and painful process. And at its
most painful it will involve recognising that, out of the rag-bag of
personal and sexual contradictions that we are, we are all too likely
to oppress the ones we are closest to, we love and we make love with.

Similar problems are raised in different ways if we consider the
question of language, especially its use in political debate. The
women's movement has drawn attention to the ways in which particular
forms of language or modes of argument can achieve their effects, not
through intellectual rigour or other merit, but by the ways in which
they structure possible responses, by forcing those who disagree into
silence, or by negating the worth of a disagreement. A particular tone
of voice, turn of phrase, gesture or pause can do more to ensure the
adoption of a proposal than any cogent argument. And even the
emphasis on cogency, on the arts of public performance, may effectively disqualify those with less rhetorical skill or who are less clear
about the precise nature of their positions or doubts. This is true
not only of the pompous, ritualised and aggressive style of much left
political debate, but also, in different forms, of academic discussion
and social conversation. At various times most people are likely to
have found themselves put down in this kind of way during arguments
and discussion. But the women's movement does more than merely direct
our attention to this aspect of personal relations and the power relations expressed in it. For the crux of the feminist argument is that
for women there is a particular consistency in the experience of these
relations as oppressive across the whole range of personal, social and
political contexts, and this experience of oppression is a political
problem and an appropriate and possible object of political struggle.

The point is, of course, not just that personal relations are
relations of power, but that they have a general result, of disad- ·
vantaging and oppressing women and privileging men. It is frequently
further argued that, since this oppression is produced at the level
of individual male behaviour, the various forms of oppression suffered
by women in their daily lives have a common cause. This identifies
the object of political struggle in the personal sphere not just as
the consequences of particular practices and relations, nor just as
male behaviour, but as masculinity itself. And thus this field of
political struggle is conceived as sexual politics, not only in that
among the forms of behaviour at issue are sexual relations, but rather
because the lines of opposition in this field are structured by a
sexual division.

In the same way as many feminists are questioning the utility of
the concept of patriarchy while accepting that the social and historical form of a whole range of practices has definitely disadvantaged
and oppressed women, so there are many who question the utility of
taking masculinity as the organising concept with which to understand
the many and varied forms of power in the personal sphere. Again, we
do not think it appropriate for us to enter that debate here. What
is clear is that many women have experienced and do experience these
relations of power in the personal sphere as deeply oppressive and
disabling. Further, if men are to play a role in political struggle
in this field, the politics of adoptive support by men is inadequate
to the task. We cannot enter the struggle for the reform of behaviour

by simply nodding our heads in quiet agreement and extending our best
wishes to feminists in struggle.

To put it at its most direct, in the personal sphere men and women
are equally at stake. To recognise that both male and female characteristics are socially constructed and fundamentally related, rather
than simply biological or natural attributes of individuals, means
that any struggle for transforming them *directly* implicates men.
Men can never merely express support for these struggles as if they
were external to us, worthy but not our own, just but far removed.
If the argument that the personal is political is accepted in the
sense in which we have discussed it, it must also be accepted that
the necessity and the responsibility for undertaking political
struggles in this field devolves just as much upon men as upon women.

Socialist men and feminism

Some feminists would argue that the failure of socialist men to
accept the centrality of these issues of power in personal relations
originates in precisely that masculinity which structures and gains
from that power. They would argue that it is no accident that a lip-
service is paid to feminism which denies the radical force of its
personal implications. Whether or not this argument is accepted,
and for many of us it is deeply problematic and unsatisfactory, it
is undoubtedly true that the modern women's movement raises a series
of specific problems *for men*.

Socialist men who accept the importance of the issues raised by
feminism face a particular and uncomfortable paradox. As we have
argued, the issues directly implicate men in a variety of ways, yet
the organisational form of the struggles conducted around them by
women is one that excludes men from its ranks. Socialist ideology
has always attempted a double appeal: not simply to those who are
oppressed and for whom it seeks to speak, but also to a wider and
more diffuse constituency of individuals able to participate in
political struggles within the same organisation. Feminism does not
organise on this basis; its political form is by definition a movement of women. We suspect that the consequences of this paradox are
particularly intense for the large number of men who are not aligned
with any single political organisation, or who are deeply unhappy
with the organisations to which they do belong, or whose assessment
of the political potential of their organisations is understandably
gloomy, especially if the general political gloom is relieved only
by the dynamism of the women's movement.

This paradox and its consequences contribute to a number of elements in socialist men's responses to feminism which prevent or
handicap the development of adequate political strategies. Some of
these - dismissing, placing or instrumentalising feminism, and the
politics of adoption - we have already referred to at length or in
passing.

A further element in many responses has been envy. The contrast
between the left's general weakness and uncertainty and the dynamism
and purpose produced by the women's movement easily leads to this
response. Feminism's apparent strength and purposefulness highlights

the inadequacy of most other available forms of politics, yet we are
by definition excluded from the movement. Clearly, this response,
like any other envy, involves an element of imaginary projection.
The women's movement's practice is, no doubt, a good deal less elev-
ated than its ideology; the challenge to left forms of organisation
may transform rather than eliminate relations of authority; the movement is split and factionalised and feminism contains theoretical and
political differences and uncertainties. But to suggest that the
unity and solidarity of the women's movement may be more a feature of
its ideology than its practice is neither to decry it nor to say it
is an illusion. For the ideology provides a sense of unity in diversity, of an accepted terrain for disputing political issues, principles,
objectives and priorities from which the left outside the women's
movement has much to learn. To the extent that responses involve
this element of envy, however, they are neither particularly noble
nor close to being politically adequate.

A different element is the converse of this envy: suspicion. Not
in the sense of doubting individual commitments: the suspicion is
directed precisely at that idealism which gives the women's movement
its strength of purpose and its ideology of unity and solidarity.
Many of us have idealised at different times the virtues of the
working class, the Soviet Union or the People's Republic of China,
only to have to learn the need to confront reality, often painfully.
Along with these idealisations went the false joys, certainties and
knowledgeable superiority which they produced, the 'scientific'
theories we embraced and the solidarity which grew out of them.
Discarding these idealisations, we have adopted various forms of
political realism which are essential to our project in P&P, to the
analysis of existing conditions and the development of strategic objectives, which are naturally being battered by those parts of the
left that still deal in various of those idealised certainties. We
all face the problem of reconciling this realism with idealism, of
producing from the fragments a coherent, committed and principled
politics which does not succumb to the old dogmas. This suspicion of
feminism must be seen in part in the light of this unresolved yet
crucial problem.

Neither a response to feminism which is touched with envy, nor even
one which includes an element of suspicion, necessarily constitutes a
response which one could designate as hostile to feminism. The problem with these and with other positions we have criticised in this
editorial is not necessarily an open hostility, but their inadequacy
for developing strategies capable of engaging in political struggle
in the areas feminism has prioritised. It may be that underlying
these kinds of responses there is a tendency to political commitment
to socialist feminism which is not matched by a personal commitment
to feminism and to the personal struggles and transformation which
that commitment demands of men.

There are, of course, various routes to a proclaimed commitment to
feminism. For men, the number of routes is large and some of them
are hideously tortuous. But a general feature stands out: if socialism is the organising principle of one's commitment to feminism, inescapable limitations are placed on that commitment. The demands of
feminism are encountered and evaluated not in their own terms but in

terms of their contribution to a different conception of politics.
The objectives of feminist struggles are selectively appropriated
on the basis of their compatability with objectives prioritised
within a different political analysis. And what is repeatedly
marginalised is what is most radical in the demand that feminism
poses for a politics of the personal: a politics of sexuality which
challenges our notions of masculinity and feminity, which requires
us to examine male experience, and which demands political analysis
and struggles in the arena of personal conduct. Feminism, that is,
can be proclaimed a good thing for what it does for our socialism,
not for what it does to us. One consequence of this can be apparently accepting that 'the personal is political', while failing to
accept the extent to which 'the political is personal'.

Most if not all male socialists have met feminist women. Many of
us have had close relationships, some sexual some not, with feminist
women. Many of us have lived through a variety of negotiations, some
successful some not, in our relations with feminist women. These
unavoidably affect the ways in which we think about feminism. These
experiences, even if painful, have often had positive effects, making
us aware both of ourselves as socially constructed individuals and of
possibilities for relationships with others we did not previously
recognise. On the other hand, particularly if there is a history of
failed negotiations with women, there can be hidden reserves of
bitterness ready to inform our politics because our lives have
touched against the diverse range of survival strategies, informed
by feminism, which women have found necessary. These experiences and
our reactions to them rest at the level of our private personal histories, yet in unstated and perhaps unrecognisable, or at least unrecognised, ways they inform our theoretical and political perspectives.

The effects of these encounters with feminist women are especially
complex because the ordinary complications of men's responses to women
are compounded by the fact that they are responses of 'aware' men to
feminist women. When men encounter women the erotic dimension is
never totally absent. It fundamentally shapes many encounters. Its
presence may be acknowledged or not, consciously or unconsciously
repressed, or explored and found possible or not. Whatever the circumstances, and however they develop, it is a fact of social life
with which it is probably equally hard for men and women to come to
terms.

At the same time, the erotic dimension is normally assumed to be
absent from encounters between men unless they already carry a specific reference to being gay. It is traditionally in the relatively
unexamined medium of friendship that men have found with one another
elements of support, solidarity and caring. Yet friendship between
men, to the extent that it has been viewed politically within the
perspective of feminism, tends to be treated with deep suspicion, as
a hotbed of male bonding and fertile breeding ground for sexist
attitudes and behaviour. But it remains true that without an open
commitment to homosexuality it is extremely difficult for men to
acknowledge or express the erotic element in their relations with
one another, let alone to recognise that such relations occur
within, and have implications for, the field of politics. To this
extent it is in our relations with women that we are able to enjoy

aspects of tenderness and the security of physical contact which we obtain less easily and more rarely in the relationships we have with other men.

We really have no way of knowing to what extent these dimensions of personal experience shape our own involvement in the issues of sexual politics raised by the women's movement, let alone how they shape the responses of the other men with whom we attempt some form of collective involvement in these issues. We also do not know to what extent it is possible to take these questions of eroticism in personal and political life as possible and appropriate objects of political struggle and transformation. For once the complexity of the issues entailed in the slogan of 'the personal is political' begin to be disentangled, the radical extension of the field and nature of 'the political' becomes clear. To the extent that these questions are raised within a politics which would seek the reform of personal behaviour, problems emerge for which there exist, to date, no adequate modes of analysis, and indeed scarcely a language within which they can be formulated. Nonetheless, a serious attempt to follow through the implications of the politicisation of personal relations requires that these difficulties are addressed.

There is, at any rate, a need for men to involve themselves in the development and articulation of strategies for political struggle within the personal sphere. Whilst this involvement, in the identi- fication of this area of political problems, will necessarily take its inspiration from the inquiries instigated by feminism, it cannot be limited by such perspectives but must be capable of identifying further dimensions and possibilities. Anti-sexist sackcloth and ashes are useless as a response to these problems and necessities. We have seen it tried and it does not work. At the same time, duck- ing and evading the problems does not work either.

What we require, both in P&P and more widely, is a way of acknow- ledging and engaging politically with these issues and a way of moving beyond them. We are still stuck with definite limitations in our response to feminism. Notably we are still stuck with having to respond. Nowhere have numbers of men managed to *initiate* a sustained engagement with the problems of sexual politics. We need to begin by explicitly acknowledging our personal stakes and investments in our sexual politics, to encourage each other in this enterprise, and to sustain each other in the inevitable difficulties.

It is, however, far easier to state this need than either to elab- orate it or act upon it. Perhaps the place where the beginning can begin is twofold: first, in taking further the exploration of the various implications of the assertion that the personal is political; second, in acknowledging that our relationship to sexual politics cannot be subordinated to or exclusively defined by socialism, not least because the meaning of 'socialism' is itself a matter of major and essential dispute. And this process must inform the ways in which we explore and develop political principles and strategies in respect of all those issues bound up in the construction of relations between men and women in our society.

Strategies for the future

How and where are these strategies to be developed? What part can
P&P play in this process? We have already noted the discrepancy
between our recognition of the mutually interacting construction of
men and women in the field of the personal and the available organisational forms within which a progressive politics on these issues
can be formulated. The women's movement is, by definition, a movement of women, and men are necessarily placed at one remove from a
construction within it of a politics of the personal. Existing
forms of political organisation on a non-gender basis - within the
labour movement, or pressure groups such as the Child Poverty Action
Group or National Council for One Parent Families - frequently support a mode of politically prioritising 'the family' which many on
the left would reject.
    However, to raise this problem is not to question the autonomy
of the women's movement, nor to demand that its ranks be opened to
men. Neither are we suggesting, as we have already argued, the construction of a single political formation to organise struggles in
these areas. We are simply registering an important difficulty in
the process of men collectively involving themselves in debating
these issues and in raising them within left politics. That is to
say, the problem of developing strategies on the issues we have
been discussing itself raises strategic problems.
    On strategy, there is something else to be learned from feminism.
Feminist strategies seek realistic and attainable changes in policies and forms of social organisation to improve the immediate
living conditions and opportunities of women. Changes in abortion
law or in provision of custody for children are two examples. But
the aim of these objectives is not to terminate political activity.
They are important in themselves, but also because they provide
conditions for a more general transformation in the social position
of women in all its dimensions. Feminist strategies are not afraid
of the details of policy; it is recognised, for example, that
children will have to be cared for in any foreseeable future, that
there will be people not in waged work to whom income must be redistributed, that social provision of health care will be needed,
and so on. But they also discuss and advocate alternative ways of
organising such provisions as one part of a more general strategy
to achieve definite political objectives such as the transformation
of family forms or relations between mothers and children. This
strategic perspective avoids many pitfalls familiar on the left,
with its careful formulation of unrealisable demands and its
repetitive permutations of reform and revolution.
    We hope P&P will contribute to the development of strategic per-
spectives in this field. Central to our project is the intention
to study, analyse and assist in formulating principles and strategies in respect of sexuality, gay politics, 'the family' and all
those aspects of political and social relations bearing upon these
issues - welfare and administration, taxation and legislation,
cultural representation and political ideology. These questions
are being addressed by recent work in the women's movement and in
feminist journals, and our own commitment represents neither a

threat to autonomy nor an attempt at colonising those issues and struggles. The problems we have raised about the development of this process are to do with coordination and alliance, of forging a coherent progressive politics. We see no utility in approaching this at the level of a single publication promulgating a correct line, a single organisation and a single theoretical doctrine. The task is one of developing a progressive ideology which can provide the medium for the necessary debates in formulating political strategy, and at the level of the links and relations between the various forces involved.

We certainly have no final answers to the many questions we have raised here about the relation between socialism and feminism, concerning strategies, objectives and principles. But we feel that, as an open and undogmatic forum for discussing the issues, as an alliance between socialists and feminists, between men and women, encouraging debate rather than foreclosing it, P&P has a part to play in finding the answers.

In many ways, the nature and significance of the problems we have discussed here have only become evident during the publication of the first two issues of P&P. In consequence, neither offers any great advertisement for the success of the project we have now outlined. It is clear that, in terms of the simplest measures, such as the number of female authors and the type and content of the articles published, reality has fallen far short of our current intentions. Indeed, these intentions have only crystallised for us in the process of debating the problems and formulating this statement. However, with this statement and with the articles in this issue, we have at least laid down a marker for those intentions. The rest is for the future.

Barry Hindess   Chris Nawrat
Paul Hirst   Mike Prior
Alan Hunt   Geoff Roberts
Phil Jones   Nikolas Rose
Alan MacDougall   Dan Smith

Diane Ehrensaft
When Women and Men Mother

Ten years ago the women's movement put the traditional nuclear
family on trial and declared it oppressive to women.   Entrapment as
housewives and mothers was targeted as key to female oppression.   A
prime focus, both theoretical and strategic, was to free women from
their iron apron strings.   Some women, particularly radical feminists,
called for a boycott of women's involvement with marriage, men, or
motherhood.   Others demanded universal child care to free women from
the home.   Some opted for motherhood but no men.   A minority of women
within the movement, who were either already in nuclear families or
still desired involvement with men and children, opted for a different
solution in their own lives - the equal sharing of parenthood between
mothers and fathers.   Contrary to traditional heterosexual relationships in which men are reported to spend an average of twelve minutes
a day on primary child care,[1] this new model of parenting assumed that
mothers and fathers would share the full weight of rearing their
children.   The model is often linked to a broader demand for fuller
involvement not just by both biological parents but by 'significant
others' in the child's life, either housemates, relatives, or intimate
friends; this article will look specifically at the relationships of
mother and father.
      Ten years later, a combination of forces pressures those of us who
chose this latter solution to talk about and assess our experience.
Recognizing the confusion and turmoil experienced by people in this
country around issues of personal life, astute new-right organizers
have responded with the rallying cry of 'save our families, save our
future' as the road to surviving contemporary crises.   The emergence
of the new right is marked very strongly by a bid for women to remain
responsible for primary child care.   At the same time, more and more
mothers are working outside the home to support themselves and their
families.   For many women, this means two full-time jobs.   The
popular press abounds with news reports, articles, and books attest-
ing to the growing interest of men in family life, accompanied by a
drop in male workaholism, while the women they live with no longer
settle for being 'just a housewife'.

Simultaneously, feminist theory, particularly two recent books,
Dorothy Dinnerstein's *Mermaid and the Minotaur* and Nancy Chodorow's
The Reproduction of Mothering, has stressed that gender differentiation and sex oppression will exist as long as women continue to be
totally responsible for mothering. The call for shared parenting
by men and women moves those of us already involved in attempting
such a reorganization of family life to reflect and analyze its
potential and actual effects on the reorganization of gender and
child-rearing structures. We are further moved by pressures from
the new right to develop this analysis within the larger project of
a left counterprogram that more effectively addresses people's
fears about crumbling family stability, lack of personal commitment,
increased social violence, and dissolution of knowable social forms.
This must come not as a romantic plea for a return to the good old
days, but as a step forward to new social structures that provide
the emotional and social intimacy and sense of community for which
people are legitimately searching.
   This article examines the experiences of a small group of men and
women. Most of us do not represent the mainstream of our society.
We are, on the whole, white, in our thirties, with a history of left-
wing involvement. Often we hold professional, non-traditional or
'movement' jobs with greater opportunity for flexible working hours
than most people have. We tend to congreate in liberal communities
(such as, in the USA, the Bay Area, Boston, New York or western
Massachusetts). While most of us hold that ideally all mothers and
fathers living together should share equally in the parenting process,
this is indeed not the ultimate solution for all people. Parenting
by women alone, by men alone, in extended families, in gay couples,
in communal situations within neighbourhood networks, are all models
to be explored and understood. Economic necessity and social context
will influence different parenting solutions. But the experiences of
our small group are important not only because they reveal the parameters and possibilities of gender reorganization within the family
at this point in history. They also simultaneously reflect and speak
to the concern of growing numbers of both women and men who find they
no longer survive in or accept traditional family roles. Shared
parenting exists not in isolation, but as part of the larger struggle
facing contemporary adults in redefining their position in (and out
of) the family.
   The political meaning of this analysis is twofold. On one hand,
if feminist theory stands correct in pinpointing enforced motherhood
as a major source of women's oppression through confirmation and
reproduction of their domesticity, shared parenting challenges that
situation. If, as Dinnerstein and Chodorow respectively argue,
misogyny and gender-divided personality structures have their roots
in female-dominated parenting, shared parenting sets the stage for a
new generation of men and women and challenges a universal structure
in the organization of gender.
   On the other hand, an examination of actual shared parenting
experiences confirms that '"production" and "reproduction", work and
the family, far from being separate territories like the moon or sun
or the kitchen and the shop, are really intimately related modes that
reverberate upon one another and frequently occur in the same social,

physical, and even psychic spaces.'[3] This article, focusing on the experiences of men and women who have taken an equal share in parenting, while also maintaining outside work identities, argues that equalisation of parenting between men and women is problematic within capitalism. The interpenetration of work and family makes it very hard to alter power and psychological structures in the family without a concomitant restructuring of power and ideology in the public world of work and politics. By looking at the general nature of shared parenting, the division of labour and male-female relationships between shared parents, and speculating about the outcome for children in these families, we can explore the tension between the tremendous political potential and the actual limitations of shared parenting today in the reorganization of gender.

Shared parenting in a capitalist context

Who is engaged in shared parenting? Any two individuals both of whom see themselves as primary caretakers to a child or children. As defined by Nancy Press Hawley, elements of shared parenting include: (1) intimacy, both between sharing adults and between adults and children; (2) care of the child in a regular, daily way; (3) awareness of being a primary care-taker or parent to the children; (4) ongoing commitment; and (5) attention paid to the adult relationship.[4] In addition to daily caretaking functions, we are talking about two individuals who fully share responsibility for the ongoing intellectual, emotional, and social development of the child.
     In the late 1960s and early 1970s, some people, coming out of new-left lifestyles, tried to establish a model of two parents each splitting their work time between part-time paid work and parenting responsibilities. Others had a vision of a 'one year on, one year off' model, with mother and father alternating primary parent responsibilities from one year or so to the next: 'We had fantasies of each of us getting half-time jobs while we had babies so we could share in their care and taking turns working once the children were older.'[5] But economic downturn smashed that vision for many. With part-time jobs hard to come by and the sum total of one income insufficient to support a family, in 1980 we are more likely to be talking about two parents absent for much of the day, using child-care facilities and sharing parenting responsibilities.
     We have no statistics on how many women and men in this country fit the above criteria of shared parenting. Those of us involved do know we are a rare phenomenon - in the left and in the women's movement, because so few of our contemporaries (until recently) were parents at all; in the world at large because of economic, social, and ideological realities which dictate that *women* mother.
     At the same time we find ourselves in a newly formed majority category of two-working-parent families. According to government statistics, 28 per cent of American households consist of both a father and a mother who are wage earners, in contrast to 17 per cent in which father is the sole wage earner and mother is a full-time homemaker. Why should shared parenting therefore be so rare?

Despite the trend of growing numbers of women in the work force, the
lack of decent child care for very young children (particularly breastfed babies), inadequate maternity policies at the workplace, income
and job inequalities between men and women, and lack of flexible job
structures leave women moving cyclically between home and workplace,
men more firmly planted as the primary breadwinner: 'The sexual
division of labour and society remains intact even with women in
the paid economy. Ideology adjusts to this by defining women as
working mothers and the two jobs get done for less than the price
of one.'[6]
     Simultaneously, the ideology of motherhood remains strong. With
even liberals and feminists such as Selma Fraiberg and Alice Rossi
arguing for the primacy of women as mothers,[7] the pressures on women
to maintain parenting responsibilities remain great. An article in
the *Los Angeles Times* (August 1977) reports that women with both
children and jobs see themselves as nearly twice as harassed as women
with no children and no job. 'The strange thing about the study,'
reports the investigator, 'is that women don't seem to mind.' In
fact, they often shooed away their husbands' attempts to help, not
wanting encroachment on their defined territory by an inept assistant.[8] Years spent within female-dominated households and within
other social institutions lead many to believe it could not be
otherwise: motherhood is woman's 'natural' calling and her obligation, or her sphere of power and expertise.
     The traditional socialist belief is that entry into the sphere
of production is the ultimate road to women's liberation. Only
through entering the socialised arena of paid work could women
establish the collective political leverage to free them from their
shackles of oppression. Instead, we find the reverse to be true.
They now have a double workload - as paid worker and as housewife
and primary parent. While many fathers have come forward to 'help
out' with kids and housework, doing more work in the family than in
our parents' time, the full sharing of parenting between women and
men remains a rare phenomenon. When we hear about mothers and
fathers gone all day at work, and dad coming home to plop in front
of the TV while mum puts in her extra day's work as housewife and
mother, we feel compelled to demand shared parenting as a mass
phenomenon rather than the rare experience it is now. At the same
time we recognize the ideological and power dynamics that maintain
the status quo. Mum will be reluctant to shoo dad away from the TV
if the consequence is that he and his larger income walk out the
door leaving her to support three kids on her own.
     What have the women's movement and the left offered as guidance
in the solution of this parenting problem? Interestingly enough,
left-feminist and left politics in the last ten years, which have
argued against this dual oppression of women as paid and unpaid
workers, have yet been vague about or blind to the demand for men's
involvement in parenting. For example, in a document drawn up by
the Mothers' Caucus at the National Socialist-Feminist Conference
in Yellow Springs, Ohio, in 1975, the demand that men and women share
equally in the responsibility for child care is not mentioned once.
The closest statement is that 'collective childrearing is an absolute
necessity'. The 1974 Principles of Unity of the Berkeley-Oakland

Women's Union were also vague on this point, going only so far as
demanding that unpaid work in the home be recognized as socially
necessary and that all productive human activity become the collective
responsibility of the whole society.   This lack of an explicit call
for fathers to come forth is again repeated in Juliet Mitchell's
Women's Estate.   Remaining vague, she calls for the diversification of
socially acknowledged relationships now rigidly defined in the nuclear
family.   As for the rearing of children, the dominant demand has been
for universally available child care for women, without an explicit
concomitant demand that men and women also share equal responsibility
for finding that child care or parenting those children.   The alteration of family relationships between men and women was most often
translated into a direct demand for sharing of housework.   The lack
of attention given to men as *fathers* in the family can likely be
explained by the childlessness of most of the women involved in the
feminist movement in the late 60s and early 70s.   Parenting was an
issue which did not hit home for the majority of the women in the
movement.   Those who were in fact parents were often afraid or ashamed
to admit it.   At that moment in history, motherhood became for many a
politically incorrect act.
    It is true that much of feminist writing and politics in the last
ten years, with the exception of sex-role socialisation and child-care
projects, has been focused specifically on *woman* and her oppression,
and only tangentially on men and the needed changes in their gender-
related experience ('leave it to the men to figure that out').   Radical
and socialist feminists, in particular, identified the nuclear family
as a patriarchal underpinning of women's oppression and therefore
often shied away from solutions, such as shared parenting, which might
ostensibly reinforce this abhorrent social institution.   Some radical
feminists have taken the extreme 'matriarchal' position that men
ought not to be involved in the rearing of children at all (men as
sons but not as fathers).   It has been liberal feminists who have
spoken most directly to the issues of fathers who parent.   While
socialist feminists have remained abstract (dealing with the larger
issues of sex, race, and class), and radical feminists avoidant of
male-female parenting issues, liberal feminists have tackled the
structural reforms that speak most directly to the actual experiences
of daily parenting life.   Liberal feminism also claims among its ranks
more mothers than any other feminist tendency.   However, as more left
feminists have children in an atmosphere where it is no longer politically incorrect and recognize that, to be effective, socialist
feminism too must connect more directly to people's daily lives, we,
too, begin looking for analyses of parenting and male-female relationships.
    The lack of attention to men in parenting is not simply a feminist
problem, but the left's as well.   In an article on the baby boom
written in 1978 for *In These Times*, Sidney Blumenthal, pinpointing
changes in parenting in the eighties, never once mentions the willingness or need for fathers to share child-care responsibilities.[9]
Instead, he identifies *women*'s desire and need to work and *women*'s
increased acceptance of day-care centres as critical differences that
will differentiate the new baby boom from that in the fifties.   No
mention of men's increased involvement in family life.   The lack of

attention to men's involvement when addressing parenting issues, both
by the left and by much of the women's movement (with the exception
of a particular radical feminist counterideology that only *women
should* mother), reflects a deeply entrenched ideology, not easily
shed, that simply equates parenthood with mothers.

From a political point of view, shared parenting between men and
women is a novel phenomenon. Most left approaches have called for the
emancipation of women by freeing them from the house and providing
entry into the public sphere of work and politics: 'The emancipation
of women will only be made possible when women can take part in production in a large social scale and domestic work no longer claims
anything but an insignificant amount of her time'[10] (Engels).
Traditional left-feminists, such as de Beauvoir, have argued a similar approach. Alice Rossi, in her 'Immodest Proposal', could only
envision the freeing of (middle class) women from their homes into the
world of the professions by calling on other (working class) women to
enter these homes as paid substitute mothers. In contrast, shared
parenting among heterosexual couples demands that men enter the feminine sphere of baby powder and diapers. It is the practical embodi-
ment of the socialst-feminist demand that women's traditional work
be socially recognized and shared. But rather than turning to the
state or to the public sphere - as in the demand for wages for house-
work/mothering or for universal child care - shared parenting challenges the mystique of motherhood and the sexual division of labour at
another critical point of reproduction - the home. As stated by a
sharing father: 'For me, the equal sharing of child care has meant
bringing the feminist 'war' home - from the abstraction it would have
remained in my mind, to those concrete day-to-day realities that
transform us as few other situations I can think of.'[12] It is a
demand that accepts the viability of heterosexuality as one, though
not the only, structure for personal life, but insists on a radical
transformation in male-female relationships.

At this moment, shared parenting has several social and political
dimensions. We have already pinpointed the pressing need to relieve
growing numbers of women from the dual oppression of paid worker and
primary parent. Also, in theory shared parenting: (1) liberates
women from full-time mothering; (2) affords opportunities for more
equal relationships between women and men; (3) allows men more access
to children; (4) allows children to be parented by two nurturing figures and frees them from the confines of an 'overinvolved' parent
who has no other outside identity; (5) provides new socialization
experiences and possibly a breakdown in gender-differentiated
character structures in children; (6) challenges the myth buttressed
by sociobiology that women are better equipped biologically for
parenting and that women *are* while men *do*; (7) puts pressure on
political, economic, and social structures for changes such as paternity and maternity leaves, job sharing, and freely available child-
care facilities.

What, though, do we know about the actual implementation of shared
parenting today? We have few models from the past, and few reports
of present experiences. A woman writing about 'Motherhood and the
Liberated Woman' urges that 'if women's liberation is to mean anything for people who have children or want to have them it must mean

that fathers are in this, too. But in what ways it must change, my husband and I don't exactly know.'[13] What can we conclude about the viability and political significance of shared parenting from the experience of those men and women who are trying to share 'mothering'?

The sexual division of labour in shared parenting

In this argument, the word 'mothering' is used specifically to refer to the day-to-day *primary* care of a child; to the consciousness of being *directly* in charge of the child's upbringing. It is to be differentiated from the once-a-week games or twenty-five minutes of play a day that characterise the direct parenting in which men have typically been involved. In relationship to shared parenting, one mother aptly put it as, 'To a child Mummy is the person who takes care of me, who tends my daily needs, who nurtures me in an unconditional and present way. Manda has two mothers; one is a male, Mummy David, and the other a female, Mummy Alice.'[14]

According to recent psychological studies, anyone who can do the following can 'mother' an infant: provide frequent and sustained physical contact, soothe the child when distressed, be sensitive to the baby's signals, and respond to a baby's crying promptly. Beyond these immediate behavioural indices, psycho-analysts argue that anyone who has personally experienced a positive parent-child relationship that allowed the development of both trust and individuation in his or her own childhood has the emotional capabilities to parent. Much as sociobiologists would take issue, there is no conclusive animal or human research that indicates that female genitals, breasts, or hormonal structure provide women with any better equipment than men for parenting.[15] On the other hand, years in female-dominated parenting situations and in gender-differentiated cultural institutions can and do differentially prepare boys and girls for the task of 'mothering'.[16] And in adulthood social forces in the labour market, schools, media, etc. buttress these differential abilities. To understand what happens when two such differentially prepared individuals come together to parent, two issues have to be addressed: parenting and power, and the psychic division of labour in parenting.

Power and parenting

Recently, in a single month, I read four articles in the popular press acclaiming a shifting in family structure - women have become more and more interested in and committed to extra-familial lives while men have fled from the heartless world to the haven of the family. Knowing that theirs is not the only wage coming in, more men walk off the job, come late to work, rebel against the work ethic. The articles speak optimistically of a new generation of 'family men' and 'career women' and a greater sharing among men and women in both family and work life.[17]

But we who know the behind-the-scenes story take a moment of pause. We women who have shared parenting with men know the tremendous support and comfort (and luxury) of not being the only one there for

our children. We see the opportunities to develop the many facets of
ourselves not as easily afforded to our mothers or to other women who
have carried the primary load of parenting. We watch our children
benefit from the full access to two rather than one primary nurturing
figure, affording them intimacy with both women and men, a richer,
more complex emotional milieu, role models that challenge gender
stereotypes. We see men able to develop more fully the nurturant
parts of themselves as fathers, an opportunity often historically
denied to men. And we develop close, open, and more equal relationships between men and women as we grapple with the daily ups and downs
of parenting together. The quality of our lives no doubt has been
improved immensely by the equalisation of parenting responsibilities
between men and women.

   Yet we also know another side of the experience, that shared parenting is easier said than done. Because it has remained so unspoken,
it is this latter reality I wish to speak to here, while urging the
reader to keep in mind the larger context of the successes, the
improvements in daily life, and the political import that accompany
the shared parenting project.

   'Men and women are brought up for a different position in the
   labour force: the man for the world of work, the woman for the
   family. This difference in the sexual division of labour in
   society means that the relationship of men as a group .to production is different from that of women. For a man the social
   relations and values of commodity production predominate and
   home is a retreat into intimacy. For the woman the public
   world of work belongs to and is owned by men.'[18]

While men hold fast to the domination of the 'public sphere', it has
been the world of home and family that is woman's domain. Particularly in the rearing of children, it is often her primary (or only)
sphere of power. For all the oppressive and debilitating effects of
the institution of motherhood, a woman *does* get social credit for
being a 'good' mother. She also accrues for herself some sense of
control and authority in the growth and development of her children.
As a mother she is afforded the opportunity for genuine human interaction in contrast to the alienation and depersonalisation of the
workplace:

   'A woman's desire to experience power and control is mixed with
   the desire to obtain joy in childrearing and cannot be separated from it. It is the position of women in society as a whole,
   their dependent position in the family, the cultural expectation that the maternal role should be the most important role
   for all women, that make the exaggerated wish to possess one's
   child an entirely reasonable reaction. Deprived and oppressed,
   women see in motherhood their only source of pleasure, reward,
   and fulfillment.'[19]

It is this power and control that she must partially give up in sharing parenting equally with a father.

   What she gains in exchange is twofold: a freedom from the confines
of twenty-four-hour-a-day motherhood and the same opportunity as her
male partner to enter the public world of work and politics, with the
additional power in the family that her paycheck brings with it. But
that public world, as Rowbotham points out, is controlled and

dominated by men and does not easily make a place for women within it.
The alteration in gender relations within the 'shared parent' family
is not met by a simultaneous gender reorganization outside the home.
A certain loosening of societal gender hierarchies (e.g. the opening
of new job opportunities for women) no doubt has prefigured and
created the structural conditions that have allowed a small number
of men and women to share parenting at this historical moment. But
those structural changes are minor in contrast to the drastic alteration of gender relations and power necessary for shared parenting to
succeed. So the world the sharing mother enters as she walks out her
door will be far less 'fifty-fifty' than the newly created world
within those doors.

For men taking on parenting responsibilities, the gain is also
twofold: he gains access to his children and is able to experience
the pleasures and joys of child-rearing. His life is not totally dominated by the alienated relations of commodity production. He is
able to nurture, discover the child in himself. But he, too, loses
something in the process. First, in a culture that dictates that a
man 'make something of himself', he will be hard pressed to compete
in terms of time and energy with his male counterparts who have only
minimal or no parenting responsibility. In short, parenting will cut
into his opportunities for 'transcendence'. Second, the sharing
father is now burdened with the daily headaches and hassles of child
care which can (and do) drive many a woman to distraction - the in-
delible scribble on the walls, the search for a nonexistent good
child-care centre, the two-hour tantrums, and so on. He has now
committed himself to a sphere of work that brings little social
recognition - I'm *just* a housewife and a mother.

In *shared* parenting, the gains and losses are not equal for men and
women. Mum gives up some of her power only to find societally-
induced guilt feelings for not being a 'real' mother, and maybe even
for being a 'bad' mother. (Remember: for years she may have grown up
believing she should and would be a full-time mummy when she was big.)
The myth of motherhood remains ideologically entrenched far beyond
the point when its structural underpinnings have begun to crumble.
She is giving up power in the domestic sphere, historically her domain,
with little compensation from increased power in the public sphere.
Discrimination against women in the labour force is still rampant.
She will likely have less earning power, less job opportunity, less
creative work, and less social recognition than her male partner.
When push comes to shove, she is only a *'working mother'*. (There is
yet no parallel term 'working father'.)

The power dynamic for sharing fathers is quite different and more
complicated. On one level he gains quite a bit of authority in the
daily domestic sphere of child-rearing, a heretofore female domain.
But by dirtying his hands with nappies he also removes himself from
his patriarchal pedestal as the breadwinning but distant father, a
position crucial to men's power in the traditional family. He now
does the same 'debasing' work as mama, and she now has at least some
control of the purse strings. Nonetheless, as the second 'mother'
the father has encroached on an arena of power that traditionally
belongs to women, while at the same time he most likely retains more
economic and social power vis-à-vis mum in the public world of work
and politics.

   The societal reaction is also double-edged for the sharing father.
Given the subculture that most current sharing parents come from, in
his immediate circles dad often receives praise for being the 'exceptional' father so devoted to his children or so committed to denying
his male privileges. In challenging a myth so deeply embedded as
motherhood, the man who marches with baby bottle and infant in arm
can become quite an anti-sexist hero. But in the larger culture
reactions are often adverse. A man who stays home to care for
children is assumed by many to be either disabled, deranged, or de-
masculinised. One father, pushing his child in a stroller past a
school on a weekday afternoon, was bemused by a preadolescent leaning
out of the school window yelling, 'Faggot, Faggot'. Some time ago my
grandmother, in response to my mother's praise of my husband's involvement with our children, snapped, 'Well, of course, he doesn't
work.' But as pressures of shifting family structures increase, popular response is rapidly swinging in the sharing father's favour, at
least among the middle classes; and the response to his fathering from
his most immediate and intimate circles is most likely a positive or
even laudatory one.

   When the results are tabulated, the gains and losses for men and
women are not comparable: women come out behind. Where does this
newly experienced power imbalance leave mothers and fathers vis-à-vis
their commitment to shared parenting? Women can feel deprived of
status both at home and at work. The experienced sexual inequalities
in the world outside the family can create a tension in the 'sharing'
mother to reclaim dominance as primary parent and establish control
and autonomy *somewhere*:

   'I was angry and I was jealous. I was jealous because he not
   only had the rewards of parenthood, he was into work he could
   relate to. I think one reason I nursed as long as I did was
   to keep myself as Amanda's most special person. It was also
   difficult to share one area of competence I felt I had....
   After all, if she prefers David, what else do I have? I am
   woman therefore mother. I held on to my ambivalent identity
   as student in order to have something of my own.'[20]

Structural forces dictate that she'll be much more successful in
claiming control in the family sphere than in the public sphere. For
some women, particularly those who start as primary parents and then
move to shared parenting, it is not a question of reclaiming, but
of giving up control for parenting to men in the first place. As
expressed by one woman:

   'Neither of us could find a satisfactory way to increase his
   involvement. The children would have nothing to do with him.
   This situation probably came about because he was home less
   often and also because for many years the children were my
   own arena and thus my main base of power. At some level I
   probably did not want Ernie to be equally important in the
   lives of the children.'[21]

The reclaiming or unwillingness to give up a more primary role in
parenting is not easy. It often culminates in frustration or anger
(self- or other-directed) when a woman sees herself as doing more or
too much parenting in comparison to her male partner.

The man, on his part, can feel a number of things when his female partner claims more parenting responsibility for herself: resistant to being shut out by mum, inadequate in his own seeming lack of parenting skills, relieved to relinquish fifty per cent of control in a sphere that he was never meant or prepared to participate in anyway. This is not to say that father merely reacts to mother's power tactics. As we will discuss more fully in the next section, he is often quite active in 'granting' women increased power in the sphere of parenting to give him the time he wants, needs, or has been conditioned to devote to extra-familial activities.

The underlying point is this: powerful tensions arise when the sexual divisions of labour and power in the family are altered without simultaneous sweeping restructuring of gender-related power relations outside the family. Women under advanced capitalism spend too much time feeling powerless to relish a situation where, under the auspices of liberation, they find themselves with less power. I have watched many a sharing mother - undervalued, sexually harassed, or discriminated against at the workplace - waffle on her outside work identity and refocus on the pleasure, reward, and fulfillment that one can find in identity as a mother. This is not to say that she relinquishes her paid work, but that, indeed, she becomes a *working mother*. Fathers, for their part, are not often prepared for the arduous, but undervalued task they're taking on in becoming the other mummy:

'I get an empty feeling when people ask me what I'm doing. Most of my energy in the last six months has focused on Dylan, on taking care of him and getting used to his being here. But I still have enough man-work expectations in me that I feel uncomfortable just saying that.'[22]

Even if he, too, balks at the alienation of the workplace, the flight into parenthood is not a likely one. (Two recent articles, one in the *San Francisco Chronicle* and one in *Ms* magazine, report on men who gave up the pressures of work and career for a year to 'find themselves'. Their children, by report, played an insignificant part in their year's activity of finding themselves.)

The tension between men and women over this issue was illustrated by the marked female-male differences in response to the first draft of this article. Women, whether mothers or non-mothers, urged me to emphasise how *rare* it is for men to involve themselves in parenting or for shared parenting actually to work. Men, on the other hand, wanted me to put more emphasis on the growing involvement of men in family life and the actual fathering that men have done historically *and continue to do*. Both are true, and both reflect the unresolved dialectic between women and men regarding parenting responsibility.

Physical vs. psychic division of labour in parenting

The tensions in shared parenting cannot, however, be reduced to power politics in personal relationships. External expectations, attitudes, and ideology collide with deeply internalised self-concepts, skills, and personality structures to make the breakdown of the sexual division of labour in parenting an exciting but difficult project. Often the

sharing of *physical* tasks between mothers and fathers is easily implemented - you feed the baby in the morning, I'll do it in the afternoon;
you give the kids a bath on Mondays, I'll do it on Thursdays. What is
left at least partially intact is the sexual division of the *psychological* labour in parenting. There is the question, 'Who carries
around in their head knowledge of nappies needing to be laundered,
fingernails needing to be cut, new clothes needing to be bought?'
Answer: mother, because of years of socialization to do so. Vis-à-
vis fathers, sharing mothers often find themselves in the position of
cataloguer and taskmaster - We really should change the kids' sheets
today; I think it's time for the kids' teeth to be checked. It is
probable that men carry less of the mental load of parenting, regardless of mutual agreements to share the responsibility of parenting;
this leaves the women more caught up in the psychic aspects of parenting.
   The more significant division of psychological labour, however, is
the different intrapsychic conflict men and women experience in integrating their parent and non-parent identities. We already looked at
the power imbalance that pulls mothers back into the home and fathers
away from it. Women often feel tremendous ambivalence or guilt in
relinquishing full-time mothering responsibilities. This is common
among all women who depart from full-time mothering, either by working outside the home or sharing parenting responsibility with other(s):
   'The myth of motherhood takes its toll. Employed mothers often
   feel guilty. They feel inadequate, and they worry about whether
   they are doing the best for their children. They have internalized the myth that there is something their children need that
   only they can give them.'[23]
   'To have children but turn over their rearing to someone else
   - even their father - brings social disapproval: a mother who
   does this must be "hard", "unloving", and of course, "unfeminine".[24]
Numerous studies negating any ill effects to children who are not
totally mother-raised pale in the public light in contrast to sensationalist reports of the delinquency, psychopathology, and emotional
deficiencies that will befall our children if they are not provided
with the proper 'mother-love'. And this love is 'naturally' *woman*'s
duty and domain. Raised in this culture, even the most committed
feminist 'sharing' mother will experience doubt. Doubts and fears are
profound because the stakes are so high. By sharing parenting we are
experimenting with the growth and development of our children, adopting new child-rearing structures in the face of reports from psycho-
logists, pediatricians, and politicians that we will only bring ruin
to our young.
   These fears are fueled by pressures from individuals in the sharing mother's immediate life. Her mother is often appalled or threatened by her daughter's deviation from her own parenting model. Relatives are often resistant to the notion that a man should hang around
the house taking care of a kid. People will inadvertently (or deliberately) turn to mother rather than father in asking information
about the children. Letters from school come addressed to 'Dear
Mother'. From the point of view of the outside world, even though
men are being given more and more attention for their participation
in family life, father remains an invisible or minimal figure in the

daily rearing of children. A feeling so deeply internalized as
'mother guilt', constantly rekindled by these external pressures and
messages, creates in the sharing mother a strong ambivalence. Our
intellectual selves lash out at the Alice Rossis telling us that we
as women are the best-made parents, but our emotional selves struggle
hard to calm the fear that our feminist views on motherhood may be
ill-founded.

If mother guilt were not enough, women are confronted with two
additional conflicts. First, the traditional structures of child-
rearing have produced in a woman a psychological capacity to mother.
With personal observations and experience to back her up, she may
have a hard time believing that a father, with no parallel long-term
preparation, is really capable of fulfilling 'mothering' responsibilities. As she watches her male partner stick the baby with a nappy
pin (even though she as a new parent may have done the same thing the
day before) or try unsuccessfully to calm a screaming child, her suspicions are confirmed. Thus, internal forces pressure the mother to
reclaim control over parenting, so she can be assured her children
survive intact. Men are often accomplices in this process: 'Some men
act out unconscious resistance to shared parenting by accentuating
their ignorance, asking a lot of questions they could figure out themselves.'[25] Sometimes women are not willing to be teachers. In the
short run, they find it easier to do it themselves.

The second conflict arises from a woman's establishment of an
'extra-mother' identity. We've already mentioned that women do not
accrue much social recognition at the workplace, that they are seen
as mothers first and workers second, and that when attempting shared
parenting, there is sometimes a retreat from the world of paid work
back into the female sphere of family life. Within her own psyche
the sharing mother has a hard time integrating a work identity with
being a mother: 'When you go out to work, the job is something you *do*.
But the work of a housewife and mother is not just something you do,
it's something you *are*.'[26]

For men, however, the experience is quite different. Historically,
since the advent of industrialization, fathers' daily involvement with
the kids in the nuclear family has been peripheral - usually concentrated on evening, weekend, and holiday play or instructional activities. There is no doubt that fathers have always been important
figures in their children's lives and socialization experiences, even
if as a result of their absence. The traditional father is very
actively involved in his child's life as breadwinner, as role model,
as disciplinarian, but not in the day-to-day nurturant fashion that
shared parenting dictates. The challenge for the man in shared parenting is to move from being a 'father' to a 'mother'.

Today the growing participation of men in the birth experience of
their children often stops at the delivery room doors. Contrasted to
mothers, the sharing father more likely enters the parenting experience with a notion that parenting is something you *do* rather than
someone you are. In early preparation for this consciousness, preschool boys in a recent study not once reported 'Daddy' as something
they would be when they grew up, while a majority of girls named
'Mummy' as a projected adult identity.[27] In popular writing today,
involved fathering is often presented as a *choice*, 'only if the man
wants to'.

Only this consciousness could yield an article in the *San Francisco Chronicle* about a football coach who 'tossed in the towel' after a 68-day attempt at mothering: 'Peters said yesterday he's convinced "motherhood" is an impossible *task* [italics mine] for a normal human being.'[28] If parenting is something you *do*, then it is something you can stop doing. But it is much harder to stop being someone you are. In the general population, the large numbers of desertions or failures to pay alimony or child payments by fathers testifies as to the male-female difference in 'parenting permanence'; the number of women who similarly desert their parenting role is infinitesimal in comparison.

The guilt that the sharing father experiences is markedly different from the mother guilt reported above. Often he feels caught up in his own inadequacies, his own lack of socially moulded 'intuition' in handling the everyday intrapsychic and interpersonal aspects of parent-child relationships. It was mentioned earlier that men often resist shared parenting by accentuating their ignorance. But often they also genuinely feel ignorant, lacking the psychological skills to meet their children's emotional needs. Learning practical skills like changing nappies or administering nose drops is one thing. Developing traits of 'empathy', 'nurturance', 'taking the role of the other' necessary to good 'mothering' is a far more challenging task. These are the very traits that often remain underdeveloped or atrophy in the man's life history and are not easily reinstated at a later developmental period. The shared father's male guilt parallels the guilt felt more generally by men who feel accountable for the oppression of women (or a woman) and for the perpetuation of sexism. But within a relational context, it can become magnified in shared parenting because the object of the father's guilt is not just the women he lives with, but also the children he loves and feels responsible for. This is not to say father guilt is limited only to the *sharing* father. Given that all fathers are involved in some parenting functions, any man who feels he is shirking his responsibilities (not spending enough time with the kids, not providing enough of an income, etc.) can experience guilt.

But the guilt is felt in relationship to something he *does*, in contrast to a more central and deep-seated guilt in mothers for something she *is*. Because of this the 'sharing' man is less likely to be consumed by father guilt, than the woman by mother guilt. Instead, he feels caught between parenting responsibilities and extra-familial identity. When people ask him what his paid work is, nobody asks him, as they do his female partner, who takes care of the kids while he works. No one is awestruck by his dual responsibilities as worker and father. But people and institutions will put pressure on him to perform as if he had no child-care responsibilities. And as a child who grew up believing he should make something of himself, that aspiration can gnaw at him. In de Beauvoir's sense of 'transcendence', being a successful parent does not qualify. Being successful or fulfilled in one's paid work or in public life does. Even when a man repudiates the work or public success ethic, which has occurred in our generation, he seldom turns to parenting as the locus of fulfillment and positive identity. This is well illustrated in the *San Francisco Chronicle* account of a financial wizard on Wall Street

a father of three, who took a year off to find himself. He spent his
time lying on the couch, talking on the phone, collecting tropical
fish, setting himself a 'schedule bristling with physical, intellectual, and cultural self-improvement projects', and 'marveling' at his
wife's frantic schedule as homemaker and mother. His only parenting
activity during this year was watching his son from behind a tree when
his class had sports in the park.[29] Does this represent, at least in
part, the actual content of 'men's growing involvement in the family'
which is making such a media splash? Coming home to a haven where
one's own psychological needs can be nurtured is a far cry from taking
on new responsibilities for the nurturance of others.

Gender-differentiated intrapsychic conflicts of sharing parents do
not necessarily remain quietly within the mother's and father's heads.
They appear in subtle male-female differences in actual parenting
among sharing parents. The obvious difference often cited is that
from years of dolls and playing house women will continue in our
generation to make better parents than men because of their preparation and social induction into parenting. The woman, grappling with
the repudiation of socially induced guilt that to mother less than
full time is to abandon one's intimate relationship with the child,
often vacillates among three stances: (1) overinvolvement with her
child, often to prove to the world, her child, and herself, that she
is 'supermum' (this is parallel to the phenomenon that many lesbian
mothers feel even more strongly - to answer society's accusations
that they are unfit mothers, they are constantly under pressure to
be even better than the best mums); (2) respectful human interaction
with her children based on her ability to explore both her parent and
non-parent self and not carry the whole weight of parenting on her
shoulders; (3) tension and frustration, or underlying resentment,
directed at the child (or other parent), reflecting her own struggle
to integrate, in the face of institutional and ideological obstacles,
her identity as both a mother and a non-parenting adult.

The sharing father is less likely to experience such a tension-
ridden relationship or overinvolvement with the children. He is not
consumed by guilt for not parenting enough; more likely, he is being
raised to the level of sainthood in certain of his immediate circles
for parenting at all. He can maintain effective boundaries between
himself and his child and provide unconflicted warmth and nurturance.
But with doing rather than being as the basis of day-to-day fathering,
and with pressures to do something loftier than change nappies all
day, the pull on the man may manifest itself instead in a psychic
(or physical) disappearing act vis-à-vis the children, a phenomenon
reminiscent of men's general coping style in other emotional relations. Instead of an overtly conflict-ridden relationship, the
father's relationship with the children may be somewhat diluted in
contrast to mother's, or it may periodically dissipate. Father, too,
may feel the same frustration as mother in trying to integrate parenting with other parts of his life. But he has a safety valve not as
easily accessible to women. With more power than women in the outside world and less indoctrination in the inevitability of parenthood
as his primary adult role, he is freer to pull back from his parenting and direct more energy elsewhere. One mother reports she had to
leave town to accomplish this same redirection of energy away from

parenting. The gender-related differences in handling this conflict
are further exemplified in the following account. A mother was responsible for arranging child care for her child one year, while the
father was responsible the next year. Because she didn't have a paid
job and felt it would allow her time with her child, the mother had
consciously limited the number of days her child would attend child
care that year. In handling child-care arrangements for the following year, with the option of three or five days of child care per
week, the father's response: 'Five days of child care, of course.
It's my freedom we're talking about.'

The above mother-father differences are most representative of
sharing couples who try to balance parenting and outside work. It is
somewhat different for the 'one year on, one year off' parenting
pair. Here, when father is 'on', he is more firmly planted in his
parenting seat - mum is out working and just isn't there to take over.
And mum, by periodically finding herself structurally in the traditional fathering role, can theoretically make a cleaner break from
being a hovering mother on her year 'off'. (The importance of this
structural position, often outweighing the saliency of gender, is
highlighted in the account of a lesbian parent who holds a paid job
while her partner, the actual biological mother of the child, stays
home to care for the baby. She reports feeling just like a father
when she arrives home, wanting to be cared for, attended to by her
partner after a long day at work.) But the advantages of this
model must be weighed against its problems: (1) It is becoming
increasingly difficult as more people discover one parent's income
to be financially insufficient. (2) Often the mother's 'year on'
is during the child's infancy, when mother is recovering from preg-
nancy and also breastfeeding.
parent bonding is developing, bonding that carries into later years
and makes mummy more central than daddy in the child's psyche.
(3) Even with the 'on again, off again' parenting model, both parents
are still integrally involved in the child's life, and, for all the
reasons cited above, mum is still often more involved in her children during her 'off' periods than dad in his 'off' times.

In sum, both women and men in shared parenting relationships find
themselves in a dialectical tension between breaking away from and
retreating back into gender-differentiated parenting. The challenge
and success in breaking away from traditional fathering and mothering
is one of the most exciting social projects for our generation. For
those of us who come from second-generation left families, our parents look at our own shared parenting relationships with admiration
and some sense of loss and frustration that their historical moment
did not open up the same consciousness and opportunities for them.
At the same time the difficulties we encounter in actually implementing shared parenting bring home to us the long-term nature of our
project and the necessity of working on all three fronts at once -
production, social reproduction, and ideology - in the reorganization
of personal life.

In this project we remind ourselves that shared parenting is necessary not just for the development of healthier relationships between
mothers and fathers. We also look to the elimination of destructive
engenderment and provision of healthier socialization experiences

along socialist-feminist principles for our children. What reflections can be made about the possible outcomes for the children of
sharing parents?

What happens to the children?

> *Jesse: Daddy, Daddy, pick me up.*
> *Daddy: No, Jesse, I'm cooking dinner.*
> *Mummy: Come on, Jesse, I can pick you up. I'm your mother.*
> *Jesse: No,* Daddy's *my mother.*
> *(Unsolicited statement from a three-year-old son of shared parents)*

We do not know that the long-term gender outcomes for the children of
shared-parenting families will be. Most of these children are still
growing and have yet to unfold their own full history. But we can
make some predictions and analytic reflections on the basis of observations and theories of parenting, socialization, and engenderment.
    According to Chodorow, 'The sexual and familial division of labour
in which women mother and are more involved in interpersonal, affect-
ive relationships than men produces in daughters and sons a division
of psychological capacities which leads them to reproduce this sexual
and familial division of labour.'[30] This is not simply a product of
behavioural modeling and imitation. It is the result of a complex
set of family structures and relationships between child and same-
and opposite-sex parent that resolve themselves in gender-specific
personality constructs. It begins early in life when mother and
mother alone becomes unique in the infant's eyes as the provider of
primary care, and unfolds as the child attempts to individuate him-
or herself from the parents and develop a self- and sexual identity.
The daughter, according to Chodorow's analysis, raised by a same-sex
parent, grows up with a sense of self as connected to the world. She
has developed relational capacities and needs, a psychological sense
of self in relationship to others. Sons, raised by opposite-sex
parents, will develop a basic sense of self as separate, not in relation to another. This construct is predicated on the notion that
object relations between like-parent and child will vary markedly
from opposite-sex parent and child, and that the child's development
of a sense of self as male or female is critical in the formation and
organization of personality.
    In shared parenting situations that begin at the child's birth,
both *mother* and *father* become equal in the child's eyes as individuals
who provide primary care. The exception is in the provision of food,
which in breastfed babies will obviously be done by women. While
food and sucking is certainly a core concern of the newborn baby,
substantial evidence from both humans and monkeys indicates that
touch, warmth, softness, and responsiveness are equally if not more
important to the infant. This allows for equal sharing of the provision of basic needs by both men and women, even when mother is the
only source of food. This is not to deny the reality that mother's
lactation has often erupted as a point of tension between parents
attempting to share equally their infant's caretaking - including
jealousy by men and resentment or feelings of added importance by
women.

In contrast to the female-raised infant, a mother and a father are
equally internalized early in the child's life. The infant's sense
of self is developed in relationship to two people, a man and a woman.
This means that later individuation of self will also be from two
people, both a mother and a father. In shared-parenting situations
fathers are no longer abstractions or once-in-a-while idealized figures to the young child. They are as real and concrete as mothers in
the child's eyes. And both girls and boys will have parallel struggles of individuation from like- and opposite-sex parents, albeit in
different combination. They will have a parental interpersonal environment that is not gender-linked: both men and women will be available for strong emotional attachments. If different interpersonal
environments for girls and boys in the family create different
'feminine' and 'masculine' personalities and preoccupations, an elimination of the different interpersonal environment through equal
parenting by men and women should eliminate those personality
differences.

But this is predicated on two assumptions: (1) that women and men
are really equally involved in the parenting process; and (2) that
families rather than the larger culture are the primal force in
gender development. Concentrating first on the former assumption,
we identified in the last section a tension that occurs in both men
and women who attempt shared parenting at this moment in history, a
tension that still draws women closer to the home and men further
away from it. What might be the effects of these subtle (or sometimes not so subtle) tensions on the children's development of gender
identity and concepts?

Because of ideological pressures, institutional barriers, and
their own psychological preparation for motherhood, many women may
experience much more inner turmoil than men in sharing parenting with
another person and in balancing parenting with a non-parenting identity. This turmoil can influence the relationship between mother and
child. Children now understand that mum does other things besides
take care of them - she goes out in the world, can be an effective
human being outside the family sphere: mummies can be anything (if
the society and internalized norms will let them). Mummy can also
have more 'quality' interactions with the child because she is not
suffocated or psychologically withered by twenty-four-hour imprisonment in child-care responsibilities. But mother is also under the
strain of a great deal of ambivalence. After a frustrating day at
work, where she spent half her day worrying about her child's day at
school and the other half ill-treated by colleagues, employers, or
internalized lack of confidence, she comes home to find her daughter
did indeed have a terrible day at school. (Father may have had an
equally rotten day at work, but remember that he is probably carrying
around less of the mental baggage of parenting.) Mother vacillates
between wanting her child to disappear, and wanting to quit her job
immediately to be the kind of mother she ought to be. The child may
experience some very schizoid qualities in mother, a dynamic in which
mother draws her child close while at the same time she resents the
child for the guilt the child induces in her. The child experiences
the mother's drift into 'taking over', the competition with father
for the parenting role which is still mother's most legitimate sphere

of power, the 'bossing' or directives to daddy who is just not as
attuned to 'mothering' as mummy. If mother herself cannot resolve
how much of a mother she is going to be, her children may concurrently
experience the parallel ambivalence - how much of a mummy is she?
And what exactly is a woman's primary identity in life?

Fathers, we have said, also feel a pull between their parenting and
non-parenting identities. The child of the sharing father experiences
intimacy and nurturance from a man. The child learns that Daddy, like
Mummy, is a day-to-day real person in the family sphere. But if the
child experiences resentment from the father for the sapping of an
otherwise productive worklife, that child must integrate the male
nurturance received with the negativity of experiencing oneself as
a drain. Equally likely, the father, rather than expressing direct
hostility, will at times slip off his fathering cape and do a psychological disappearing act. He simply makes himself less accessible to
the child.

But relating to children involves more than the behavioural manifestations of conflicts and ambivalences around parenting. There is
also the laundry list of things daddies do with the kids vs. things
mummies do with the kids. In my own observation this varies so enormously from one shared-parenting family to another that it is near
impossible to generate a common profile. But if I had to identify
some salient differences that repeatedly appear, they would be as
follows. Sharing mothers get more involved in their children's peer
relations, worry more if their children are well-liked, spend more
time talking to friends about their children, buy the children's
clothes, wash dirty faces and comb hair more, and do more things *at
home* with the kids. In contrast, sharing fathers take their kids on
more outings, take more overnight trips away from home (often work-
related), spend more time reading in the same room as the child, put
kids' clothes on backwards, do not 'fly off the handle' with the
children as much, are able to distance themselves more from the children's squabbles and peer conflicts, and (sad but true), engage in
more rough-and-tumble play with the kids. These differences accurately reflect the dynamics of a somewhat more involved mother and a more
'balanced', but sometimes more distant father.

There is also the more complicate issue of whom mum and dad are
modeling their parenting after. Shared parenting involves moving men
away from the social definition of fathering into the sphere of
socially defined mothering. Whereas mum, too, moves away from traditional mothering in taking on a non-parenting adult role as well as
sharing primary caretaking with another person, her actual *parenting*
behaviour will be more like *mother* than like father. It is more
likely that the sharing mother thinks back, both consciously and unconsciously, to her own *mother* in developing parenting skills. But
who does the man reflect back on, identify with, when he 'mothers'?
One sharing father reports he thinks of both his mother and his father
when he conceptualizes himself as a parent: more of his mother for
everyday situations, more of his father for a global conception of
himself as a parent. Sharing fathers may present to their children
a more integrated identity of parent, resulting from a more complete
merging of elements of both mother and father from their own
childhood.

   For both men and women in shared parenting situations, these
patterns are not universals. But they are commonly observed and
reported patterns in my own experience and collection of accounts.
Inasmuch as these patterns do exist, the implication is that gender-
differentiated interpersonal environments are not easily eliminated
in shared-parenting families. The children of the 'fifty-fifty'
generation will experience, in a much more reduced or subtle form,
the difference between the more involved mother and more distant
father. To what extent this will affect the children in these
families or reproduce gender differences remains to be seen. There
is no doubt that male children, given the models and relationship
with their sharing father, will grow up more prepared to 'mother'
than their own fathers:

   'Our child Blake is now in fourth grade. One of the most
   touching things about him is that he "instinctively" loves
   to take care of younger children. This isn't for approval
   or even for show. It's because his early memories include
   not solely his mother, but as far back and just as often,
   this grumpy lovable old shoe of a person who snored sometimes
   when cuddling his baby to sleep.'[31]

But within the structural family context, their sisters may still
have at least a slight edge over them. And both boys and girls may
still retain a notion of mothering differentiated from fathering, as
opposed to a global notion of parenting. In the quote above, it is
not insignificant that three-year-old Jesse made daddy into a
'mother' as the one who would pick him up and care for him.

   We are not only concerned, however, about our children's ability
to parent. We are also concerned about what kind of human beings
they will grow up to be - their sense of competence, their empathy
and capacity to love, their sexuality, their political and social
consciousness, etc. Here is where we must look at the second
assumption. The child of sharing parents, like other children,
does not grow up in a family vacuum. She or he is socialized in
day-care centres, schools, and other institutions in which women
remain primary caretakers and sex-typing abounds. The media are
also a constant and pervasive force in children's lives. It is
probably true that outside their own father, close friends, or relatives, and occasional successes in drawing men into day care or
early childhood settings, young children will meet up with very few
men in their everyday life. (Despite ideological commitments or
policy statements striving towards equal involvement by men and
women, I have never been involved in a parent co-op day-care programme where men have been willing or able to participate as regularly as the women.) Notes coming home from school addressed to
mother or inviting *mother* to participate in class reinforce this
tendency. And whereas definite gains have been made by the feminist
movement in alleviating sexist practices and structures in social
institutions, the fact remains that sexist divisions are still pre-
valent - in the job market, in the school curriculum, in most
people's families, in media content, etc. TV, in particular, bombards
the child with sex-role stereotypes and presents a world where shared
parenting is virtually unknown. Extra-familial institutions are
strong forces in the child's life, not just in the behavioural shaping

or reinforcement of the child's actions, but in the development of the
child's cognitive and emotional constructs of 'who I am' in the world
as a male or female. For the child of sharing parents, these influences are often in direct contradiction to the intent and effect of
non-gender-divided socialization at home.

What effects do we see of these influences on the child of shared
parenting? Superficially, sitting in a day-care centre or classroom,
you cannot easily pick out a shared-parented child in a crowd. They
know that girls can be doctors and boys play with dolls, but so do a
lot of other kids exposed to nonsexist education curricula. They know
that mummies can go off to work in the morning, but so do children of
single mothers or of working mothers in non-sharing two-parent households. Despite all conscious practices to the contrary at home, the
girls may look as 'fem' and the boys as 'macho' as any of their non-
shared-parented classmates. Influenced in the cognitive organization
of their experience by the normative structures of the world around
them, at preschool age they may look you straight in the eye and tell
you only men can be lawyers (even though their own mother is a lawyer)
or that mummies stay home and do all the cooking and daddies go off
to work (even though daddy made meals all week while mum was off at
a conference). In a society where more and more of a child's socialization experiences occur outside the home, societal norms and
standards cannot help but organize a child's self-concept and organization of social experience.

The influence of gender-based ideological, productive, and repro-
ductive forces impinges on the child not just as he or she leaves the
sanctity of the home to face the outside world. The parents also
become mediators of the culture, either intentionally or unintention-
ally, as it relates to gender development. For example, if the
children are aware that daddy's paid work receives more social recognition than mummy's, this may well affect their self-identity and
their concept of gender. If mummy's work is more marginal or seasonal,
the children may integrate that into their concept of who a mummy is
and who a daddy is. If the sharing mother is in an ill temper, her
child may accuse her of being a witch or a mean old stepmother. No
similar social insult falls off the tongue for a mean male parent.
Also, the parents' own ongoing process of transcending their own
gender-linked socialization is witnessed and possibly absorbed by the
child. The child cannot help but notice that daddy may be clumsier
with the sewing machine and mummy a bit more awkward with the tools.

But the children are not passive in all this. They bring to the
situation a cognitive and social set which is largely determined by
experiences in their most intimate environment. The child is then an
active participant in making sense of that situation. Scratching
below the surface of appearances, we do discover some distinctive
characteristics of shared-parenting children. Illustrative is the
example of a six-year-old daughter watching *The Brady Bunch* on TV.
Alice, the maid in *The Brady Bunch*, is in her apron washing the
dinner dishes:

> Sharing Mother: What do you think about Alice working for the
> Brady's, getting paid to do all their cooking and cleaning?
> Daughter (in irritated voice): Mum, she doesn't get paid. She
> just lives there.

Mother: Oh, well what do you think about her *not* getting paid
    and doing their work?
Daughter (in a tolerant voice): Mum, they all take turns. This
    is just Alice's night to do the dishes. And then the mummy
    takes a turn, and then the daddy. She just likes living
    with them.

In other words, Alice is just a collective member (who happens to wear
an apron) in this sharing household of both parents and nonparents.
While any child today exposed to 'Free to Be You and Me' can spout a
rhetoric of expanded options for women and men in the world, it is
the children of sharing parents who deeply internalize these understandings from exposure to their own family experience. In their
developmental progression they indeed may go through a preschool
stage mentioned earlier where normative societal features appear
more salient than intimate family experience, but over the long term
they reveal a clear and 'taken for granted' conceptualization of both
mothers and fathers as parents and as non-parents. Whereas many
children of single parents also grow up with an internalized concept
of *one* parent (usually mother) as also outside worker, it is in
shared parenting where the children are presented, within their
family experience, with parenting reorganization for both men and
women. They not only know that mothers can go out and work, they
also know that fathers can nurture, cuddle, and run the house for
days at a time.

In the great burst of studies supporting nonsexist education, numerous findings pointed to the greater cognitive competence and creativity in children who were not sex-typed.[32] This did not refer only
to children of shared parents, but to any child who was not socialized
into sex-stereotyped functioning. By extrapolation, however, it
makes sense that a low degree of sex-typing within the family would
occur where women and men both actively merge socially defined
aspects of 'masculinity' and 'femininity' into their own functioning.
Inasmuch as shared parents do this, their children ought to have
high levels of competence and creativity. While the family's class,
social position, and content of parental practices, not to mention
school experience, are obviously also strong determinants of a
child's competence and creativity, my observations do attest to the
sense of assuredness, initiative, and innovativeness with which many
children of shared parents move through the world. They not only
receive messages of what men, women, and therefore any person *can*
do, they actively watch and experience their own mothers and fathers
doing it. In a society where gender is still so important, these
internalized experiences become critical to an expanded notion of self.

One problem, however, is that we may be creating family structures
where boys and girls both get to observe directly what was traditionally 'feminine', albeit now done by women and men, while the traditionally 'masculine' functions remain abstract. Most modern households in which shared parents (and non-sharing parents) live do not
necessitate a large number of heavy physical activities. Either outside experts are called in or mechanical devices do the work that was
traditionally 'masculine' and done in the home (e.g. carpentry,
plumbing, heavy yard work). What is left for the children to observe
and experience is mothers and fathers actively involved in tradition-

ally 'feminine' tasks - child-rearing, housekeeping, etc. Then mum
or dad disappear each day into the abstract world of paid work, which
is for the most part separate from the child's direct experience.
What opportunities do the children have to *directly* observe mum and
dad functioning in traditionally 'masculine' tasks? Compared to
direct observation of feminine tasks, very little. If we accept that
gender reorganization should include a blending of the socially
defined masculine and feminine, in addition to bringing children to
their workplace (which, unfortunately, often tends to be sex-
segregated), shared parents (as well as any other parent) must also
be conscious of infusing into the child's immediate experience a
greater degree of mum and dad functioning in spheres stereotypically
of main domain.[33]

We can speculate that children of shared parenting will develop a
greater sense of trust in the world than children with only one
primary parent. They grow up with a confidence that at least two,
rather than one, persons can offer them basic nurturance and security.
One could also predict that monogamy would not be as deeply ingrained.
If monogamy is in part shaped in the child's psyche by the original
mother-infant possessive dyad, breaking up the dyad with basic nurturing from another person conceivably shapes in the child a concept of
love beyond a pas de deux. We can even predict an expanded notion of
sexuality, perhaps a greater incidence of bisexuality. With primary
care coming equally from women and men, and with individuation from
both a father and a mother, rapprochement will also be toward a man
and a woman for children of either sex. If gender becomes less of a
central factor in who these children are, then sexuality may be more
loosely tied to whether the object of love is male or female. But
these are areas in which we must wait patiently for the children to
grow into adulthood to unfold their own story.

Both the new right and left-wing critics of feminism condemn
children growing up in anything but traditional nuclear families to
a life of narcissism, neurosis, or psychopathy, stemming from the
breakdown of authority in the family. What becomes confused in their
argument is the differentiation between *authority* and *authoritarianism*.
Children of shared parents indeed understand a hierarchy of responsibility and the 'leadership' position of their parents in the family.
What they do not experience is the unilateral power base of the patriarchal father who offers conditional love in exchange for unconditional submission. Because children of shared parents continually observe
two adults democratically negotiating decision-making and division of
responsibility in the home, they are presented with a new model of
authority based on collectivity and flexibility rather than un-
challenged power. Since two people fully share the parenting responsibility, one cannot simply criticize the other's parenting as a role
foreign to him- or herself. The criticism comes within a joint
endeavour in which they must mutually arrive at a parenting solution
satisfying to both. Thus mutuality and consensus, rather than directives and compliance, further inform the child's internalization of
democratic processes. In the actual parent-child interaction, the
child learns quite early that authority does not lie in just one
person's hands. There are always two, rather than one person, with
whom the child can equally approach or consult on matters requiring

parental decisions or guidance. Neither parent unilaterally holds the purse strings, manages the household, or enforces disciplinary actions. With authority more diffused than centralized, the child has more room to move as a meaningful participant in family decisions and functioning.

Shared parenting alters authority relations not only between parent and child, but between males and females. With all the qualifications noted above, shared-parenting families substitute 'unisex' parenting for the 'instrumental-emotional' gender division of traditional families. Girls and boys develop new understandings of equal authority among males and females. Even though all children in our culture have no doubt been affected by the Wonder Woman mystique, girls and boys of shared parents understand at a concrete level, not just in surreal fantasies, the strength and independence of women vis-à-vis men, the possibility of equality, rather than dominance-submission, in female-male relationships. This is often translated into peer relationships in which daughters are pugnacious, audacious, and stalwart in their interactions with boys and sons have a healthy respect and acceptance of the social power of girls.

While trust, democratic impulses, and balancing of social power between females and males may be outcomes for children of shared parents, a smothering from over-parenting is also possible. An ostensible advantage of shared parenting is that with two (or more) primary care-takers, one of the care-takers can comfortably take 'time off', have space for oneself away from the children. The reality, however, is that shared parenting often leads to a consciousness of 'on all the time' for both parents. From the point of view of the child, not just one parent but two parents are actively ego-involved in the child's development. Not just one but both parents tell the child to drag an umbrella to school on a rainy day. The potential for overprotectiveness, overinvolvement, or stifling of autonomy is obvious. Also, the implication for *two* parents now totally absorbed in parenting consciousness is potential 'parent burn-out' not just by one, but by two people, leaving the child with two strung-out parents.

There is no doubt that children growing up in a shared-parenting household are exposed to a different socialization experience than children from other family structures. When daddy and only daddy can be mother, something crucial has changed. But we must wait to see what the *adult* personality outcomes of these children will be. In the reorganization of gender, the degree of reduction in the female-male division of psychological capacities can help us understand the significance of family structure and processes in producing gender. If female and male differences are indeed reduced in these people, compared to people who did not experience shared parenting, we will find validation for the primacy of family structure in gender development. If these children grow up with psychological capacities undifferentiated from families where parenting is more conventional, this will reflect either the greater primacy of extra-parental forces or the ineffectiveness of shared parents in successfully re-organising gender-related parenting (or both). These experiences help us to understand the ways in which reproduction, production, and ideology interpenetrate and can thus inform our strategy for transforming gender relations.

Conclusion

I have analyzed the experiences of a very small group of people. At
the same time, all signs show a rapidly changing family structure in
which parents do not live in nuclear families at all or when they do,
both continue in the labour market. Disequilibrium is great right
now: the concurrent pressures of work and what is experienced as
'family upheaval' overwhelm many. For these reasons a reorganization
of parenting becomes for many not a 'choice', as it has been for many
attempting shared parenting, but a necessity. It is this necessity
that gives us on the left the leverage to introduce a new concept of
family structure that challenges both the sex-gender system and capitalist modes of reproduction. The new right has been built partly
through addressing people's fears about the rapidly deteriorating
quality of life. Recognizing people's concern for the future, particularly the well-being of their children, the new right offers reactionary programmes which, retreating to old patriarchal forms, claim
to save unborn offspring from murder, shield families from untoward
homosexual influence, and put the money back in the family's pocket
where it belongs. The left and the women's movement have to address
the concerns that underlie these issues. Many of us have begun to
look more closely at issues of family or personal life. Some have
taken the tack of defending or rebuilding the family in the face of
capitalist attack. Others of us feel wary of an approach which by
uncritically 'defending the family', tends to reproduce the romantic,
anti-feminist thrust of the new right. We need to demonstrate the
ability of *new* social and family structures to provide the satisfactions that people legitimately long for - emotional and sexual intimacy, child-rearing by caring people, a sense of community.
    In the latter context, share parenting is an important political
effort. It challenges an oppressive feature of the family - the universality of motherhood. Shared parenting frees women from the dual
burden of paid and unpaid work, affords men access to the growth and
development of children and children access to the growth and development of men, and helps to eliminate gender-linked divisions between
males and females that reproduce the sex-gender system. But shared
parenting must also be seen as only one aspect of the larger demand
for new forms of personal life to replace the decaying traditional
nuclear family and provide solutions to the problems of personal
tension, violence, and loneliness experienced by so many. We need
to restructure social responsibility for children so that not just
mothers and fathers but also non-family-members have access to and
responsibility for the care of children. What is labeled by many as
a crisis of the family should more aptly be approached as a historical
shift in family structure. In this period of flux, we can try to
create and sustain a new fluidity between family and non-family for
the responsibility of children, a greater involvement of men in this
process, new kinds of authority relations between parents and children, and forms other than the traditional nuclear family in which
people can choose to live. These goals necessitate addressing the
interpenetration of reproduction, production, and ideology. These
goals will not be achieved overnight. Yet we know much *can* be

accomplished, and such efforts will be an increasingly important part
of political and social life in the coming years.

NOTES

* This article was first published in the USA in *Socialist Review* 49,
January/February 1980. While based on research into experience in
shared parenting in the USA, it is nonetheless most relevant to
similar experience in Britain. The Editorial Board of *Politics & Power*
is extremely grateful for permission to reprint the article here with
a small number of minor changes, and we hope it may spark off a much
needed debate of these issues in this country.
     The author wishes to thank Nancy Chodorow, Jim Hawley, Barry
Kaufman, Gail Kaufman, Joanna Levine, Elli Meeropol, Robby Meeropol,
David Plotke, Marcy Whitebook and the *Socialist Review* West collective for their criticism and support in writing this paper.

1 Joseph Pleck, *Men's New Roles in the Family: Housework and Child
   Care* (Ann Arbor, Mich.: Institute for Social Research, December
   1976).
2 See, for example, Betty Friedan, 'Feminism Takes a New Turn', *New
   York Times Magazine*, 16 November 1979; Caroline Bird, *The Two-
   Paycheck Marriage*; Jane Geniesse, 'On Wall Street: The Man Who
   Gave Up Working', *San Francisco Chronicle*, 11 November 1979;
   Lindsy Van Gelder, 'An Unmarried Man', *Ms.*, November 1979.
3 Rosalind Petchesky, 'Dissolving the Hyphen: A Report on Marxist-
   Feminist Groups 1-5', in Z. Eisenstein, *Capitalist Patriarchy and
   the Case for Socialist Feminism* (New York: Monthly Review Press,
   1978), p.376.
4 Nancy Press Hawley, 'Shared Parenthood', in Boston Women's Health
   Collective, *Ourselves and Our Children*, Random House, New York
   1978; this framework differentiates shared *parenting* from shared
   custody, in which two parents, separated or divorced, share the
   children back and forth.
5 Alice Abarbenal, 'Redefining Motherhood', in Louise Kapp Howe,
   ed., *The Future of the Family* (New York: Simon and Schuster, 1972),
   p.349.
6 Z. Eisenstein, 'Developing a Theory of Capitalist Patriarchy and
   Socialist Feminism', in Eisenstein, ed., *Capitalist Patriarchy*, p.29.
7 See Selma Fraiberg, *In Defence of Mothering: Every Child's Birth-
   right* (New York: Basic Books, 1977); and Alice Rossi, 'A Biosocial
   Perspective on Parenting', *Daedalus*, Spring 1977, pp.1-31.
8 Susan Steward, 'Working Women Don't Get All the Breaks', *Los
   Angeles Times*, 31 August 1977.
9 Sidney Blumenthal, 'A Baby Boom in the 80s'?' *In These Times*, 30
   August-5 September 1978.
10 Frederick Engels, in *The Women Question* (New York: International
   Publishers, 1951).
11 Alice Rossi, 'Equality between the Sexes: An Immodest Proposal',
   Daedalus, Spring 1964; reprinted in Robert J. Lifton, ed., *The
   Women in America* (Boston; Beacon, 1967).

12 Kenneth Pitchford, 'The Manly Art of Child Care', *Ms.*, October 1978, p.98.
13 D. Baldwin, 'Motherhood and the Liberated Woman', *San Francisco Chronicle*, 12 October 1978.
14 A. Abarbenal, 'Redefining Motherhood', p.366.
15 Cf. Ann Oakley, *Women's Work*, ch.8, 'Myths of Woman's Place, 2: Motherhood' (New York: Vintage, 1974); Wini Breines, Margaret Cerullo, and Judith Stacey, 'Social Biology, Family Studies, and Antifeminist Backlash', *Feminist Studies*, February 1978, pp.43-68.
16 Nancy Chodorow, *The Reproduction of Mothering: Psychoanalysis and the Sociology of Gender* (Berkeley, University of California Press, 1978).
17 Cf. articles cited in reference 2.
18 Sheila Rowbotham, *Woman's Consciousness, Man's World* (Baltimore: Penguin, 1973), p.61.
19 Oakley, *Woman's Work*, p.220.
20 Abarbenal, p.360.
21 Quoted interview in Hawley, 'Shared Parenthood', p.134; this desire to maintain parenting within woman's sphere as a source of power might have some influence, conscious or unconscious, on the feminist movement's tendency to avoid demands for fathers' involvement in parenting.
22 Steinberg, p.370.
23 Oakley, *Women's Work*, p.211.
24 Ibid., p.189.
25 Hawley, 'Shared Parenthood', p.139.
26 Rowbotham, *Women's Consciousness*, p.76.
27 Barbara Chasen, 'Sex Role Stereotyping and Pre-Kindergarten Teachers', *Elementary School Journal*, 1974, pp.74, 225-235.
28 'A Father Who Failed as a Mother', *San Francisco Chronicle*, 6 September 1978.
29 Jane Geniesse, 'On Wall Street: The Man Who Gave Up Working', *San Francisco Chronicle*, 13 November 1979.
30 Chodorow, *Reproduction of Mothering*, p.7.
31 Pitchford, 'Manly Art', p.89.
32 Cf. Eleanor Maccoby and Carol Jacklin, *The Psychology of Sex Differences* (Stanford, Calif.: Stanford University Press, 1974).
33 My thanks to Nancy Chodorow for her thoughts on this aspect of shared parenting.

I&C

"Political analysis and criticism have in a large measure still to be invented."

(M. Foucault)

I&C (formerly titled Ideology & Consciousness) began in 1977 by taking stock of new intellectual currents available to left politics: radical critiques of social science, Marxist theories of ideology, and approaches via psychoanalysis, feminism and theories of language, signs and discourse to the 'subjective' dimension of power, domination and struggle.

Recent issues of I&C have moved towards a re-examination of the custodial-governmental functions of the 'human sciences' and the relations of power and knowledge they entail. As a journal, I&C sees its role less as building a manifesto of imperatives than as offering an exploratory space for questioning, reflection and research. For I&C political analysis entails a sceptical attitude to ready-made blocs of theoretical doctrine, but not the rejection of theory itself as a tool for grasping the real. One of I&C's particular strengths is the presentation of work by new writers in other countries, mostly outside the established international of the new left, who pursue a more intellectually open and honest confrontation with their political present.

I&C 7 : TECHNOLOGIES OF THE HUMAN SCIENCES. Our latest issue includes: 'What is psychology?', an essay by the celebrated French historian of science George Canguilhem; a new introduction by Michel Foucault to Canguilhem's work, its political influence and originality; 'Psychiatry as a Political Science', a review article by Peter Miller; a study of the roots of criminology, science of 'social defence', by Pasquale Pasquino; Beverley Brown on the updated liberalism of the Williams report's proposals for law and pornography; Jenny Somerville's evaluation of Nicos Poulantzas's last major work to be published in English; State, Power, Socialism.

Some articles in previous issues: Nikolas Rose, 'The psychological complex: mental measurement and social administration' (I&C5); Jacques Donzelot, 'The Poverty of Political Culture' (I&C5);Diana Adlam and Angie Salfield, 'A Matter of Language', review of Language and Materialism by Rosalind Coward and John Ellis(I&C3);Michel Foucault, 'Politics and the study of discourse' (I&C3),'On governmentality' (I&C6); Colin Gordon,'Other Inquisitions', an introduction to Foucault (I&C6);Pasquale Pasquino, 'The genealogy of capital - police and the State of prosperity', Giovanna Procacci, 'Social economy and the government of poverty' (I&C4).

I&C is published twice yearly in spring and autumn by I&C Publications Ltd.

Bookshop distribution: Full Time/Southern Distribution.

Personal subscriptions (UK): £2.80 for two issues (students/claimants £2.25). Back issues (nos. 1-6) £2 each.

Address: I&C (SP), c/o G.Burchell, Westminster College, North Hinksey, Oxford OX2 9AT

Jill Hodges
Children and Parents: Who Chooses?

(A review of *Beyond the Best Interests of the Child*, Free Press, Macmillan, 1973; *Before the Best Interests of the Child*, Free Press, Macmillan, 1979
both by Joseph Goldstein, Anna Freud and Albert J. Solnit)

One thing is evident throughout *Before the Best Interests* ... and its predecessor. It is a discussion of policies concerning children which starts resolutely from the position of the child, and sticks to it unswervingly. One may argue that traditional social policy starts from exactly that same position, which indeed is embodied in the successive pieces of legislation affecting children. Most recently the Child Care Act 1980,[1] which brings together many previous enactments, begins with the 'General duty of local authorities to promote welfare of children' (Part 1, Section 1, subsection 1); 'It shall be the duty of every local authority to make available such advice, guidance and assistance as may promote the welfare of children by diminishing the need to receive children into or keep them in care under this Act or to bring children before a juvenile court...'. The Children Act 1975[2] (Part 1, Section 3) not only instructs that in decisions relating to adoption 'the court or adoption agency shall have regard to all the circumstances, first consideration being given to the need to safeguard and promote the welfare of the child throughout his childhood' but also that it 'shall so far as practicable ascertain the wishes and feelings of the child regarding the decision and give due consideration to them, having regard to his age and understanding'. However, the discussion in this review will indicate some of the ways in which the position put forward by G F & S differs from the traditional one with, in particular, its conflicting emphasis on the rights of the parent - rights which operate in a different register from the one with which G F & S concern themselves, and which we shall return to consider later.

An important point resulting from G F & S's taking up the standpoint of the child in this way, is that theirs is a discussion of the family which, though in many respects radical, differs sharply from the many other radical critiques of the family which start from the standpoint of the position of women. Indeed, it almost takes for granted many of the positions they put forward. It makes no assumption that it is women any more than men who should be concerned with child care, let alone women as part of a couple in which each partner fulfils a stereotypic sex role. It assumes neither that a single

parent of whatever sex is inadequate, nor that a wider group of parenting adults is necessarily undesirable. It deals in the categories of
'parent' (to be discussed below) and child, and the only programmatic
assertion critical to its argument is that a child needs a continuing
relationship with at least one psychological parent. Indeed many of
the debates which preoccupy feminism in relation to the family and
childrearing seem fairly irrelevant to the issues raised in Goldstein,
Freud and Solnit's analysis. This is not to say that these debates
are unimportant or irrelevant in themselves; rather it is to register
the fact that they are built largely around *adult* roles, around the
privilege of the man and the 'open or concealed domestic slavery of
the wife' in Engels' phrase - part of that slavery being the burden
of childrearing. Different adult roles, and different divisions of
the physical and emotional work of childrearing are argued for primarily as ways of revolutionising adult relationships, adult sexual
divisions, adult internalised gender identities, stereotypically male
or female; as ways of overcoming the oppression of women in the family.

As well as the focus around the *adult* domestic relationships,
another feature of this particular form of feminist analysis might
be noted. 'Domestic labour' covers a wide range of work; within this
range certain jobs have very differentiated requirements. Some sorts
of housework could in theory be done by a different person every day
without any problem. But there are some jobs, and childcare par
excellence, where it has to be the same constant adults to do the
job adequately. Subsuming childcare under the more general heading
of domestic labour or of housework may be polemically necessary, to
make the point that the hand that rocks the cradle is a hand which is
working - and not being paid for it, either. But it may also tend to
blur the specific nature of childcare, into a more general part of
women's oppression. It is still the level of adults which is the
primary one. The question 'What happens to the children?'[3] comes
later; and even when this is the focus, it is difficult to bring the
discussion into much of a relationship with G F & S's approach. The
reason is not so much that radical and feminist discussion of the
effects upon children deal with issues like the socialisation of
particular forms of gender identity - issues which G F & S do not
address. Rather, the basic difficulty lies in the fact that the
radical and feminist discussions are programmatic. They outline goals
to be struggled for, new forms of identity to be attained, new forms
of relationship to be created; or at the very least, old traps of
oppression, not to be fallen into. But this programmatic approach,
which indicates what is positively to be required of a family, is a
form rejected by G F & S's analysis. Instead of setting out what
they regard as the characteristics of the desirable family - a utopian
view of what they would ideally approve - they define, rather, the
negative criteria of what can no longer be regarded as falling within
the wide limits of a functioning ('psychological') family.

All three authors are psychoanalytically trained. (Goldstein is
a professor of law, and Solnit of paediatrics and psychiatry.)
However, the content of their books will come as a surprise to anyone
expecting prescriptions about 'proper' childrearing based on their
personal or psychoanalytic opinions. Let us now begin to examine
what they *do* deal with.

In their first book, *Beyond the Best Interests of the Child* (1973),
G F & S argued for changes in the practices affecting children whose
custody had *already* become a matter of State concern. Their recommendations were aimed at child placement procedures which would, in
their words,
  - safeguard the child's need for continuity of relationships;
  - reflect the child's, not the adult's, sense of time;
  - take into account the law's incapacity to supervise interpersonal relationships and the limits of knowledge in making
  long-range predictions;
  - provide the least detrimental alternative for safeguarding the
  child's growth and development.
Some at least of their formulations have become widely accepted as
part of social work thinking although not embodied in legal provisions.
'The child's sense of time' is a case in point, and one which illustrates the most striking feature of the book - an approach which is
consistently and singlemindedly *from the point of view of the child's
interests*. They point out the asymmetry of the child's and the
adult's sense of time and the importance of recognising this asymmetry
in child placement decisions. To adults, such as lawyers, social
workers or parents themselves, delays of a few months or even longer
while the appropriate placement is debated and decided may seem
relatively brief and inconsequential. To the infant or child who
(depending on her age) has a relative lack of the adult's emotional
and cognitive ability to cope with uncertainty, loss and disruptions
of continuity, the time may be overwhelmingly long. Not only may the
delay be hell for the child while it lasts, but it may permanently or
temporarily damage the ability of the child to make satisfactory new
relationships once the placement eventually materialises. Goldstein,
Freud and Solnit point out that child placement procedures are not
such as to assure prompt and final decisions like those possible in
other areas of intervention - in cases where the risk to well-being
is physical rather than psychological and where for example parents
who refuse to authorise a blood transfusion necessary for their
child's survival may be legally - and urgently - overruled. Similarly a person's right to an education, property, or free speech may be
promptly and decisively upheld, in contrast to the delays and provisional arrangements which characterise child placements.
  G F & S's second book (confusing called *Before the Best Interests
of the Child*) moves to a discussion of the stage which comes prior
to discussion of placement. 'What must have happened in the life of
a child before the state should be authorised to investigate, modify
or terminate an individual child's relationship with his parents..?'
They express two basic convictions. One continues the argument of
Beyond the Best Interests ... in stating that once justification for
intervention *has* been established, it is the wellbeing of the child
which should be paramount, and not that of the parent, the family or
the child care agency. The other is an expressed preference for
minimum state intervention into the family, on the grounds that so
long as a child is a member of a functioning family, his paramount
interest lies in the preservation of that family, as likely to fulfil
his need for continuity of care from parents who are generally
'autonomous' in the sense of being 'entitled to raise their children

as they think best, free of state interference'. Safeguarding the
privacy of the family is seen as a way of safeguarding the continuity
and development of the psychological parent-child relations necessary
to the healthy development of the child.

The question of the privacy and autonomy of the family is an important one, and one which will recur as a problem throughout this discussion. G F & S confine themselves to discussion of what they term
coercive state intervention, concerned largely with the placement of
children, and explicitly exclude from discussion laws concerning e.g.
education or child labour. In so doing they exclude from consideration the many forms of state intervention into and regulation of the
'private' family. Instead there is an over-simple view in which the
family is autonomous and in general external to state regulation;
and state intervention, G F & S argue, should be minimal in order to
preserve this autonomy, and limited as far as possible by carefully
codifying the grounds for intervention.

What this fails to deal with is the necessity for surveillance.
This necessity is implied, but not admitted and its implications for
the 'privacy' of the family are consequently left unrecognised. Any
policy which has both a societal-level concern for children's well-
being, and an emphasis on the private family as the best means to
achieve that well-being, is faced with the necessity of policing
those private families, intruding on their 'privacy', to ensure that
they continue to provide what is seen as adequate for the child.
This surveillance, itself an intervention, may or may not lead to
direct moves to rectify some state of family affairs which is regarded
as undesirable; but it is the continued possibility of such a state
of affairs which allows the continued regulating surveillance. This
policing is carried out through a very wide range of policies and
agencies. Some, though not necessarily coercive in G F & S's sense,
are nonetheless relatively direct, as with the contact between the
family and doctors, health visitors, social workers, educational
welfare officers etc. Other mechanisms, as Donzelot[4] describes, may
be much less direct and may involve a much greater element of self-
regulation by the family according to the norms. This has an important implication, which is left out of G F & S's discussion because of
this over-simple notion of the private family and which will only
briefly be outlined here. The degree of privacy and autonomy granted
the family, in the sense of the degree to which the family is permitted to police *itself*, varies with social class. The class aspect
tends to be less visible if one looks only at the 'coercive state
interventions' with which G F & S concern themselves, since intervention in (e.g.) a case of child abuse is likely to be relatively
independent of social class. It is the 'softer' forms of surveillance
and supervision which mark class divisions much more clearly.

To return now to the psychological ties between child and parent,
which the assumed privacy and autonomy of the family is seen as
safeguarding. Psychological parental ties usually overlap with
legal rights over the child, by biological or adoptive parenthood.
But this overlap is not inevitable; a child may be separated from
biological parents, so that emotional links are never established or
disappear through over-long separation, or conversely a child may
have strong emotional ties with parenting figures who have no legal

claims over her. G F & S argue that legal right - in the sense of the
adults' right to have the child with them and to bring her up as they
wish - should accompany or follow the development of psychological
ties. 'Thus rights which are normally secured over time by biological
or adoptive parents may be lost by their failure to provide continuous
care for their child, and earned by those who do.' And these new
relationships between child and 'psychological parent' should have
the same safeguards against state intervention as G F & S would accord
to relationships in 'natural' or adoptive families. Thus, and importantly, they reorganise the notion of the family around psychological
ties rather than birth or the 'blood tie'.

A further reason for protecting the parent-child relationship is
the inability of the State, the legal system, etc., to substitute for
flesh-and-blood parents and their complex ties with the child. However, the very family privacy which is intended to protect and promote the child's well-being may sometimes become a threat to that
well-being. Not all families provide the ideal setting for development, and 'emotional neglect', 'psychological damage' etcetera may be
put forward as grounds for the removal of a child. In rejecting
these as grounds for intervention, G F & S point to the lack of consensus regarding what constitutes such damage, the difficulties in
assessment, attribution of causes, and treatability. The vagueness
of the concepts, they say, give too great a licence to authorities
which can exercise coercive powers of intervention 'based on a wide
range of child-rearing notions about which there is neither professional nor societal consensus.'

It is worth underlining this rejection of 'psychological damage'
criteria for intervention, because it amounts to a radical intended
curtailment of the grounds for intervention currently employed, by
social workers, educational welfare officers and similar personnel.
Further, it would amount to even more of a curtailment on grounds
for 'softer' forms of intervention, than on the forms which G F & S
recognise and discuss; with, as suggested above, consequences which
would differ depending on social class. In addition, there are other
political implications. If grounds for intervention are not to
include 'psychological damage' criteria, this sanctions the development of caregiving units which violate existing 'psychological'
norms. These might include, for example, lesbian or homosexual
parents and collective forms of childrearing.

G F & S cite examples of the scope given by grounds of 'psychological damage', to the personal views and norms of judges or social
workers as to what constitutes a setting from which a child should
be removed. One concerns the removal of a (white) three-year-old
from his (white) mother, who was living with a (black) man to whom
she was not married, in Montgomery, Alabama. The Family Court judge
who ordered the child's sudden removal had no evidence that the child
was in any way ill-treated and knew nothing about the mother except
that she was white, unemployed, and living with with a black man;
about whom the judge again knew nothing except that he was not
married to the mother. The judge testified that the race of the
man with whom the mother was living was relevant to his decision to
order the removal of the child, particularly because they were living
in a black neighbourhood. He 'concluded that this habitation in a

in a black neighbourhood could be dangerous for a child because it was
his belief that "it was not a healthy thing for a white child to be
the only (white) child in a black neighbourhood".' Just to underline
the point that such gross displays of prejudice, in the guise of
preventing emotional damage to the child, are not safely past and
gone, it is worth noticing how recent this decision was - 1975.

Even where the family situation is one where there would be more
consensus on its shortcomings, the state's intervention may make a
bad situation into a worse one as far as the *child* is concerned -
though judges or child welfare personnel may feel differently.
G F & S make it very explicit that however unsatisfactory the State
may find a family situation, it cannot always offer a better one.
Temporary foster placements or a children's home may well be even
less satisfactory alternatives.

G F & S propose a framework of grounds for coercive state intervention into the parent-child relation. These grounds, they say,
must meet the requirements of 'fair warning and power restriction'
in the same way as do laws concerned with child labour and compulsory
education. In the latter there are well-defined limits to the state's
power to intervene, and advance warning to parents. In contrast,
statutes concerning questions of child care have much vaguer criteria
and scope of intervention, and give great discretion to courts and to
state agency personnel in areas usually under parental control.
Standards of intervention may be ad hoc and reflect the personal
views of those with the authority to deal with disfavoured families.
G F & S recommend that statutes should prospectively define what must
be established to justify intervention, that a heavy burden of proof
be placed upon those with the power to intrude, and that procedures
be such as to make highly visible the function and degree of intrusion
at each point. Given this, they separate out for discussion the
three critical decision points for procedures of child placement -
stages of invocation, adjudication and disposition which usually are
'answered in a continuous, though often muddled, flow of decisions by
legislators, child care agency personnel, and judges'.

(1) What events are reasonable bases for authorising an investigation into the relationship between an individual child and parent(s)?
For example, is the death of a parent sufficient grounds? or
parental divorce? or a child's poor school performance? This raises,
of course, the important general implication, which is that *all*
families are open to surveillance and potential intervention. As
already indicated, in upholding the privacy and autonomy of the family,
G F & S tend to treat it as a private area outside the law, and not
to take into account the ways in which this autonomy is constructed,
granted, regulated, and sometimes withdrawn again by the law.

G F & S go on to pose the second decision point of this stage;
once such an investigation has been authorised, what should it be
required to find, before the state can *seek* to change or terminate
a parent-child relationship - that is, before the parents must defend
their entitlement to care for and represent their child?

(2) Once such an investigation has been set in motion, what would
be sufficient evidence to authorise a court to end or modify a parent-
child relationship?

(3) If grounds are shown for thus changing the existing situation, which is the 'least detrimental available alternative'?

In the rest of the book, G F & S go on to discuss the grounds they consider to justify intervention, and to suggest provisions for a model child placement code which extends the model statute given in their earlier book. Essentially, grounds for intervention include: parental requests to place the child; this may seem obvious and un-questioned until one recognises, for example, how many women who wish to relinquish their children for adoption are instead pressured into 'keeping' them - which may mean the child remaining for years in a children's home, with minimal contact, while the mother decides when or whether to reclaim the child. (More dramatic, through not neces-sarily more damaging to the child, is the case cited by G F & S of a woman who requested adoption of her son, whose request was refused and who then battered the boy in order to demonstrate to the agency concerned that she was in earnest in wanting him removed from her, and to provide grounds for his removal.) Grounds for intervention also include loss of parents if they have made no other provision for the child, bodily injury or attempts at injury to the child by the parents, conviction of a parent of a sexual offence against the child, and the refusal to authorise life-saving medical care. In contrast to these interventions leading to the removal of the child from parental care or, in the last case, the overriding of one area of parental autonomy, intervention is also proposed to uphold the rights of 'longtime care-takers' other than the biological parents to keep in their care a child who has been with them for a long period (varying with the age of the child) and thus to preserve psychological parent-child relations.

Clearly, such a discussion is not just a set of recommendations about child placement. Children occupy too central a place in notions of the family to allow discussion in the abstract of their care and placement. Whatever the form of care in which children are brought up, its point of reference is some idea of the family. There may be a conscious rejection of traditional family roles within a small group consisting of parents and children and looking from the outside very like the conventional family. At the opposite end of the spect-rum would be forms of institutional group care where the adults see themselves as trying to approximate as closely as possible to the ideal and idealised 'normal' family relationships of which the children have been deprived. Though in the form of a set of guide-lines for statutes and legal revision, what the book does, by system-atically privileging certain of the elements involved in notions of the family, and ignoring or undermining others, is to demonstrate con-cretely that the family is not only a complex idea, not only defined by a large number of different criteria, but that these criteria and the practices they represent come into conflict with each other. (And both politically and in particular strategically, such re-definition of the idea of the family may be more significant than positions which are either anti- or pro- 'the family'.)

Now these potentially competing or conflicting claims may often to unnoticed, but they can become highly visible in cases of family pathology; it is via these cases that the complexity of non-patho-logical families too can be approached. Freud, from the starting

point of a view of sexual pathology, arrived at a theory of sexuality,
normal as well as pathological. Appropriately, Freud's daughter and
her co-writers can also be seen as approaching the study of marginal
children - cases of family pathology - in a way which can lead to a
clearer view of the position of children in *non*-pathological families.
   A good example is provided by their treatment of the crucial central
concept of 'parent'. In *Beyond the Best Interests* ... they distinguish
the biological parents, who physically produce the child; and the
psychological parent, who may be a biological, adoptive, foster,
'common-law' parent (see below), or any other person. 'There is no
presumption in favour of any of these after the initial assignment
at birth'; for at birth a child is placed with the biological parents, and 'unless other adults assume or are assigned the role, they
are presumed to become the child's psychological parents'. The
emphasis on the separability of 'psychological parenthood' from the
legally formalised varieties of parenthood underlies the category of
'common-law parent'; 'A common-law parent-child relationship is a psychological parent ... wanted child ... relationship which develops outside of adoption, assignment by custody in separations or divorce
proceedings, or the initial assignment at birth of a child to his
or her biological parents.'
   This definition of the 'common-law parent' is based in turn on the
category of 'psychological parent'. G F & S define this in a way
which raises an interesting point about their analysis. In the def-
initions accompanying the 'Model child placement statute' in *Beyond
the Best Interests* ..., which *Before the Best Interests* ... extends,
the psychological parent is 'one who, on a continuing, day-to-day
basis, through interaction, companionship, interplay and mutuality,
fulfills the child's psychological needs for a parent, as well as
the child's physical needs'. This is very much a normative definition, and it echoes something of the introductory chapters to either
book, which include some discussion of these 'psychological needs for
a parent', as G F & S see them. The interesting thing is that this
normative element is very much at odds with the analysis of the
family which is embodied in their recommendations. For this analysis
amounts to a *negative* definition of an adequate family; one where
none of the grounds for intervention apply. And as already described,
G F & S specifically exclude the grounds of 'psychological neglect'
or 'emotional damage'. The quality of 'interaction, companionship,
interplay and mutuality' is thus not the touchstone of 'parent'hood
so far as G F & S's proposals go. Rather, in so far as their proposals do carry a positive definition, it is one in terms of specified
chronological periods over which the adults have cared for the child.
They discuss the difficulties of schematising in this way, and the
exceptional case of older children who may have retained ties to previous parents despite a prolonged placement in the care of other
adults; but in general they suggest that 'it would be unreasonable
to presume that a child's residual ties with his absent parents are
more significant than those that have developed between him and his
long-time care-takers' once a child placed under the age of 3 has
been with these care-takers for one year, or for two years if placed
over the age of 3. In this negative definition of an adequate
family, and exclusion of very definite criteria of actual desirable

childrearing practices, G F & S do not differ significantly in their
proposals from the approach of existing legislation. Where they do
differ, as already stated, is in their attempt to limit very specifically the grounds justifying intervention, and to reduce the scope
for those with the power to intervene to do so under the influence of
their own personal preferences regarding desirable childrearing.

Let us now return to the question of the distinction between the
different notions of 'parent'. G F & S's emphasis on the separability
of 'parent' in the biological sense, the legal sense (e.g. adoption)
and the 'psychological' sense, might seem to be belabouring a rather
obvious point. Unfortunately, the point has been very far from obvious to those responsible for child placement decisions. For example,
Christopher Bagley, reviewing judicial decisions concerning custody in
adoption cases, concluded that 'judges have given considerable weight
to the ties of blood which apparently bind a child to his natural
parents, and have given much lesser weight, despite the statutory
guidance about the welfare of the child, to the strength of the
attachment between a child and his foster parents'.[5] Like the
judiciary, social workers also give evidence in their decision processes of a belief in the importance of the blood tie at the expense
of other criteria of parenting. The study reported by Tizard,[6] for
example, made it clear that many of the parents involved had been
subject to pressure of various sorts to keep their children rather
than relinquish them for adoption, and the child had sometimes been
kept 'on ice' in an institution for years on end, with minimal contact with a parent who might or might not in the end reclaim the
child. (Further, if the parent did disappear, or insist on giving
the child up, there would often be an attempt to keep the child in
'his family', by placing the child with other relatives, with little
consideration of whether they were either able of willing to care
adequately for the child.)

Legal and social-casework decisions, then, strive to keep the
family together; so do G F & S. But a different 'family' is at stake
in the two different cases. Legal and social-work decisions priorit-
ise criteria of the family, such as birth and the blood tie, which
G F & S set aside as irrelevant to the criteria which they put forward, to do with the psychological development of the child. In a
sense, their criterion is at its simplest an architectural one, in
terms of a unit of habitation; a group which continues to share the
same roof or succession of roofs. The primary thing is continuity
of close care for the child from one or more adults.

The family which social casework and the law seeks to keep together
is thus not the same family which G F & S seek to keep together. And
the distinction is of a lot more than academic importance. In April
1973, William Kepple was found guilty of the murder of his seven-year-
old stepdaughter in January that year. Her name, if not his, will
be familiar: Maria Colwell. The 'Report of the Committee of Inquiry
into the Care and Supervision Provided in relation to Maria Colwell
(1974)' brings a number of issues to light; not only the tension
between too little or too much supervision and intervention, not
only the delays and lack of coordination, not only the reluctance to
remove Maria from her biological mother's care once the evidence of
maltreatment had begun to accumulate, but the *pre-history* of this

tragic placement. It is this which is most relevant to the present
discussion; how, at the age of six, she came to be removed from the
only parents she knew and placed with the couple who within fourteen
months had killed her.

Briefly, the history is this. Maria, the youngest of five, was
privately placed by her biological mother in the care of a sister-in-
law, shortly after the death of the biological mother's husband.
Maria was four months old at the time. (A few months later, the four
older children were removed from their mother under a place of safety
order.) Maria remained with the sister-in-law, Mrs Cooper, and her
husband, until she was 11 months old, when the biological mother re-
claimed her, having visited only spasmodically. Only a week later
the biological mother again relinquished the care of Maria, leaving
her not with the Coopers but 'with another woman in circumstances and
conditions which Inspector Curran of the NSPCC ... immediately recognised as requiring at once the obtaining of a place of safety order'.

Under this order, Maria was returned to the Coopers, an interim
measure which was formalised when Maria was placed by Juvenile Court
order in the care of the local authority and boarded out with the
Coopers as foster parents. '(A)t the time it was clearly explained
to them that the long-term plan was for Maria to return to her
mother'. But for the next five years Maria remained with her aunt
and uncle and the statutory six-monthly reviews showed her progress
and development to be entirely satisfactory. The Coopers were
extremely attached to her, and expressed a wish to adopt her.
However, Maria's biological mother, now remarried and starting her
second family of children (the others still in Local Authority care)
resented the Coopers having care of Maria and did her best to maintain some claim over her in ways certain to be resented by them; for
example, vetoing their proposal to have Maria christened, only two
days before the ceremony, on the grounds that she herself intended
to become a Catholic and intended to have all her children baptised
- though consenting to her social worker that her other children,
still in care, could be brought up as non-Catholics. Mrs Kepple,
as the biological mother had now become, began to express her intention to have Maria back. Maria was over five years old by this time,
and it is clear from the report that, although earlier visits to her
biological mother had passed off without incident, once she knew of
Mrs Kepple's intentions she became distressed and uneasy. 'When,
with the aim of final return in view, visiting was intensified, she
answered with kicking and screaming, clinging, hiding, repeated
running away, deterioration in behaviour and health'. Despite this
clear indication of who for Maria were her 'real' parents, the local
authority decided, although with difficulty, not to oppose Mrs
Kepple's application to have Maria restored to her.

The Coopers were not present at the hearing in November 1971 which
established Mrs Kepple's right to have Maria restored to her after
growing up with the Coopers for the first six years of her life; they
were told neither the date nor the result of the hearing, as legally
they were not parties to the proceedings.

Thus Maria was restored to her biological mother and her stepfather.
This despite the fact that the four other children of Mrs Kepple's
first marriage were still in care under a place of safety order; that

there were complaints of her neglecting and sometimes ill-treating
the three children of her second marriage; and various other aspects
of the family which would without doubt have ruled the Kepples out
as prospective adoptive or foster parents for any other child. As
G F & S point out, 'Had Mrs Kepple been a stranger without the pre-
rogative accorded to a biological parent, Maria would never have
been put into her care.' But placed she was, despite her desperate
efforts to run away and her distress; and after this point the
remaining pages of the Report document the increasing maltreatment
of Maria, the numerous complaints by neighbours and the school (not
by the Coopers - they never saw Maria again) and the lack of effective intervention by the authorities. In January 1973, Maria was
taken by Mr and Mrs Kepple to the hospital where she was found to
be dead, with massive bruising of the head and body, severe internal
injuries, and a body weight 10-15 pounds underweight for her age
and height.

Apart from all the other lessons to be drawn from the case for
judicial and social casework procedures, it provides the clearest
possible indication of the weight still attached to the biological
parents' claim to the child, and the assumption that this right
somehow coincides with the intention of the Childrens Act that the
welfare of the child be paramount. (In the Colwell case there was
at one point an attempt to justify removing Maria from the Coopers
to her biological mother, on the grounds that in adolescence the
Coopers might be unable to deal with Maria's feelings about her
'natural' parents and that Maria herself might wish to return to
her 'natural' mother at that time - in which case it was better
for her to build relationships with the Kepple family by being
placed there earlier rather than later.)

One further point; in one respect the Colwell case does fall
short of providing a complete example to illustrate G F & S's
arguments. The biological mother can be seen, even before the later
events, as culpable - she did not care for the child, left her in a
highly unsatisfactory second placement, failed to look after her
other children adequately, and so on. Under such circumstances, as
G F & S point out in their earlier book, many judges may be more
willing to find against the biological parent who claims possession
of a child; the judge may well feel that losing the child is the
result of the parent's own deliberate neglect or abandonment. This
is to say that the parents can fairly readily be seen as having
forfeited their right to the child, and so the question of the
parents' rights and of the child's can quickly be brought into
realignment.

But there is one category of cases which demonstrates that
parental rights to the child, and the child's rights to belong to
a family in G F & S's sense are rights within two very different
registers, whose alignment cannot be taken for granted. This category consists of those cases where the parent's neglect or abandonment of the child is indisputably involuntary, and where the judge
will see the parent as the innocent victim of *force majeure* - war,
for example, or illness. The parent not only still has a claim on
the child, but has all the support felt for the innocent person who
has encountered hardship (including the loss of the child).

Such a case occurred at the close of the Second World War when, in
Holland, Jewish parents who had survived the concentration camps returned home looking forward to a reunion with the children they had
left behind in the care of non-Jewish families. Yet meanwhile many
of the children had become closely a part of their foster families,
and their biological parent meant little to them. In such a situation, whatever the decision, someone is going to suffer 'unjustly'
- the biological parent if denied the child, the child (*and* the child's
psychological parents) if the child is removed. While G F & S recognise that a case can be made for giving such biological parents an
overriding right to reclaim the child whom they had lost against their
will, they argue against this and in favour of applying the same
guidelines as in other cases. That is, that parental rights belong
to those who have actually cared for the child and, tragic though
it may be for the innocent biological parent, he or she should be
granted no more rights than any other individual to claim the child.
(To answer the question which is no doubt preoccupying the reader
at this point: the Dutch Parliament decreed that all the children
would be returned to their biological parents.)
And yet, despite this disentangling of 'psychological' from biological parenthood, G F & S do not completely question the biological
relationship. There is the presumption that most biological families
care reasonably well for their children and that the initial assignment at birth of a child to the care of her biological parents is
justifiable on those grounds. Were this not so, the whole form of
the recommendations would be different; positive prescriptions defining desirable childcare practices, rather than a strictly delimited
set of negative defining features - features, that is, which state
the extremes beyond which a family cannot go and still retain care of
the child. Linked to this negative method of defining the family,
with its assumption of the adequacy of a very wide range of child-
rearing approaches, is the authors' ignoring of the whole range of
policies and forms of state intervention which relate to children who
remain within the family where they have been placed by birth or by
adoption - education being an obvious example. That is, they deal
with policies relating to children who *cannot* be brought up within
the biological family, not those relating to children who can.
A second point to be made, concerning this presumption of the
adequacy of the biological family unless there exist defined indica-
tions to the contrary, is that the authors are not making a utopian
or trans-historical statement about desirable ways of bringing
children up. They are by implication accepting a very wide diversity
of childrearing methods, including of necessity many which (psycho-
analysts all) they would personally disapprove. The point is that
theirs is a policy statement, and it begins from present conditions
in Britain and the USA. So in asserting as they do that a child's
best interest lies in being a member of a functioning (psychological)
family, they are not stating an ideal and idealised norm, so much as
arguing a programme based on existing conditions in which, first,
families are recognised to be thoroughly diverse and, second, the
alternatives are recognised to be generally a good deal worse.
With this question of the primacy of the biological parents, we
come to the traditional view of the family. And if, as suggested

earlier, the radical and feminist view of the family is built largely around *adult* relationships, e.g. conjugal, its focus is by no means accidental. It is a response to the traditional view of the family as it is constructed through many other practices. Though these are far too complex to try to detail here, it is the legal which seems most relevant to the discussion, and brings us back to the question of the rights of adults over the child they have produced.

One should note, first, that many measures which may quite fundamentally affect the position of a child are aimed at the safeguarding of adult rights or regulation of relations between adults. Access rights of one separated parent to a child in the custody of the other are a case in point; there are certainly cases where access and visits could be seen as detrimental to the child's interests, but it would be unlikely for a parent (particularly, perhaps, the 'injured party') to be denied their rights. They are entitled to a share in the child - rather like any other possession - and it can be extremely difficult to reverse this presumption where the child's interest seems to conflict with it. It is a similar claim which allows the biological parent to reclaim a child from foster-parents - as Maria Colwell's mother did - even in cases where the foster parents are the child's *only* effective parents. G F & S quote the judgement given in one such case, this time in the USA. The court agreed that the county child care service had custody of the child, a 5-year-old named Tom, including the authority to determine what was best for him; and that 'if ... the best interests of the child received paramount consideration, this court could readily determine that young Tom would obtain greater advantages and benefits' by remaining with his foster parents (of four years' standing). However, the judge ruled that Tom be removed from the foster to the 'natural' parents. He argued a contract theory; the foster parents had 'accepted the child with knowledge of the terms of the agreement and received money compensation for their services. The agreement also provided that the (foster parents) were not to institute any proceedings with a view to adoption or placement'. This they had done, by asking that the child remain with them instead of being 'returned' to his biological parents. The judge went on to say, 'While a child's custody should not rest alone upon a contract and a child regarded as mere chattel, the natural parents have natural rights and obligations and are entitled to their child.' The court concluded piously that thus it upheld the principle stated in the Juvenile Court Act that 'the unity of the family whenever possible is to be preserved. The family itself is an institution whose sanctity must be preserved'.

Commenting on this decision, G F & S make the point that 'Even if a contract theory deserves recognition, there is no reason why the child must be sacrificed to the injured party. In any other breach of contract case involving personal service the court can aware no more than money damages. When adults are concerned it cannot require specific performance of personal services as the Court did when it ordered Tom to leave his home to live with people who, from his point of view, were strangers.' They add that 'Courts must begin to distinguish between finding a violation of parental rights and fashioning a remedy for that violation'.

Now, given the extraordinary strength of the parents' legal claims over the child, it is worth glancing, however schematically, at what underpins these claims. There is a tactical importance for this, for if the law relating to children is going to change in the direction of reducing the 'natural rights' of the biological parent and increasing those of the child and those who actually look after the child, it will have to identify the very powerful opposing forces which maintain the position as it is at present. And as suggested already, the child's rights and the adult's are in very different registers.

One of the major underpinnings of the parents' rights over the child is property, and more specifically inheritance. Although in England parental rights duties and liabilities were inalienable until the passing of the Adoption Act in 1926 (1930 in Scotland), it is worth noting that the very earliest forms of child welfare legislation, where in however limited a way parental rights were infringed upon, were in the form of provisions respecting workhouse children. Thus one element - by no means the only one - is the fact that parental right begins to be eroded precisely where the parents are paupers and legally recognised as having no property to pass on.

A policy like that advocated by G F & S, were it suddenly to be implemented outright, would pose an enormous threat and difficulty for the whole system of inheritance and the descent of property to the heir. For by devaluing the rights of the biological parent, distinguishing the function of giving birth from the 'psychological' parenthood which Goldstein et al argue should be earned by actual care and legally recognised, they render a whole other area of legal regulation shaky. From which parent does the child have the right to inherit, within which family do the parents pass on property? It is interesting to look at some of the foreshadowings of this problem which are happening currently even in the present state of the law.

For example, adoption law currently solves the problem by blotting out, effectively, the biological parents and making the child equivalent to the biological child of the adoptive parents. The legal context provided by current adoption law is such as to limit very narrowly the information about the biological parents available to the adopted person. Until the age of 18, it is up to the adoptive parents to give the child what information they choose, on the basis of what little they have been told by the adoption agency. An adopted person over the age of 18 may have access to a copy of the original birth certificate, which gives the name of the biological mother, her address at the time, and perhaps the name of the father if known. (A new birth certificate is given on adoption which does not contain this information.) Even this degree of access is comparatively recent in England. The biological parents have *no* right to information about the child once relinquished. Thus the legal context provides a close restriction.

But there is now increasing emphasis on an adopted child's right to know more about the biological parents, and also, at least in the USA, signs of moves on the part of biological parents to demand some knowledge of the child they relinquished. (Not to mention countermoves to each of these.) Thus, although in fact the legal situation remains unaltered, there is a sense that there may arise real and competing sets of parents. And what becomes of the orderly descent of property? It is striking that at a recent gathering of social workers in the USA, many concerned with adoption, a new kind of fear was raised. Potential adoptive parents are beginning to express anxiety that, should they die and their adopted child inherit their property, and should the child then die without heirs of his or her own, then would the child's biological parents not be able to claim the property? That is, property would cease to descend *within* the family and instead pass outside it and into the hands of strangers.

Having briefly suggested the property/inheritance underpinning of the existing primacy of parental right, one should add that there are many other practices which equally uphold in various forms some degree of parental right. Perhaps religion should be mentioned; for it is the one vestigial legal remainder of the days of inalienable parental rights and obligations. The one right retained by the biological mother when relinquishing her child for adoption is to state the form of religion in which she wishes the child to be brought up. Though social workers may implement this fairly broadly, one could still see custodianship of the child's soul as the last right to go.

The point of outlining some of the practices which do perpetuate and uphold parental right is, as said before, partly a strategic one. The complexity and the diversity of these practices offer an enormous diffuse resistance to any major change. One must note however that successive pieces of legislation - Childrens Acts, Adoption Acts, etc. - have slowly moved towards a recognition of greater rights for those who actually care for the child. (Here is an example of the strategic importance of gradual redefinitions of the *idea* of the family.) The position of foster parents is considerably strengthened by the Childrens Act of 1975 which allows foster parents to apply for a custodianship order once the child has been with them for three years, and prevents the biological parents from removing the child pending the hearing of their application. Once custodianship is granted, the child cannot be removed from the foster parents without a court order, and they have many of the rights usually accompanying parenthood - e.g. deciding on schooling, taking out passports. However, the bio-logical parent still has access, and it seems likely that this will perpetuate some of the confusion and uncertainty which foster children experience about their status within their family.

A final point in conclusion, leaving aside the question of tactics - of *how* biological-parental rights become curtailed in the interests of children's rights - and turning instead to the underly-ing principle. G F & S base their belief that it is the interests of the *child* which should be paramount on a cycle-of-deprivation argument: ' ... by and large, society must use each child's placement as an occasion for protecting future generations of children by increasing the number of adults-to-be who are likely to be adequate parents. Only in the implementation of this policy does there lie a real opportunity for beginning to break the cycle of sickness and hardship bequeathed from one generation to the next by adults who as children were denied the least detrimental alternative'.[7]

However, it is possible, and indeed G F & S recognise that it is possible (the Dutch concentration-camp example) to decide *not* to

make the child's interests paramount, and to choose to uphold the
rights of adults. As things are, the two are somehow expected to be
always capable of alignment, as I have suggested. The rights of the
adult may be justified or rationalised as being in the child's best
interests (thus returning Maria Colwell to her family before the
difficulties which being apart from it in adolescence might notion-
ally cause her). It is rare that a court will state so explicitly
as in the case cited of Tom that, in upholding the biological
parents' rights it is choosing to act against the child's best
interests. Even where the difference is not part of *legal* rights,
it perhaps is worth making explicit that there is no reason why the
needs or rights of children and of adults must infallibly be non-
conflicting. And a choice of either can be made. One can argue, at
the simplest level, that an infant has a need and a right to be
comforted and got back to sleep when it wakes at night, and equally
that a parent has a need and a right to adequate sleep. The two are
not necessarily compatible. What this is saying is that, in any
argument for rights which affect adults - changes in women's rights
for example - there may well be an issue affecting children, and
there may be a contradiction to be recognised and a choice to be
made - whose rights will be recognised and at the expense of whom.
It is true that this problem illustrates something of the difficulty
of posing political demands or calculations in terms of rights; if
the right of the child to a 'psychological' family is to be given
priority over the right of absent parents to 'their' child, what
about the foetus' right to life as opposed to the woman's right to
choose? Equally it is true that such are, currently, the terms of
debate for many issues of importance to women and to the left, and
that for an effective outcome the claims have to be clearly differentiated and their different foundations taken into account - for
example I have tried to emphasise the different registers in which
parental rights and the child's rights are situated. One of the
achievements of G F & S's book is to have clearly made this differentiation and to have given such an uncompromising voice to their
view of where the child's interest lies.

Notes and references

* I am grateful to Athar Hussain for discussion of several of the
points made, and to Fran Bennett and Nikolas Rose for their
comments.

1 Child Care Act 1980, Chapter 5, London, HMSO.
2 Children Act 1975, Chapter 72, London, HMSO.
3 The question as posed by Diane Ehrensaft in 'When Women
   and Men Mother', reprinted in this volume.
4 J. Donzelot, *La Police des Familles*, Paris, Editions de Minuit,
   1977. See Paul Hirst's review, this volume.
5 C. Bagley, 'The welfare of the child - an examination of judicial
   opinion about medical and social work evidence in adoption cases'
   in *Child Adoption*, Association of British Adoption and Fostering
   Agencies (no date given). Bagley's assessment does not represent

the unanimous opinion, especially it seems of lawyers. See e.g. Ormrod's article in the same collection, and Leo Goodman, 'Aspects of Law in relation to non-accidental injury to children' in *Non-accidental injury to children*, DHSS publication, London, HMSO, 1975. Both feel that the practice in courts is substantially changing.

6 B. Tizard, *Adoption: A Second Chance*, Open Books, 1977. Again, social work practice is not static.

7 *Beyond the Best Interests* ..., chapter 8, discusses their reasoning.

Routledge & Kegan Paul

POLITICS & POWER is a bi-annual series of articles,
surveys, reviews and discussions focussing on the
problems and possibilities for socialist strategy in
contemporary Britain. As a forum for serious and fruitful debate, it is intended to draw together socialists
from a wide range of intellectual and political perspectives in sustained analyses of the political,
economic and social questions facing the British left
today.

The first issue of **POLITICS & POWER** was published in
May and contained 14 contributions collectively described as 'New Perspectives on Socialist Politics'. It
considered such topics as socialist feminism, the
alternative economic strategy, nuclear power, the Trade
Unions and the Labour Party, the 'Gramsci boom' and
socialist journalism. Tribune praised the 'intelligent,
careful and original contributions to socialist discussion', the Leveller considered it to be 'strong on
libertarianism', and Labour Weekly found that it 'raises
vital issues and deserves to be widely read.' Socialist
Worker thought it to be 'Old Fabianism in a new plastic
wrapper' !

The second issue, subtitled 'Problems in Labour Politics'
promises to be just a controversial, containing a wide
range of articles looking at the Labour Party and its
politics:

CONTENTS

Problems in Labour Politics/Holland, Field and Meacher
A 'Left' Labour Government/Hindess
The Labour Governments 1945-51/Fishman
Tripartism and Beyond/Sassoon
The Communist Party, the Labour Party and Representation/
Newrat and Roberts
Politics and Social Policy: An Interview/Townsend
Socialism and Social Policy/Rose
The Thatcher Experiment/Jones
Ten Years of Gay Liberation/Fernbach
The Politics of Workers' Plans/Rustin
After Polaris/Smith
Multinationals and the Third World/Smith
Togliatti and Politics/Laclau
Parliamentary Democracy: The Limits of Hindess/Jessop

- -

POLITICS & POWER 1   £4.95   0 7100 0593 8

For publication 27th November 1980:
POLITICS & POWER 2   £5.75   0 7100 0716 7

ORDER FROM YOUR BOOKSELLER, or in case of difficulty use the Order Form below:

TO: ROUTLEDGE & KEGAN PAUL, Broadway House, Newtown Road, Henley-on-Thames, Oxon. RG9 1EN

Please supply ..... copy/ies POLITICS & POWER 1 @ £4.95 each + 10% post & packing

Please supply ..... copy/ies POLITICS & POWER 2 @ £5.75 each + 10% post & packing

I enclose my full remittance of £.............. (Cheques should be payable to ROUTLEDGE &
KEGAN PAUL).

NAME ....

ADDRESS ....

Paul Hirst
The Genesis of the Social

(A review of Jacques Donzelot, *The Policing of Families*, Hutchinson, London, 1980)

Donzelot is concerned with what has by now become a familiar topic, the formation of the 'modern' family. But his book is unlike any of the historical or sociological works concerned with this question which have begun to appear in increasing numbers. It is neither a history of the family, concerned with the evolution of patterns of kinship and sentiment, nor a sociological account of its place as a social institution, treating it as a necessary concomitant of capitalism or industrialism, as one of a number of functionally necessary components in a coherent ensemble of social relations. Rather Donzelot's work consists of a series of studies of how social interventions *in* the family have been formative and transformative *of* it. The modern family is not an enclosed basic 'social unit', it is open to the outside, to social interventions which deal differentially with its various members and accord them distinct statuses. Donzelot is concerned with the transformation of the enclosed, self-governing family of the *Ancien Régime* in France,[1] an institution primarily concerned with the transmission of property through marriage alliances and with the maintenance of its honour in a series of relations of dependency, into the modern family as a socially supervised educative and consumption centre, concerned with what he calls the 'social promotion' and self-realisation of its members. He examines an important and neglected component in this change, 'outside' interventions in family practices and against traditional patriarchal prerogatives in order to combat various social evils or to attain desirable social objectives.

Let us begin by considering the social 'evils' out of which these interventions emerged. They are a compound of the effects of the decay of the social fabric of the *Ancien Régime* and the consequences of the early stages of industrialisation. Donzelot begins in the 18th century with the deleterious consequences of leaving children to the education and care of servants among the nobility and bourgeoisie and the high death rate among children of the people occasioned by the practice of putting children out to wet nurses or of abandoning them to foundling homes because of poverty. One may add to this starting point that lethal combination of conditions, characteristic of the

first half of the 19th century: the prevalence of socially fostered
infectious and contagious diseases, mass alcoholism, slum housing,
widespread pauperism and vagrancy. A regime of life which, for all
our current economic and social difficulties, we can barely compre-
hend and one whose evils were recognised across the spectrum of
'social' reformers and commentators, from representatives of the
established order like Chadwick or Shaftesbury, sympathetic observers of the poor like Mayhew and Gustave Doré, to Engels. This
recognition was made the basis for a 'magnificent journey' of reform
which continued throughout the century into its culmination in the
welfare state today.

Such views are currently unfashionable. The sources of the displacement of social evils are now placed not in the actions of reformers but in patterns of economic development. In industrial
preoduction, which provided on a mass scale the materials means to
public health and private hygiene. In economic growth and rising
standards of living, which made possible the transition from starva-
tion wages and pauperism to mass consumption and social welfare. This
view is shared by economists of different persuasions, from liberal
apologists of the logic of industrialism to marxist critics of the
logic of capitalism. This explanation is by no means wrong, but it
is partial. The economic logics in question are dependent on certain
forms of social organisation and intervention, and these forms do not
come into existence as mere reflections of economic necessities. In
the first place, the application of the means to public health was
conditional on appropriate means of social organisation and supervision. Second, the working population needed to reconstruct itself
so as to be capable of supporting economic growth and mass consumption;
attitudes, skills and a certain level of wellbeing are the social
preconditions for an advanced industrial civilisation. Meeting
these necessities depended on specific organisational and institutional innovations for which industrial production and the money
economy provided no blueprint.

It is with certain of these innovations that Donzelot is concerned,
the limit to the scope of his analysis being those interventions
which directly touch on the family. But his book is as much concerned
with the genesis of the 'social' sphere as a whole as it is with the
family in particular. With the 'social' in the senses we associate
with *social* problems, *social* reform, *social* welfare, *social* work and
*social*isation. The 'social' is a distinct domain for Donzelot, not
the whole of society. It emerges at a historically specific moment,
in the attempts at solution to the so-called 'social question'. His
point is that the 'social' is the product, the coming together of a
series of innovative interventions directed toward particular social
evils. The 'social' realm is an *artefact*, conditional on the appearance of certain forms of social organisation and certain objectives:
mass education, the supervision of 'private' conducts in childrearing
and health, public health measures, and attempts to eliminate pauperism. This realm is the realisation of no single political ideology
or programme, it had no unity of design or single locus of direction.
'Social' interventions are by no means the product of state action
alone, nor do the various forms of state intervention have an institutional coherence or common objectives. A stratum of disciplinary

powers and social interventions which came into existence during the
19th century formed the basis for the ideology of the 'welfare state'.
But 'welfarism' is a subsequent political construction placed on those
artefacts of social organisation which had already formed the 'social'
domain.   This domain exceeds the proper limits of state action in
liberal ideologies, and falls short both of demands for self-management and comprehensive planning in socialist ideologies.   The 'social'
is thus neither the realisation of a political programme nor the
necessary reflex of economic development.

Donzelot challenges four currently influential ways of accounting
for the 'modern' family.   He rejects none of them outright and yet he
sees limits to and problems in all.

First there is Marxism.   Donzelot is here concerned with the various marxist functionalisms which attempt to explain the family as an
apparatus contributing to the preservation of the capitalist mode of
production in general and bourgeois property relations in particular.
He shows that the various interventions aimed at the preservation of
children and the improvement of public health *weakened* the traditional
proprietorial rights of the family.   The family in France was a far
more direct support of the established order and private property
under the supposedly 'feudal' *Ancien Régime* than under the 'bourgeois'
republic.   Further, Donzelot shows that, far from acting as a smoothly
running transmission belt of bourgeois ideology or as the necessary
means of reproduction of labour power, the family has always 'failed'
to a substantial degree to educate, care for, discipline and train
its members.   These 'failures' are the points at which social agencies
intervene.   Yet there is no sense in which Donzelot believes the
apparatuses of the 'social' make up for these deficiencies.   These
apparatuses exist because of, and they *manage*, but they do not eliminate these 'failures'.   Donzelot thus refuses to consider the family
as a functional appendage of capitalism, or to regard social welfare
agencies' interventions as leading to effective social control.

Second, in relation to modern feminism, Donzelot is concerned to
qualify the relevance of the category of 'patriarchy' to his analysis.
He points to a sustained displacement of the patriarchal rights and
powers of the *Ancien Régime* father.   The transformation of the family
was effected with the active participation of women.   The woman was
selected from the beginning as the partner and collaborator of various
forms of disciplinary, medical and educative intervention.   These
interventions strengthened women's domestic power, reinforcing and
reconstructing the role of wife and mother as agent of socialisation
and moralisation of her family.   Interventions in the family selected
particular family members as their targets and agents; they differentiated between family members, generally to the enhancement of the
rights of women and children against men, and to the educative influence of women over men.   Donzelot further argues that in the latter
half of the 19th century the feminist movement allied itself with
philanthropy in promoting the possibility of a healthy home and family
life as a desirable objective for the mass of women.[2]

Third, there is psychoanalysis.   Donzelot refuses to take part in
the pro- and anti- theoretical and political battles that have raged
around this discipline.   He chooses not to judge the scientific or
political status of psychoanalysis, but, rather, seeks to explain its

practical effect, its adoption as the key component of what he calls
the 'psy' complex. The 'psy' complex is central to the working of
diverse modern educational, welfare and supervisory practices. He
asks how it is that psychoanalysis comes to supplant religious,
medical and psychiatric techniques in the management of personal
conflicts and relational difficulties. His answer is that these
older established techniques magnify and elaborate rather than manage the 'failures' of the family. They suspend the workings of the
family, remove members and unequivocally pathologise them. Psychoanalysis, on the contrary, leaves the members in their place, it
treats normality and pathology as a continuum, and does not set
rigid norms of conduct; rather it seeks to manipulate the discrepancy between ideals of family life and the reality of the situation.
Unlike the heavy handed religious or psychiatric impositions of
norms psychoanalysis allows standards of normality or competence to
'float' (a metaphor borrowed from the EEC currency 'snake', which
permits limited variation between exchange rates) and to reach an
equilibrium level of adjustment in relation to family reality.[3]

Donzelot points out that for all the critiques of psychoanalysis
as patriarchal and sexist, it alone of the socially accepted forms
of intervention avoids pathologisation, eugenic conceptions of de-
generation and racism. Unlike much of orthodox medicine and medical
psychiatry it can sustain a 'liberal' order of welfare interventions
which minimises coercion and formal social segregation. In fact
what Donzelot means by 'psychoanalysis' is something far broader
than Freud's theories or individual psychotherapy - although he is
less than clear about this. The 'psy' complex includes the ideas and
techniques used in counselling and guidance, from family planning
clinics and marriage guidance centres, to educational counselling
and sex education.

Finally, Donzelot argues that the historical analysis of the
transformation of the family in terms of the development and diffusion of patterns of consciousness and sentiment is not wholly in-
accurate but does have a serious flaw. It converts the family into
an entity which evolves autonomously, spontaneously, under the direction of the 'mentalities' which govern the actions and sentiments of
its participants. He cites as pioneering examples of such histories
Philippe Ariès' *Centures of Childhood* and Jean-Louis Flandrin's
Families in Former Times. In fact these two French works suffer less
from this flaw than two American works influenced by Ariès' approach
which Donzelot does not mention, Edward Shorter's *The Making of the
Modern Family* and Lawrence Stone's *The Family, Sex and Marriage in
England 1500-1800*. What Donzelot demonstrates is that the modern
family is not formed by the downward diffusion of patterns of sentiment from the bourgeoisie to the working classes, as Shorter would
argue. Rather there are quite separate routes to the attainment of
'domesticity' on the part of the bourgeoisie and the people. The
modern family is neither the realisation of chosen personal values
nor a 'liberation' of its members - its development involves definite
forms of coercion and control, by family members over one another and
by social agencies over the family. Donzelot points out that from
the 18th century well-to-do parents were encouraged to convert the
home into an 'educative' environment, in which the child could

develop his potential. The bourgeois child was allowed a closely
policed 'freedom' in the interest of the development of his manners
and abilities. The child *and* husband of the proletarian family
were to be enclosed in domesticity as a form of discipline, a curb
on their unsupervised freedom to squander themselves in idleness in
the streets and taverns respectively. The mother was to serve as an
agent of moralisation and control, restricting freedom in the interests of family life and sobriety. Together the respective enclosures
of the home and the school would contain and watch over the conduct
of the proletarian child, in the interest not so much of the formation of abilities as the confinement of vices. 'Domesticity' is an
ambiguous value and one with very different significances in the
different social classes.

But Donzelot by no means treats the family as a mere 'mechanism',
as the mere recipient of interventions from without. There is an
important lesson in the work of Ariès and his successors. Donzelot
asks the following challenging question of the family's critics:

'If today's family were simply an agent for transmitting
bourgeois power, and consequently entirely under the control
of the "bourgeois" state, why would individuals, and particularly
those who are not members of the ruling classes, invest so much
in family life?' (p.52)

To the predictable answers in terms of 'ideological' conditioning he
offers a tart reply:

'To assert that this is the result of an ideological impregnation
comes down to saying, in less delicate language, that these
individuals are imbeciles, and amounts to a not too skilful
making of an interpretative weakness.' (ibid.)

Given ample opportunities for 'failure', the massive difficulties in
the way of maintaining a happy, stable and prosperous home for large
numbers of working people, why is it that so many people try so hard
to 'succeed'?

This question is a challenge to contemporary feminists no less
than it is to marxists. If the modern family is one more manifesta-
tion of an essentially unchanging phenomenon of 'patriarchy' and male
oppression, why is it that a loosening of the legal obligations and
formal subordinations which marked the family of the *Ancien Régime*
was combined with an increasing investment by men *and* women in the
family and the rearing of children as a means of personal realisation?
Patriarchy from being a manifest structure of law becomes a diffuse
ideological conditioning. As in the case of marxism, the reality of
popular aspirations is evaded by using the category of 'ideology'.

The modern family is both a legal institution, the target of
various health, education and welfare practices, *and* a product of
voluntary association. The decline of kinship obligations, arranged
marriages, and the most severe obstacles to illegitimacy means that
families are, like it or not, formed by acts of choice of the partners. Ideology, capitalist or patriarchal, is being given an over-
load of work to do when it is asked to explain both the social
necessities of the formation of families *and* the mass investment in
the values of family life. High rates of divorce in modern industrial countries confirm rather than subvert this question because
they are combined with high rates of remarriage. Likewise the fact

that the 'typical' nuclear family, beloved of advertisers and sociologists, accounts for less than a majority of households confirms
rather than challenges the predominance of familial values.[4] Other
types of households are to a considerable degree preparations for,
consequences of, or products of the breakup of 'typical' family
associations: couples deferring marriage or childrearing, pensioners
or couples whose adult children have left home, and divorced or
separated men and women with children. Single parent families are
increasingly common, but at the same time there is a strong pressure
from state agencies and charities to 'familialise' them as the price
of recognition and support. Family units and family values are not
undergoing some spontaneous process of decline or crisis.

Donzelot also points out that, whilst political radicals are once
again questioning the family, in the crucial period of intervention
in and transformation of the working class family most radical ideologues and movements accepted the family as a necessary part of the
social order. In the first half of the 19th century the battle lines
were clearly drawn. Supporters of the restored French monarchy -
Catholics and authoritarians - supported the traditional patriarchal
legal order of the family as a continuation of the old regime, and
liberals supported the autonomy of the family as a proprietal unit
as the basis for the bourgeois order. Both could therefore accept
the *Code Napoleon* because it restored and strengthened the rights of
the father. Most anarchists and utopian socialists challenged it
for these very reasons, and because they favoured the thoroughgoing
socialisation of life (a conception which reaches caricature in the
'Phalansteries' of Fourier).

In the latter half of the 19th century there is a complete re-
grouping of the political forces in respect of the family. The
socialist parties accepted the family as: 'at the same time the point
where criticism of the established order stops and the point of
support for demands for more social equality' (p.53). Thus, for
all the apparent influence of Marx and Engels, the SPD remained
committed to the notion of the family as a 'natural' institution
which would form the basic unit in a reconstructed social order,
once it had been stripped of the hypocrisy and legalised prostitution
forced on it by bourgeois private property. Socialism and feminism
far from opposing philanthropy and intervention moved in company with
them. The worker and the housewife both have a right to a stable
family life, something denied to them by the unchanged workings of
capitalism.

But philanthropic and state interventions were by no means socialist or feminist in conception or application. If they did have a
politics, it was a deviation from classical liberalism enforced by
social necessities. They were in conception attempts to meet the
problems of misery and poverty without displacing bourgeois private
property or civil liberties. But the *effects* of intervention ex-
ceeded the proper limits of state action in classical liberal
political theory and subverted the ideological division of the
'public' and 'private' spheres. Donzelot considers this subversion
of liberalism as occurring not merely or mainly in terms of state
encroachment on the 'private' sphere, but, rather, on the one hand,
through the assigning to charitable and philanthropic bodies of

'public' powers of supervision and control, and, on the other hand,
through the differentiation in status and treatment between kinds of
family, a differentiation whose at best quasi-legal status differs
entirely from the formal feudal divisions into 'estates' but is none
the less real. We should remember that modern centralisations of
'welfare' agencies under the state are relatively recent in both the
UK and France. 'Private' hospitals, assistance, insurance schemes
(for the mass of the population, rather than the well-heeled) have
been steadily diminished in their role since 1945. But in Italy and
other - particularly Catholic - countries, a good deal of the welfare
system remains 'private'.

Donzelot argues that the poor in 19th century capitalism could
neither be merely repressed nor ordered from above. At the same time
their needs could not be ignored. The political and economic consequences of the mobility of labour and the realities of mass organisation prohibited the social programmes of the Restoration reactionaries
as much as they threatened the political order of liberal ideology.
The poor had to be made the active and cooperative accomplices of
philanthropic interventions. Without intelligent cooperation schemes
for the reform of manners, the imposition of new hygienic norms, the
encouragement of saving, the proper use of 'social' housing, etc.,
were bound to fail. Invariably social agencies sought the cooperation
of particular family members as agents of the diffusion of new norms
and practices, the housewife-mother being chief among these, and, to
a lesser degree, the child through the influence of the school.

Likewise, it was difficult within the framework of the liberal
order to devise a *legal* basis for the power to intervene which did
not convert *all* families into clients of a patriarch-state. Such is
the problem posed by the contradictory demands of the 'bourgeois'
family for autonomy and the necessities of intervention in the families of the working class and this in a context where laws are supposed to be general norms applicable to all. The problem can be highlighted by the contrast between the explicit recognition in the *Ancien
Régime* of the family as part of the order of government and the place
of the family in the liberal state. The patriarchal head in the older
scheme is master of his household and answerable for them, he could
appeal to the King to imprison members who threatened family honour and
caused public scandal. The family was located between ties of alliance
to other families through marriage and property and relations of
dependence and association to feudal superiors and local corporations.
The family was a formally recognised part of the system of public
statuses and mechanisms of government. In theiry the family under the
'liberal' state is treated as a private association, a   may enjoy his
property and peace without interference. All free men are equal before
the law, and every man, whether rich or poor, enjoys the same rights
in respect of his home and property. This scheme would prevent intervention if it could be actually applied. It is through the *failures
and deficiencies* of families that the state and public powers find the
means and the cause to intervene. Parental deficiency and juvenile
delinquency provide routes for intervention, pretexts under the liberal
order whereby children can be removed from their families or families
placed under supervision.

The autonomy of the family comes to depend not on law or proprietorial right but on *competence*. It enjoys a loosely supervised

freedom to the extent that it meets social norms. Control from above
is coupled with the active commitment of the majority of families to
'social promotion', the economic and cultural betterment of their
members. Supervision falls lightly on those families who succeed in
this commitment. This combination of control through deficiency and
mass voluntary commitment to 'social promotion' permits the state and
public bodies to deal with marginality through a 'near total dis-
possession of private rights' (p.94). The active commitment of most
families to the pursuit of wellbeing, their attempts to collaborate
with social and hygienic norms, means that the state can exercise
government *through* families, through the cooperation of their members.
Families are tied into networks of supervision through the school,
through the juvenile courts, through public housing and social security. Failures in relation to or *claims upon* these institutions bring
the family under what Donzelot calls the 'tutelary complex'. This
complex attempts to manage the effects of 'failures', to supervise
conduct and to adjust family members and units to social norms.
Increasingly the deficiency of or claim by *one* member of the family,
for example a truant child, or a mother in need of special assistance, becomes the ground for the supervision of the family as a
whole. In relation to this 'tutelary complex' the father ceases
to count as a figure of authority or as a bearer of rights.
     Donzelot treats the 'modern' family as a correlate of parliament-
ary democracy, although not as functionally necessary to its workings. The modern family is open to the interventions of authority,
but because most families accept the norms it polices they do not
feel this authority. The generalised pursuit of personal autonomy
and consumptionism minimises the degree of intervention and coercion.
And, we might add, keeps the demand for interventions to a level
where welfare agencies can 'police', and even then barely cope with,
failures. Parliamentary democracy implies a sphere of individual
'liberties', however circumscribed, rather than the detailed social
and authoritarian supervision of all elements of life. The modern
family enjoys the 'liberties' to educate and consume, within the
limits set by relatively flexible norms of conduct and competence
and by the operation of the market economy. It works as an 'autonomous' agency for the organisation and expression of consumption
needs, and for the acquisition of social competencies. The 'liberalisation' of family law, breaking down the proprietorial rights of
the father and the parents, is both a condition of the family's new
promotional tasks *and* for state action when it fails in them - it is
no unequivocal 'freedom'. What this 'liberalisation' does imply,
however, is a reduction in the significance of the family as a
proprietorial institution (which goes hand in hand with the increase
in its significance as a unit of mass consumption), and the consequent
conversion of social expectations as to the role of the father from
that of paterfamilias into the 'educative parent' and cooperator
with the wife. The 'social work' image of the adequate father -
in non-economic roles - is as a support of and auxiliary to the wife.
     In dealing with the 'tutelary complex' Donzelot avoids the classic
poles of the debates about welfare and rights. He fails to take
'sides' in the issue of whether social welfare interventions are to
be regarded as displacing individual rights, leading to a state

manipulation of life, or as a rational and necessary way of meeting human needs which the formal possession of legal freedoms by individuals does nothing to satisfy. Likewise he does not take 'sides' in the thorny question of the rights of parents versus the needs of children for care and protection. He subscribes neither to the ideology of liberal individualism nor to that of welfarism. He asks instead what relations *exist* between law, psychiatry and education, and how does social work actually operate as a crucial component of the 'tutelary complex'?

The law, far from being negated and set aside, plays an important double role in relation to the 'tutelary complex'. First, the 'liberalisation' of family law and changing views as to the criminal responsibility of juveniles bring psychiatry and social work into the operation of the law itself. Along with greater legally-sanctioned tutelary authority over the poor or incompetent family comes a greater role of 'psy' knowledges in the decisions of the courts. Thus Donzelot notes the tendency toward the 'dematerialisation of the offence' in juvenile courts, which increasingly concern themselves with the child's character and home circumstances rather than merely establishing the 'facts' of an offence. Second, this former process implies no displacement of the organising role of law and the courts. The law sanctions surveillance. Social work agencies have the authority necessary to their operations from the courts, and apply to obtain the powers they need in individual cases. But, in addition to this licensing role, the courts serve as a back-up to the social welfare institutions. The law serves as a filter for failures of normalisation by 'psy' and social work practices to be passed over to repressive institutions. The courts, therefore, provide the welfare apparatuses both with a threat over and a means of expulsion of the intractable and unruly.

Law and welfare, far from being in opposition, fit together and intermesh. Law could only be considered to be displaced if its procedures are conceived solely in terms of the ideology of 'individual rights'. But, we may add in support of Donzelot, there never has been a time when this ideology has been realised - the heyday of classical liberal political theory being no exception. The legal apparatuses have never waited for definite offences when urgent matters of social control are at stake, and the character of the accused has always counted for a great deal. What differs now are the forms in which that character is assessed and the relations between the law and the complex of 'tutelary' institutions.

Donzelot argues that the 'tutelary complex' could never attain its present scope, and social work could not enjoy the place it does in it, if its organising knowledges were confined to religious, medico-hygienic and medico-psychiatric norms. He poses the reason why in the form of a question: 'How could the family be divested of a part of its ancient powers - over the social destiny of children in particular - yet without disabling it to a point where it could not be furnished with new educative and health-promoting tasks?' (p.199).

Religious supervision worked by dividing families into legitimate and illegitimate, assessing them by their conformity with *religious* norms (confession, attendance at mass, etc.). Thus a certificate

from the priest would be needed to qualify for forms of assistance
operated by the Church or bodies run by Catholic notables. But for
modern social work and educational conceptions there is no such
division of *status*, every family is potentially 'illegitimate' and
can encounter difficulties. Children from religious and bourgeois
homes can be slow learners, truants, exhibit 'personality difficulties'.
Conformity and certification fail to meet the demands for assessment
of competence the modern 'tutelary complex' requires. Likewise with
hygienist norms or psychiatry. They are limited to inspections for
definite 'illnesses' and forms of restriction and isolation of the
'sick'. But the key problem is difficulties *in* the family not a
pathology of individuals that requires them to be removed from it to
the isolation or psychiatric hospital.

'Psy' meets these more complex requirements of discipline, supervision and control. Psychoanalysis mediates between familial and
social authority. Instead of imposing rigid norms of conduct, hard
and fast categories of health and illness, it permits an intervention
which manipulates the gap between the family's performance and social
norms by re-adjusting the objectives and outlook of family members.
Further, it permits social norms to 'float' (in the sense of a floating exchange rate), they are not rigidly applied but adjusted to
circumstances. Thus individuals are counselled to make the best of
their lot in relation both to their real circumstances and their
aspirations. Thus in the sphere of the regulation of sexuality, in
place of rigid religious observances or strictly medical conceptions
of health (which, for all their claims to 'science', long proscribed
'onanism' and declared homosexuality to be a disease, and are only
slowly adjusting to more liberal, 'psy'-informed conceptions of
sexual normality), there is the increasing predominance of marriage
guidance and family planning clinics which operate with an ideology
of 'relationships' and making them work through mutual adjustment.

'Psy' intervenes in an increasingly large number of families without disbanding or disabling the family as an autonomous agency. It
minimises the application of social power whilst at the same time
reinforcing the image of the non-patriarchal, cooperative, educative
family. Donzelot identifies 'psy' with psychoanalysis; an error in
my view, especially in the British context. He makes clear that his
assessment of the social role of psychoanalysis implies no condemnation of it: 'I have not expressed any hostility in principle to
psychoanalysis, not in the least' (p.253). Indeed, such hostility
would only make sense if one thought that 'psy' was only an ideology and one which could be easily displaced, but Donzelot has spent
a great deal of time explaining, in my view persuasively, why 'psy'
is such a pervasive feature of modern societies. *The Policing of
Families* ends with no call to 'freedom', with the invocation of some
other set of ideal social relations in which problems of supervision
and control would become unnecessary. This would involve subscribing
to the very 'poverty of political culture' he has criticised elsewhere.[5] At the same time the tone of his work never gives the
impression that he believes that all is for the best in the best of
all possible worlds. Nevertheless, his avoidance of condemnation of
these dominant and unavoidable forms of social organisation should
be emphasised because his work is all too likely to be taken up in

the Anglo-Saxon countries by a current of libertarian 'anti-welfarism' amongst radical social scientists.

Donzelot links Freud with Keynes as the joint saviours of liberal democracy. Keynes in this view mediated between state authority and the autonomy of the capitalist firm. In creating through the actions of the state, through demand management, a suitable economic climate, the autonomy of the business corporation was preserved. Without such a climate mass unemployment and poverty would create demands for socialisation which would be irresistable within the framework of parliamentary democracy. Freud mediated between familial and social authority. His conceptions of normality and techniques of adjustment permitted the family to remain an autonomous agency, to limit disabling and heavy handed forms of intervention. Freud and Keynes are the fairy godfathers of advanced liberal capitalism.

I do not for a moment accept this account of the influence of either Freud or Keynes. Freud, for all the proliferations of 'psy', for all his immense intellectual 'influence', remains a prophet as ignored and slighted as ever. Maynard Keynes is at best a dubious father for the economic measures which bear his name. 'Keynesianism' is a set of policies only loosely related to Keynes' theories[6] and these policies came into existence, in the UK at least, for reasons that have little to do with his 'influence' and a great deal to do with the reorganisation of the British monetary and fiscal system and the institutions directing the economy as a consequence of the 1930s and during the last war.

If we take the proper names away there is some sense in Donzelot's point, nevertheless. Demand management, post-war growth and social welfare did assist in the elimination of mass unemployment and poverty, and the alleviation of a great deal of personal misery. The British people lived not merely better than they have ever done before during the last three decades, but in a qualitatively different way. This cannot be written-down merely to 'economic growth'. And the British economy has grown slowly and unevenly relative to its major industrial competitors. Sustained growth needs to be organised and promoted as present circumstances all too easily illustrate. The present crisis makes it clear that what passes for Donzelot under the labels 'Freud' and 'Keynes' is not enough. This is not intended to imply that social-ism is the only 'solution' to the present crisis, it is rather that the management of modern capitalist economies is a socially and poli-tically far more complex problem than was ever imagined in post-war 'Butskellite' ideologies. What I am implying is that additional tech-niques of economic *and* social management are necessary to keep advanced liberal capitalisms to an acceptable level of failure. These new techniques relate directly to the role of the family.

Donzelot implies in his concept of 'social promotion' that families are committed to the enhancement of their material and cultural well-being. The family serves to provide the economy with personal motiv-ations and expectations as to its performance, it provides the social back-up to sustained demand and high mass consumption. Interestingly enough this is also the view of the now deeply unfashionable American sociologist Talcott Parsons - for all his status as a right-wing bogeyman his writings on the family are of great interest and anti-cipate themes taken up by left-wing writers. The problem with this

view of Donzelot's as to the economic role of the family is not that
it is false but rather that the expectations so generated create as
many problems as they solve.

What follows must necessarily be speculative given the limited
compass of a review, the arguments advanced here cannot be fully
elaborated or substantiated and I hope the reader will be generous
enough to bear this in mind.

A full-employment economy based on demand management requires the
adjustment of expectations of income to the likely prospects of
growth. Until recently mass expectations have been schooled to ant-
icipate steadily rising levels of private disposable income. In an
economy with full employment and effective free trade unions this
will - arguably - tend to produce wage-fuelled inflation. This undermines the prospects of sustainedly maintaining full employment through
'demand management' techniques like tax cuts and credit creation.
I have argued elsewhere that the answer to this problem of maintaining a full-employment economy is, neither a destructive and ultimately ineffective monetarism, nor a call for a socialism which is
politically unattainable under current electoral conditions, but an
incomes policy.[7] A crucial aspect of incomes policy, however, is the
motivations and expectations of the mass of wage workers. Wages
freezes do nothing to socialise or adjust expectations as to levels
of incomes and the form in which they should be received. Wages
freezes can never be more than short-run expedients rather than a
long-term technique of economic stabilisation.

In the long run - Keynes' famous aphorism notwithstanding - the
economic prospects of advanced liberal capitalisms will be closely
tied to the *quality* of expectations as to living standards and the
motivation to acquire levels of culture they can instill into their
workforces. Arguably - and this involves no conversion to Daniel
Bell's *The Coming of Post-Industrial Society* - economic growth in an
advanced industrial economy depends to a high degree on the knowledges,
skills and expectations of the population. In this respect mass
education in Britain, far from 'reproducing' a labour force appropriate to advanced industrialism, has failed to motivate the majority
of working-class children even to acquire the knowledges and skills
available to them. We remain the worst educated advanced industrial
country. Schooling is not the main source of this failure, rather
it is the family and peer-group sponsored expectations and motivations which lead to school being devalued. Most manual workers, in
one sense not unreasonably, tend to identify well-being with personal
disposable income and material satisfactions. To the extent that
British working-class families aspire to Donzelot's 'social promotion' it is spelt out primarily in private terms and material goods.
I am certainly not implying that it would be better if we were a
nation of monkish ascetics, a high demand for consumer durables is
an important and desirable part of an advanced industrial economy.
Rather the issue is that this demand is accompanied by a relative
indifference to the acquisition of complex cultural skills and to
social consumption. The British economy thus lacks, to a greater
degree than some competitors, certain crucial - if immaterial -
'inputs' which come ultimately from families. If people come to
accept the receipt of a higher portion of their income through a

more equitably distributed social consumption - in health, welfare, education, culture and leisure - and are drawn more fully into economic management *then* there are prospects for a planning of incomes which will be accepted as something other than a wages freeze, as more than a temporary expedient acquiesced in through fear of the consequences of inflation. An interventionist full-employment economy, of which an incomes policy is an important part, requires the generalisation of skills and competencies now commonly thought to be confined to the 'middle classes'.

It is useless to say that this is pie in the sky because 'capitalism' or 'capitalist schooling' has denied working people both cultural skills *and* the motivation to acquire them. If that is true and continues to be true then nothing can ever change.

In a curious way these points about the limitations of the Freud-Keynes combination confirm rather than invalidate Donzelot's analysis. The argument I have been advancing here is that the concept of 'social promotion' must be accepted and that the objectives it refers to must be broadened in their scope. Further, that something like the diffusion of 'bourgeois' expectations downwards which Donzelot argues *did not take place* in the 19th century is a necessity today. The expectations are, of course, no longer the same as they were then and are not merely matters of interpersonal sentiment. It is a necessity not because the middle classes are the repository of morality which needs to be brought to the great unwashed, but because those very strata *should not* have a monopoly of certain kinds of skills, competencies and expectations. Donzelot's analysis points to one way in which this extension of the social expectations and cultural objectives of the mass of the people may come about. Through a further extension of the place and powers of women in the family. Here the Women's Movement in striving to change women's expectations and competencies, to challenge passivity and the acceptance of secondary domestic roles, can have a potentially enormous social influence. But in order to do so it must take full account of that mass investment in the values of family life to which Donzelot is so concerned to draw attention, and of the fact that this investment is unlikely to cease under present social conditions. It is precisely by supporting and extending ordinary women's aspirations and actions *in* the family that modern feminism can have most effect *on* the family.[8]

This seems to be the major lesson of Donzelot's important book. This process involves, as the 19th century feminists who allied themselves with philanthropy did, treating women as a potential source of education and enlightenment for their men and children. In the contemporary case the objective is not new norms of hygiene, sobriety and thrift, but demands for culture, social facilities and de-facto in addition to de-jure equality with men. These things are not important because they may make certain kinds of economic policies possible, rather they may make economic management easier *because* they are so important to masses of women.

There are, however, no immediately obvious equivalents of the 'philanthropists' today with which feminism could ally even if it wanted to. The orthodox socialist movement remains blind and deaf to the sorts of issues raised in our discussion of why 'Freud' and 'Keynes' are not enough - for all its endorsement of feminism. The trade

unions are dominated by men and by calculations of individual take-
home pay, again primarily for men. For this reason women, whether
employed or not, because they tend to put the actual material and
non-material standards of living of their families first, may serve
as an alternative channel for the expression of demands for income
planning and social consumption. The Women's Movement, precisely
because it is not locked into established organisational practices
like the unions, could (and has to some extent) take up and formulate these demands. In doing so, in expressing neglected interests,
it has the prospect of winning mass support.

If feminists wish to improve women's lot in contemporary capitalism, rather than wait for some completely socialist social system
which is no nearer now in the advanced capitalist countries than it
was a hundred years ago, then they must adjust their politics to the
place of the family in capitalism that Donzelot outlines. By commit-
ting itself to a narrowly anti-familialist ideology modern feminism
could all too easily alienate itself from the majority of women.

It is interesting in this respect that both feminism *and* modern
familialism should be strongest in advanced liberal economies like
the USA or Scandinavia. Donzelot points out why modern familialism
and parliamentary democracy are so closely correlated. This is not
to say that in the USSR the pre-revolutionary family remains intact
or that there are Phalansteries on the steppe. In the Eastern Bloc,
whilst there are modern nuclear family patterns, the 'liberalisation'
of family norms and parental authority has taken place to a lesser
extent than in the West, social inteventions and supervision remain
heavy-handed, and the 'private' sphere of consumption and 'autonomous'
social promotion is relatively restricted. The pressures for reform
are directed toward making the Eastern countries more like the
capitalist West, precisely because in the West opportunities for
consumer choice are greater and social controls less visible and
oppressive. A comprehensive state organisation of socialised child-
rearing and personal consumption is impossible. Under advanced
industrial conditions the modern 'educative' family and the 'psy'
complex go together, permitting a definite autonomy in personal
relations.

It is just this autonomy that the Women's Movement seeks to extend, particularly for women who devote a great deal of their lives
to raising children. In this respect it is following and reinforcing
a major line of social development, rather than setting its face
against it in an irrelevant radicalism, that is, the tendency toward
the elimination of the proprietorial position of the father in the
family. Again, by intervening in practices of counselling and challenging authoritarian conceptions on the part of professionals,
modern feminism has recognised the importance of 'psy' and the need
to struggle over its content. 'Psy' is the counterpart of family
autonomy but there is no reason why its supervisions and interventions should be fixed in their form. Feminism can thus be viewed,
in one of its aspects at least, as contributing to a long process of
'liberalisation' of family norms and structures. The more extreme
forms of 'lifestyle politics', however, set themselves against this
trend because they seek to impose new and rigid norms of sexual and
relational 'normality' (albeit of a libertarian kind). The mass

pursuit of autonomy and the 'floating' of standards of personal conduct in countries like the USA both make these forms of politics
possible (they would get short shrift not only in the USSR but in
formally democratic and socially conservative countries like
Switzerland) and yet condemn them to marginality. The Women's Movement is *not* marginal precisely because it is capable of moving in
conformity with the main lines of development of the modern family
and taking up issues vital for society as a whole which are neglected
by other forms of social organisation. If there is value in
Donzelot's book it is in helping us to see why this is the case.

Notes

1 This refers to the 'feudal' system prior to the revolution of 1789.
   Donzelot relies on his reconstruction of the *Ancien Régime* as a
   point of contrast throughout. This contrast would not work so
   well in the case of England. Institutional changes, particularly
   in the sphere of law, were less clear-cut in England. English
   family institutions were radically different from those in the
   majority of French regions. Alan Macfarlane in his *The Origins
   of English Individualism* (Basil Blackwell, Oxford, 1979) argues
   that there is no easy contrast between traditional and modern
   family types to be found in England, important elements of the
   'nuclear' family can be traced back well beyond the 16th century
   in England.
2 This point is taken up and confirmed by Christopher Lasch in his
   review in the *New York Review of Books*, 12 June 1980.
3 Psychoanalysis is by no means so influential in welfare and
   medical institutions here, and certainly takes second place to
   behavioural and strictly psychiatric theories. For a discussion
   of this point and for generally interesting comment on Donzelot see
   the Jill Hodges and Athar Hussain review in *Ideology and Consciousness* No.5, Spring 1979. One point in particular is very important, they point out that by concentrating on the home Donzelot
   ignores the labour market and that no corresponding diminution
   of the place of the man has taken place there. This review is
   also well worth reading because it thoroughly summarises an often
   difficult and inconclusive book.
4 For relevant data on households and families see *Social Trends*
   1980, HMSO, London, pp.77-82.
5 See Donzelot's essay 'The Poverty of Political Culture' in
   Ideology and Consciousness, No.5, Spring 1979.
6 See for example Axel Leijonhufvud, *On Keynesian Economics and the
   Economics of Keynes*, Oxford University Press, New York, 1968.
7 I have tried to argue the necessity of an incomes policy from a
   socialist standpoint and the substantial social changes in the
   framework of British capitalism needed to make it possible in
   'On Struggle in the Enterprise', see Mike Prior (ed.), *The Popular
   and the Political*, Routledge and Kegan Paul, London, 1981.
8 These aspirations are by no means consistent and can be taken up
   in various ways; for an attempt at thinking through the political
   implications of feminism for families in just one area, personal

taxation, see Fran Bennett, Rosa Heys and Rosalind Coward, 'The Limits to "Financial and Legal Independence"...' in *Politics & Power One*, Routledge and Kegan Paul, London, 1980.

politics of sexuality

DOUBLE ISSUE   no 5 & 6   1981

A Feminist Interest in Pornography
                              Beverley Brown

The Assertion of Homosexuality
                              Jeff Minson

Rape - Sexuality in the Law
                              Delia Dumaresq

Women and Shi'ism in Iran
                              Mina Modares

Psychoanalysis and Social Relations
                              Paul Hirst

Mary Kelly's Post-Partum Document

Introduction to Post-Partum Document
                              Elizabeth Cowie

Translation of Julia Kristeva On Motherhood

Introduction to Julia Kristeva
                              Claire Pajaczkowska

Translation of Moutafa Safouan on the universality

of the Oedipus Complex

Review of Fcucault's History of Sexuality
                              Athar Hussain

m/f

£2.95

22 Chepstow Crescent
London W11

Fran Bennett, Beatrix Campbell, Rosalind Coward
Feminists-The Degenerates of the Social?

A reply to the review by Paul Hirst of Donzelot:'The Genesis of the Social'

> 'The more extreme forms of "lifestyle politics" ... seek to impose new and rigid norms of sexual and relational "normality"...'
>
> 'It is precisely by supporting and extending ordinary women's aspiration and actions *in* the family that modern feminism can have most effect *on* the family.'
>
> 'If feminists wish to improve women's lot in contemporary capitalism, rather than wait for some completely socialist social system ... then they must (sic) adjust their politics to the place of the family in capitalism that Donzelot outlines...'
>
> (Paul Hirst, *Politics & Power Three*)

'The Genesis of the Social' is an article which has proved that, for feminists, there is no ready basis for an alliance with socialists who have criticised so-called reductionist Marxism. Paul Hirst's review proves, rather, that anti-feminism and ignorance of the discussions and aims of feminism is as rampant among some socialist men as it ever was. The review damns the extremists of 'lifestyle politics' and appeals, with a tedious familiarity, to the 'ordinary woman' who only wants the best for her man and children, and who will only be alienated by the anti-familialism of the women's movement.

The review starts, therefore, from an ignorance of the basic tenets of feminism, and ends with a reactionary prescription for the salvation of liberal capitalism. There are many strands in the article that we could follow up to reveal that Paul Hirst's views on the family and the current social situation exhibit nothing more than the well-known male preference for a certain kind of family and a certain kind of woman within it. In the following three sections, we try to draw out these strands; to dispute his (and Donzelot's) assessment of history and the current situation; to challenge his assessment of what the family is; and to dissociate ourselves completely from his conception of feminism.

History from the male standpoint

Paul Hirst's preference for Donzelot's approach to histories of discourses surrounding the family, and his particular interpretation of
this approach, reveal how ideological preferences can sift and distort
historical and contemporary evidence. His interpretation of Donzelot
concentrates on how feminism developed in the context of social
changes which favoured the family as the institution by which an
explosive society could be regulated. This account attributes the
emergence of feminism to women's newly acquired status as mothers,
guardians and educators. Feminism is seen almost exclusively in
this new-found status within the family.
    That 19th-century feminism can be characterised by the language
and aims of philanthropy is hardly news to feminists today. But
contemporary feminism is also aware that we cannot limit the aims
and criticisms of our predecessors merely to those social developments.
Right from the earliest days of 19th-century feminism, there has been
an accompanying critique of the oppression entailed in the structure
of the family itself. Even men like Gissing were sufficiently aware
of this critique to include it in their representation of feminism.[1]
    Feminism by then included criticism which saw women's confinement
to domestic roles and domestic obligations, and their confinement to
emotional dependence on one man, as a source of structural oppression.
In other words, feminists had already begun to develop a critique of
the family which saw it as a site of conflict and differential interests for men and women. The period characterised by Donzelot as
giving women status as 'partners and collaborators' was in fact the
period when women were fighting to gain elementary rights of citizenship - and these rights were won, not through gaining advantages
for the family, but by rejecting the laws of the country as patriarchal. The suffragettes often stated openly that they refused to
listen to the courts or be judged by them; the laws were made by
men for men, they said, and women had their own interests to pursue
against such laws.
    It is important to emphasise this alternative account of the
history of feminism, for the arguments about women's position within
the family, their moral strength, and their interest in elevating
their menfolk and children, were precisely the arguments made in
the rulings which barred women from certain occupations and the
right to citizenship.[2] These were the judgments which the feminists
opposed as patriarchal. Paul Hirst, however, takes them at their
face value. The language of law and social policy describes women's
position as equal but different, remote from politics and the sordid
public realm, but triumphant in their domestic dominance. That such
discourses exist is not in dispute; what *is* in dispute is whether
they describe the everyday reality of oppression which was created
by women's confinement to this role.
    The reason why it is important to expose this reading of history
is because he uses it to indicate that feminism has already been
used once to save an ugly social crisis, in which class conflict
and social deprivation might have provoked a revolutionary situation,
had it not been for the 'family'. He glosses over the fact that,

for the women who won us the advantages which we now share, the family
itself was a source of oppression. To demonstrate the partial nature
of such a view of history is also to reveal the particularity of his
assessment of the contemporary situation. He suggests that liberal
capitalism solved some of its problems by constructing the family as
a relatively autonomous unit, an area of personal freedom, which
could be loosely policed, and backed up by other State interventions
when it 'failed'.

Now, this suggestion could perhaps be a useful one; it could show
us the way in which women were coerced and forced into the 'family'
form. It could in fact demonstrate the exact opposite of his proposition, by revealing that State intervention and social policy were
directed towards achieving the 'success' of this social unit - even
though feminists had, in many instances, recognised it as an area of
conflict and oppression. Paul Hirst, however, uses the suggestion
to indicate that the family could once more be mobilised as a solution to a contemporary social crisis.

It is feminism as a mass movement which for Paul Hirst could
initiate and substantiate the elevation of the family as the solution to today's crisis, with women fighting to 'restore their position and power in the family'. But it never occurs to him that he
sees both history and the contemporary crisis and solution entirely
from a male viewpoint; it never occurs to him that the solution he
proposes might be the source of social oppression and deprivation
for women. Because the problem concerns men, and the solution is
for men.

The 'crisis' to which Paul Hirst seems to be responding has several elements for him: one is mass unemployment; another is the
deterioration of British products; a third appears to be a nebulous
sense of social disintegration. All these phenomena can be viewed
very differently if your account of society *includes* within it the
history of the oppression and subordination of women. The elements
specified by him in the current crisis are all elements which accept
men as the prime subject of history.

Take the example of unemployment. No one would remotely want to
throw doubt on the seriousness of the present levels of unemployment,
or on the social effects which they are having, and are likely to
have in the future. However, it must be stressed that women as a
group have always had a structurally different relationship to employment from men. Even in the periods of so-called full employment,
many women have remained out of the labour market, or have entered
it only sporadically under the exigencies of domestic responsibility.
Feminists have begun to realise that until the ideology of the male
breadwinner (increasingly incompatible with the realities of existence) has been challenged, no real advances will be made towards
transforming women's status.

This point will be discussed in greater detail in the subsequent
sections. Here, it merely serves to indicate that the usual horror
at - male - unemployment is predicated on a blindness to the frequently 'hidden' unemployment of women and their oppression within the
family. It seems to be regarded as a moral disaster if so many men
are unemployed - yet women are frequently and regularly expected to
be just that. We need to rethink the concept of 'full employment',

which - unexamined and merely put forward as a fetish - ignores the
changing social relations under which production could take place,
and demotes the necessity to transform women's relation to paid employment. The *Financial Times* is full of letters suggesting that married
women move 'back into the home' in this time of high (male) unemployment. Although Paul Hirst does not of course suggest this himself,
doesn't this reflex reaction reveal what is actually thought of
women's 'position and power' within the family? Surely, if there is
any real commitment to feminism among socialists, it must be based on
both a realistic assessment of what kind of economy we could have,
and how women's domestic subordination can be overcome and women's
position be promoted within such an economy?

The horror of social disintegration, which emanates from his analysis of the present crisis, has implications which should be rejected
by socialists and feminists alike. On the one hand, Paul Hirst seems
to be regretting that the working classes are not taking up the
opportunities open to them to turn out skilled workers (i.e. men);
on the other, he paints a picture of under-socialised youth - perhaps with the spectre of Brixton muggings and street crime in mind?
But his fears are not our fears. We fear systematic violence against
us by men: middle class, working class, single and married. No
feminist will be surprised if the so-called Yorkshire Ripper turns
out to be a church-loving, family man; certainly his campaign of hate
against women has been conducted in the name of morality and family
decency against the extremes of 'lifestyle politics' (prostitutes and
students).

Paul Hirst's advocacy of the acquisition of middle class 'competences' as a solution to the crisis must seem equally ridiculous to
feminism. Although the concept is left unexplained, presumably what
is thought to be necessary for the working classes is the acquisition
of the capacity for self-achievement; the capacity to acquire a
decent home and standard of living; in fact, the capacity to become
a good consumer. To many feminists, this is *the disease rather than
the cure*. To many of us, the behaviour of middle class men is nothing
less than a pathological repression of emotions and responsibilities,
and a defence of the right to exploit and mistreat the other sex.
It is not surprising, then, that he should see nothing wrong with the
existing education system, if only the working class family could get
it together to push their offspring through it. For, in his eyes,
there is nothing wrong with the male authority, hierarchies and forms
of petty egotism which are so rampant in academia and the other
professions.

The two points, therefore, which are designated as signs of
social crisis are unemployment and under-socialisation. We have
tried to suggest that both these 'crises' could be seen differently
if we examine social structures from the perspective of the relations
between men and women, the hierarchies which are constructed, and
the forms of power and gratification which men can extract from
women's dependence. Once posed in this way, Paul Hirst's 'solution'
becomes a nonsense; it depends and builds upon the very structures
which themselves reinforce women's subordinate position in employment, in the home and across society.

The family from several standpoints

Although Paul Hirst suggests that for feminists to consider what it
is that binds us ideologically to the family would be too much of
a problem; we would in fact claim that for the last ten years much
of feminism has been concerned precisely with investigating what is
involved in the dynamic of so-called family relations. This, indeed,
is the most disingenuous part of his argument. It does not seem
long since he himself was defending the need to pay attention to the
ideological aspects of society, and encouraging an attack on forms
of economistic Marxism which neglected such aspects. Now he argues
that the fact that women 'freely' aspire to family relations undermines
the idea of ideology: 'the reality of popular aspirations is evaded by
using the category ideology'. Suddenly, if people are racist, they
are so for a reason; and if people want to live in the family, there
must be a reason. The implication is, of course, that this is a good
reason. Paradoxically, however, he peppers his paper with references
to how Freud has been misunderstood by Donzelot, and that there is
more to him than a 'psy' complex. We would suggest that, in fact,
psychoanalysis does begin to show what is at stake in family relations: how the anxieties which often lead to the miseries of family
life - jealousy, dependency, masochism - have their roots in childhood experience. In our society, we are brought up investing all our
emotional energy in one or two people; we are conditioned to invest
our sexual relations with the same familial significance and intimacy.
Again and again, the disappointments connected with these emotional
forms can be found at the bases of women's sense of personal frustration and defeat within the family.
   It must be said, however, that to defend the possibility of understanding, and therefore challenging, the emotional structures which
dominate our society is to accept the terms of Paul Hirst's arguments.
It is possible to challenge the very assumptions from which he starts.
It is clear that, despite the emphasis on 'discursive constructions'
of categories and so on, he in fact thinks that the family, once constructed by State policies in the 19th century, has remained largely
unchanged until now. It would be possible to take the logic of
Donzelot's argument in other directions, however - directions which
correspond with the facts.
   This family as agent of socialisation, with mother, father and
offspring, is a grouping, marked out by policy, which does not necessarily correspond to the reality of people's lifestyles. It is only
economic and social policy and legal representation which produce
the picture of women with primary investment emotionally in their
husbands and children. On the negative side, for example, women are
frequently (and increasingly) as burdened with elderly parents as
with young children; or, more positively, their primary emotional
commitments are not with the family, but with their friends and work-
mates. And there is plenty of evidence in popular culture of extreme
sex antagonism and disillusion within the family.
   Paul Hirst's insistence that all women are either on their way in
or on their way out of the nuclear family is a point which by no
means necessarily proves the eternal grip of family ideology on the
populace. It argues, rather, for a re-examination of the ways in

which people are actually living and the different responsibilities
and commitments which govern people's lives. The only reason for
focussing on one moment where groups coincide with the policy stereotype is because for some reason it is thought that this unit should
be privileged.

In fact, he (après Donzelot) wants the masses' social expectations
and cultural objectives to be achieved through 'a further extension
of the place and powers of women in the family'. Such language is at
best vague and at worst misleading. However, we can only interpret
him to mean that he shares the current imperatives of the Conservative
Government to return to the 'family' (i.e. unpaid women) the functions
which have become social, and waged. Nothing in Paul Hirst's piece
refers to any transformation of men's role in the family; so the
extension of these places and powers must be to women. But women
have them already, and many of them seem not to want them - as witnessed in surveys carried out by the government, the TUC, One-Parent
Families and so on, into women's demands for an extension of their
'place and powers' *beyond* the family.

Paul Hirst regards a politics based on the transformation of the
economic, sexual and political relations between men and women as
ridiculous, because women en masse reject that project (just as they
apparently reject socialism). He thereby demonstrates his isolation
from, and lack of knowledge of, current debates within feminism about
the family and women's 'place' and (lack of) 'powers' within it. He
takes it for granted that there is no contradiction between genders,
which results in his piece attending to those givens in women's attitudes to the family, and proposing that feminism routes itself along
these givens. Thus, feminism would provide a movement of continuity
with family forms, rather than a movement which is radical. Of
course, it is 'irrelevantly' radical, in his view, to be anti-
familial, because he ignores the very destabilisation and contradictions within the family upon which feminism is based.

Feminism simply seeks to act upon those contradictions, and to
engage with the construction of femininity and masculinity - to
transform women's position in the family, and in waged work, AND IN
RELATION TO MEN in general. Men are by and large absent from his
article. We are told that women *are* familial; they like the family;
they choose it. He doesn't tell us that they are subordinate in the
family, so that often it is Hobson's choice for them. And we are
not told whether men like it, choose it, are good for it, or experience contradictions within it.

Moreover, his is essentially a static view of the family. It is
no coincidence that Talcott Parsons is invoked, in a sentence which
praises with the faintest degree of blame. If we look instead at
women's relation to the family historically under capitalism, we can
see that it developed under a patriarchal imperative. The socialising
tendencies of capitalism in the field of production were not matched
in the field of domestic or urban reproduction. In some instances,
the development of the State is associated with the efforts to confront and mitigate the social crisis attendant upon this. In others,
patriarchal sexual relations asserted an alliance with capital to
enforce women's expulsion from waged labour and their re-entry into
the home. Women have rarely accepted this lying down. It has always

been secured coercively, by women's exclusion from jobs upon
marriage and their exclusion from trades unions.

Men secured this purge, at the ideological level, by an insistence
on the family wage: a wage sufficient to maintain the wife, who maintains the husband and dependent children. Thus, by means of enforcing
dependency on their subordinate spouses, a certain problem of day-to-
day reproduction was solved. Since the Second World War, and especially since the 60s, women have moved back into the labour market in
large numbers. Now the only full-time dependants are women with
small children. And yet the labour movement - and Paul Hirst - have
nothing to say about this development. They have nothing to say about
what transformations of working time, familial relations and social
child care provision might be sought to alter this relation of dependency - because, in the end, they don't see anything wrong with it.

Feminism from a feminist standpoint

Women's re-entry into waged labour, therefore, is characterised by
their own full-time relation to parenthood, and by men's passive
relation to parenthood. This means that both domestic and waged work
are characterised by a sexual division of labour, in which women are
always relatively impoverished. This must affect fundamentally a
feminist attitude towards the wage, the social wage, and the relationship between them.

Paul Hirst's references to incomes policy and wages militancy are
familiar. They are drawn from the work over the late 60s and throughout the 70s by dissident Communists such as Bill Warren, Mike Prior,
David Purdy and Pat Devine. Like Paul Hirst, we too have drawn on
their work. In the last two issues of *Red Rag*, we have initiated
debate among feminists on wages strategies.

It is by now conventional wisdom on parts of the Left to criticise
wages militancy as the sole thrust of socialist politics. It is also
widespread, from NALGO leftwards, to stress the importance of the
social wage. We as feminists share this conventional wisdom; but
this should not be taken to mean that we are against wages militancy
per se. On the contrary, we are *for* a major wages offensive to stem
the relative decline of women's already unequal earnings in relation
to men's. In 'United We Fall' (*Red Rag*, 1980), some tentative suggestions were made about a possible approach to wage strategies for women.

The first point is that, still within a free collective bargaining
context, the percentage increase must be dropped in favour of flat
rate increases. Secondly, it is necessary to campaign against differ-
entials; thirdly, increments (long-service and others) which tend to
accrue to men because of their uninterrupted career path, must be
opposed. There is a whole range of other aims related to wages,
which amount to a transformation of the priorities of free collective
bargaining. Thus, feminism cannot simply be appropriated by Paul
Hirst, in his critique of traditional Left economism and its accompanying stress on wage militancy, to collaborate on a joint project to
preserve the status quo. Feminists certainly *do* question the legitimacy and efficacy of both typical patterns and priorities within
wage bargaining, and the primacy and resources given to the individual

wage within our society. However, we would question them on rather
different grounds from his. We would demand some radical rethinking
of patterns of wage bargaining - whether within free collective bargaining, or comparability exercises, or incomes policy - which are
premised upon the priority given to the characteristics of male work
patterns: a full-time, long-term, uninterrupted presence in the
labour market, with opportunities to work overtime untrammelled by
other commitments. We would make a critique of free collective
bargaining, not, as he does, because it is a major determinant of
wage-fuelled inflation, but because so far it has not transformed
any of the areas in which feminists - let alone socialists - demand
to see changes: the relationship of wage to wage, the relationship
of wage to social wage, work to domestic life, or even wage to capital. Collective bargaining is simply a form of negotiation between
labour and capital; it cannot be abolished; it is part of that way
of life. What we are challenging is not only its traditional significance for the Left or socialism, but also the inherent sexism
of its financial priorities.

We would argue that a further dimension of the feminist approach
is to equalise women's and men's relation to working time - and,
furthermore, to equalise adults' relation to working time with
those typically spent by children in their own institutions, such
as schools and nurseries. This means abolishing contractual differences between full-time and part-time workers, and launching a major
campaign to reduce the working week - despite the fact that, at
present, most men's response to shorter working time is that it
gives them more overtime opportunities.

In other words, far from capitalising on women's financial
dependence (as Paul Hirst does) to suggest that individual wage
bargaining is not important to them,·and that they can be persuaded
to go for 'demands for income planning and social consumption', we
would respectfully suggest that the problems we face are rather more
complex than that. For example, wage militancy among women has
always been constrained by the question of the appropriate and
relevant levels of militancy for women. In *Red Rag*, we challenge
certain concepts of militancy: butch militancy and smash and grab
politics, rather than militancy in general. We are concerned in
particular that women, particularly in the service and caring
industries, are inhibited from the industrial action of withdrawing
their labour. Furthermore, women's relation to earnings is complicated in any case by their own relation of financial dependence.
We agree with Paul Hirst that the range of women's demands may be
more comprehensive than men's - but not for the essentialist reasons
that he advances.

Rather, we believe that women's material and financial demands
can only ever be met partially through the individual wage. There is
also a crucial component of income - the social wage - which bears
directly on the labour of women, and which under present British
conditions can only be struggled over at the national (sometimes
municipal) political level. Paul Hirst's position tends to suggest
that because women aren't greedy (like men) and because they care
about people (which men don't) they will opt for the social wage.
We would suggest, rather, that because of the sexual division of

labour, a whole range of demands does not occur to men, because they can rely on women's labour. Women, however, have a different political imperative, precisely because their responsibility for that labour is the means by which their oppression and domination by men is secured.

We would argue for priority to be given to the social wage, then, as the means by which women's 'places and powers' within the family are relieved. We see the development of the Welfare State as being (amongst other things) an expression of, and a response to, the destabilisation of the family, which has been endemic since the Industrial Revolution. And we would reject the trade-off which Paul Hirst seems to be offering between pressure for a higher social wage and decreased wage militancy. At the time of the introduction of family allowances, in fact, it was argued that non-wage family benefits would *prevent* the (male) worker from being blackmailed into docility by the prospect of his family starving due to his own desire for 'material satisfactions'. We would argue for the removal of the costs and care of children from wage bargaining altogether, by means of a collectively funded child benefit to cover both. Only by removing the calculation which exists in wage bargaining ideology that the male breadwinner's wage has to cover the cost of children's subsistence and care, can you approach an equalisation of men's and women's earnings.

Conclusion

Let us take a closer look at what kind of society Paul Hirst would like to see. Socialism is out; people won't vote for it. Unemployment and inflation are bad for male egos. The answer must be liberal capitalism, with the family as the basic unit and agent of socialisation. Presumably he would claim that the advances that women should win for the family are connected with gaining the conditions under which women themselves will be more fulfilled. This is no more than the traditional 'Leftist' formula of revolution now, liberation later. He wants a stable liberal capitalist economy, full employment and decent chaps who play with toy soldiers; women will get a look in when, and only when, they have got the family back in good order. He forgets that the end will be a product of the means. The feminist cause will not take off itself when society as a whole is back on its feet, because feminism is about transforming what society is. We will not achieve anything until domestic relations are transformed; however 'good' the man in question, however high the benefits, the individual family reinforces structures of isolation and oppression which must be transformed.

Of course, everyone has to be domestically grounded, but it is clear from the evidence of the atypicality of 'normal' families that the family is not the only form of domestic life available, and that familial relations are not the only possible and satisfactory relations between the generations. Paul Hirst's attempt to elide domestic relations into the familial cannot be accepted.

Neither do we accept his elision of women's manifestations of resistance to their familial role, with 'irrelevant' sexual extremism, radicalism and lifestyleism. He describes rigid lifestyle extremists (Lesbians for example?) trying to 'impose' new normalities

of sexual behaviour. It is difficult to imagine how one imposes
norms without a certain modicum of power. In fact, the first Lesbian
to win a custody case recently had to promise to 'impose' heterosexuality on her son. In his view, the new sexual and relational forms
which have developed within the sexual politics movement since the
60s are merely rude interferences in an otherwise 'normal' - or
'natural'? - heterosexual, monogamous, nuclear family. But he cannot
deal adequately either with the evidence (ranging from Criminal Law
Revision working papers, to Royal Commissions, divorce statistics and
endless sociological archaeology on the family) of the escalating
instabilities and contradictions between genders and between generations.

Feminism has been concerned to restore domestic conditions of
existence to politics, because women within the family are subordinate
and dependent. 'Ordinary women's aspirations and actions' in the
family are thus grounded in that relation of domination. What ordinary women want, no one knows - unless we abandon the theory of ideology,
and assume that what they've got is what they want, or indeed that
what they say they want is what they want. The implications for
radicals in politics of Paul Hirst's conclusions are horrific. We
obviously do not need movements to advance demands; we certainly do
not need a women's movement, because, by his account, we know what
women want already, and they want what they get.

By feminism's account, however, we have to have an autonomous
political space in which to construct our political desires, and the
means of expression of our 'aspirations and actions'. Paul Hirst's
article and its assumptions make it quite clear that feminists who
thought they could share a platform with anti-economistic Marxists
were wrong. His anti-economism is theoretical. Nothing differentiates his position from old-fashioned Labourism (or is it conservatism?). Clearly, feminism has made little impact on what he considers
social priorities to be.

Footnotes

1 Gissing, G., *The Odd Women* (1893), reprinted Virago, 1980.
2 See Sachs, A. and Wilson, *Sexism and the Law*, Martin Robertson,
   1978.

Paul Hirst
Reply

I am saddened by the spirit in which my fellow members of the
editorial board have chosen to read this article. They have 'read-
in' whatever seems to suit the stereotype of a conservative, anti-
feminist and anti-socialist supporter of the family as a bulwark of
the social order. To call it a caricature would be to exaggerate
its resemblance to my article; they have had to invent views I
neither hold nor express to sustain their stereotype.

The main misunderstanding concerns the *spirit* in which my piece
was written. I am neither a supporter of the family as an institution nor as a set of values and aspirations. My point is, and it
has been reached reluctantly, that there is no prospect of a shift
away from family forms or values on the part of masses of 'ordinary'
people. I tried to argue that feminism must register social and
economic circumstances which are not within its control and which
cannot be transformed, just like other political movements must do.
I have argued elsewhere that the issues, struggles and forces out
of which socialism must be made are not distinctively socialist ones.
In the same way feminism must work with issues and institutions
which are neither of its making nor to its liking. Feminists cannot
treat their objectives as a set of 'values' to be unambiguously
realised any more than socialists can. Feminism must, as a condition of its political success, address itself to and proffer solutions to general problems of social organisation, ones which must be
confronted by any political force whatever its values. In doing so
it must seek to convince and win the support of non-feminist men and
women and to form alliances with other political organisations and
social forces. However, the whole implication of my piece is that
recognising that the family is not going to disappear and that many
'ordinary' people will continue to subscribe to goals and values very
different to feminism is a condition for working to *change* the family.
My position is predicated on the need for radical changes in the
family and the position of women and is concerned with the very real
obstacles in the way of such changes, obstacles which will not vanish
by persuasion or abuse. Not one line in my article could lead an
unprejudiced reader to conclude that I favour a complacent acceptance

of the generally inferior position of women vis-a-vis men in
domestic and economic roles.
    Where my critics could have got the following ideas from I do
not know.

    (i) That my concern with full employment is a concern with *men*?
Full employment as I understand it means a condition in which everyone
who is able and willing to participate in waged labour can do so, men
and women. My concern with full employment does not mean I favour
the current position of women in the occupational structure.

    (ii) That I am concerned with 'social disintegration' and that I
paint a picture of 'under-socialised youth' engaged in 'street
crime'? My concern with the failure of working-class children to
get the full benefit from education, to press for better and more
interesting work, etc., is not voiced because I am concerned with
them turning to crime. My concern is the waste of talents and possibilities, education *is* a precondition for many skills and pleasures.
My concern is the support for conservatism and the status quo that
indifference to education and indifference to achievement (in its
broadest sense) silently and unknowingly offers. A population that
actively demanded the best in education, housing, health, culture
and so on, and had the organisational and political skills to get
it would pose a revolutionary threat to the existing order.

    (iii) That I am concerned to inculcate in workers 'the capacity
to become a good consumer'? The mind bends at such a reading. I
have stressed throughout the importance of *social* consumption and
the political and economic limitations of workers striving for short-
term money and material benefits alone. I do *not* want everybody to
be a status-mad, competitive middle-class professional. Everybody
cannot win in such a competition.

    (iv) That I have done a u-turn on the question of ideology which
makes a mockery of my previous anti-economism? Indeed, I have
become an old-fashioned economistic Labourite. A funny 'Labourite'
who argues for an incomes policy and is primarily concerned with the
non-economic social relations that condition economic performance.
I have not changed my position on ideology or ideological social
relations. I have always been opposed to theories which conceive
'ideology' as a means of motivating individuals to act in ways
functional to the social order. I have also challenged the notion
that social agents are merely 'subjects' constructed in ideology.
Popular beliefs, however repugnant, cannot be treated as illusions
or 'false consciousness' for the very reason that they *are* popular
and people 'believe' in them. However, I do not say that the
family is a matter of 'free-choice' and OK for that reason:
'... the modern family is neither the realisation of chosen personal
values nor a "liberation" of its members - its development involves
definite forms of coercion and control by family members over one
another and by social agencies over the family.'

I have already exhausted the limited space allotted to me, and the points I would have liked to make in correction of the distortions and inaccuracies in the critique are legion. I will ignore the slur that I have abandoned socialism. I am no more of an antifeminist than are the authors of the critique. I hoped my piece would provoke debate, not shadow-boxing with an imaginary enemy.

Elizabeth F. Kingdom
Sexist Bias and Law

<u>Introduction</u>

A considerable variety of claims to the effect that law has a sexist
bias can be found, explicitly or implicitly, in radical and feminist
literature. This working paper is an attempt to organise the disparate debates and struggles surrounding such claims, on the grounds
that some such organisation is an essential part of developing
socialist/feminist policies and strategies relating to, among other
things, campaigns for women's rights, in or out of law. To facilitate this organisation, three models of the claim that law has a sexist
bias are outlined together with an examination of some of their
theoretical problems and political implications. The three models
are as follows:

    Model 1 Sexist bias as intervention in law
    Model 2 Sexist bias in law
    Model 3 Sexist bias as effect of law

Before moving on to discuss these models, two preliminary points
need to be made. The first concerns the scope of the claim that law
has a sexist bias as examined in this paper, and the second explains
the use of models in this respect.

(i) Bias and discrimination

At least four specific issues might be suggested by the claim that
law has a sexist bias. The first is the reference to bias which is
found in jurisprudential analyses of natural justice. The second is
the scope of the Sex Discrimination Act 1975 (SDA). The third is a
problem about legal notions of sex as they appear in SDA and in other
areas of law. The fourth is the equal treatment of sexes under current legislation. But for purposes of this paper the claim that law
has a sexist bias is not reduced to any one of these issues.

It is commonplace to read that the Common Law operates with a notion of natural justice, not in the sense of an abstract ideal deriving from extra-legal considerations of morality, but in the sense of a number of criteria for the conduct of trials. It has been argued, for example, that the rules of natural justice 'enunciate ... the minimum standard that the Common Law sets for all manner of hearings and tribunals, public or domestic'.[1] These rules, it is further argued, can be 'summarised in the form that no man should be condemned unheard and that every judge must be free from bias'.[2] It is true that two examples of sexist bias and law given under the heading of Model 1 are concerned with possible bias in judges but the claim of Model 1 is that law as a whole has a sexist bias. Its claim is not directed specifically at the operation of the standards for a fair trial, although it might include that question. It is for this reason that no further reference will be made in this paper to the specific question of natural justice in law.

Secondly, the point of discussing sexist bias rather than discrimination in the context of law is that discrimination too readily suggests SDA. SDA makes it unlawful to discriminate in a limited range of fields, for example in employment and education.[3] Under the heading of Model 2 some attention is paid to the fact of this limitation, but it is enough here to point out that exclusive concern with SDA and its workings could not do justice to the generality of the claim that law as a whole has a sexist bias.

Thirdly, the claim that law has a sexist bias could suggest the problem of the ways that SDA and other parts of law treat the notion of sex. In SDA 'woman' includes a female of any kind and 'man' includes a male of any age.[4] In a short, cryptic and sometimes sensationalist article, Terrence Walton identifies a number of problems and anomalies resulting from the failure of current sex law to recognise relations which may hold between persons who do not fall easily under the headings of male and female.[5] In failing to recognise unions not between men and women but also between males and female trans-sexuals and between females and male trans-sexuals, law could be said to have a sexist bias. This is an important issue for the investigation of law's construction of sexuality, but it is a specific issue. It therefore receives no further attention in this paper, which is concerned with the general question of law's sexist bias.

Fourthly, SDA recognises that, in the fields it is concerned with, discrimination on the basis of sex can occur to the disadvantage of men as well as women,[6] and men have successfully pursued cases under SDA. Discrimination against men is alleged in other areas of law too. For example, the Law Commission's Working Paper No.4 on Family Law and Illegitimacy suggests that 'from a strictly legal point of view, the father of an illegitimate child is today probably at a greater disadvantage than the child himself'. It supports this allegation in two ways. First, the father's consent to the marriage of the child during the child's minority is not required unless he has been granted custody of the child or has become the child's guardian under the mother's will. Secondly, there is no legal procedure by which the father can establish paternity without the consent of the child's mother.[7] It is this sort of issue that has led to the setting up of groups such as Fathers Need Families.[8] In this way the claim that law has a sexist bias suggests the specific problem of the equal treatment of sexes in current legislation. Under the headings of Models 1 and 2 there is brief discussion of the problems involved in arguing that law ought to be impartial as between sexes. But once again, important as this issue is, it is only one aspect of the general question of how law's sexist bias is to be characterised.

(ii) Models

The preceding section emphasised that for purposes of this paper the claim that law has a sexist bias is not reduced to any one of four specific issues, including that of the equal treatment of men and women. But the general presumption of the claim that law has a sexist bias is certainly that law's sexist bias works to the disadvantage of women. The three models shortly to be considered are intended to facilitate a theoretical ordering of claims made in the light of that general presumption, together with an examination of some of their political implications for campaigns for women's rights.

The use of the term 'model' in this paper follows that of C.B. Macpherson. He defines a model in a broad sense as 'a theoretical construction intended to exhibit and explain the real relations, underlying the appearances, between or within the phenomena under study'.[9] Accordingly, it is not claimed in this paper that the models of law's sexist bias serve as standards or ideals against which feminist practices are to be assessed, even if they carry implications for the direction of such practices. It is not claimed either that these models exhaust the variety of claims made about law's sexist bias or that any one author is exclusively identified with any one of them, or that elements of all three models do not appear in a single work. Rather the models are intended both as a means of exhibiting some major themes in these contemporary debates and, through their theoretical and political assessment, as a means of suggesting more coherent analyses and strategies.

Briefly, I shall argue that the serious theoretical and political drawbacks of Models 1, 2 and 3a point to a need to develop an analysis of law's sexist bias along the lines indicated by Model 3b. The paper concludes with a summary of these discussions in terms of women's rights and with a brief proposal for their analysis. A full development of this analysis would involve much more work both on the general analysis of legal rights and on the possibilities of intervening in law with a view to achieving socialist/feminist objectives.[10] These tasks are clearly beyond the scope of this working paper, since its limited purpose is to assemble and clarify arguments which focus attention on law and the allegation of its sexist bias.

Model 1   Sexist bias as intervention in law

The starting point of this model is a distinction which is in fact
shared by all the models under consideration. The distinction is
between a legal sphere on the one hand and a non-legal sphere on the
other. The legal sphere will include the body of Statute Law, Common
Law, legal practices in courts, the processes of legal education and
professionalisation, and the ideologies attendant on and incorporated
in those laws, practices and processes.
   In contrast with this legal sphere is a non-legal sphere. This
will be identified in a number of ways: a psychological sphere, a
psychoanalytical sphere, a biological sphere, an economic sphere,
and so on. These various non-legal spheres have as their content
human desires and motives, human physiology, interests and organisations, or whatever.
   What is distinctive about Model 1's employment of this distinction
is that law's sexist bias is conceptualised as the appearance or
expression in the legal sphere of elements deriving from one or more
of the non-legal spheres. The usual presumption is that these elements
intervene in the legal sphere in ways which are, in some sense, improper or undesirable in that they work to the disadvantage of women.
   Model 1 offers a variety of examples. First, Jerome Frank's brand
of legal realism posits a pre-legal reality, namely the conditions of
childhood understood in a semi-psychoanalytic way. Elements of this
pre-legal reality are said constantly to affect legal practices.[11]
On such a view, sexist bias in law would have to be traced to the
mental and moral upbringing of judges, court clerks, Law Lords, and
so forth.
   Secondly, Albie Sachs and Joan Hoff Wilson conceptualise sexist
bias in law as the appearance in law of interests which are variously
described as male, upper-class and basically economic.[12]
   Thirdly, early forms of Marxist theory of law identify laws as the
representation of economic struggles, so that, for example, property
disputes in law can be read as a map of the class struggle over the
means of production and consumption.[13] On such a theory of law, sexist bias in law could be identified as the appearance in law of
women's economic status, for example in the division of labour.
This type of relation between Marxist analyses of capitalism and
legal institutions on the one hand and the position of women on the
other has received more specific treatment in socialist/feminist
literature by means of the concept of patriarchy. So, for example,
Annette Kuhn argues that patriarchy is a structure which intervenes
in social relations and institutions in ways which are determined
by the prevailing mode of production. Legal institutions can then
be characterised as biased against women through the support of those
institutions for the mode of production, currently through the appro-
priation of property by men.[14]
   To initiate discussion of the theoretical problems and political
implications, if any, of Model 1, it should be noted that, if sexist
bias in law is conceptualised as intervention in this way, the appearance or expression of the intervening elements can be characterised
as inevitable or as something which can be avoided, and, even where
it is seen as inevitable, as something which is proper or improper,

that is, as something to be content with or as something which, even if
it cannot be wholly eradicated, should at least be corrected. Frank,
for example, sees the intervention of all forms of bias in law as inevitable. He also sees it as the duty of a judge 'to act in accordance
with those basic predilections inhering in our legal system (although,
of course, he has the right, at times, to urge that some of them be
modified or abandoned).'[15] Sachs and Wilson, on the other hand, see
the intervention of male, upper-class and economic interests as something which is inevitable under present circumstances but they insist
that it must be remedied through gender struggle.[16] And Steven
Goldberg sees patriarchy as universal in the sense that there has
never been a society in which hierarchical authority and leadership
have not been associated with men in its political, economic, religious and social systems. He adds, however, that he is uncertain if it
makes sense to describe the inevitable as unfair but that it would
certainly be utopian to believe that the sort of laws which can prevent occupational discrimination can have much effect on male and
female stereotypes.[17]

In fact, the conceptualisation of law's sexist bias as intervention
of non-legal elements in law poses general theoretical problems regardless of whether the intervention is seen as proper or improper, but
special political problems are posed if the intervention is seen as
improper or as a breach of law's impartiality.

The general theoretical problems stem from Model 1's use of the
initial distinction between the legal and non-legal spheres. It seems
to involve a conception of law as a social practice independent of, for
example, economic or political practices. On this view, it would seem,
law operates - or ought to operate - according to its own devices but
is subject to interference by economic or political elements. The
problem here is not so much the *prime facie* absurdity of conceptualis-
ing law as insulated from other social practices as the difficulty of
actually identifying the occasions on which the alleged economic or
political elements make their appearance. This problem can be illustrated through a brief discussion, first of a legal event which has no
obvious feminist interest, and secondly of one which does.

Consider, first, the outcome of appeals made in June 1980 by members of the 'Operation Julie' drug gang against forfeiture orders.
The five Law Lords unanimously allowed the appeal, in Lord Diplock's
words, 'with considerable regret'. Lord Scarman pointed out that the
forfeiture provision of S.27 of the Misuse of Drugs Act 1971 (MD) did
not apply to the proceeds of the crime in question. It followed that,
while the Director of Public Prosecutions was not to be required to
hand back the seized property, the appellants might seek to recover
the proceeds of their activities.[18]

On Model 1, it could be argued that here is an obvious case of
the intervention of the economic interests of a significant proportion
of the population (villains) to flout the otherwise just course of
law. But it could equally well be argued that a different economic
interest is at work here, namely the economic interests of another
significant section of the population (the police, to whom, it seems,
the proceeds might otherwise go). These interests find their expression not in the Law Lords' actual decision, it might be argued, but
in their regret at that decision, the implication being that perhaps

under only slightly different circumstances the intervention of the
police interest could produce the reverse decision.

At least three problems are raised by these alternatives. The
first is the difficulty of ascertaining the mechanism whereby either
of these rival interests might manage to gain expression at the cost
of the other, and even with the advantage of hindsight it is impossible to produce a theoretically determinate account of why, in any
particular instance, the one should prevail over the other. The
second problem is the difficulty of reconciling either alternative
with another sort of explanation, one which need not invoke non-legal
elements at all. In this case, for example, it could plausibly be
argued that the outcome of the appeal can be entirely explained by
reference to the intra-legal debates relating to the confused status
of conspiracy under S.27 of MD, and, indeed, the Law Lords pointed
out that conspiracy was not an offence under the Act. The third
problem is more pertinent to those versions of Model 1 that identify
patriarchy as perpetually intervening in legal institutions. The
question here is one of speculating about how 'universal' patriarchal
interests or structures could have been suppressed in this case. In
any event, it is difficult to see how precisely they could even be
thought to have a bearing on it.

The theoretical problems of Model 1 can be made more pertinent to
feminist analyses by considering a legal event which, as Sachs and
Wilson point out, has been described as 'a milestone in the march
of women to equality'.[19] According to Sachs and Wilson's conception
of sexist bias as the intervention in law of male, upper-class and
basically economic interests, however, the passing of the Married
Women's Property Act 1882 must present an anomaly in the otherwise
predictable march of male supremacy. Consider the explanatory options: male partiality momentarily displaced by female partiality,
male partiality miscalculating its economic interest, male dominance
in the legal profession briefly overcome with guilt at its history of
male partiality, male partiality shrewdly calculating a mere gesture
at female equality,[20] the belated appearance of gender-free impartiality, and so on. Now Sachs and Wilson claim that partiality and
impartiality can each be seen as significant determinants of legal
institutions and practices. But their claim provides, and can provide, no solution to the theoretical problem of producing analyses
of legal practices which can differentiate the appearance either of
various competing interests or of the conflicting values of partiality and impartiality. This criticism of Sachs and Wilson's position
as theoretically indeterminate in the manner just described can be
extended to all verions of Model 1.

But, as indicated in the description of Goldberg's position above,
there are also important political implications of Model 1 for purposes of developing policies and strategies for the elimination of
sexist bias from law. The distinction between legal and non-legal
spheres characteristic of Model 1 is frequently accompanied by the
suggestion that law, subject as it is to intervention of economic
or political elements, ought nonetheless to be disinterested in its
rules, procedures and decisions. The notion of sexist bias in law
as breach of law's impartiality is set against the notion of law as
neutral, fair and impartial and, by implication, as working to the
advantage of nobody on the basis of sex.

It is commonplace to note, however, that the notion of law as impartial is highly problematic for policies of positive discrimination, since such policies necessarily involve discrimination to the advantage of some people, usually women, on the basis of their sex. Put in this way, the problem seems insoluble, but two solutions which might be advanced are worth brief mention.

First, it might be argued that positive discrimination is desirable as a temporary expedient to restore 'balance' to law and that, just as special measures can be introduced to cope with hitherto sexist bias against women, so those measures can be phased out as and when gender-free impartiality is established. The difficulty with this attempted solution is not just that it has an air of sexual millenarianism - looking forward to the day when civilisation emerges from its pre-history of sexual injustice. It is rather that the 'temporary expedient solution' for purposes of establishing impartiality 'in the long run' involves the retention of the very conception of law as impartial which Model 1's characterisation of bias is expressly designed to challenge.

The second possible solution to the problem of positive discrimination as outlined above is more radical. It might be argued, in accordance with Model 1, that the intervention in law of political and economic interests working to the disadvantage of women is so extensive that, far from attempting to remedy it through the introduction of positive discrimination, law should not be considered a site of feminist politics. The political dangers of abstaining from, for example, resistance to attacks of abortion rights or to attacks on women's employment rights are obvious. It should be noted, however, that support for the view that law should not be a site of feminist politics might be found in the observation that, even where positive discrimination has been allowed in law, it has been largely ignored, and also in the observation that SDA has been used in ways which positively advantage the position not of women but of men.[21] These sort of observations, pointing to the limitations of law reform, will be discussed more fully in connection with Model 2.

Model 2 Sexist bias in law

This is perhaps the simplest of the three models seeking to account for law's sexist bias, since it focuses attention entirely on the legal sphere and postulates no non-legal elements which have to be related to it. Rather the claim here is that law's sexist bias is to be conceptualised in terms of law's intrinsic discrimination against people on the basis of sex, normally to the disadvantage of women. The restriction of the analysis of law's sexist bias to the claim that law per se - in Statute Law, for example, and in courts - discriminates against women suggests the corollary that the elimination of sexist bias from law is simply a matter of the more or less complex processes of law reform.

On Model 2, attention is likely to be paid to the advances made by the passing of SDA and the Equal Pay Act 1975 (EQPA). It will be conceded that SDA has removed a great many examples which could formerly have been given in support of the claim that law has a

sexist bias, since SDA makes it unlawful to discriminate against men
or women in a range of fields: employment, education, the provision
of goods, services and facilities and the disposal of premises, and
discriminatory advertisements. But it will also be argued that there
is still a vast area of law which remains sexist. So, it has to be
pointed out that SDA does not make it unlawful to discriminate in the
private sphere. Tony Honoré, for example, provides much information
on the unequal treatment of men and women in sex law, the most notable
and well known example being the possibility of criminal prosecution
in the case of male homosexuality but not in the case of female homosexuality.[22] Again, SDA does not apply to service in the armed forces.
The NCCL booklet *First Rights* alerts people to the fact that boys can
volunteer for the armed services with their parents' consent when they
are 16 but that girls have to wait until they are 17 for that particular privilege.[23]

By identifying areas of law still exhibiting sexist bias, Model 2
poins to the possibilities of eliminating sexist bias from law
through law reforms. So, for example, it would be appropriate to
investigate Honoré's proposals for the rational reform of law in
connection with homosexuality. Among other things, he proposes the
substitution of the phrase 'sexual act' for the phrases 'buggery',
'gross indecency', 'unnatural act', 'crime against nature', and so
on. He proposes too that the present laws regarding male buggery be
changed so that it would be an offence only in the case of a male
over 18 with of in the presence of a male under 18. It is interesting that he makes no proposal for the introduction of similar criminal
legislation for female homosexuals. He recognises this as offending
against the principle of equality between sexes, but he defends his
position in three ways. First, he says that people mind less about
female homosexuality. Secondly, he claims that women are less adven-
turous than men. And thirdly, he says that in any case it is not a
good practice to introduce unnecessary legislation, especially in
this case when female homosexuals generally have a much harder time
of it than male homosexuals do.[24]

Whatever reservations might be entertained about Honoré's particular proposals and his defence of them, there seems to be no serious
theoretical problem either about the claim that law *per se* discriminates against women or about the status of the claim that legal reforms
can remove instances of such bias from law. What is in question is
the claim that the elimination of sexist bias from law can be
achieved solely through law reforms. That claim can be challenged
first at the level of the practical implementation of legal reforms
aimed at the elimination of sexist bias from law and secondly at
the more general level of the recognition of rights in law.

With respect to the first challenge, at least four complaints have
been made, mainly in connection with SDA. First, even a cursory
reading of SDA reveals that it is a morass of exceptions and provisos
to exceptions.[25] Secondly, it is by no means clear   SDA relates
to EQPA.[26] Thirdly, SDA cases have produced what appear to be
farcical decisions. There is the celebrated case, referred to by
Sheffield Rights of Women (SROW), in which an Employment Appeal
Tribunal 'dismissed a woman's claim that she was dismissed from her
job because she was pregnant. The Tribunal argued that SDA did not

apply because there was no man a pregnant woman could compare herself
with as men cannot become pregnant.'[27] Fourthly, although SDA was 'in
spirit' aimed to help women, it has been used to the advantage of men.
The case of Ministry of Defence v. Jeremiah is relevant here. At the
employers' factory, male volunteers for overtime were periodically
required to work in certain shops and because of the dirty conditions
they were paid extra. Female volunteers for overtime were not
required to work in these shops. A male worker successfully claimed
discrimination on grounds of sex because under SDA S.6(2(b) he was
seen to be subject to detriment by the employers' practice. When the
employers appealed, his case was upheld on the grounds that if women
only had been required to work in these shops it would have been unlawful discrimination against women.[28]

What these four complaints point to is the problem of whether the
attempt to remove sexist bias from law by means of legislation can do
more than produce further examples of sexist bias in law, and they
therefore reinforce a scepticism about the possibilities of eliminating sexist bias from law solely by means of law reform. This scepticism can be transformed into the second challenge to the claim that
legal reforms by themselves can eliminate sexist bias from law. The
challenge here can be put in the form of rhetorical questions. What
grounds are there for supposing that the existence of formal equality
in law guarantees non-discriminatory practices in law? What grounds
are there for supposing that legal recognition of rights guarantees
the enjoyment of those rights by virtue of due process of law?

But the most serious obstacle to acceptance of Model 2 as an
account of law's sexist bias is that, by restricting attention to
the business of legislation and court practices, it fails to recognise
the complexities of social relations which pertain outside the legal
sphere. So, even if it were accepted that it is possible to remove
all obviously sexist legislation, it by no means follows that substantive law,which makes no reference to treating people differently
on the basis of sex,and legal practices which are not obviously sexist, have no sexist implications. To put it crudely, legislation and
procedures need not be overtly sexist for them to have sexist implications. It can be argued, for example, that an act with implications
for the level of the rate support grant, indirectly requiring cuts in
social services staff, ancillary workers in the health service, and
school meals and cleaning staff, need not directly identify women as
targets but will nonetheless have the effect of eroding ground
supposedly won by the passing of SDA and EQPA. To argue in this
way, however, is to look for an alternative model, one which is concerned not so much with the elimination of sexist bias from law
through legal reforms alone as with the capacity of law to have
effects reaching beyond the limited area of the legal sphere itself.
It is this concern that provides much of the impetus for Model 3.

Model 3   Sexist bias as effect of law

This model of law's sexist bias identifies it not in terms of prior
determinants of law, nor in terms of intra-legal practices, but in
terms of law's capacity to have effects which are unfavourable to
women in contexts much wider than that of law itself. But while the
claim that it is law's effects that are the most serious for women
may seem intuitively clear, more than one interpretation can be
placed on that claim. Accordingly, two versions of Model 3 are
distinguished here. They are different with respect to the way that
law is supposed to have such effects.

Model 3a claims that law actively perpetuates social conditions
and attitudes which differentiate between people on the basis of sex
and that it does so in a way which is systematically to the disadvantage of women. So, for example, Sachs and Wilson argue that
'in a modern society it is *the law above all* that defines social
issues and constructs models of appropriate and inappropriate
behaviour' (emphasis added).[29] The argument here is that law's
sexist bias, both in Statute Law and in the practices of the legal
profession itself, is the prime determinent of social relations
which are unfavourable to women. Similarly, within the general
theoretical framework of the inevitable relations holding between
capitalism, patriarchy and the modern nuclear family, SROW argue
that 'the law plays a role in perpetuating and reproducing patriarchal relations within the family (as well as in the public sphere).
It does this by legally enforcing women's economic dependence and
sanctioning, in varieties of ways, behaviour that does not fit with
the heterosexual, monogamous nuclear family mould (*viz.* lesbian
workers and prostitutes)'.[30] For Model 3a, law is permanently
suspect in its inevitably and systematically oppressive effects on
the status, legal and general, of women.

Model 3b, however, claims that, while law can and does have unfavourable effects on the legal and general status of women, it can
also have favourable effects on it. So, for example, both the NCCL
in its fights for women's rights and SROW acknowledge that legislation has its place - that it is worth fighting for the elimination
of sexist bias from law by means of law reform - but they claim that
legislation by itself is not enough. What is urged here is that law
can be a help to women, so that attacks on women's rights (in the
case of the Corrie Bill an attack on existing abortion rights) must
be resisted and should not be relegated to the status of irrelevant
or peripheral site of socialist/feminist politics. Further, Model 3b
pursues the argument that non-sexist legislation can be seen as a
means for the creation of 'an ideological climate that is more
receptive to feminist arguments on a woman's right to choose or on
equal pay and non-discrimination etc.'[31] In this connection, Carol
Smart argues that redressing the balance in favour of women, in the
context of their traditional legal status as comparable to children
and animals, will not be achieved without a transformation of basic
forms of ideology and social practices. This can be done not only
through legal remedies but also through the promotion of women's
studies in criminology. She rejects all analyses which rely on
'a determinate model of female behaviour' and makes a strong plea

for specific analyses of the struggles of women in law, for example
in the context of the Abortion Act 1967 and in the context of 'the
impact on women of having their men put in prison'. Her position
then, is that anti-discrimination legislation must be combined with
attempts to make existing discrimination obvious and visible if
women's traditional roles can even be questioned.[32]

The strengths and weaknesses of both versions of Model 3 as models
of the claim that law has a sexist bias are varied and complex, but
they both have advantages over Models 1 and 2. They have the advantage over Model 1 in that they do not require the postulation of non-
legal elements making theoretically incalculable appearances in the
legal sphere and they do not require the retention of the ideology of
law as impartial. They have the advantage over Model 2 in that they
point to the limitations of law reform as the sole means for the
elimination of sexist bias from law and in that they identify that
elimination as something more complex than the simple removal of
archaic or naturally unjust legislation. On the other hand, both
versions are far from being unproblematic, and this applies particularly to Model 3a.

The weakness of Model 3a derives from the fact that, according to
it, law is conceptualized as the, or a, prime determinant sphere of
all social relations or as perpetuating a total social structure
such as patriarchy. In this way, the effects of law are characterised as the, or a, prime determinant of the total movement of society.
One might say that, according to Model 3a, there is no stopping law
- it is inextricably caught up in its necessary relations with
economics, politics and ideology. The problem with Model 3a can be
identified by pointing to its strong theoretical similarity to
Model 1, since they both conceptualise law in terms of necessary
social relations. In terms of patriarchy theories, Model 1 identifies
patriarchy as intervening in law, with or without the reinforcing
agency of capitalism, so that law becomes the inevitable expression
of patriarchy; Model 3a identifies law as inevitably reproducing
patriarchy, with or without the reinforcing agency of capitalism.
The theoretical difference between them is only that for Model 1 law
is necessarily determin*ed* whereas for Model 3a law is necessarily
determin*ing*. In that case, all the problems which were identified
above in connection with Model 1 for purposes of producing specific
analyses of legal events and for developing a policy for the elimination of sexist bias from law can also be attributed to Model 3a.

Model 3b challenges Model 3a, however, in that it questions the
inevitability of law's systematically unfavourable effects on the
position of women. Rather, it emphasises the need for specific analyses of relations holding between prevailing legal and social practices. A defender of Model 3a and an opponent of Model 3b might
argue immediately that, in denying the systematic relations inevitably holding between law, capitalism and patriarchy, Model 3b is unable to produce any systematic policy or strategy for dealing with
sexist bias in law. On this argument, Model 3b is forced into the
position of adapting ad hoc and even opportunist policies, thereby
weakening the force of campaigns for women's rights. Defenders of
Model 3b can reply to this objection by questioning both the desirability and the possibility of developing any such systematic policy

and by pointing to the political dangers of ignoring the highly
specific nature of different issues which are grouped together under
the general heading of women's rights.

Model 3b, then, claims the advantage of permitting and encouraging
the investigation of the complex relations between, for example,
Statute Law, tribunal practices and conditions of work. An example
here is the analysis of whether it is more promising for people in
different occupations to bring a case of unfair dismissal under SDA,
EQPA or current employment protection legislation.[33] Also, Model 3b
allows for a complex analysis of women's rights. For example, W.B.
Creighton gives a useful account of the opposed views of a Working
Party of the National Joint Advisory Council to the Ministry of
Labour submitting its report in 1969, of the CBI, of the TUC, and of
the TUC Women's Advisory Committee over whether to retain, abolish
or extend protective legislation for women in connection with
restrictions on overtime, night work, etc.[34] Creighton describes
the position taken by the TUC Women's Advisory Committee - that
special measures protecting women be retained until such time as
other safeguards in matters of health and welfare are established.
Creighton's description shows that the defence of women's rights
cannot be a universal package deal, not only because of the sheer
complexity of particular issues but also because the defence of
women's rights in one context may well be inseparable from the
struggle to improve working conditions for men as well as women.
In this respect it is also worth noting that the removal of one of
the rights of women, such as the former right of married women to
make reduced insurance contributions, can be seen as a progressive
measure, in that particular case because it removed the possibility
of married women diseqipping themselves for various forms of independence. The removal of one right becomes the assertion of another.

The considerable advantage of Model 3b, then, is that it allows
for a complexity of analysis in relation to the effects of law and
in relation to decisions about whether or not to fight for the legal
recognition of particular rights of women. It is not encumbered with
the claim that sexist bias in law must inevitably frustrate those
struggles, nor with the claim that sexist bias is a permanent and
inescapable feature of all social conditions. In this respect it is
important to note that it is open to Model 3b to claim that, while
special measures may be needed to overcome past and present discrimination, it follows neither that those special measures must become
a permanent feature of social relations nor that different special
measures might not become desirable in future. In other words,
Model 3b is not restricted to claims about the inexorability of
female oppression, nor is it committed to a vision of a future non-
oppressive society in which there is no need for regulation of
relations between sexes. Rather, its emphasis on the need for
specific analyses must allow the possibility of future social conditions in which regulation and legislation may still be necessary,
albeit for the achievement of socialist/feminist objectives that are
different from those now held.

To argue the advantages of Model 3b in terms of its allowing and
encouraging specific analyses of social relations and in terms of
its permitting complex analyses of struggles for women's rights is

not to argue in an opportunistic way. It is not a matter of working from an existing commitment to certain women's issues and casting about for a theoretical analysis to accommodate that commitment. Instead, it is to argue for Model 3b as a theoretical/political framework with three main advantages. First, it can escape the theoretical problems of the other models discussed in this paper. Secondly, it can do justice to the complexity of the relations between women's issues and other socialist concerns, thereby avoiding the segregation of 'women's issues' from other socialist struggles. For example, the publication of the government Green Paper on Family Taxation in December 1980 generated considerable debate about the effects of the current tax allowance system, in particular its bias in favour of married working women. But it also raised questions about how that tax system is related to the general concept of negative taxation, to the Treasury's alleged prejudice against cash benefits, and to government policy on unemployment, three issues which are sites for the development of socialist analyses and strategy irrespective of their particular relevance to women's issues.[35] Thirdly, Model 3b suggests a direction for the analysis of women's rights, and a proposal for such an analysis is outlined below.

Conclusion

This working paper has adopted the device of exhibiting three models of the claim that law has a sexist bias in order to clarify the great variety of theoretical and political debates and struggles surrounding that claim. It has argued, if all too briefly, for the advantages of Model 3b. A short summary of these issues can be done through an exploratory analysis of the concept of women's rights.

It has been argued that Model 3b holds out greater hope for a useful characterisation of women's rights in the context of legal institutions and practices. There seems little to be gained, and perhaps a lot to be lost, by Model 1's characterisation of women's rights as the intervention in law of non-legal elements such as justice or impartiality, and there is even less to be gained by explaning the appearance in law of women's rights as the somewhat surprising successful outcome of the struggle to bring about the non-sexist upbringing of legal practitioners. Secondly, there are serious drawbacks to Model 2's characterisation of women's rights as entirely a function of their legal rights. Thirdly, there is little to be gained, and much confusion in, the characterisation of women's rights as the presumably miraculous effect of struggles against a total system of non-legal relations necessarily holding between capitalism and patriarchy.

The type of analysis of women's rights required by Model 3b, however, should be one which can satisfy at least two requirements. First, it should resist the temptation to adopt the traditional philosophical conception of rights as axiomatic or inalienable possessions owned by virtue of principles transcending prevailing social and legal conditions. That sort of conception cannot account for at least three important features of debates about rights. First, it manifestly cannot account for the fact that rights certainly can be alienated. Secondly, it cannot account for the fact, noted above, that the loss of a right may be positively desirable. Thirdly, it cannot account for the fact that the gain or loss of rights by persons or groups is a function not of any universal feature of human nature but of the criteria by which persons or groups are identified. Persons or groups have rights by virtue of their age, sex, nationality, income, physical health, and so on. It is obviously possible to have a right by virtue of being one sort of person or a member of one sort of group, only to lose it through being identified as another sort of person or as a member of another sort of group. An example here is the fact that wome women, having won the right not to be discriminated against in employment under SDA, find that their claim is frustrated or subverted by alterations in job descriptions or by practices which discriminate against them in new ways.[36]

The second requirement of a Model 3b type of analysis of women's rights is that it can present an alternative to those deficiencies of the traditional conception of rights that can be summed up simply by pointing out that 'possession' of a right is no guarantee of its enjoyment. The 'all-or-nothing' connotation of the traditional con- ception of a right must be replaced by an analysis which can accommo- date the different and sometimes overlapping ways in which people's rights can be assigned, modified or withdrawn. Now, if it is agreed that an appeal to some abstract or transcendent notion of right is inadequate for the characterisation of women's rights, and if it is also agreed that the phrase 'women's rights' seems to invoke some such notion, then it follows that a new rights vocabulary is needed.

It can be argued that there are considerable advantages in a vocabulary which conceptualises women's rights in terms of women's capabilities, capacities and competences, and in terms of the social practices whereby those capabilities, capacities and competences are constructed and modified. The nature of this proposal can be indi- cated through a discussion of three main advantages of this vocabulary.

First, the terms capabilities, capacities and competences are useful because they are general. They are general not in the sense of describing any sort of basic human attributes constitutive of human nature. They are general in the sense that they are used in a number of areas of law. Take 'capabilities'. The Social Security Act 1975 (SSA) defines a person as incapable of self-support 'if, but only if, he is incapable of supporting himself by reason of physical or mental infirmity and is likely to remain so incapable for a prolonged period'.[37] SSA also defines a person incapable of work as someone who cannot work 'by reason of some specific disease or bodily or mental disablement, or deemed in accordance with regula- tions to be so incapable'.[38] Again, under the Trade Union and Labour Relations Act 1974, industrial tribunals have been asked to consider the capabilities of claimants in cases of unfair dismissal. A person can be dismissed if the qualifications on the strength of which that person was appointed can be shown to be date, a matter of some interest to women hoping to return to work after a period of leave. Now consider 'capacities' and 'competences'. Legal capacity in general is defined in terms of legal power or competence. For example, the Law Reform (Married Women and Tortfeasors) Act 1935 was explicitly an act to give married women full legal capacity in contract

law by repealing certain sections of the Married Women's Property
Acts 1882 and 1893. Again, the Aliens Employment Act 1955 enabled
aliens to be employed in a civil capacity under the Crown and it
removed previous disabilities for employment in any such capacity.
Finally, in cases of bigamy the spouse of the accused is a competent, though not a compellable, witness for the prosecution.[39]

Secondly, although the terms capabilities, capacities and competences are general in the sense of being recurrent in different areas
of law, they are, at the same time, as the above examples show, defined in highly specific ways. This specificity gives them an advantage over the loose phrase 'women's rights' in two ways. First, they
can help to focus attention on the ways in which specific women's
struggles can be brought to law. They can do this by directing
campaigns to the task of formulating desired extensions or modifica-
tions of women's capacities or, which comes to the same thing,
desired removals of disabilities. It is easy to see how the two
types of incapability cited above could be modified so as to take
account of the specially difficult circumstances of women. Secondly,
since the specification of capacities is inseparable from the specification of restrictions and limitations, this vocabulary can help
to clarify the ways in which the different criteria by means of
which women are defined in law can have the effect of assigning,
modifying or withdrawing competences and capacities.

The third advantage of the vocabulary of capabilities, capacities
and competences over the general phrase 'women's rights' relates to
the fact that, although they are both general and specific legal
concepts as illustrated above, they are also central to a number of
contemporary debates *about* law. For example, the mental and physical
capacities deemed necessary for *mens rea* (the mental state which is
a necessary condition of criminal responsibility) have been much discussed, in particular with respect to the assessment of legal practices in the light of desirable social consequences.[40] Smart has
shown the importance of those debates to cases of rape and 'delinquent'
sexual behaviour, since they draw attention to the grey area between
law and morality, and they are also pertinent to her note about the
sex-specific offence of infanticide.[41]

In conclusion, something needs to be said about the status of the
proposal outlined here for a new rights vocabulary. The proposal for
this 'new' vocabulary might be interpreted as the claim that the
traditional conception of a right as an abstract and inalienable moral
possession owned independently of prevailing social conditions can be
reduced in a strict philosophical sense to statements about social
agents' capabilities, capacities and competences. No such claim is
made here, not least because that thesis, in so far as it involves
the reduction of an entity which is characterised *ab initio* as something irreducible to statements about prevailing social conditions, is
doomed.[42] Nor is it proposed here that clearly defined legal rights,
such as right of appeal on a point of law against a decision of an
industrial tribunal as provided by S.88 of EQPA, stand in need of re-
description. In particular, the proposal is not intended to deny that
campaigns for 'women's rights' may have considerable political force.
What is being urged is that campaigns under the banner of rights, if
they are to be successful either in resisting attacks on existing

rights or in establishing new ones within the context of law, require the formulation of specific objectives which are at least
potentially assimilable into law. As emphasised above, the use of
the vocabulary of capabilities, capacities and competences can help
to focus attention on the complex task of identifying those objectives and the strategies which may assist in their achievement.

Notes and references

1 Alice Erh-Soon Tay, 'The sense of justice in the Common Law',
   in Eugene Kamenka and Alice Ehr-Soon Tay (eds.), *Justice*,
   Edward Arnold, 1979, p.84.
2 *Ibid*. Tay goes on to point out that these canons are 'to some
   degree and in some areas under attack as allowing formal justice
   to impede substantial justice, but the basic tradition remains
   and is strong' (p.86).
3 Michael J. Beloff, *Sex Discrimination Act 1975*, Butterworths
   Annotated Legislation Service, Vol.237, Butterworths, 1976,
   Introduction, p.1.
4 *Ibid*., Interpretation (2) p.97. For a brief discussion of this
   sort of issue, see Ann Oakley, 'Sex Discrimination Legislation',
   British Journal of Law and Society
5 Terrence Walton, 'When is a Woman not a Woman?', *New Law Journal*,
   30 May 1974.
6 Beloff, *loc.cit*., p.1 and S.2 Sex Discrimination against men (1).
7 Law Commission Working Paper No.74 on Family Law and Illegitimacy,
   pp.14-16.
8 Cf. Beatrix Campbell, 'Divorce', *Time Out*, 21-27 March 1980,
   p.11.
9 C.B. Macpherson, *The Life and Times of Liberal Democracy*, Oxford
   University Press, 1977, pp.2-3.
10 An example here is the dilemma posed by the case of Helen
   Whitfield, reported in *Spare Rib*, March 1980. With the support
   of the Equal Opportunities Commission, Helen Whitfield and her
   mother planned to bring a case against a local authority for
   failing to make carpentry, woodwork and technical drawing available to girls. After various legal and non-legal exchanges, the
   Appeal Court is due to hear the case, the first to be brought
   under S.22 Discrimination by bodies in charge of educational
   establishments. The precedent established if she loses could
   make S.22 at best unusable and at worst an obstacle to future
   attempts through law to make 'boys' subjects', and hence access
   to craft employment, easily available to girls.
11 Jerome Frank, *Law and the Modern Mind*, Stevens and Sons, 1949,
   p.29n. For a brief comparison of Frank's views and those of
   Sachs and Wilson, see by 'Women in Law', *m/f*, No.4, 1980.
12 Albie Sachs and Joan Hoff Wilson, *Sexism and the Law*, Martin
   Robertson, 1978, pp.8-9.
13 Cf. P.I. Stuchka, *The Revolutionary Part Played by Law and the
   State - A General Doctrine of Law*, in H. Babb (ed.) *Soviet
   Legal Philosophy*, Harvard University Press, 1951.

14 Annette Kuhn, 'Structures of patriarchy and capital in the
family', in Annette Kuhn and Ann Marie Wolpe (eds.), *Feminism
and Materialism*, Routledge and Kegan Paul, 1978. It is impossible
in this working paper to do justice to the important and greatly
varied literature on patriarchy. For a useful critique of works
on the relation between capitalism and patriarchy, see Diana
Adlam, 'The Case against Patriarchy', *m/f* No.3, 1979. It seems
fair to say, however, that developed theories of patriarchy
have not paid very much attention to the precise relation
between patriarchy and modern legal institutions. References
to patriarchy certainly appear in criminology literature on
women and the law but they tend to be rather brief scene-setters
or rounding-off devices. Rhian Ellis, 'The Legal Wrongs of
Battered Women, in Z. Bankowski and G. Mungham (eds.), *Essays
in Law and Society*, Routledge and Kegan Paul, 1980, includes a
section on family, patriarchy and law at the end of the article.
The emphasis in the article, however, is on legal solutions to
the problem of battered women, and patriarchy is described as
a hierarchy which is based on male dominance and which pervades
the social, economic and political structures reinforcing the
nuclear family.
15 Frank, *loc.cit.*, p.xx.
16 Sachs and Wilson, *loc.cit.*, p.x.
17 Steven Goldberg, *The Inevitability of Patriarchy*, Temple Smith,
1977, p.26, p.178.
18 *Guardian*, Friday 13 June 1980.
19 Sachs and Wilson, *loc.cit.*, p.137.
20 Sachs and Wilson do in fact argue that 'in reality' men continued to control the property of women.
21 *Rights!* The Newspaper of the National Council for Civil
Liberties, Vol.4, No.5, May/June 1980, special issue on unemployment. It is interesting to note that the suggestion is made
here that, given the history of relations between unions and
the law, it might be more promising to pursue the issue of
genuine equality in labour through negotiation.
22 Tony Honoré, *Sex Law*, Duckworth, 1978, pp.89-100.
23 Maggie Rae, Patricia Hewitt and Barry Hugill, *First Rights*,
NCCL, 1979, p.105.
24 Honoré, *loc.cit.*, p.110. See also the recommendations for changes
in sex laws made in the recent Working Paper on Sexual Offences,
HMSO, 6 November 1980.
25 Beloff, *loc.cit.*, p.iii. For a critical discussion of SDA and EQPA,
see P. Byrne and J. Lovenduski, 'Sex Equality and the Law in
Britain, *British Journal of Law and Society*, Vol.5, 1975.
26 W.B. Creighton *Working Women and the Law*, Mansell, 1979, p.175,
and *Rights! loc.cit*
27 Sheffield Rights of Women, *Women, Sexuality and the Law*, Workshop
1980, c/o 70 Steade Road, Sheffield 7.
28 Ministry of Defence v. Jeremiah (1979) 3 All ER 833 (CA),
reported in Butterworths Weekly Law Sheet, 14 December 1979.
It was this case that prompted the following comment from Lord
Denning: 'Equality is the order of the day. In both directions.
For both sexes. What is sauce for the goose is sauce for the
gander.'

29 Sachs and Wilson, *loc.cit.*, p.ix.

30 SROW, *loc.cit.*

31 *Ibid.*, and cf. Tess Gill's comment on the importance of giving SDA cases a public airing, *New Society*, 14 August 1980.

32 Carol Smart, *Women, Crime and Criminology*, Routledge and Kegan Paul, 1977, pp.176,179.

33 See note 26 above.

34 Creighton, *loc.cit.*, pp.31-7. The case of Ministry of Defence v. Jeremiah, cited in note 28 above, is also relevant here since it too was concerned with the exemption of women from 'dirty work'.

35 Cf. discussion in the *Observer*, 7 and 14 December 1980.

36 Cf. the case of Shirley Boyle, reported by Tess Gill (see note 31 above). Boyle's medical report, detailing backache, was used against her, not at the time when she was refused a job as porter in a hospital but only later when she complained to an industrial tribunal. It is also important to note that SDA does acknowledge the existence of indirect discrimination and discrimination by way of victimisation (see Beloff, *loc.cit.*, p.1). There is evidence, however, that neither SDA nor EQPA have been adequate to the problems of women in part-time employment. Cf. *Rights!* *loc.cit.*, p.9. But cf. also Beloff's report on the importance of forthcoming proceedings in the European Court when it will be asked to decide 'whether it is contrary to European Community Law to pay a lower hourly rate to female part-time workers than to full-time male workers, although the women do the same work and have the same productivity', *Observer*, 23 November 1980.

37 L.B. Curzon *A Dictionary of Law*, Macdonald and Evans, 1979, p.164.

38 *Ibid.*

39 O.K. Metcalfe, *General Principles of English Law*, revised by John Westwood, Donnington Press, 1962, pp.60-5.

40 H.L.A. Hart, *Punishment and Responsibility*, Oxford University Press, 1968, Ch.VI.

41 Smart, *loc.cit.*, pp.124,128,190n.2.

42 For a discussion of this and some related issues in philosophy of law, see Christopher Arnold, 'Analyses of right', in Eugene Kamenka and Alice Ehr-Soon Tay (eds.), *Human Rights*, Edward Arnold, 1978.

Lorraine Culley
Women's Organisation in the Labour Party

The object of this article is primarily to provide information about the current structure and activities of women's organisations in the Labour Party, although some general questions concerning socialist feminist practice and the Labour Party will be raised. The information presented is a combination of official documents plus a description of some of the activities in one Party region. Clearly it is impossible to generalise about the practices and ideologies of women's organisations throughout the country, and there are undoubtedly many variations in forms of organisation, activities and effectiveness. I have made an attempt to assess the activities in one region - the East Midlands Region which covers 41 constituencies.

The article is concerned with the following:

1 The structure of the women's organisation and its relationship with other sections of the labour movement.

2 The organisational forms of Women's Sections, Councils and Conferences.

3 Political activities at local, regional and national levels.

4 Socialist feminism and the Labour Party.

1 STRUCTURE

The Women's Organisation of the Labour Party was founded in 1906 as the Women's Labour League, with the objectives of pressing for better conditions of labour and hours for women workers, the provision of school meals and medical inspections in schools, free education with a leaving age of 16, and campaigning for women's franchise and representation in Parliament and local bodies. In 1918 the League merged with the Labour Party and women's sections were established.

(a) Women's Sections

The Party constitution provides that in addition to being attached to their Branch party, individual women members may be organised in Women's Sections. The sections are organised on a basis as may be

decided by the Constituency Party concerned (who have the right at
the present time to refuse to allow the formation of a Women's
Section). A section may cover a branch, more than one branch or any
part of a branch. The sections are entitled to representation on
the General Management Committee (GMC) of the Constituency Party.
Representation is governed by the rules of the party concerned, but
is usually two members from each section. There is also provision
for representation, usually one seat, on the Executive Committee of
the Constituency Party to be allocated to a representative of the
Women's Organisation, nominated and elected by the Women's Organisation delegates to the GMC annual meeting. Sections have the same
right to nominate candidates and to take part in the selection of
candidates as the other organisations represented on the GMC.
There are currently 920 Women's Sections throughout the country
with an average membership of 20.

(b) Women's Councils

Women's Councils are usually established on a Constituency basis.
A Council is composed of women delegates from Sections and Party
branches, Trade Union branches, Young Socialists branches, Labour
Groups, Fabian Societies, Co-operative Parties and any organisation
affiliated to the Labour Party. Women's Councils send delegates
to GMCs, District and County Labour Parties and Regional Councils.
They may make nominations to the panels of Local Government candidates and to the B list of prospective Parliamentary candidates
and take part in selection procedures. There are currently 154
Women's Councils with an average membership of 30.

(c) Regional organisation

The Regional Executive Committee of the Party has reserved places
for women elected from the Regional Council Annual Meeting by the
delegates from the Women's Councils. Sections cannot participate
directly in this process. At Regional level there is a Regional
Women's Advisory Committee which co-ordinates and organises women's
activities throughout the region. Sections and Councils nominate
and elect most of the members of this committee.

(d) National organisation

The National Labour Women's Advisory Committee (NLWAC) consists of
2 representatives from each party region plus 6 (female or male)
representatives from the National Executive Committee (NEC) of the
party. It is responsible for carrying out the decisions passed at
the Women's Conference. It also reviews the organisation generally,
conducts surveys, liaises with the NEC and other party bodies and
acts as a pressure group generally within the party. Since the
1979 Women's Conference, for example, the activities of NLWAC
have included the submission of Conference resolutions to appropriate departments, Shadow spokespeople and the NEC, submissions
have been made to the Party enquiry and the Rolling Manifesto.
The committee has been active in lobbying Labour MPs over abortion
rights, proposed changes in the nationality rules and employment
protection, and has provided evidence to various commissions, e.g.
the Law Commission's report on illegitimacy. The committee held

joint meetings with the NEC to discuss advancing the policy-making role of women in the party and several important recommendations were accepted. A new sub-committee (of the NEC) on Women's Rights has been established and NLWAC has been given the right to nominate members of other sub-committees and study groups and to come forward to various sub-committees with policy papers and contribute to the preparation of draft discussion documents and statements issued by the NEC.

National Women's Conference

Each year there is a 3-day National Conference of Labour Women. Delegates come from sections, councils, constituency parties where there is no women's organisation, trade unions and national organisations with women members who are affiliated to the Labour Party. Resolutions may be submitted on any issue. The 1980 conference included debates on women's rights, nuclear arms, public expenditure, new technology, party democracy and many others. Conference decisions are not binding on the party.

National Executive Committee

There are five places on the NEC reserved for women members elected by the Annual Labour Party Conference as a whole (i.e. overwhelmingly by Trade Union votes). The Campaign for Labour Party Democracy Women's Action Committee argues that the Women's Section of the NEC should be elected by the Women's Conference.

Staffing

In each region there are Assistant Regional Organisers who are responsible, as part of their duties, for co-ordinating the work of women's organisations in their region and acting as the secretary of the Regional Women's Advisory Committee. Some of these organisers are favourably disposed to women's organisation and others somewhat lukewarm. In the East Midlands the organiser is actively encouraging the establishment and extension of the women's organisation.

At Head Office, the Chief Women's Officer is an Assistant National Agent whose work includes not only responsibility for the women's organisation but many other aspects of party work. There are demands from the women's organisation to increase this staffing. The Youth Section, for example, has more full-time staff and secretarial help, although it is considerably smaller than the women's section.

2 FORMS OF ORGANISATION

Women's Sections and Council's are usually advised to adopt the model rules and standing orders as outlined in the publication *Women's Organisation in the Labour Party*. These rules allow for the usual formal structure of party officers (Chairwoman, Secretary, Treasurer, etc.) and the formal conduct of meetings, with minutes etc. Most organisations work within these rules, although they can be and often are amended as the individual group requires. Even where these rules are formally accepted, meetings in fact vary in their character according to the issue in hand. Meetings to plan campaigns, support local issue groups, organise social events, form resolutions for branches or GMCs will often be organised differently. On the whole, the atmosphere of meetings is much less formal or competitive than in the party in general, with much freer debate. Some sections and councils organise on a non-hierarchical basis, similar to meetings common in the women's movement. In this case there is usually one person to whom party correspondence can be addressed and an emphasis on collective organisation. In effect, a diversity of forms are possible and can be determined by the members themselves according to their particular objectives and activities.

One of the aims of many sections is to familiarise women who have had little experience of political meetings or who lack confidence in speaking, with party structure and functioning as well as policy. The use of formal organisation of meetings is regarded as an opportunity for women to acquire skills in chairing meetings, making interventions, forming and moving resolutions etc. This is seen as important if women are to make contributions to policy making and be represented in the party on a larger scale. Often it is agreed within sections that offices be rotated on a regular basis to allow as many women as possible to gain experience.

3 POLITICAL ACTIVITIES

Most members of Women's Sections seem to take an active part in branch affairs generally and there is little evidence that the women's organisation diverts energies from branch activities. Members of women's sections are often engaged in activities locally with which the party is not directly concerned and may bring into the branch parties requests for branch support for various campaigns (e.g. NAC). The sections and councils can act as an effective caucus for attempting to direct party discussion and action on issues which would otherwise possibly not be discussed. Meetings may be organised by the sections and thrown open to the whole party, or resolutions and discussion items brought before branch meetings, GMCs or Executive Committee meetings. Since women's sections have direct representation on the GMC it is possible for them to bypass the branch altogether if this is regarded as expedient.

The range of activities varies according to the particular political perspectives of the group in question. Some groups conform to the 'tea-makers and fund-raisers' image, although this is something of a stereotype of even the traditional sections. They may well be the organisers not only of most of the (important) fund raising and social events for their branches, but also are commonly the only section of the party undertaking any political education and debate in an organisation so often dominated by meetings confined almost totally to party business. In fact the contribution of the women's

organisation in terms of its political education activities is widely
recognised in the movement. The meetings of sections and councils
are rarely purely business meetings but are devoted to political
discussion of various kinds. Many invite speakers from Party and
non-Party organisations and some groups undertake research projects.
Several organisations are also actively involved in local community
politics, working with organisations such as Women's Aid, tenants
groups, National Abortion Campaign, Chile Solidarity, etc. In
addition to activities at branch level, many women take part in
weekend and day schools and conferences organised by the Regional
Women's Committee, who also organise an annual Regional Women's
Conference. In the East Midlands, for example, two recent events
were a weekend school concerned with training women to take office
in the party, to stand as candidates for local and national elections,
to handle the media (giving interviews, drafting press releases, etc.)
and a day conference on the effects of the recent Employment Act on
women's rights.

In addition to general political activities some groups are concerned with activity aimed to enhance the position of women within
the Labour Party. The under-representation of women in party and
public office is striking. There are currently 11 women Labour MPs
out of a total of 267, and there is little sign of any improvement
in this situation. Women are virtually absent from the A List of
potential parliamentary candidates (nominated by affiliated organisations, mainly Trade Unions), and are approximately 8% of the B List
(unsponsored candidates, mostly nominated by Constituency Parties).

```
WOMEN LABOUR MPs
1945    21      1974 (Feb)   13
1955    14      1974 (Oct)   18
1966    19      1979         11
1970    10
```

The number of women parliamentary candidates has increased
slightly since 1970 but the percentage of women candidates elected
is always significantly smaller than the percentage of male candidates
elected, which indicates that women are less likely to be selected
for safe seats. In 1979 approximately 43% of men were elected
compared with 21% of women candidates.

There is an increasing militancy of women in the Labour movement
which has arisen in the context of the disillusionment of many women
with the effects of the 'Equality Legislation' and the performance
of recent Labour governments, the explicit attacks on women by the
present Tory government and the general debate concerning democratisation of the Party. This militancy has been expressed in the formation
of two new groups in recent months - the Campaign for Labour Party
Democracy Women's Action Committee (CLPD-WAC) and Fightback for
Women's Rights.

CLPD-WAC are concerned primarily with campaigning for changes in
the Party in order to increase the representation of women, particularly in Parliament. Their campaign includes demands that Parliament should operate a normal working day, that the NEC should adopt
a target of 50% places for women when co-opting members for its

sub-committees and for positive discrimination for women on
parliamentary shortlists. They are proposing a Constitutional
amendment to provide for the mandatory inclusion of women (and a
manual worker) on every Parliamentary shortlist. Fightback is a
group which includes active Labour Party and Trade Union women and
also women from groups outside the Labour movement. Its aims are
to campaign against the current attacks on women's rights generally
as well as in the Party and Trade Unions.

The NLWAC has also been active in publicising the problem of the
under-representation of women and has made several proposals in the
document 'Women Candidates in the Labour Party' which has been
approved by the NEC and distributed to CLPs and affiliated Trade
Unions. This document recommends that the party produce a list of
public bodies and committees which women should be encouraged to
stand for, and that regional courses be provided to train women to
serve on such bodies. It proposes that more practical help be given
to women by, for example, providing the facilities for them to attend
meetings. It asks parties to regularly monitor names coming in for
parliamentary lists and to hold discussions with the trade unions on
ways of encouraging more women to stand for election. It reminds
parties that they should be responsible for payment of expenses both
for candidates when attending meetings during the selection process
and for carrying out their work as parliamentary candidates and it
requests the NEC to instruct parties that questions of a sexist
nature be not admissible either at preliminary meetings or at
selection conferences.

4 SOCIALIST FEMINISM AND THE LABOUR PARTY

Is the Labour Party an important arena of struggle for socialist

feminists?

There are those socialists who argue that the Labour Party is not and
never can be a vehicle for socialist change. There are those feminists who argue that the Labour Party, as an institution dominated by
men, is not and never can be truly concerned with feminist struggles.
The limitations of the current nature of the Labour Party with
respect to socialist feminist struggles should not be underestimated.
I would not argue that the Labour Party is either the only or
necessarily the most effective way of fighting for specific objectives. To argue this would be to essentialise parliamentary forms
of struggle and party politics and to ignore the advances made outside these forms. Nevertheless, the parliamentary and local government arenas are crucial spheres in British politics and must be
taken seriously by socialist feminists. To take these arenas
seriously in Britain means recognising the Labour Party as the only
possible party to have any chance of organising electoral support
and creating a left parliamentary and local government.

It has not been the intention of this article to analyse Labour
Party policy in relation to socialist feminism. This would indeed

be a complex task since policy decisions in all areas (not simply
those designated as 'women's issues') will have effects on sexual
inequalities, e.g. public expenditure policy, incomes policies,
policies for the democratisation of institutions, etc. There are
women (and men) in the Labour Party who are engaged at all levels
in activities which could be described as attempting to further
socialist feminist objectives. Perhaps the most important point in
the current state of British politics is that the Labour Party is an
arena where the debate concerning what socialist feminist aims might
be (by no means clear at the present time) can occur and where concrete objectives can be formulated within the context of a party
which can command electoral support and which does engage with the
wider labour movement and with many thousands of ordinary women and
men with whom the women's movement has not engaged. Moreover,
because it is a political party it can be forced to debate issues
in a manner which accommodates interrelated policies (for socialism
and feminism) and which may produce a wider and more general strategy
than any likely to emerge from a single-issue campaign.

Should there be separate organisation of women in the Labour Party?

There is some (currently muted) opposition to separate women's organisation within the Labour Party. There are party members (men and
women) who advocate the demise of the women's organisation. This
opposition commonly takes one of two forms. Firstly, it is argued by
some that the women's organisation is *unnecessary* since either there
is sufficient consideration already given to women's issues and/or
sufficient opportunity for women to occupy positions of power in the
Party without having separate groups. Secondly, and more seriously,
there are those who argue that separate organisation is undesirable
since it means that important issues are taken out of the centre of
political debate, labelling them as 'women's issues' to be debated
by women among themselves. This argument does highlight a potential
drawback to the existence of separate women's groups, but there is
no *necessity* for the existence of women's organisations to result in
the ghettoisation of 'women's issues' as *women's* problems. Whether
or not this occurs will depend on the political practice of women's
groups in this respect. Indeed, separate organisation can provide an
excellent opportunity for ensuring that there is *more* debate about
socialist feminist ideas in all forums of the party. Women's sections
can force debate at branches and GMCs; women's council representatives
can initiate debates at County and District Party meetings where local
policies are discussed, and at Regional Council and Executive Meetings.
The NLWAC can bring issues directly into the NEC.
The women's organisation can take advantage of opportunities that
separate organisation affords in terms of giving women confidence and
knowledge of politics, allowing effective caucussing and directing
party debate on issues not necessarily the current priorities in the
Labour Party. Those who defend the women's organisations argue that
the advantages from the point of view of the party as a whole are
that more women can be drawn into the party by first becoming involved
through the women's organisations in discussions and campaigns which

relate to their immediate interests and experiences, and that the party is more attractive to women by having the option of women's meetings.

The women's organisations of the Labour Party must, however, be wary of any separatist ideology. It may be an unpalatable fact for some in the women's movement, but it is nevertheless clear that socialist feminist objectives at the levels of legislation and national or local government policy must be constructed within, and supported by, the Labour Party if they are to have any chance of being carried out - and to achieve that they must involve both women and men working together in the Labour Party.

Fran Bennett, Lorraine Culley, Barry Hindess
Interview with Frances Morrell

(Frances Morrell is on the executive of the Campaign for Labour
Party Democracy [CLPD] and played a major role in establishing its
Women's Action Committee [WAC], and she was one of the founders of
the Labour Coordinating Committee. During the last Labour Government she was political advisor to Tony Benn.)

*Q. You've been associated with the Labour left for a long time, but
you haven't been associated with anything like the Women's Action
Committee or women's issues until very recently.*

FM: I have been interested in women's issues for a long time. For
example, together with Molly Meacher, I put in evidence to the
commission for women's rights that was set up between 70 and 74.
We argued that the hours in Parliament should be changed, obviously
in the first instance to suit women but actually because the hours
of work should be such as to enable parents to be with their children when they were out of school. That is one of the demands that
is in the WAC proposals.
  I personally have been thinking about women's issues, like many
other women, for a long time, and like very many other women in the
Labour Party, I've become more politicised about women's rights over
the past few years. That's something we're all aware of, things are
happening differently, and it's happening in other countries too.
And because it's happening in Britain, it's happening in the Labour
Party, understandably. So what I'm saying about myself simply
reflects what's happening to lots of women in parallel: we've all
been politicised. The specific seed was Germaine Greer's book
which, funnily enough, my husband went out and bought, read and said:
"You really ought to read this." I was absolutely astonished when
I read Greer's wonderful writing. I know she's not necessarily
considered the greatest thinker in the women's movement, but she's
a very very good writer. I was instantly convinced; she articulated
something that I felt, but hadn't been able to express.
  But for everybody in the Labour Party, and for every woman in the
Labour Party, there's a special problem: the Labour Party is oriented
towards class, as we all know, and I myself having come from a very
poor working-class home am very orientated towards class, and certainly
my strongest feelings of indignation are bound up with the visible
signs of class in all its complexity. I certainly don't have feelings
to the same degree about the women's situation. However, the point-
less resistence to our set of demands for change is rapidly developing
this.

*Do you see the relationship between the position of women and tradi-
tional socialist ideas as socialism being primarily concerned with
class, while other things are often just tagged on as secondary
issues? So there is a divorce between these two sets of ideas?*

FM: Oh no, I wouldn't say that. There was a gap between reading *The
Female Eunuch* and other literature, and being able to feel that I had
a coherent position myself. I had to reconcile my feelings that
wherever I looked women were being exploited, that this was self-
evident, but at the same time working people were being exploited.
I was very strongly held back by that strand of the women's movement
thinking which is anti-men, anti-trades union, and actually anti-
working people - although they don't say so. Some of the comments I
hear about trades unionists are so lacking in sympathy and understanding of the suffering imposed on working men, as to be anti-working
class. That's how I perceive it, and I was put off very strongly
because I could never, never bring myself to associate with any
movement that had, however subtly, an anti-working class component.

*Can we turn that on its head and look at the record of the British
labour movement? The TUC has from the very beginning been committed
to full equality for women, and the Labour Party has been to some
extent committed as well. Yet their record has not been terribly
impressive. It's been better than the Conservative Party and other
political parties. But in terms of their positive action to improve
the position of women we'd have to say that the British labour
movement hasn't gone all that far, and hasn't taken seriously the
oppressed position of women in our society. Now there are women
organising independently, and forcing them to take it seriously.*

FM: You've forced me into a defence which in other circumstances I
wouldn't be prepared to make. When I listen to you, I think this is
the sort of person who didn't stand a chance of converting me into
thinking I could do something about women's rights. The primary
source of oppression in our society is the British ruling class;
it's not the labour movement. If you lose sight of that primary
truth you can't get anything done because you don't even know where
the source of oppression lies. Therefore this obsession with saying
that the labour movement hasn't done enough suggests that the source
of oppression in our society is the labour movement, whereas the
source of *hope* in our society is the labour movement. It is very
important to get one's mind clear about that.
    What we know in the Labour Party is that it is possible to
campaign within the labour movement on the grounds of justice, and
attract support. It is not possible to argue with the ruling class
on the grounds of justice and get support. And you must know that
or you don't know anything about politics. We are campaigning in
the labour movement. The women's campaign requires us to revolutionise the way we look at society; there is nothing to be gained by
pretending that it isn't difficult to see society in a wholly
different way.
    But I want to take up your principal point, having made all those
caveats. It is of course true that the labour movement has not been

successful; it has not really issued the kind of challenge it ought
to have done to the kind of exploitative society we live in. But we
live in such a backward soceity and part of our weakness is that we
don't recognise how intimidated we all are by the kind of class
society we're in - we live in Ruritania and don't realise it - that's
how I perceive it, it's like living in India and not knowing what a
maharaj is, or that there's a caste system. We've persuaded everyone
that we're a modern society when we're actually in many ways very
backward. It's very difficult for people to stand back from all that
and see it. Instead, they're intimidated. We all are. And the
minute you start pressing for change the ferocity of the response is
so colossal that it's easy to understand why people are intimidated.

In terms of work within the labour movement you've had two kinds of
tasks. One is to work with the labour movement for wider changes,
and the other is to try and get changes within the labour movement
and in particular, with the Women's Action Committee, changes inside
the Labour Party. Could you tell us what you saw as likely allies
for the demands of the Womens Action Committee in the Labour Party
and what you saw as the sources of resistance to those demands?

FM: Very plainly, women must be our allies, men must be our first
opponents. But I suppose what the CLPD would think, and I agree, is
that unless the LP can change itself with regard to the position of
women, it's pretty meaningless to think it's really going to take on
the opponents of change in favour of women outside the LP and I don't
think we need this in just a superficial way. We don't mean only
that we need women on all the representative and policy-making bodies
in order to use that influence, although we do need that. But, as
I said earlier, because it requires a mental revolution which is very
painful and difficult in order to understand exploitation, it involves a political struggle. And unless the Party faces the struggle
inside itself first it won't have altered its view. The struggle for
change within the Party will be the change in the Party without which
it's difficult to believe it's going to change anything else.

There is a fairly extensive women's organisation inside the Labour
Party already. How do you view the existing women's organisation?

FM: Well, the existing women's organisation means first that every
party has the right to establish a women's section, or rather that
women in every Party have a right to establish a women's section;
and secondly, the women's section has the right to send two delegates
to an annual conference for women. That is, so to speak, the outward
and visible sign that the Party is at least formally committed to
equal rights for women. If that structure didn't exist we would
have had to invent it. So I'm jolly pleased we won't have to invent
it and that it's there already. It's one step along the road.
Increasingly, radical women are joining those women's sections and
wanting to go to the women's conference and wanting to make the
women's conference a genuine campaigning voice for women in the Party.
And some of the proposals we're putting forward are to do precisely
that. For example, we're proposing that the women's conference as

a right should be able to table five motions to the annual conference, to come up wherever is appropriate on the agenda. Secondly,
we're arguing that the women's section on the NEC should be elected
by the women's conference. The women's section at the moment is
composed of women, certainly, but their views on women's rights are
not part of the criteria for which they are selected. We're proposing that the Women's Advisory Committee should become the executive
of the women's conference and be elected by the women's conference
itself, which it isn't at the moment. These proposals are to make
the women's conference genuinely active and to give it power within
the Party.

*How do you see the WAC working with the existing organisation? In
setting up something which is new, which is different and separate
from the existing women's organisation, are you implicitly critical
of either the form of organisation or the kind of demands that
they've been making, the kinds of positions they've been taking?*

FM: Obviously if we felt that the existing women's structure within
the LP produced the sort of demands we wished to see, we would just
be working for that straightforwardly. But it's because we feel
that much tougher demands should be made we've formed this committee.
The CLPD is an anti-establishment body within the LP, dedicated to
changing the Party, but it's also dedicated to changing the Party
constitutionally. In other words, to change the rules in order to
shift power within the Party and so far it's been dedicated to
shifting power from the Parliamentary Party to the rank and file.
Broadly, the WAC would be dedicated to shifting power between men
and women in the Party.

*So you see the WAC as attempting to transform the existing organisa-
tion, to make it more radical?*

FM: We aim to make the existing women's organisation more powerful.
It may be potentially radical but it doesn't matter if it's radical
because it hasn't got any power at all. It's quite often said, and
it should be said, that the women's conference is in many ways a
radical conference. Unfortunately it just doesn't push any buttons,
because they pass the motions and that's the end of it. Leading
male figures in the Party frequently say to me: "My goodness, what
a tremendously radical conference it is, very influential"; and I
keep on snarling: "We don't want to be 'influential'." That is the
name of the game - either you have power or you don't; but being
influential is the same as not having power.

*Many of the demands of the WAC are at the national level, in terms
of conference and the national women's committee and the issue of
parliamentary short-lists. Do you see that as being the crucial
level? Because at the local level the women's organisation does
intervene in General Management Committees, and it does have a
certain power.*

FM: At the CLPD national women's conference the list of demands was amended and added to. People said that women should have a right to set up a women's section in their party even if the GMC did not agree, and that is now one of the demands; that is right because we're not concerned only with changes at the national level. That would be hopeless as a position. We're concerned to make it possible for women to play an equal role at every level of Party life. So if you start at the GMC, then all of us have the power to set up women's sections, send representatives to the GMC, whether the Party agrees or not. That provides a forum locally. We've also demanded positive discrimination on short-lists. We've earmarked Parliamentary short-lists because of the complexities about demanding positive discrimination on local government short-lists. We'd like to see positive discrimination there, but we do recognise that parties often find difficulty in getting people to stand, and you can't lay obligations on them that they can't fulfil. We also want to see positive discrimination on the policy-making committees of the Party. We have positive discrimination on the National Executive already because there's a women's section, but we want women to do the electing. And that's quite a structural approach, to favour rather than handicap women.

How do you see the mechanism of positive discrimination working, say, if you had a situation where there weren't actually any women coming forward, which is sometimes the problem?

FM: I don't really accept that there's this tremendous problem about getting women to come forward. If you go to the women's conference and the women's rights rallies there really are a lot of very able women. I think that obviously positive discrimination would force the parties to look out for women and that is exactly as it should be. Because if you take that issue alone, it seems to me that the Party doesn't understand the nature of the selection system it's running. It's frequently said within the Labour Party that the kind of person who tends to have a very good chance at a selection conference tends to be a member of the professional/managerial middle class. People often comment on this with an air of "what a mystery this is, you know, we can't understand it!" Now it's obviously true, as the composition of the Parliamentary Labour Party shows. But it isn't a mystery at all because the nature of the selection process is geared to producing that sort of situation. Anyone who wishes to be a candidate is obviously helped by being in the first instance well-known, which means that they must have had the opportunity to become well-known, which is something that men have and women haven't. And often a person will be selected who's offered themselves at several selection conferences all over the country. In order to be able to offer yourself at selection conferences all over the country, you have to have large sums of money, *large* sums of money. If you think of the train fares and all the rest of it, simply to make yourself available requires cash. Then it requires freedom from home ties, it requires the little woman at home looking after the children and running the home or not having any ties at all. So it's absolutely geared against women, but it's also geared for the managerial middle class.

But it has also come to mean the concept of a career structure.
Many men of that class think in terms of career structures, and there's
nothing wrong with that, it's just that nobody else does. They think
in terms of all the things you can do first to get on to that rung
of the ladder. Going into Parliament has become for many well-educated
middle class men an alternative to reading for the bar or becoming a
journalist or something like that. I don't wish to criticise those
people who offer themselves, because they've got a perfect right to
do so; open selection implies that, and it's silly to criticise those
who put themselves forward under the current system. I'm criticising
the Party for being so unaware that there is a system in operation
which will favour one group rather than another. Positive discrimination will begin to impede that process because it will force the
parties to look for the people who at the moment are handicapped.
    The WAC is fighting for women, obviously, but it's impossible to
campaign solely for women because working people and women and ethnic
groups are all in the same position. All the conditions of handicap
that we are describing are experienced by all of them. They're all
exploited and though the rationale for their exploitation differs,
the method, the mechanism for exploitation is the same, and so it
would be quite wrong and inappropriate for us in the Labour Party to
say that we're only concerned to advance the cause of women. What
we do feel is that each group has to fight for its own cause
because that's part of the meaning of the struggle. Women have got
to do it for themselves, men can't do it for them, and indeed won't.
And also the ethnic groups have got to do it for themselves, and
indeed are doing it, I'm glad to say. They took up some of the
proposals that we'd already made for women at their conference, and
said: "Splendid, we'll do this." Obviously we are stretching out our
hands in comradeship towards them and would support them for the
reasons we hope they'd support us, and we hope that within the trades
unions there will be increasing consciousness of the need to give
working people a chance. One of the things that you don't see on
the short-lists are the shop stewards who've been engaged locally in
the most tremendous struggles, who have really gained responsibility
and experience highly appropriate to being a Labour member of Parliament. But for some reason Labour parties do not put them on the
short-list or seek them out or even think about it. So we do have
a comprehensive approach towards positive discrimination. Obviously
women must fight for women but at the same time they must encourage
the trades unions and the parties generally to look at the class
aspect as well, and the ethnic groups to push for themselves.

*You highlighted the problem of domestic responsibilities which
hinder women's activities in the Party. How do you think the LP
could be organised to minimise that kind of problem?*

FM: The practical answer is that already the provision of creches
at the LP conference by the women's conference, dare I say it, and
by bodies like the CLPD at its own meetings and other institutions,
is a hopeful indication that within the LP people are beginning to
recognise that if women are to attend meetings then the provision
must be there to enable them to do so. Now plainly, there would

be a tendency to think that you provide a creche and you've solved
all the problems. You haven't, but it is the beginning of a thought
process. Now how do we solve it? What I would like to feel as
campaigning goes on is that you alter people's awareness. There
isn't a direct relationship between campaigning, say, on the hours of
Parliament, positive discrimination and the provision of a creche and
making facilities available for women. But there is a very strong
indirect relationship. You can campaign for change, particularly
change that's going to be resisted very, very strongly, and we can
guarantee that positive discrimination on Parliamentary short-lists
will be fought to the death, because it's an area of tremendous
privilege for men. As you specifically fight in an area of privilege
to get it changed, you tend to stimulate the most tremendous discussion and debate.
    The example I would give would be mandatory re-selection. Theor-
etically you might have thought that mandatory re-selection was a
modest little proposal that might have just gone through without
anyone noticing. But not at all; it's been fought over several years
during which the whole relationship of the Parliamentary Labour Party
to the movement has been debated and, in my opinion, a consensus
forged that there should be a shift of power, they should be more
accountable and, in addition, that they had not behaved as they
ought. Now some of the proposals we're putting forward we know will
meet with just as much resistance as those simple proposals for
mandatory re-selection. The debate that will ensue will be about
the whole relationship between women and men in the LP, naturally,
and during the course of that all sorts of proposals will come up.
Now that's not to say that fighting for change inside the Labour
Party is enough. Another organisation has been set up, Women's
Fightback, which is going to look much more at the policy side, and
rightly. The CDLP and WAC's impetus is to change the LP in order
that it will then carry out policy. We felt that if you didn't get
mandatory re-selection and some accountability for your local MP,
you could have all the wonderful policies in the world but you'd
never get them carried out. In the same way, we feel that unless
the LP undergoes a process of changing itself in relation to men and
women then you can get the most wonderful policies for women in the
world, but after going through the LP conference, nobody notices them.
That's the most sinister thing. At the local GMC, at the LP conference, people don't even bother to state a debate and oppose it. No
one dare oppose it, but don't think those people who are silent are
converts, and are going to do something about it. They are just
sparing themselves the trouble. Nobody opposed the abilition of the
House of Lords when it was passed by a two-thirds majority, but it
was still vetoed by the leadership when it came up. The Party's got
to be made to face the problem, and it will face the problem when
privilege within the party is touched. And then they won't go for a
cup of tea when those issues come up, they'll stay and have to take
a view, so they'll learn about themselves. That's very important.

*It seems perfectly possible, because each local party selects its
own candidate, that you could have positive discrimination on the
short-list without having an overall effect on women getting*

*elected or even selected. And so it's possible for that kind of issue
to go by without setting up the fight which you're saying is necessary
within the LP.*

FM: I already know that there's going to be resistance. It's a very
controversial proposal. People do not simply say on the left of the
Party: "Goodness me, how right and proper" - not at all. They normally say that women must fight on their merits, which is an old
argument. It has a sort of superficial attraction, I suppose; if
women had any opportunity to demonstrate their merits and if there
wasn't prejudice against women as well. That's the other thing which
is difficult really to engage in, because until you have a debate
about a tangible change that you want, no one will admit to being
prejudiced. Find me a prejudiced person in the LP! Since nobody
has any prejudice, how can you discuss it? People have got to start
arguing, they have got to start articulating their feelings in order
to become aware of them for themselves and to change them. And you
can only do that by making tangible proposals for changes in the
rules that will favour women at the expense of men. Otherwise
you'll have a clutch of wonderful policies, no-one will have opposed
them and they won't get carried out. That will be the situation
we'll get into.

*So you think that these proposals will flush out your enemies in the
LP and also flush out your friends?*

FM: I would rather say that it will be an educational process for
all of us. It'll be an education for us as women because women will
have to think where they stand. After all, take the proposal to
change the hours of Parliament. It would be ridiculous to assume
that the massed ranks are going to come forward saying we've been
wanting to do this for such a long time and since you ask ...
That proposal alone has a whole underlying ethos embedded in it -
about how the organisation of work, even political work, ought to
take into account family life - that will have to be argued through.
If we're into the politics of persuasion, which we are, then we have
to be prepared to struggle and argue and change people's minds. It's
a big process, and we've already said that to fight the women's cause
involves revolutionising one's view of what's going on in society.
It involves altering the institutions that you're involved in.
People don't like either of those processes and if you have to take
the two together, it will be a very big struggle.

*Could we ask you now about the relationship of the WAC and its
proposals to the women's movement? You were talking about women
being able to represent their own interests best, similarly with
ethnic minorities and so on. A lot of women in the women's movement,
who are not necessarily active in the LP or in any other party,
would agree. But the conclusions they draw would be very different
from yours, that there has to be a separate organisation and pressure
within the LP for women. They would rather direct their energies
towards building a strong autonomous women's movement outside the
LP and then try to put pressure on the LP to try and change policies*

*from that position.   How do you respond to that kind of argument?
What kind of relationship do you see between the women's movement,
particularly women who are not active in a political party, and the
kind of thing you're trying to do within the LP?*

FM: Well, in the first instance people are in the LP because they
believe that it's the only viable means of changing society.   So
therefore by definition we don't believe that activity which is exclusively outside the party can be successful.   Obviously the women's
movement has had a great influence and it would be silly to say
that it hadn't.   So it's a question of striking a balance.   I'm
in the LP because I believe that it's the political institution
most likely to change an exploitative society, not only by its
legislative power but through its campaigning work.   I keep coming
back to this analogy: we want to shift power to the constituency
LPs in order to make it worthwhile for people to join the party, to
feel that they could change society through their membership, locally and nationally.   It would be an instrument that people could
use.   We want to change the Party in relation to women because we
hope that women who seek change will join the Party.

*We were talking just now about the politics of persuasion.   There
are people in the women's movement who would say that they no
longer believed in the power of persuasion to change the structures
of dominance in society between men and women.   So that in a
structure like the LP, which is male-dominated, they don't believe
that just by talking to people and trying to persuade them it will
work.   They would rather be in a structure which can be organised
along very different lines, and exert pressure from without.*

FM: There are two different questions there.   First of all, can
women who are organsing themselves inside the LP organise themselves
in a way that the women's movement has come to favour, or will they
have to conform to the traditional structures of the LP?   The
answer is yes and no.   Firstly, women's sections are showing a
strong tendency to want to have a different form of organisation
itself, very much reflecting the thinking of women.   For example,
although the rules of the party probably lay down that there has
to be a formal chair, they will rotate it.   I know some women would
argue that there shouldn't even be that figure at a meeting, even
if it's rotating.   But there are different ways of understanding
the role of the chair.   The women's movement has understood the
chair as an oppressive figure.   On the other hand, the chair can
be the friend of the weak at a meeting and the person who is
empowered to cut short people with lots to say, not too rudely,
but to actively encourage the people who haven't spoken - there's
lots of ways of understanding that sort of figure.   That's merely
one example of the fact that within the Labour movement people
won't necessarily agree with the women's movement, about the best
form of organisation - although certainly a lot of the feeling of
the women's movement has been absorbed.   Part of what they've said
is we don't see meetings as places where people come along and
make great speeches and go home.   A meeting is for us all to talk

to one another. Well *that* process has not only been going on in the
women's movement and the women's movement ought to take that into
account. It's been going on within the LP between the rank and file
and those who hold any sort of formal position, so that the nature
of meetings has altered within the LP in general. The compromise
we had at our women's rights rally was to open with speakers from
the organisations like CDLP and Fightback, to give them a brief
period, and then to have a discussion, and we had twenty speakers
who were people who'd come to the meeting. It would be a mistake
to think that the only kind of thinking for change that has occurred
has occurred within the women's movement. I would challenge that,
the labour movement may well have something to contribute on women's
rights campaigning because within the labour movement we would certainly expect the support of men. Even though we say we're fighting
privilege, we would nonetheless expect the support of many men in
doing it.

*And you're saying that would be a challenge to some of the thinking
that's gone on in the women's movement?*

FM: I certainly wouldn't wish to issue a challenge to anybody.
Thinking evolves, situations change, what's an appropriate posture
at one time isn't necessarily an appropriate posture at another
time. My sense is that women's thinking has come a long way in
the last decade. First of all, women, radical women, have made this
tremendous leap of understanding, that we are actually exploited,
and can clearly articulate it. That is the kind of 'Black is
Beautiful' syndrome where you draw back and you say: "I'm all right,
I'm just being exploited and all the things they say to me are just
to persuade me to carry on being exploited and like it." That's
the great leap of understanding. Related to that is the understanding that you don't have to conform, and the next leap is that you've
got to challenge it. Advanced women have gone through that sort of
process and have reached the point where they wish to challenge.
It's not particularly sensible to organise that challenge outside
a party in order to put pressure on it. If you're not aiming to put
pressure on it, fine. But if you do, it stands to reason it's easier
inside than out.

*But haven't you taken on at least something from the women's movement
and their form of organisation by having, for example, a meeting for
women only. You said the opposition is men in the Party. But you
also said that we have to work with men, with people to be persuaded.
Isn't one of the criticisms of the women's movement that they do
organise separately, have separate meetings?*

FM: I think I'm being put in a false position of criticising the
women's movement, and I'd like to make it clear that I have no
criticism whatsoever to make of the women's movement. The women's
movement has articulated the feelings of women in a very positive
way, they have given a political lead to women and have given them
hope and encouragement, and so I wouldn't wish to criticise them at
all. Now, I would like to see that struggle take place inside the

LP. Some women will feel that that's not the sphere in which they can work most usefully. Well, fair enough. But for me, it is, because all my beliefs revolve around that.

Say that the changes that you're proposing do happen, so that women have a much stronger influence inside the LP. What differences would that make to what the LP sees as its socialist aims? Women's Fightback is much more concerned with the policy issues, but presumably you would see some policy being changed if what you want to see does come about.

Policy changes will follow through automatically. It's part of the perception that the struggle is the change just as much as the changes you make. It's easier to look at the example of what is past than guess at what might happen. The struggle for mandatory re-selection has changed the LP. It isn't just that now there's a little routine change. It's a fact that it's altered the perception of the rank and file about themselves and their relation to their MP. That's the shift embodied in the rule change, but the rule change would mean nothing if members of parties had not themselves altered their whole perception. It's this which is the important thing. MPs are weakened and members of parties strengthened in their own perception. So it's the struggle that changes people.

You're saying that you can't foresee what changes in priorities there will be because it will depend on what kind of strength people think they've gathered from working towards that change.

FM: What are the priorities? You tell me what you think are the priorities women should want. If you ask me what the change in priorities will be, I will ask you in return what should they be?

A vision of socialism which didn't have fundamental changes in social and sexual relationships would not be enough for the kind of socialism they want.

FM: I don't know if we're not talking at cross purposes. I assume that the struggle for a shift in power between men and women in the party will, if it's successful, produce the most tremendous debate. Discussion won't simply concentrate on each little change that's being put forward but will be precisely around all the issues that you're describing. Obviously it would amend the Party's vision of socialism, which is class-based to a vision of socialism which relates to class relationships, sexual relationships, emotional relationships and move toward a much more mature understanding of what there should be.

So you argue that an influx of women into the Party and into powerful positions in the Party will necessarily strengthen the fight for sexual politics?

FM: No, although that is plainly helpful. For example, if half the PLP were women, I think the abortion rights campaign would have

found it easier. The idea of men all clustered inside and you out
there shouting is not my ideal situation. But what I'm arguing is that,
in demanding those changes, the demand is based on a philosophical
position, and in fighting for them people will endlessly be explaining their philosophical position, will endlessly be challenged on
that position. It's the whole process of changing the hearts and
minds of people in the Party that has to be done. The change that
comes at the end of the day is merely the ratification of the changes
in hearts and minds, and that's the important thing that's got to
happen.

*But a criticism that some women in the Party would make is that,
although we do have some women Labour MPs, not enough in anybody's
terms, they haven't always been in the forefront of the struggle for
sexual equality.*

FM: It can't be part of anybody's case that women should hold a
substantial proportion of the places on all representative and
decision-making bodies, and that those women when they get there
must be perfect people. Men don't have to be perfect people to hold
these positions. That argument depends on the basic rights argument.
It is the right of women to hold those positions. 50% of the population have the right to 50% of the places. They don't have to be
better people as well. Whoever puts the argument forward, it would
seem to me to be this: because those few women MPs have not always
fought for women's rights as hard as they should (*if* that's the case
and I don't know person by person), it would follow that we might as
well not be here at all, and it wouldn't matter. Do they really wish
to argue that? It's a false argument. They can't really say that
women should have 50% of the places because they're going to be
better people and more socialist and more feminist and all the rest
of it. They merely have a right. Full stop. We don't say about
black people that there should be black people in Parliament but
only if they're wonderful socialists and all the rest of it. Black
people have a right to be represented in Parliament, and that is all
there is to it, as far as I'm concerned. I argue that there should
be more working class people in Parliament. Now my preference obviously is for figures like the sort of shop stewards who are not being
pushed by the trade union hierarchy but are carrying out the burden
of the battle. I can't also specify that they've got to have views
to suit me.
    I trust that of the wide selection of women, black people and
working people put forward, the Party will choose socialists from
amongst them. But that's the *second* point. But the first is that
they've got a right to be there. And the women's movement, or those
people who put forward the idea that you're putting forward, are on
very dodgy ground and they should think about it a little bit. But
thirdly, do I suggest that the world's going to be altered if the
composition of all these bodies is changed? I've no idea. My guess
is that, if the GLC were 50% women, it would be a very different body.
At the moment it's very difficult to change the world to suit women
when there's only small numbers there. Let me give an example. I
worked at the DoI which was all male. It was very difficult to argue

for institutional changes to suit women when it means just you, and
everybody else is going to have to be inconvenienced to suit you.
You aim really to change it first and simultaneously demand that
large numbers of women should be in the PLP, because then they'll
be able to behave like women because there'll be enough of them. The
honorary man syndrome relates to the woman who's surrounded by men.

*But what you said about women representing women best and blacks
representing blacks best does suggest that you did have the idea
that when they are there then there will be the kind of changes ...*

FM: I did cherish the hope. My experience tells me that only those
who've experienced exploitation understand what it is. I do think
that. The most imaginative person in the world can't really understand
the limitations of our present situation when they haven't shared it
at all. But I also know the colossal pressure that the establishment
can bring to bear on whoever's in Parliament. So I simultaneously
wouldn't hope for too much. A big part of what I was trying to say
is that the struggle for change is the process of change. The most
important thing is the struggle for change and then the prizes you
collect at the end, having altered things, just ratify that. But the
people themselves who are doing the jobs have changed, who have
participated in the struggle.
  The reality of the situation is that the proposals we have made
will not be achieved without a struggle. Suppose, for example, you
radically altered the balance between men and women in the Parliamentary Party as a result of a struggle. Then the people at least who
first went there would be radicalised themselves, and the people who
sent them there would be radicalised, the expectations of what they
would do would be higher, the whole situation in which they went would
be different. Whereas if you could wave the magic wand and suppose
that the Party tomorrow passed an edict saying, we're going to change
the rules, you wouldn't have the same situation. The women who went
as the result of the Party passing an edict would not go in the same
way and with the same result, and therefore the effect would be
different. However, the Party won't pass an edict and therefore
we'll have to have the struggle first. We're struggling to make the
Party pass an edict and that's how you change things.

*A point you made at the very beginning is that the labour movement is
an area of politics where people will take seriously arguments for
justice and rights and equality. What that means is that in arguing
for changes in the position of women within the LP and within society
generally you have to make an appeal within the LP to men as well.
And you have to expect men to come on to your side. But you said
earlier, and you were right, men haven't been making those appeals
or those arguments themselves inside the LP. That suggests that
maybe the number of allies among men will be relatively small at
this stage.*

FM: You create the allies as you go along. Initially we will
campaign across the constituency parties, obviously because they
have been a spearhead of radical thinking within the Party. But it

would be stupid to overlook that there have been women in the trade union movement campaigning for some time now, making change within the trades unions. I hope we will be able to link up with them, so that we can each, as it were, add momentum to the other's struggles. I find it hard to answer your questions because I don't see myself looking for allies in quite that way. What we have done so far is to build up or assemble a programme of demands for change to be agreed by Labour women themselves. That was our first step; to say, well here's a consultative document, here's some suggestions we're putting forward, please read it, come to the conference, and you, by either rejecting or amending or adding, will be responsible for drawing up that list of demands. Now, the CLPD executive at the moment is dominated by men, but it is very likely indeed that they will support the whole package that's come from the Labour women's conference, because they will say we've backed the idea of having a Women's Action Committee, we've backed the women's conference, so now we're going to back the women in what they say they want. So already we've assembled a whole set of allies, people who were not necessarily involved in the women's movement before but they're involved in the CLPD and they'll be loyal I know, and support all these things. And all the year that we've been campaigning just for the proposal we've already put forward, it's been the men in the CPLD who've been doing quite a lot of the work. And then it will go to the AGM of the CLPD for ratification and I'd be very surprised if there was any serious change in it. So, it will be men who will be accepting it already in the Party and men who will be confronting the fact that the organisation they're involved with and have done a lot of work for, is now going to expand the democratic argument into a different sphere. It's been men who have been arguing for it on the CLPD executive. That's why we have to hold some sort of a balance between the fact that we aim to provide a situation where women can organise themselves but at the same time we have looked for and have had support of men in this activity. It is a balance between the two. Women must do it but we must understand that men are supporting us. We have to understand that it is not a simple thing for people to see that society is exploitative in relation to women. It requires a lot of thought and a lot of understanding and a real shift in the way we see society. If that's what you're really aiming at, you must understand that it's difficult to do.

Diana Adlam, Barry Hindess, Dan Smith
Interview with Jo Richardson

(Jo Richardson is MP for Barking.)

Q: What is it like to be a woman in an overwhelmingly male institution like parliament?

JR: There are 19 women members, 11 of whom are Labour. I'm not quite sure, but I think it's fewer than we've had since the war. Certainly a reduction on the last period. On the face of it, strangely enough, there is very little difference between being a woman and being a man. The men do, after the initial hiccup, accept you on an equal basis and they try hard not to be patronising. Certainly on the Labour side they mainly succeed - while we're in the building I'm talking about. The Tories tend to go out of their way to pretend that you're equal,although they can't stop themselves from ostentatiously opening doors and things like that. But the whole building is absolutely male oriented. Every corridor is studded with doors marked 'members only' which turn out to be the gentlemen's lavatory. We have three so-called 'lady members' rooms' which are sort of lounges where we can go and kick off our shoes and have a bath if we want and things like that. You can find yourself in a committee room and you're dying to go to the toilet and you've only got a couple of minutes before you've got to speak and it's miles to find a ladies'. This is true also for all the staff. It isn't just that there are 19 women MPs, there is a large number of women who work in the building, in the library, the catering staff. There's a very high proportion of women but they're not really catered for at all. But as I say, once you get over the initial bottom-pinching or hair ruffling ...

That actually happens?

JR: Well, one woman MP had her bottom pinched two days after she got in by a policeman. She turned round and haughtily looked at him and he said: "Oh, madam, I'm very sorry, I thought you were a secretary". She didn't know quite how to reply to that, so she swept away. You still do get a lot of people, even on our own side, who are unconsciously condescending and patronising and who will ruffle your hair - which I absolutely loathe, and say: "Ah, she's at it again," if

you've said something or done something which they think is a bit
outrageous. Of course the place isn't set up for mums or would-be
mums, so it's hard for young women to cope with being an MP. But
basically we are treated with a fair amount of equality.

Do you find condescension undermines your own effectiveness as an MP?

JR: I don't notice it any more but perhaps that's because I've been
there for a few years. I did at the beginning. We've still got the
same system whereby if it's considered to be a women's issue, i.e.
maternity rights or employment or social security effecting women,
they always look at me or whoever happens to be on the committee and
say: "Well, that's your speech of course". I keep saying: "Well,
it's your speech too because we're all people, and you've got a lot
of women constituents, and we are half the population." We recently
had two social security bills which are now law, which ran on for
several months in committee. They very much affect women, in terms
of cutting benefits, and with one or two exceptions (there were some
on our side who were willing to make speeches about this), when we
were considering our tactics for the week, and it came to an issue
specifically affecting women they'd all look at me and say: "Of
course that's yours." When I dreamt up a few of my own, like we
should have more women on the Social Security Advisory Committee,
they all leapt up and down: "We can't have every minority group
represented"!

We had a semi-jocular, but really quite serious row on the committee.
I got up and said: "We are 52% of the population, we're not a minority. You have got disabled representatives who are in fact a minority. You don't think of women as being a majority." And they
seemed surprised to realise that women were 52% of the population;
they'd never thought of us in those terms. All I'm really trying to
say is that we do tend to get lumbered with the women's issues. Not
that I mind because I think they're very important, but I do wish
that it could be spread around so that it was felt that it wasn't
a special thing.

*Isn't it a contradiction that they turn to you for sensible
information on the topic, yet resist the idea of more women on
the committee?*

JR: Sure. We are all statutory women. There's only one occasion
I can remember when they did put on a lot of women, and that was on
the Sex Discrimination Act, which was the first big Bill I went on
when I arrived at the House. The majority of members on our side
were women, for one reason or another. We had a woman minister,
Shirley Summerskill, a woman whip, Betty Boothroyd. That was a conscious effort - it's your problem so you'd better get along and do
it. And in a way that's also wrong. They don't necessarily choose
you because you're good at the subject or because you've got ideas,
but because you're a woman.

On a lot of committees there's one woman member. But with a small
number of women it is quite difficult to cope. If one wasn't careful you would find yourself on every committee - simply because you
wanted to take on more or you wanted to have two or three women on
a committee. By and large there's usually just the one, the statutory one. Funnily enough, the Tories on the Social Security Bill
had two - we only had one. They had Linda Chalker, who was the
Junior Minister, and Peggy Fenner, who never said anything much anyway. Again, sometimes they forget to include a woman when it really
is a women's issue. There was a bill in the last Parliament which
covered the conditions of nurses and midwives and there was no
woman on the committee. They all went beserk when they discovered
they'd forgotten.

There needs to be a lot more women so that we could spread the job,
but also the men must positively take up the issues. We take up
issues that are not women's issues - why shouldn't they take up our
issues as well? When we had the report stage of the Employment Bill
which of course affects women too, because they're trades unionists,
but especially because of the maternity provisions which have been
cut, the Whip on the Bill - there had been no women on that Bill
although I know they were very well briefed on our side - the
Whip, when we came to the report stage, rushed around finding three
or four women saying: "This is *your* debate, we'll all keep back."
We said: "We don't want you to keep back, we want *you* to say something as well." "No, we'll make this a women's debate." So they
got Oonagh McDonald and Joan Lestor and me and one or two others
to make speeches about maternity rights. The whole thing is
unbalanced.

*Have these problems ever been raised as issues for discussion in
the PLP?*

JR: No they haven't. I've never thought of raising them to be
quite honest.

*Is it impossible to raise or is it just that the PLP works in a
way that makes it very difficult?*

JR: They wouldn't know what we were talking about. They wouldn't
see it in the way we see it, they think they *are* doing something
about women. But they're not. There are about a dozen honourable
exceptions Particularly amongst the younger and newer members of
parliament. People like Reg Race, Clive Solley, John Tilley really
understand and will make an effort. And of course on the Corrie
Bill there were a number of male MPs who became very interested
and reversed what I've been saying. They were very very good about
that.

That was the third of the efforts. Did you feel it had built up?

JR: Oh yes, very much so. The women in the constituencies
initiated Campaign Against Corrie groups in a much more organised

way than they'd ever done before, and this pressurised them. So they
felt they could speak because they had the backing. And they found
they wanted to and they got very, very interested in it. People
like Alex Lyon, whose instincts were okay, but who had never joined
in before and Willie Hamilton, Stan Thorne and Ian Mikardo, for
example, were all very good and really got absorbed by the situation.
I hope that will mean that eventually they will come to think of
other things as being general subjects.

*With those kinds of MPs, who have all been in the House for quite a
time, is there a feeling that over an issue like abortion or others
that come under the bracket of women's issues, that they would be
sticking their necks out? That their constituency, their GMC or
whatever would think they were wasting their time?*

JR: On the previous Abortion Bills there had been a *great* deal of
pressure from the other side. MPs with some guts have taken no
notice of it and have spoken or voted against it. I don't care in
this case, if they voted - that was enough. I had MPs coming to me
and saying: "For god's sake, don't you know anybody at all in my
constituency who could write me a letter saying I approve of your
stand about abortion, because I've had a thousand letters from the
other side and I feel really threatened and as if I should keep my
head down because I've only got a tiny majority." And it is difficult, I appreciate that. But I think that two or three of the older
ones did it because they believed in it and because they were very
experienced in procedure; people like Ian Mikardo, for example, who's
got a safe seat. He hadn't taken any particular interest in it but
then became interested and he had a lot of pressure from his constituency, which he was very pleased about. And he has the London
Hospital which has an abortion unit in his constituency. So there
was another bit of interest. And he got absolutely fascinated and
absorbed by the whole thing, and learned a great deal, I think,
about it. There were others who were even more courageous because
some of them don't have such safe seats, yet were willing to do it.
Stan Thorne has a very, very marginal seat indeed and has always
taken a very level-headed and good view about it.

There are a number of my women colleagues on the Labour side who do
not feel there is any discrimination against women, any patronising
or condescension or anything like that. I don't entirely share that,
but most MPs would say that they don't particularly see any difference between men and women once you're in there. *Getting* there is a
different problem.

*Before we talk about getting there, is that different over defence
because that's something you've specialised in? Looking through the
community of scholars and writers on defence there is an extraordin-
arily small number of women. It is seen as a particularly male subject.*

JR: Yes I do feel that about defence and to a certain extent about
one or two other subjects. But on defence, apart from Audrey Wise
who took a close interest, I'm the only woman who has consistently

played a part in defence debates. I always have the feeling when I
get up to speak in the Chamber on defence that a glazed look comes
over people's faces. Particularly on the other side but sometimes on
our side too. It's infuriating - they think here comes the CND and we
better just listen, or we don't even have to listen, we know what the
line is. Some of the interruptions you get from the Tory side are
very patronising, rather as if you can't possibly know what you're
talking about. The other woman who takes a close interest in the
nitty gritty of defence is on the other side and that's Janet Foulkes.
But she's listened to with more respect on her own side certainly,
because she happens to represent Plymouth where of course she's got
a naval dockyard. So they can see that as good old Janet defending
the rights of her constituents to have a job. But certainly I'm not
really welcome in defence debates. They put up with me there as the
voice of CND.

*You're saying you're not really welcome because you're treated as
the voice of CND; not because you're a woman?*

JR: Well, there are men who are close to CND but they listen to them.
It's a combination of CND and being a woman that makes it: "Oh dear,
she's on again, she's totally unrealistic." You can see it. To a
certain extent that sometimes happens with other subjects, but less
so.

*Could you tell us a little about the subjects you've specialised in
- especially defence and civil liberties. Why you picked that
particular range of subjects rather than some other?*

JR: I've always been interested in defence. Before I was in the
House, I was a long-standing member of CND. To be perfectly honest,
when I first went into the House, I wasn't terribly involved in a
day-to-day sense in women's rights. It was there. But the kind
of women who had been in parliament had been women who tended to
get given "women's subjects". And I don't mean in the sense in
which we now see it. The shopping basket, the cost of living, consumer protection and so on. I vowed that I wasn't going to take
the slightest interest in those, except in the most general sense.
And I certainly wasn't going to specialise in the Sally Oppenheim
way in the price of bread today because women always do the
shopping. I didn't want to do that and most of my women colleagues
on our side felt much the same. But then everything changed in
74-75 with the Sex Discrimination Act. It got more exciting in
the women's rights sense and a number of us got involved. But it
was a different approach and a different kind of women's issue.

Oh yes, why did I pick defence and things like that? Well, I
didn't pick defence, it was something I had always been interested
in. Civil liberties are terribly important. The growth of police
powers and the fact that I was a member of the NCCL - these things
just hit me as ones we ought to be making a noise about.

The Labour MPs who take up these issues tend not to be MPs who've come up classically through the labour movement. It tends to be people who've been academics or journalists.

JR: It is but I don't really know that I can explain it. It is fundamental to the whole of socialism that our civil liberties should be preserved and extended. But you're right, it's not a subject which all that many people think is relevant.

Do you think it's going to become, as economic questions get more and more to the forefront, more difficult to pursue civil liberties issues? And also for women's rights issues?

JR: It is going to be more difficult because in a male-oriented society, and particularly in a working class area where jobs are threatened, where it's always been the man's job to go out to work to earn the *principal* part of the income - then it's going to be back to the old competitiveness that women's jobs have got to go first. They won't really think that that's wrong, that will just be in the natural order of things. The man must have the job and it would be nice if the woman had one too, but it's still hers that has to go first.

We've been set back a long way by this government. I'm not saying there were many steps forward with the previous government but there were a few. It's the same with civil liberties. As people come to accept the 'discipline' of unemployment, of perhaps not settling for such big wage increases, as Thatcher wins on that field, however much they may resent it, they'll think less and less about their rights as individuals. They'll be more scared of the establishment and of the police and the SPG, and this is a very dangerous trend.

You've discussed this trend as if the problem arises from the way people are reacting to economic and political circumstances. But there is also the point that the Labour Party and the labour movement in general hasn't campaigned on these issues. So it's not surprising if labour supporters in the population don't take them very seriously.

JR: Certainly, we've been *awful* in the Labour Party and in the trades unions. Although the trades unions are now getting more aware of women's rights because they've got more women members. There are a larger number of women who are trades unionsts and almost every union or every large union has a women's rights officer. But by and large the Labour Party has regarded this as one of these issues that you put in on a good day but you don't regard it as central to the whole business of living. We had to watch like a hawk to make sure there was some reference to women's rights in *Peace, Jobs and Freedom*. And in our draft manifesto. It's pretty minimal as it is, but at least it's there. But I think that is now going to change.

Could we talk now about being a woman trying to get into parliament?

JR: Oh, it's awful. It really is terrible. I don't know whether
I'm typical but I stood four times in four general elections before
I got a seat, a safe seat. The others were all Tory - I knew before
I started that I wasn't going to win. In fact, I'd given up. I
fought in 51 and 55, 59 and 64. I didn't fight 66 or 70 because I'd
packed it in. Then several people said: "Why don't you have a go in
Barking?" and I said: "Oh, what's the point?" But I decided I might
as well have a go, completely convinced that I didn't stand a chance.
The irony is that I got on to the short list in Barking because I
was a woman. I don't actually know if I would have got on if I
hadn't been. There were over a hundred applications for the seat, in
some cases people who were quite well-known, including ex-MPs. I was
put on the short list, although I had several nominations, because
they thought: "We've got to have a statutory woman." Parties don't
think about having two statutory women or five on the short-list
being women. That's a bit beyond the bounds of possibility, though
I think that's going to change in the future too. It was good luck
that I got it. It was very much due to the women's section in Barking
who had invited down four people who had applied from the list that
was circularised of the people who had put their names in - all men,
and they didn't like the look of any of them. At the very last
minute, a couple of days before the close of nominations, I had a
call from the secretary who'd happened to be at a ward meeting where
I'd spoken and she said they'd discussed it at the women's section
and they didn't like any of the men that they'd seen. She told them
about me and made my speech for me, so they decided to nominate me.
They've been very good supporters and friends ever since. What I've
said about Barking in some respects doesn't totally apply to the
Party because the women's section, although it's an older women's
section, not a young one, are very much in favour of women's rights
and want to continue to have women MPs. They have a healthy contempt
for many men.

Basically the Labour Party, which pays lip-service to having women on
the short-list and women candidates, writes a letter once or twice a
year to every party to that effect and doesn't really do much more.
The National Labour Women's Committee is very well into women's rights
and we should get that committee raised to the status of a proper sub-
committee of the NEC because it will help the issues. We now have a
study group on women's rights but it's taken about twelve months to
get it off the ground. The Party has thought it was enough to include
a few words here and there or to take up individual issues like
maternity rights and so on. Aside from the need for a policy there
are a lot of women who would find their natural home in the Labour
Party if we could show we were serious about women's rights.

*A number of women who came into politics through the women's movement
are now moving into or thinking of moving into the Labour Party. You
said that the women's section in Barking is very insistent on women's
rights but many women say that the women's sections in their local
constituencies are just dreadful.*

JR: I don't believe that's true.   There are some who do more than
the traditional thing of making the tea and running the bazaar.   Indeed
my own women's section does that; it's relied upon to do it.   But they
are much more aware of the fact that they can have an input in a
different direction.   Some feel they could do a councillor's job.   I
used to take the view that the women's sections were an anachronism
and that we all ought to stand on our own feet, and if we were good
enough we would get elected as councillors or be able to represent the
party at Conference or on other bodies.   But I realise that we've got
such a long way to go that we've got to have some positive discrimination.   Women do need a women's section in order to be able to talk out
their problems and to get a new perspective on their own lives which
they can't always do through the branch meeting or a GMC largely
dominated by men.

*Do you see that as a shift in the role of the women's sections in
providing necessary political support to women gaining political
confidence?*

JR: Yes.   There are a lot more women's sections springing up and a
lot of them are young women who want to meet together without men.
And there's a lot of resistance in some local Labour parties to the
setting up of women's sections.   Cold water is poured from a great
height on some of them - some say it's sexist to be separate.   But
I don't take that view.   If women want to meet separately they should
do so.   They'll find themselves, through being able to discuss political issues with other women, gaining confidence to put their views
at branch and GMC level.

*Has the women's movement influenced both your own position and will
the women's sections perhaps begin to play that kind of role?*

JR: Very much so.   Quite a lot of women are now coming into the
Labour Party.   I hope a lot more will, because I think they are
beginning to see that it is a major party which can, if it's pushed
in the right direction, really achieve something.   It's up to them
and us to see we are taken seriously.   The present trend to have
women's sections, to promote women, to constantly bring up the subject of women's rights in resolutions and so on has been very much
influenced by outside women's groups.   For example, 'Fightback for
Women's Rights', which is excellent and has a socialist perspective, is
becoming better and better known.   I spoke at their first meeting and
was very impressed that a lot of women there had not been associated
with any political party, and rather despised political parties, but
were beginning to see that the only way to achieve the kind of
society they were working for in groups outside was through a major
political party.   Whatever criticisms they may have about the Labour
Party, and we all have criticisms about it, many are now turning to
it as the only way to achieve what they want.   And in doing that
they're getting interested in other subjects: civil liberties; the
economic situation; defence - not just as they impinge on women but
generally.   But I absolutely accept that the Labour Party's been awful
about women's rights. I was looking the other day for a pamphlet and

came across some 1945, 1950s pamphlets and I was just flipping
through them: *everything* is about men, every single thing. They're
all Labour Party pamphlets and they're all written for men, they're
all about men and not a single mention of a woman in them.

*Now you watch like a hawk and get in the mention there. But you've
still got to do that. Moreover, if the number of women MPs and
women candidates is an index it seems not only that progress has
not been made, but there's actually been a slip.*

JR: A lot can be done by encouragement by the NEC and by a bigger
proportion of our manifesto being slanted not just towards women,
but slanted in terms of this being a fundamental part of the progress
towards a socialist society. You can't have it without. I can't
think what we were all dreaming about in the 40s and 50s by ignoring
it, and ignoring the civil liberties angle which was just as dangerous in those days as it is now. Perhaps not quite so much. Things
are more sophisticated in terms of attacks on civil liberties now.
At the same time, of course, we mustn't forget that *we* are also more
knowledgeable than we were in those days, more people know about
files and telephone tapping and mail opening. If anything, the party
is more oriented nationally towards civil liberties than it is
towards women. Partly, I suppose because civil liberties affects
everybody.

*It wasn't just a question of omitting women, there were positive
factors at work. Such as the question of what to do about the jobs
that women had done while men were at war and making sure that the
men got those jobs back.*

JR: That's right. But if you think back to the war time, which I
can remember, it's amazing how quickly we adapted then to the fact
that women went to work. Nursery places sprang up all over.

There were all those propaganda films of women doing heavy work.

JR: Not only propaganda films. I saw some copies of *Woman* and
Women's Own from that time where there was still the pretty face on
the front cover but she was wearing a headscarf to tie her hair back
and she was working a lathe. It was great, it was the working woman.
But there was a move in the other direction too, dismantling all
the day nurseries, and for a long period after the war most women
would give up work on getting married. Although funnily enough in
Barking, for instance, most women continued to work because they
needed the money.

But did they go into different kinds of jobs?

JR: Yes, into low paid jobs with bad conditions. The school jobs,
the school secretary and the dinner ladies and so on, the part-time
workers in hospitals. They weren't unionised, the jobs were there
that could be done while they looked after the children and fitted
in with the school holidays.

*How was it that in the 40s and 50s the Labour Party was still dream-
ing while all these things were happening around it, indeed during a
period when it was in office for six years?*

JR: In the 40s and 50s we had tremendous problems in the aftermath
of the war. I'm not saying they just forgot it because of that.
It just wasn't within their view.

*There were other things as well like trades union strategies around
notions of a family wage, embodying a conception that if women are
going to work it's for pin money. The argument is still now in terms
of a family wage and at the same time there are demands for equal
pay and equal opportunities.*

JR: Women are still conditioned to that kind of role but they were
more conditioned then than now. When you were talking earlier about
the immediate aftermath of the war when women had to give back the
jobs to men, there was very little protest from women.

There was from some of the women's unions.

JR: Yes, but it was very marginal. There was an acceptance: "OK,
back I go to the kitchen sink and having the kids, and I'm glad to
have my old man back from the war, and of course my role is back
there." What's happening with this government is the same thing.
All the cuts, not just the obvious cuts in maternity rights, the
sex discrimination in immigration, but that people are sent home
from hospital before they're completely well on the assumption that
the woman at home, whoever she is, will look after the mother or
the father or the child. The idea is that, with charges for home
helps, the daughter will come round and do for mum, or the home help
stays on and does it for nothing because she likes the old lady.
All this is becoming an accepted part of life today in the same
way, though not quite so starkly, as it was after the war.

But it is meeting a lot more resistance?

JR: Meeting a lot more resistance because there are a lot more
articulate people who are not willing to sit down under it, and
the more they discuss and the more they have meetings and conferences about it, the more other women who are on the periphery of
politics and trades unionism will come to understand it.

*A lot of issues have been marginalised, not just by the Labour
Party but within the labour movement, because economic policy has
tended to dominate everything else. Certainly with Crosland and the
Gaitskellites there has been the idea that we can't really do anything until we get the economy right – we have to pay for everything
out of growth. The effect of that has been that all sorts of other
policy issues were set aside by saying that we can deal with them
once we've got a certain amount of growth in the economy. Why has
the Labour Party been like that for so long? Because it's obvious
that, although any kind of policy instituted by a government must*

*cost some money, many wouldn't cost government very much, so that
for a lot of issues paying for it isn't going to be a major problem.
Yet the Labour Party's taken it that we can't do these until we can
afford to pay for them.*

JR: It's at least partly, perhaps wholly, because of a general
acceptance that things like women's rights and civil liberties are
marginal issues. As far as the left is concerned, some far left
groupings take the line that until you get the economy right, when
you get a socialist society - I'm oversimplifying it - but when you
nationalise the principal companies, all other things will fall into
place *then*, so therefore please don't bother about it now because
it's all a waste of time. They do a lot of harm. Some take the
lofty view that it's all rather an extraneous diversion which we
oughtn't to have to be bothered with and it'll all come right in the
end.

*But as you say, it's at one level comprehensible in the case of, for
instance, Trotskyist groups because they have a definite position on
what the transition to socialism must look like. But that can't
account for the views of other sections in the labour movement.*

JR: I agree with you. If you go back to the right wing, I think it's
just innate conservatism and fear, and fear because women are an unknown factor. The Gaitskells and the Croslands could predict more or
less, not that they were always right, but they could predict what was
going to happen because it was their kind, i.e. men, who were making
the decisions. Even some of the people on the left of the party -
I'm not talking about the Trotskyist groups now - on the NEC, for
example, have no idea and they're very patronising and condescending.
They wouldn't dream of saying anything out loud but basically they
don't understand it.

*It's as if it's endemic to the Labour Party to marginalise issues,
that getting the economy right must come first and the result is that
you ignore a whole series of issues which are not only to do with
women or civil liberties, but anything which doesn't fall under the
purview of the Chancellor of the Exchequer. On the other hand, it
isn't exactly marginalisation, because it's easy to get people worried
once you raise things like the 'breakdown of the family'. There was
a discussion a couple of years ago about a Ministry of Marriage as if
there was a problem of civil order that had as its axis a breakdown
in traditional forms of the family. So when it's raised the other
way round rather than in terms of women's rights, then there is a
lot of concern and debate.*

JR: The family was a political football in the 77-79 period, with
Patrick Jenkin talking about 'the family' and Jim Callaghan about a
Ministry for Marriage. In practice, after the election the Tories
had forgotten it altogether. They want the family to be the wife
back home with the least appetising aspects of the kitchen sink in
front of her. The only encouraging thing I find is that I think
we've gone past the point of no return. Things will never be the

same again because the present generation of young women will never
let it. I hope not.

Why do you think we've passed the point of no return?

JR: Whatever is done by government against women, by this government
or even by a Labour government, in the interests of the economy and
all that, women won't wear it forever. There's a temporary competitiveness between women and men. The job of the principal breadwinner
is the job to be saved, though that breadwinner is often the woman.
So many women are better educated in terms of what their rights are
and in feeling they have a real stake in the future of the country
that they won't let it go. The new awareness of women has been underestimated, people are more educated into demanding more rights and
more say. Look at the change in the family. You can't really say
that the nuclear family is typical any more. It isn't just man, wife,
married with two and a half children. There are one-parent families,
and people choosing to live together and not to get married but
having children anyway. I don't think we'll ever go back to the
other image.

*Clearly, women's organisations are part of the general changes
you're talking about. How far would someone like you go to women's
organisations now in a way that you wouldn't have ten years ago?*

JR: I follow anything which is pushed through my door on women's
rights. Women's groups all over the country send me a copy of their
bulletin which they may have just put round a few houses where they
live. I read them avidly, I'm so pleased that they're doing something. I take out subscriptions to all the things like Women's
Fightback. I'm very excited about our own new women's rights study
group.

*Apart from the post, how much direct contact do you have with
women's organisations, and do you initiate or do they?*

JR: Works both ways. I know people in most of them. I have sometimes initiated contact and sometimes they get in touch with me.
Probably the second is more usual than the first. Not because I'm
unwilling but because I don't have time. But I try to keep up to
date. When there's some specific issue in parliament, I get in
touch immediately.

*Like the Abortion Amendment epic. Do you find yourself working
quite closely with them?*

JR: I never heard a peep out of some of them. Campaign Against
Corrie, yes. National Abortion Campaign and Labour Abortion Rights
Committee, yes. The nitty gritty work was done by Co-ord, which is
the Coordinating Committee on Abortion, and is made up of various
abortion rights or charitable sector organisations. They had been
keeping together since the Benyon Bill. And they were the people
who actually sat down Monday after Monday and drafted hundreds of

amendments. That and the campaign outside parliament was what kept
the Bill off the statute book. We had 7 or 8 lawyers, 2 or 3 doctors,
2 or 3 people representing the charitable sector, and we worked it all
out every week. The outside job was done by NAC and IARC and a lot
was done by some unions and by the National Labour Women's Committee
of the Party.

But with all the mobilisation from outside, if we hadn't had the
possibility of moving amendment after amendment after amendment, the
Bill would have gone through. We kept the report stage going for
four Fridays - unheard of. Parliamentary tactics were essential but
those parliamentary tactics were helped by being supported by MPs
who were bolstered up from outside. The two dovetail together.

*What do you think about groups within the women's movement that don't
want anything to do with parliament, like the people who objected to
the whole way the TUC demonstration was organised?*

JR: Personally, I think they were counter-productive. The fact is
that if we had done what they wanted us to do, Corrie would be on the
statute book today. No question, it would be. Because the outside
pressure was not enough. The fact that we had to go through a
committee stage and a report stage and we had to keep it going for
four Fridays made the parliamentary side crucial. I was terrified
it was going to go through. Groups who say we shouldn't have anything to do with parliamentary procedure are taking a ridiculous
position. While you've got parliament you've got to fight through
it, important though outside pressure is. I was very upset by what
happened at the TUC demonstration. It took us weeks to get the TUC
to agree and they were not too keen at the beginning. But the women
who are on the TUC, or close to it, worked hard to get them to agree
to it. It was no mean thing to have the trade union movement involved and to make them all aware of it. It was a very good demonstration in terms of size, and the women who tried to take it over
simply undid a lot of the work that had been done. The fact that
they got to Trafalgar Square long before everybody else and hogged
all the main positions meant that other people coming along could
only hear them shouting: "Get out - men, get off". I was physically
attacked by a woman afterwards. She said: "You should be ashamed of
yourself, being on the platform with men." I can understand women's
groups and women's issues sometimes being discussed in meetings where
no men are allowed. I think that's fine. But you've got to persuade
men on some issues and on the abortion issue it is absolutely vital.
Indeed, arising from the TUC demonstration a lot more unions wrote
to their sponsored MPs saying: "We hope you will oppose the Corrie
Bill" - that was very useful.

*Inside the Labour Party now there seem to be a number of moves to
resurrect the question of equality, rights of women. Things like
the Campaign for Labour Party Democracy proposing that all short-
lists for selection should have at least one woman and one member
of the manual working class. Or Frances Morrell's proposal that
50% membership of all Labour Party committees should be women.*

JR: I thought I was the first one to say 50%!   But I'm not competing
with Frances.   I am very much against having just one woman, because
that just institutionalises the statutory woman.

*You were saying earlier than no-one thinks of having more than one
woman.*

JR: That's it.   It reminds me of that story about panel games.
Apparently the BBC laid it down that one woman was OK, two, well,
OK if they were both famous, but three and it must be relegated to
Woman's Hour.   It's just like that.   I want to see us having power.

*When you floated the 50% idea what were you suggesting?   In Frances
Morrell's article in the Guardian she was suggesting that there
should be constitutional changes so that it should be laid down that
at least 50% of the membership of every committee should be women.
Is that what you were suggesting?*

JR: I think you've got to do it in a positive way.   You've got to
legalise it as it were.   You'll never get it otherwise.   It will be
very difficult to achieve because there will be the usual arguments
saying: "We don't want just any woman".   The labour movement, as
society does, overlooks the fact that there is enormous talent, as
much talent among women as among men.   And that women have always
been oppressed.   I just want to see women in their proper role in
society - which means playing an equal role in making decisions.
I don't care if they get into parliament and never mention women's
rights, although I'd be very happy at the moment to spread the load.
But all the major decisions, all the important decisions in this
country and in the world, are taken by men.   It's really involvement
in decision making that I'm after.   Society loses a tremendous lot
by overlooking women, and women lose a lot by being put in the position of unequal partners.   If you look at the House of Commons and
at other representational bodies, what you need is people with common
sense and an idea of the kind of society they'd like to achieve.
There are as many women who have something to say about that as
there are men.   I don't want to see a House of Commons with half
women in it, all of whom do nothing else but talk about women's
rights.   I want them to talk about defence and civil liberties and
employment and environment and energy.   All of which are generally
regarded as men's topics.   I want more women involved in decision
making.   I don't see that they should get there only to concentrate
on women's rights, important though that is.

*So there must be other mechanisms for making sure that women's rights
are constantly to the fore.   Which includes convincing the men.*

JR: A lot of men will be convinced when we achieve a bit more
equality in numbers.   At present the general cry from men at all
sorts of levels, when there's a call for a delegate to a conference,
is: "Women don't put themselves forward, so there aren't any women
to choose anyway."   This overlooks the fact that there are plenty
of women who never had a chance to open their mouths about anything.

One feminist reason for being suspicious of the Labour Party is that,
if we join and work within it, then we have to do it on their terms,
and if we do it on their terms then we'll get nowhere - so let's
stay outside.

JR: Yes, I suppose that's true. At the same time, we need those
people inside the Labour Party because they will give us a lot of
help and a lot of people to draw on. If, for example, we had all the
women who are involved in the women's movements and women's groups,
suddenly joining the Labour Party and being regular attenders at
their branch meetings, this would revolutionise the whole thing.
We wouldn't achieve 50% overnight, but there would be so many more
women who would be willing to come to meetings and put themselves
forward, who would have a voice and an angle on whatever was discussed.
The Labour Party, to be fair to it, is not against articulate women,
if they're there and show themselves. I agree that you've got to
work very hard, work twice as hard at it, but if you're there and
you're pushy enough, then they'll give you a chance. So to that
extent, from a purely practical point of view, I'd rather see them
inside than outside. But I agree that innately the Labour Party is
conservative and we've got to get over that conservatism. The Labour
Party is really only a reflection of the whole of society because,
until we get more acceptance that the father or the husband has as
much duty to stay at home looking after the kids while his wife or
his partner goes to meetings, until we get that acceptance generally,
you won't get more than a few women in the Labour Party being able to
participate. Unless they're very pushy about it, or unless they've
got a very good relationship with their husband. It's true of the
trades union movement too.

Or unmarried?

JR: Or unmarried. It's the same in the trades union movement.
You've got too few shop stewards who are women largely because they're
either too tired to take on the extra job or the branch meetings are
held at times which are inconvenient. It's all very well, as someone
said to me the other day: "It's easy enough, we make it a rule that
branch meetings are at lunchtime." Most of the women workers in
Barking who are members of the union have to go and do the shopping
at lunchtime. They barely have time to eat. At Fords Dagenham,
there is one plant composed almost entirely of women and very militant they are too. Their lunch hour, which is 45 minutes, is spent,
10 minutes rushing up Chequers Lane - full of potholes which they're
constantly complaining about - to the big supermarket on the corner
to get the old man's tea, and then rushing back again, and if they're
lucky when they get back they've got time for a sandwich. They cope
with this by having their branch meetings in the middle of the morning, but that's very unusual. Part-time workers, mostly women, are
usually not there anyway when a branch meeting takes place. So they
never get a chance. That is difficult to solve.

What kind of flurry if any was caused when Margaret Thatcher became
first head of the Tories and then Prime Minister? It is extraordin-
ary for a predominantly male institution such as the Conservative
Party to elect a woman.

JR: They don't think she's a woman. They think she's a pretend man. She'a a woman but no sister, and she has no idea of what it's like. She has no conception of women's rights. It was terribly embarrassing for us because the women on our side were all asked by the Press: "Aren't you pleased that there is a woman Prime Minister?", and it was a very difficult question to answer at the time. Some women MPs went overboard and said: "Oh, it's absolutely marvellous, so good to see a woman there" - they soon changed their minds. I hate all this, she's done harm in a number of directions because you get more and more people saying: "Britain's first and last women Prime Minister", and the sort of "ditch the bitch" sexist remarks don't do us any good. They just turn men against women. She's a horror, I must say. But then so's Heath. All Tory Prime Ministers, give or take a bit, are bad. But she's particularly dedicated to being tough.

Gideon Ben-Tovim, John Gabriel, Ian Law and Kathleen Stredder
Race, Left Strategies and the State

INTRODUCTION

The arguments presented here rest on the assumption that the development of effective Left strategies to combat racism and racial disadvantage requires a knowledge of policy formation at central and
local levels and an assessment of those political forces addressing
themselves directly or indirectly to policy issues. It is in this
context that we explore once such policy initiative, the 1976 Race
Relations Act. We begin with an assessment of its origins and
principal enforcement agency, the CRE. The discussion moves on to
a more detailed consideration of both formal and informal political
structures which, if not responding directly to the Act itself, have
done so indirectly through their involvement in race issues.
   The selection of the two areas Liverpool and Wolverhampton has
been made on the basis of our involvement as a group in local
politics in these areas. Such involvement is seen as a necessary
precondition for an effective contribution to any conjunctural analysis and hence to policy development. The two areas provide a
useful focus for comparison insofar as they establish variations and
unevenness resulting from local conditions. Specific interventions
in which the group has been/is involved play a central role in the
analysis of these conditions and in particular the identification of
those forces responsible for shaping politics at a local level.

I RACE THEORY AND THE STATE

The revival of interest in Marxist theory, now over a decade old,
has only recently concerned itself in any detail with questions
pertaining to socialism, Left strategy and political theory. The
initial interest in philosophy, theories of culture and ideology, and
economics has shifted towards a series of more explicitly political
debates. Much of the rationale underpinning our own work in Liverpool
and Wolverhampton rests on a series of problems identified with respect to certain hitherto ascendent interpretations of the state,

ideology and socialist strategy within Marxist political theory.
There are certain implications which might be drawn from this discussion that are relevant both in terms of analysis and intervention
in the field of race relations. Together these problems and their
implications provide the starting point for the substantive issues
raised in the latter part of this paper.

(i) The concept of the monolithic state

One central focus of recent debates within Marxism concerns the
character of the state in contemporary capitalism. In conventional
terms the state is conceived as a combination of repressive and
ideological apparatuses employed by the ruling class to secure its
own reproduction. Drawing on polemical and rhetorical remarks from
classical Marxism, the modern state is thus perceived as the political arm of the Bourgeoisie, the means by which the dominant
economic class rules politically. This monolithic or instrumentalist conception of the state and state power has been called into
question by a series of authors whose positions ultimately diverge.
Marx and Lenin themselves acknowledged the contradictory and
complex character of state forms. Contradictory in the sense that
state power by no means always coincides with dominant class interests (e.g. in 19th century Britain); complex in the sense that a
whole variety of forms become possible through the presence and
intervention of other classes and class fractions out of which
alliances emerge at different levels of the class struggle. Such
factors as these affect the balance of class forces at a given
moment in time and space (Hall, 1977).
   Others following Marx have developed the conceptual means by
which these complexities might be grasped. Gramsci for instance
made one such contribution through his concept of integral state:
   '... the general notion of the state includes elements which
   need to be referred back to the notion of civil society (in
   the sense that one might say the State = political society
   + civil society, in other words hegemony protected by the
   armour of coercion). (*Prison Notebooks*, p.263)
The extension of the state to include arenas of struggle conventionally conceived to be outside its boundaries thus serves to break
down the straightforward state/masses opposition. The latter are
now incorporated within this extended definition of the state whose
forms can now be seen as the product of struggles waged by classes
and class fractions. The war of position, where the 'siege is
reciprocal' (cited by Sassoon, in Hibbin, 1978, p.20), is waged on
the terrain of the state itself. Although it is true that the subordinate classes have not themselves selected those terrains, the
latter, nevertheless, are the product of compromises necessitated
by class struggle. It is important to note here that Trade Union,
Social and Welfare legislation constitute, in part, the parameters
within which these struggles ensue. What is more, it is important
to note that the parameters themselves are the result of previous
struggles, a point to which we shall return in our consideration of
the 1976 Race Relations Act.

Poulantzas, too, is critical of restrictive conceptions of the state of the sort referred to above, where the state is seen exclusively in terms of what it 'forbids, rules out, prevents, or in its capacity to deceive, lie, obscure, hide and lead people to believe what is false' (Poulantzas, 1980, p.30).

Apart from failing to provide the mechanisms by which such ideologico-political relations are constituted, the above conception also inevitably fails to acknowledge the role of dominated classes within the state. Once this latter point is recognised, then it becomes possible to identify certain material measures as being of 'positive significance for the popular masses, even though those measures represent so many concessions imposed by the struggle of the subordinate classes' (ibid, p.31).

We might conclude this section with reference to Hindess's critique which is aimed not only at instrumentalist conceptions of the state but also those which rest on the assumption of state sovereignty. Since there is no general mechanism of connection (or non-connection) between economic relations, political arenas of struggle and ideologies, then there can be no general theory of such connections. The latter is thus rejected in favour of an analysis which focuses on the specificity of particular struggles and forces (Hindess, 1980).

Divergencies between the above mentioned positions have already been acknowledged, and indeed at one level, Gramsci, Poulantzas, and Hindess make strange bedfellows. What is important for us however is the generalised critique of a certain conception of the state which emerges from these positions, and, as we shall see shortly, its implications for political strategy.

(ii) Race theory

It is not altogether surprising to find a certain uneven development within the various branches of the social science disciplines in terms of the acknowledgement paid to debates pursued beyond their immediate boundaries. It could be argued that race analysis is surprisingly backward in this respect, far more so, for instance, than recent debates within the feminist movement. It is thus revealing to note that some of the most recent contributions to the politics of race and the politics of race research continue to make precisely those assumptions with regard to the state, ideology and political practice, which have been acknowledged as problematic and deficient, and which have been referred to above.

In a recent review of the sociology of race in Britain by Jenny Bourne, the ideology of race which is mediated through state institutions is said to reflect the needs of capital. The collapsing of racist ideology to an appendage of the economy has been the subject of critical discussion elsewhere and need not concern us in detail here (Gabriel and Ben-Tovim, 1978; Ben-Tovim, 1978; Ben-Tovim and Gabriel, 1979b). What can profitably be drawn attention to from the point of view of this discussion is the explicit reliance on an instrumentalist conception of the state to support this position. Ideas of racial superiority are thus seen to have been 'honed into a fine tool of exploitation' by 'political parties and governments (Labour

and Tory alike) and came to inhere in every institution of British
society' (Bourne, 1980, p.350). Once the state/masses opposition is
invoked, albeit implicitly, and the former is conceived as being inevitably and universally racist, then certain political consequences
necessarily follow. Authentic anti-racist political analysis and
action somehow have to find a place outside the confines of the racist
state. Consequently an emphasis is placed on analysis undertaken by
independent institutions and organisations (e.g. the Institute of
Race Relations) and, in terms of action, on industrial struggles and
those opposing directly the various manifestations of state racism
(e.g. police harrassment, immigration laws etc.). This position
thus provides the basis for critiques of policy-orientated research
on the one hand and intervention within official statutory and semi-
statutory bodies on the other.

It should be clear from the previous section and the reference to
our own work in this section that we find this position untenable.
If we accept the extended conception of the state offered to us in
the previous section, then those struggles referred to above must
fall within its parameters. Furthermore the context in which each
struggle ensues is contingent in part on the results of previous
struggles of subordinate classes, and their allies. The struggle
for union recognition, for instance, which has become a central
issue for black workers in recent industrial disputes, must take
previous legislation as one point of reference. The same is true
for those recent campaigns against police harrassment, which have
crystallised around pressure to repeal the 'sus' law. The role of
research here too is important and evidence ptoruced by such 'paternalistic' bodies as the Runnymede Trust (Demuth, 1978) and the
Home Office itself (Home Office, 1979) has been influential in
bringing the present Conservative government to the point of ultimately repealing the law. In this sense to reject policy per se
(trade union, social policy or whatever) is both mistaken and unthinkable. It is mistaken insofar as it assumes the initiatives
have been imposed unilaterally in order to deceive, conceal etc.
It is unthinkable since any struggle of subordinate classes must
acknowledge at least implicitly the legally defined terrain on
which the struggle is waged. The elucidation and clarification of
that terrain must constitute an important precondition for an
effective struggle. The question of who carries out this 'research'
task is not necessarily that important, in our view. What matters
is the use to which that research is put and the effects of its
incorporation into concrete political struggles (Ben-Tovim and
Gabriel, 1979a).

(iii) <u>Political strategy and the local state</u>

The opposition between 'radical' and 'pragmatic' research on race
(Mullard, 1980) and the confinement of the anti-racist struggle to
quite restricted forms of activism (see section III below) corres-
ponds closely to the conventional distinction made between insurrectionism and reformism. There are, however, good grounds for
abandoning this distinction in the context of a consideration of

Left political strategy in contemporary Britain, as recent authors
have argued. As Miliband rightly points out:
    'The rejection of insurrectionism is the largest and most
    important fact about the working class in advanced capitalist
    countries since 1918... no doubt there has always been a
    section of the working class of different proportions from
    one country to another and from one period to another which
    has found such an option and commitment acceptable but it has
    always and everywhere been a very small section of the whole;
    and the overwhelming majority of the working class, not to
    speak of other classes, has always rejected the politics of
    revolution. (Miliband, 1978, pp.161-62)
This does not mean to say that the road to socialism is necessarily
trod via parliamentary and representative institutions, at least not
exclusively. Furthermore, the rejection of insurrectionism does not
necessarily lead us back to social democracy. Rather, the acceptance
of the insurrectionist/reformist distinction and the resulting imposition of one political strategy does not recognise that advancement
of socialist struggle must start from the present conditions of that
struggle. The anti-racist struggle must recognise the ideological
diversity and the specific objects of the activities of the black
community. Only then can internal and external obstacles to political organisation and mobilisation be identified and steps taken to
produce the conditions for their resolution. As Jones point out,
what is required is a form of calculation which acknowledges the
role of certain intermediate reforms 'which may themselves be
insufficient [but] require as a necessary corollary further reforms
the effects of which would be a significant process of transformation' (Jones, 1980, p.146). It is interesting to note that Jones
illustrated this with reference to industrial democracy and the
scope offered by the Youth Opportunities Programme of the Manpower
Services Commission for the formation of co-operative forms of production and distribution. Intermediate reforms of the sort referred
to by Jones can arise out of popular movements, prefigurative
struggles or in more formal institutional contexts (cf. Prior and
Purdy, 1979; Rowbotham et al, 1979). Poulantzas refers to planning
bodies as one mode of access and intervention (1980, p.259) as one
example of the latter. The Race Relations Act affords others, and we
shall refer to these below.
    What is required from the point of view of political calculation
is 'a precise knowledge of the complex processes of [the state's]
formation' (Mercer, 1980, p.135). The 'liberation' of such concepts
as monolithic state, and the rejection of such oppositions as
insurrectionism/constitutionalism provides the possibility for the
sort of conjunctural analysis and calculation required by Mercer and
Jones. This enables the evaluation and utilisation of the radical
potential in certain reforms and provides the criteria for the
rejection of those reforms which are purely pragmatic or regressive.
Such analysis may facilitate the anti-racist struggle to articulate
its demands in such a way as to win resources, popular support and
political power to provide the conditions for further advancement in
this sphere.

The local state, for instance, can now be seen as a potential
scenario for 'popular democratic' struggle (Laclau, 1977). It cannot
be conceived simply as a mechanism for the reproduction of capital,
the local arm of the bourgeoisie, replicating the efforts of the
nation state to secure the conditions for capitalist survival
(Cockburn, 1977). The more general analysis of the state referred
to above thus permits a more detailed consideration of local conditions. As Corrigan (1979) has rightly acknowledged, the local state
is an important arena in the struggle for democracy. For those Left
organisations and groups in Liverpool and Wolverhampton it is initially at the local level that real participatory intrusion into the
state will be made, and from local struggles that popular movements
will emerge. The materialisation of race ideologies in local state
practices has developed unevenly and subject to a series of local
constraints: community ideologies, economic, demographic, political.
Of course, these are subject to broader constraints which transcend
local boundaries. The articulation of national and local political
structures is central to the subject-matter of the article. In
particular we are concerned with those conditions effecting varying
responses to the most recent piece of anti-discrimination legislation in Britain: the 1976 Race Relations Act.

II THE 1976 RACE RELATIONS ACT AND THE COMMISSION FOR RACIAL
    EQUALITY

In terms of the original White Paper 'Racial Discrimination' which
preceded the 1976 Act (Cmnd 6234), the ultimate aim was the equalisation of opportunities for groups regardless of colour, race, ethnic
or national origins. The White Paper acknowledged, however, the
need for more extensive provision in other areas of public policy
for this long-term objective to be realized (paras.25-26). The Act
was thus conceived as providing the legislative framework within
which such policies and practices might be pursued. In principle it
sought to strengthen existing legislation (the 1968 Race Relations
Act) through an extension of the legal definition of discrimination
and a strengthening of the enforcement powers conferred on the
newly established Commission for Racial Equality.
    The limits of the Act must not only be seen in terms of the need
for wider provision through an extension of existing social policies.
The elimination of racial discrimination and disadvantage implies a
goal of equal opportunity for racial groups. In a general sense
problematic aspects of this principle have been cogently argued by
Westergaard (1978). Inequality of treatment militates against any
realization of equal opportunity not only for the black but also for
sections of the white population. Inequalities in terms of wealth
and income distribution, access to public and private housing, education, health provision, inevitably limit the potential impact of
any anti-discriminatory measure, particularly if such measures are
introduced alongside initiatives designed to reduce public expenditure at national and local levels. The Act then at the very most
aims to equalise opportunities for racial minorities. Its intention
is to ensure that such groups at least have an equal chance on a

group basis to end up more or less equal than others on an individual
basis.

These limits inevitably affect the impact of the Act however strong
its provisions and the machinery established to enforce it. What we
shall argue in this paper is that, given these limits, the Act nonetheless provides scope for constituting an intermediary reform in the
sense defined above. The continuing acknowledgement of racist discrimination and disadvantage and the need for equal rights and
opportunities for racial groups, however ill defined, provide scope
for further initiatives and interventions at a number of points in
the political process.

The consideration of the Act begins with a discussion of its
origins. The arguments presented there not only shed considerable
doubt on the social control/conspiracy interpretations of social
legislation. They also serve to indicate where political pressure
from below has the potential for influencing the extent and shape of
legislative reform. In this case black militancy inside and outside
the workplace as well as submissions of evidence to the Select
Committee both contributed to the acceptance of the principle of
reform and to the ultimate shape of that reform. Research evidence,
too, in this case the PEP reports, strengthened the case for reform.
The analysing of the origins of the legislation thus in principle
provides a basis for future political calculation.

(i) The origins of the 1976 Race Relations Act

The impetus to reform the 1968 legislation on race relations appears,
in our view, to have come from five principal sources.

(a) The Liberal-Academic Lobby: The PEP reports

Widely publicised by the then Community Relations Commission and its
journal *New Community*, these reports principally covering housing and
employment became the major touchstone against which deficiencies in
the previous legislation were measured (Smith). The 1968 law for
instance placed an unreasonable onus on the complainant to prove his
case requiring an extension of the concept of discrimination. One
report in particular (Smith, D.J., 1974/75, p.60) provided the legal
framework within which an extended definition of discrimination could
be accommodated.

(b) Administrative expedience

If the various PEP reports confirmed the weaknesses in the 1968
legislation and provided the principal 'knowledge resource' on which
legislative reform was justified, then the impetus for administrative
reform came from the then recent Sex Discrimination Act and the White
Paper 'Equality for Women' (Cmnd 5724) which preceded it: indeed the
White Paper referred to the government's intention to harmonise
legislation on race with that proposed on women (Rendel and Bindman,
1975, p.2). The Runnymede Trust, too, favoured bringing race relations legislation into line with legislation on women to provide the

basis for a coordinated attack on discrimination (Runnymede Trust,
evidence to Select Committee, 1975). This was the view perhaps more
importantly of Whitehall officials involved directly in drafting the
Bill (Home Office Interview, 1979). The particular provision or
issue here was the merging of the former Community Relations
Commission with the Race Relations Board to form the Commission
for Racial Equality in the mould of the Equal Opportunities Commission established under the Sex Discrimination Act.

(c) Judicial decisions

Two cases in particular have been cited as crucial in exposing flaws
in previous legislation. One was the House of Lords' decision to uphold the operation of a colour bar in a Preston Dockers' Labour Club.
The other was the failure of the particular clause of the 1968 Act on
incitment to racial hatred which was highlighted in the Scarman Report
on the Red Lion Square disorders (Labour Party, 1978, p.28). Particular attention was subsequently paid to these two aspects of the
1968 legislation in the drafting and debate on the 1976 Act.

(d) Ethnic minority demands

In their evidence to the Select Committee on Race Relations and
Immigration (HMSO, 1975), organisations representing minority groups
reaffirmed some of the inadequacies in legislative provision referred
to above. Others went further. The Indian Workers' Association,
for instance, believed the Race Relations Acts to be a sop to the
blatantly discriminatory racist immigration legislation. Nevertheless, this organisation and others, including the Standing Conference on Pakistani Organisations, acknowledged the need for more
effective legislation to combat discrimination, and for a much
stronger body to conduct investigations and solicit information
which in principle were largely met in the statutory powers conferred on the CRE. Some supported an analogous administrative
structure to that envisaged to deal with sex discrimination while
the West Indian Standing Conference opposed any merger of the CRC
and RRB. Instead it campaigned for a consultative council of
immigrant groups, a position which reflected a general dissatisfaction with the representative and democratic structure of the present
and proposed apparatus.

We shall assess the extent to which these demands were met in
the 1976 Act shortly, but it is worth making one point here. Although black groups were both cynical and suspicious of existing
legislation, this scepticism did not lead any group to campaign for
the dismantling of race relations machinery. If previous acts were
simply diversionary and retrograde in their effects, then legislative reform could only strengthen their control function. Minority
group organisations were clearly not as dismissive as this in
response to proposed changes. At this time at least they saw the
potential efficacy of race relations legislation and hence contributed themselves to submitting detailed proposals for its reform.

These formal pressures should not eclipse the effects of a growth
in industrial and political militancy. The threat of racial violence

taken in conjunction with the American experience of racial dissent
in the 1960s certainly facilitated some sort of political response.
The columns of *Race Today* and *Black Liberator* in particular publicised this unrest, an aspect of which was the growing unemployment
amongst black groups. Such conditions as these, insofar as they
became publicly acknowledged, certainly facilitated some sort of
political response.

(e) Parliamentary pressure

The collective strength of these pressures was ultimately responsible
for the achievement of a Parliamentary consensus which was necessary
to ensure the successful passage of the Bill. At the risk of over-
simplification, it is possible to detect three ideological strains
running through parliamentary debates on race related issues. The
first combines a strong demand for immigration controls with the need
to protect the interests of the indigenous (white) population. This
sometimes assumes a laissez-faire approach (e.g. when it comes to
legislation defending minority rights) and sometimes assumes an interventionist position (e.g. when the indigenous (white) population is
thought to feel threatened by minority groups). The second retains
the demand for immigration controls but combines it in this case with
some pressure for antidiscrimination legislation. The final rarely
articulated position opposes those aspects of immigration legislation
which discriminate either by design or effect against New Commonwealth
immigrants and advocates a range of policies including strong anti-
discrimination legislation required to protect minority rights and to
respond to the specific needs of particular ethnic minority groups.
  Present policies on race relations and immigration have evolved,
at the parliamentary level, through alliances between these groups
which, to some extent, although not altogether, cut across party
boundaries. Thus, the 1976 Act has been the result of a dominant
liberal consensus principally to be found in the Labour Party (whose
governments were responsible for all three race relations acts) but
not absent from elements in the Conservative and Liberal Parties.
What weaknesses there are in the legislation can be attributed at one
level to the restraining influences of that group advocating a
laissez-faire approach to discrimination and a strong interventionist approach from without and control of minorities from within.
Its weaknesses might also be attributed to the lack of any coordinated challenge from the group articulating the third position
identified above. The support for immigration control has been
established remarkably and most successfully in both political
parties (the score to date being two pieces of legislation each).
  Opposition to the 1976 Act, principally from the Conservative
Party, reflects the first of the broad ideological divisions. There
were five main objections to the race relations legislation. Firstly,
and predictably, it was claimed the Bill diverted attention from the
real issue, that of restricting the numbers of immigrants and the
detention of illegal immigrants (House of Commons Debates, Vol.906:
1569). Secondly, revisions to the incitement clauses were seen to
contain 'more than a hint of censorship' (ibid: 1576). Thirdly,
that the Bill's scope should not be extended to clubs and, fourthly,

that there was no means of redress for those wrongly accused of discriminating. Overall, the Bill, if passed, would stir up prejudice and resentment by conferring more rights on immigrants and that, in view of this, the consent necessary to secure its successful operation would be absent. (Most of these objections were raised explicitly by Wolverhampton Conservative MP N. Budgen (ibid: 1634), who voted against the Bill in its second reading. David Lane, too, now Chairman of the CRE, criticised the Bill for its failure to allay the anxieties of the white majority.) These objections to the Bill are worth noting for two reasons. Firstly because they effectively mollified some of the more radical proposals suggested for inclusion in the Bill. Secondly because they shed further light on where the impetus came and did not come from within Westminster. We shall return to this latter point shortly.

On the other hand, there were five principal reasons articulated in defence of the Bill. Firstly that integration requires not only limiting the numbers of immigrants but the need to guarantee equality of treatment for all British citizens (ibid: 1547-8). Secondly, experience in the USA had revealed the need to strengthen the Civil Rights legislation in 1972, parallels being often drawn between 1960s race riots in the USA and various racial disturbances and problems of social order here in the UK. Invariably these are invoked at Westminster as a sober reminder to those less enthusiastic to the principle of liberal reform. Thirdly, evidence from PEP publications and reports from the Runnymede Trust, the CRC and RRB, on continued discrimination and the failure of existing machinery and legislative provisions to deal with it effectively. Fourthly, the need expressed by the Home Secretary to coordinate anti-discrimination legislation and hence to bring race relations legislation into line with that concerned with women (Rendel and Bindman, 1975, p.2). Finally the lack of confidence in the then existing legislation expressed by sections of the immigrant community. This demanded some fresh lead by the government on this issue (House of Commons Debates, Vol.905: 1579).

There were efforts from certain sections of the Labour Party to strengthen the Bill's provisions as it passed through Parliament. The unity of this challenge was paradoxically undermined from within the ranks of the Labour Left itself. Attempts to strengthen obligations on employers to keep ethnic records for instance were opposed by Eric Heffer (Liverpool, Walton) (ibid: 1637). Housing records, too, were considered unnecessary by the same MP, thus pre-empting any opportunity to reorganise local provision and allocation to meet the requirements of particular groups.

Conclusion

In conclusion, then, we might say that the passage of the Act was a result of a combination of factors brought to the attention of the 'liberal' lobby within Parliament who were in a position to win the support of the Labour Government and a handful of Conservative and Liberal MPs. These factors included: the need to coordinate anti-discrimination legislation; the American experience and the threat of escalating militancy in the presence of growing industrial unrest and unemployment and in the absence of reform; evidence of continuing discrimination and finally one or two key judicial decisions which identified weaknesses in the then current legislation.

In the light of this evidence, the Act cannot be considered as a device for strengthening political control over the black community. If it was then the black community themselves were amongst those supporting the principle of legislative reform, while those most likely to be seeking their control were opposing the Bill and voting against it in Westminster. It was the result then not of capital's needs but of a complex combination of administrative, judicial, academic and political pressures which were collectively responsible for the successful passage of the Act through Parliament.

The evolution, then, of the 1976 Race Relations Act needs to be seen, as with other forms of statutory provision, in terms of struggles that have been waged within the terrain of the state between various specific organisations and social forces. In order to assess the actual strengths and weaknesses of the legislation, we now turn to an examination of the structure and functioning of the machinery developed to implement the Act, in particular the Commission for Racial Equality and the associated local Community Relations/Racial Equality Councils.

(ii) The Commission for Racial Equality

The current radical wisdom with respect to the CRE is to view it as suffering from an inevitable paternalism, characteristic of official race relations bodies of the late 1960s and early 1970s (Dummett, M. and A., 1969; Dummett, 1973; Rex, 1979); as acting as a referee standing between the black communities and the government (Coote and Phillips, 1979); or acting as a buffer, protecting the state from direct forms of black militancy and, at the same time, co-opting some of their most effective spokesmen and potential leaders (Mullard, 1973; Katzneslon, 1976) and thus helping to reproduce capitalist relations of production (Sivanandan, 1976; Lea, 1980; Bourne, 1980; Bridges, 1975).

Our own investigations in Liverpool and Wolverhampton, however, reveal that this is not altogether the case. We would suggest that there are specific reasons for the widely articulated failure of the CRE (a 'flop' - *Guardian*, June 1980) and local Community Relations Councils to make serious inroads into racial inequality, especially at the level of the local authority.

(a) Accountability at central and local levels

A consistent demand from ethnic organisations in their submissions to the Select Committee on Race Relations Administration was the need for democratic control of any new race organisation. The inadequacies of the old Community Relations Commission were seen very much in terms of its failure to represent and meet the expressed needs of ethnic minority groups. These problems persist with the new body.[2]

The question of the accountability and representative nature of
the Commission for Racial Equality is frequently associated with the
question of colour. Thus the lack of black personnel in senior positions in the CRE and among its Commissioners, or the failure to use
black speakers at the recent abortive Nottingham Conference organised
by the CRE may be invoked as indicators of the CRE's lack of representativeness.

But in our view the question of the blackness or otherwise of key
CRE personnel is in fact beside the point with respect to the accountability of the CRE, which needs to be conceptualised in terms of the
extent to which ethnic minority groups have secured some form of
genuine democratic representation within the CRE, its staff,
Commissioners and Regional Advisory Committees.

Thus the issue at stake is not one of race, but rather the absence
of any formal democratic control of the CRE by outside bodies (with
the exception of course of the Home Office, which is responsible for
appointments of Commissioners and CRE staff). There is consultation,
it is true, as the CRE annual reports point out, but no formal and
continuous mechanism for involvement. So long as this remains the
case, then it seems likely that there will always be the potential
for suspicion and conflict. The recent suggestion by a number of
individuals or organisations that the CRE should be scrapped and replaced by a representative, grass-roots ethnic minority body in fact
overlooks the problem of making an official national body more
accountable and more representative in favour of arguing, in effect,
that there should be no official, or statutory, race relations
machinery.

In Wolverhampton, the question of whether the CRE should exist
has not been taken up. What does currently preoccupy the Council
for Community Relations (and this organisation has the backing of
local black activists) is the extent to which the CRE should have
control over it. The matter which has brought the WCCR into direct
confrontation with the CRE is to do with the appointment of officers.
In the course of advertising, short-listing and selecting for the
post of Senior CRO, the WCCR was advised by the CRE, without any
explanations or reasons, that certain interviewees were unacceptable
for the post and, if selected, would not therefore be eligible for
CRE funding. The WCCR took objection to what they took to be the
unjust interference of the CRE and proceeded with the selection process, the candidate finally chosen being one of the original interviewees over whom the CRE had issued their warning. The deadlock
that resulted has yet to be resolved, and a number of issues including constitutional and funding arrangements have further complicated
the dispute.

One important justification for the position adopted by the WCCR
is that the CRE is exercising power which ultimately has a very
strong influence on the type of race relations campaign that can be
mounted locally. In particular, the local organisation has been
concerned to attract an individual to the post of Senior CRO who
would espouse those anti-racist ideals which are now widely represented on the Executive of the Council. The intervention of the CRE
has accordingly been perceived, in the absence of any other explanation by the CRE, as an attempt to impose its own (differing) ideas

about how local race relations activities should be conducted (CRE, 1980).

While clearly there are a whole series of problems about the relationship between the CRE and local CRCs that have been raised as a result of this matter, the issue of the accountability and representativeness of the CRE cannot be overlooked. That is, from the WCCR's point of view, if the CRE had been more responsive to the need of the local organisations and more accessible to them, then this situation might never have arisen. As a consequence of this confrontation, both organisations have been prevented from pursuing what must be considered common aims, i.e. the removal of racial injustice and the promotion of equal opportunity.

Again, the CRE's apparent disregard for local minority group organisations was seen in the visitation by the CRE's national promotional team to Liverpool in July 1979. The CRE made a flying visit to discuss the 1976 Race Relations Act with a team of senior local authority officials, but had made no plans whatsoever for any consultation with or briefing by local minority group organisations. It was as a result of grass-roots pressure that a late-night meeting was organised at 10 pm in the senior CRO's flat to attempt to provide a rather uncomfortable group of CRE officers with some detailed ammunition with which to approach the local authority.

The accountability of a body to those organisations and groups whose needs and rights it seeks to represent is also pertinent in the case of local organisations. Thus in Liverpool, one of the most serious weaknesses of the Merseyside Community Relations Council was, at least until recently, its failure to adequately represent the largest minority group in Liverpool, the Liverpool-born blacks, not one of whom was elected to the CRC executive until 1980 (when 5 were elected including the Chairman). In addition, members of that community have frequently accused the MCRC of failing to consult them on issues that concern them, or of speaking *for* them rather than ensuring that they are themselves consulted and involved in discussion and decision-making with respect to their interests. Similarly in Wolverhampton, although the Executive might be seen to be more representative of local black organisations, the organisational structure and constitutional arrangements militate against an involvement of the whole Council in policy discussions and decisions.

There is, however, nothing necessary or inevitable about the undemocratic strcture of either the CRE or CRC organisations, whatever their current severe limitations. Indeed the CRE advocates an ideology of active black participation in its policy recommendations to local authorities; whilst the CRCs do provide scope for intervention and change by radical black groups. Thus it is interesting to note that in the Wolverhampton Community Relations Council just over a year ago, the 'white liberal' controlled Executive was overthrown by a 'black radical' faction within the Council. In Liverpool, members of the locally born black community organised, via the Liverpool 8 Action Committee, a militant picketing and boycott of the MCRC offices in 1977 precisely because the appointment of a Liverpool 8 Fieldworker was *not* made from those active in the local black community. As a result of this pressure, a further appointment was made, and the worker appointed has in fact been able to use his position

and the resources of the MCRC to help form and consolidate Liverpool's
most radical black organisation, the Liverpool Black Organisation,
the only local group directly and exclusively representative of the
locally-born black community. There is no substantial evidence, at
least from Wolverhampton and Liverpool, to suppose the CRE are guilty
of 'creaming-off' potential leaders from black organisations: indeed
it is the very top-heavy whiteness of the CRE that is frequently used
against it - thus 5 out of the 6 CRE team visiting Liverpool were
white; whilst the blocking by the CRE of appointments to the Wolverhampton CCR and the recent sacking by the Home Office of the CRE's
more militant black members surely suggests that the problem of
creaming off is hardly the major one.

(b) Organisation and co-ordination

A second factor limiting the effectiveness of the state's interventions in the race relations field must rest with the failure of all
the sections of the CRE to co-ordinate with each other and with the
local community relations councils and minority group organisations.
    Thus, an absurd situation developed in Liverpool whereby both the
North West office of the CRE (Fieldwork section) and the Head Office
(Promotions) were making, during 1979, approaches to the local authority with respect to the Race Relations Act (section 71). This
culminated in the cancellation by the North West CRE of a conference
owing, in part, to problems with head office in London over the
division of responsibility. Head Office itself made a number of
dates for its own visitation, ranging from a week to several days,
to a single day, and in the end paid a visit so superficial and dis-
organised as to cause a severe set-back in the outlook of an already
unresponsive authority. This low estimation of the efficacy and
seriousness of the CRE, and likewise of the Race Relations Act, was
confirmed by the failure of the CRE to have organised any follow-up
whatsoever after a whole year.
    In Wolverhampton, again, investigations are being carried out by
the CRE in the lock industry, without prior consultation with the
CCR, so that the knowledge of those members of staff working in the
local organisation is to some extent being ignored. In this event,
duplication of work is a real possibility (as occurred in the North
West), which suggests that the limited resources frequently offered
by the CRE as a reason for their lack of co-ordination (e.g. in *Plan
80*) is not necessarily as much of a problem as how these resources
are distributed between the various levels of the organisation. The
failure then of the CRE to make adequate use so far of the 1976 Race
Relations Act with respect to local authorities must lie in part
with the CRE's own current practice and organisation. This has involved the failure to develop the co-ordinated strategy amongst
national, regional, and local organisations as is required by the
legislation itself, i.e. the very careful planning and detailed
knowledge of the local situation. Such an approach has been undermined by the CRE's internal structure and conflicts, and also by its
apparent failure to develop positive working relationships with local
CRCs and minority groups based upon ongoing forms of dialogue,
consultation, and participation in decision-making.

(c) The role of the CRE viz. statutory and non-statutory agencies

A third basic problem with the CRE, as with all community relations organisations, has been correctly identified, in our view, by Hill and Issacheroff (1971), and more recently by Layton-Henry (1980). This is the ambivalent and contradictory nature of their status. The structural position of the CRE or CRCs, as outside central or local government, deprives them of much of the status and authority of a government department (and pay, viz. the Cinderella income of community relations officers compared to other local government workers). At the same time, their role as a pressure group working outside the government machine is limited by their semi-statutory status and their financial dependence on central or local government.

This ambivalent role is captured in attitudes to the CRE. Government officials we have interviewed have referred to the CRE as 'unprofessional', 'interfering' and 'aggressive', while many local black organisations regard the CRE as 'soft', 'elitist' and 'undemocratic'. Similar contradictory criticisms have been made of the local CRCs.

The problem might be reduced by the total abolition of any kind of statutory agency with responsibility for removing racial inequality, an alternative favoured by sections of both the right and the left, but which, in our view, would make still more remote the development of rigorous official measures to eliminate racial discrimination and disadvantage. In the meantime, what is crucial for the CRE is to develop a close and detailed knowledge of local political agencies, through close liaison with councillors, officials, black organisations and anti-racist groups, as well as CRCs, in order to establish the key sources of local influence and an accurate assessment of the means by which successful pressure can be brought to bear (Interview, North West CRE).

Conclusion

Our analysis of the community relations apparatus suggests some form of conceptualisation is required which takes account of a range of political and ideological issues which cannot readily be accommodated within the notion of a homogenous state bloc. It must take account of real oppositions e.g. between the Home Office and CRE, between central and regional CREs and between CRE and local CRCs. In each case our analysis suggests the need for a more dynamic and realistic picture, which enables at each level and within each institution, struggle, change, opposition and involvement to be encapsulated. Within the limits of the existing community relations apparatus and the limits of the 1976 Act (e.g. the vagueness and tentativeness of Section 71), there exist nevertheless opportunities to engage at each level in a struggle for greater democratisation and accountability as well as resources. The realization of such opportunities would in our view effect changes in local political structures which go beyond the existing community relations framework.

III   RACE AND THE LOCAL STATE

(i) Local government

Our investigations and involvement in local politics in Liverpool and
Wolverhampton endorse the form of conceptualisation of state apparatuses developed in the opening section. Our analysis of the local
state points to a series of contradictions and conflicts within and
between state agencies and local race relations apparatuses. It
suggests that such conflicts should be conceptualized as arenas of
struggle, contestation and points of potential change and democratisation, rather than as inherently ineffectual or agencies of co-
option and diversion. The sorts of factors developed in Peter
Saunders' recent study of Croydon (Saunders, 1979) might be extended
to provide a basis for contrasting variations and an unevenness of
development at the level of the local state. These include the
political complexion and ideology of the controlling group, particularly its dominant faction, the ideologies of key groups and
directorates; the relationship between the local authority and the
local CRC, local ethnic and political organisations as well as the
CRE; local cultural traditions and finally economic constraints.
      The object of this section of the paper, then, is to apply this
framework of analysis to the two local authorities where we have
been working. The identification of factors which exist within local
government structures and which affect the development of race-
related policies and issues will be our starting point. We will
extend this analysis to take account of the implications of local
limits for political organisation.

(a) Factors affecting local race relations policy

In the Annual Report (1978), the CRE noted that several local authorities were beginning to develop committee structures to coordinate
and lend direction to race relations policy, a process facilitated
by the development of corporate strategies in local government
following the 1974 re-organisation. This has not, however, been
the case in Liverpool and Wolverhampton, where policies on race
relations remain ad hoc and unconnected. There are a series of
reasons for this, but the lack of co-ordinated administrative and
organisational structures through which decisions can be made and
local policies can be implemented should be seen as an important
factor in influencing how race relations initiatives originate in
these two authorities. The absence of a coordinated approach to
policy-making has resulted in a number of key directorates having
considerable strength and independence, and this in turn has meant
that initiatives (or the lack of initiatives) on race-related issues
in both Wolverhampton and Liverpool reflect the position adopted
within these individual departments.
      In addition to these organisational factors, however, the ideo-
logical predispositions of the councils concerned are also significant in the development of strategies on race. Our present knowledge,
based on participant-observation and interviews in the two authorities, suggests that there are two dominant positions on the councils:

there is firstly the position, articulated originally in Wolverhampton
by former local MP Enoch Powell, which links the race issue integrally
with the 'problem' of immigration, the major issue being the threat
to the rights of the local indigenous white population. Secondly,
there is in both places the view held by both the traditional industrial Labour Left and general liberal opinion which equates race
problems with the problems of urban deprivation faced by the rest
of the working class community. As a result it is generally regarded
that measures which tackle economic and social problems of the inner
city are adequate solutions to the problems faced by ethnic minority
groups. Special measures to benefit ethnic minorities, on the contrary, are seen as divisive: thus Wolverhampton's Labour leader and
Education Committee Chairman has recently referred to the Indian
Workers' Association as being racialist 'and reactionary' in the
context of their demands for multi-cultural education provision
(*Wolverhampton Chronicle*, March 1980).

The dominant ideologies of the mainstream political parties (left,
right and centre) preclude, then, the need to develop overarching
policies aimed specifically to deal with the special needs of ethnic
minorities. This is a consensus frequently echoed by leader-writers
in the local press ('The situation in Liverpool is simply this.
There is no racial problem. There are problems of unemployment ...
etc.' - *Liverpool Post*, 24.11.78) and by and large accepted by
senior officials in many of the departments of the local authorities.
Thus Liverpool's Director of Education stated, in a public meeting
organised by the Merseyside Anti-Racialist Alliance on 28 September
1978 that he 'did not believe the local school system was any more
rigged against blacks than against Liverpool Irish, Welsh and Scots'
(*Liverpool Echo*, 29.9.78; cf. MARA, 1979).

The general lack of open acknowledgement paid to race means that
a key official is in a position to ignore, defuse or sit on pressure
from his Committee and local groups or organisations. Thus, the
Ethnic Minorities Liaison Committee in Liverpool, a potentially
important sub-committee of the Housing Committee which includes
ethnic minority representatives, councillors and officials, which
was set up around the MCRC's Housing Officer (funded by the EEC
and the CRE), has in fact met only four times in eighteen months,
and statistical information on black employees in the Housing Department collected by the Authority for this sub-committee is being
withheld. In Wolverhampton a liaison committee, including councillors, officials and local black representatives, set up after the
'race riot' in 1978, ceased to function after several meetings.

Given then official conservatism as well as a general lack of
political will to develop overall race relations policies, and given
also the lack of a corporate mechanism within the local authority
structure, responsibility for pursuing some initiative falls onto
individual departments and committees within the authorities. It
is at this point that the two authorities, Wolverhampton and
Liverpool, become noticeably distinct from each other. This is
because each initiative differs in terms of its origins, its content
and its potential effectivity. The unevenness of these initiatives
is a reflection of a combination of circumstances peculiar to
individual authorities and departments.

In Wolverhampton, a fairly detailed set of housing initiatives
(including an adjustment of the points system of allocation, record-
keeping and the appointment of a special member of staff) were
implemented as the result of negotiations between the WCCR and the
then Chairman of the Housing Committee and the manager of the Housing
Department who shared a similar concern over the fairness of public
housing arrangements amongst ethnic minority groups. While these
changes represent a major step forward, they have not been used as
extensively as they might be. For example, the ethnic records of
housing allocations have not as yet been monitored. Again, though
a number of staff have been appointed under Section 11 of the 1966
Local Government Act,[3] no monitoring takes place of the allocation
of these resources.

In Liverpool the setting up of a Black Social Work Project developed from several sources, i.e. pressures on the Social Services
Department from local welfare agencies, concern over the disturbances (so called 'race riots') on a new housing estate, and Home
Office Urban Aid circulars: but it is interesting to note that this
project was originally described by the Authority as the 'Non-
European Social Work Project' (in a city of 3rd and 4th generation
blacks!), and initially recruited immigrant graduates rather than
locally born blacks (see Sommerfield, 1979; Rooney, 1980). Again,
the local authority funds an employment agency serving a predominantly black clientele, yet takes no explicit initiatives to combat
racial discrimination or disadvantage in its own ranks, e.g. by the
adoption of a full Equal Opportunity Policy.

The analysis of local conditions developed in terms of the above
factors provides the possibility of constructing more coherent and
effective local political strategies on race issues.

(b) Local limits and local access points

Detailed knowledge and information about how the local state operates in relation to race issues is a precondition of effective
struggle. It allows calculated political intervention to take
account of where and how pressure can be applied. An analysis
such as the one above suggests that the local state is not a
cohesive impenetrable block, but that it is unevenly developed,
varies in its strengths and weaknesses and has a range of access
points. These must be identified for the purpose of establishing
how any intervention must be formulated.

To illustrate this, we can refer to several of the factors discussed above. In both Wolverhampton and Liverpool, it has been
suggested, the left and liberal factions of the council have adopted
the position that an open acknowledgement of race is tantamount to
professing racial prejudice. Furthermore, they are apt to see
race-related initiatives as acts of discrimination against the white
population. Whatever the origins of these ideas, it is important
that the counter-argument be made, not only to those in official
capacities, but also to those organisations and individuals within
the informal political sphere. Evidence is required which demonstrates that ethnic minority groups are subject to racial discrimination and disadvantage and that this results in inequality of

opportunity. Government legislation, Select Committee reports and research, both national and local, play an important role for establishing these facts. An intervention of this type does not by itself ensure change, but in effect it could broaden the popular support for new initiatives and perhaps develop a new consciousness amongst some local politicians who do play an important part in the formulation of local policy.

A different type of political calculation is required in the case of race-related initiatives which have already been taken but which can also be seen to be undeveloped or limited. In these cases official political will may or may not exist, but at least the initiative stands as a local acknowledgement of race-related needs. The form and content of the existing initiative indicates the direction in which further reforms may develop. One important distinction, however, must be made at this point with regard to types of race-related initiatives at the local level. Our research suggests that there are projects and schemes which have been established as the result of funding by central government and also by other national and focal organisations. These have secured some sort of independent status and are different from those local authority initiatives which are usually a part of the internal local government structure.

In the case of the former category, the implications for political calculation are more clear cut. For instance, the Black Social Work Project in Liverpool and the Caribbean Culture Centre in Wolverhampton (an initiative funded under the Inner Area Programme) have both facilitated the development of grass-roots orientated management committees by local organisations. Where political calculation would seem to be more difficult is where initiatives are concentrated almost exclusively within local government structures. The privacy of internal decisions and information make the formulation of political interventions a more complex procedure. For instance, in the case of Wolverhampton's Education Department, information on how and where Section 11 funds are spent remains largely inaccessible. Nonetheless, it is clear that a combination of activities is needed to press for change. First, the issue needs to be popularised, and following this some political pressure needs to be exerted by local councillors, who have the responsibility for ensuring that the Council remains accountable to its constituents. Councillors might be lobbied to raise questions in committee and council meetings; and other local pressure groups (particularly those concerned with education) might be lobbied to press the Education Department for specific information on Section 11. Political activities such as these can only be successful if they are carefully planned and sustained. On the other hand, at least they have potential effectivity.

Issues of defence, such as the 'turban case' in Wolverhampton (this refers to a particular incident where a local head-teacher refused to allow a young Asian boy to attend school because he was wearing a turban), or the closing of Paddington School in Liverpool, naturally require some political intervention which is initially distinct from more policy-oriented reforms such as those mentioned above. The success of oppositionist tactics (demonstrations, petitions, etc.) on these issues relies on a well-informed and active community base for popular support. It also depends on the

existence of a framework for negotiation within local official
structures, if the issue is not to emerge over and over again, and
sometimes in ways which are so subtle that it is difficult to oppose
them.

The components of any political strategy then must be devised as
the result of careful analysis of the local situation. Alternative
aims and the most appropriate means for achieving these aims must be
considered. As has already been suggested, this may involve collecting evidence, using existing initiatives to press for further reform
and using forms of demonstration and petitioning. It is in this context that confrontation over political issues can be most effective.
Confrontation in this context maximizes the potential for involvement
of local organisations, as well as the community at large. If
struggle is for change and change depends on increased political
consciousness and broadened political support, as well as concrete
material developments, then strategies must realistically take into
account how these are to be secured.

In Section II we have suggested that the Race Relations Act and
the CRE permit some potential political leverage at the local level.
These and other national policies and organisations should be fully
exploited for the contribution they can make to local campaigns and
issues. It is clear that they can and do act as reference points
for local decision-makers and the value of this should not be overlooked. Initiation of political activity, however, at this point in
time, depends very heavily on local political organisation. The
relationship between local anti-racist and ethnic minority group
organisations and political parties on the one hand, and the local
state, on the other, complete our picture of race, left strategies
and the state.

Conclusion

The local state constitutes the framework within which political
struggle takes place. The direction of local political ideology,
the structure of bureaucratic organisation and the individual will
or whim of officers or politicians (or Chairman/Director alliances)
within a particular department or committee are just some of the
factors which affect the development of race-related policies and
influence the local official opinion on race-related issues. An
acknowledgement of the complexity of the structure of the local
state suggests that political strategies must be devised which take
account of these factors. They are crucial for affecting the choice
of political aims and therefore the alternative political activities
which may be employed at any given time.

(ii) Local anti-racist and ethnic minority organisations

Despite a shift towards a more authoritarian consensus in the latter
half of the 1970s, legislation on immigration, vagrancy, police
power and Habeaus Corpus remains unchanged. What has changed considerably, and where popular authoritarianism has been accommodated,
is in the interpretation and implementation of those statutes and

legal precedents. Key agencies are indeed here: the courts and the judiciary, the police and the Civil Service are the most notable. It is in these 'less open' areas of the State where the exercise of dis- cretionary power has wielded its particularly potent influence. The opaqueness and inaccessibility of such areas of State administration is clearly a priority for the development of coherent and effective Left strategies and policies. The price of failure can be high if attempts to defend and extend civil liberties only leads to their curtailment and the consolidation of discretionary powers in the reverse direction to that intended by left groups. This is not to deny the role of defensive or oppositionist campaigns on issues relat- ing to civil liberties. What has to be calculated however are the conditions and limits of each struggle as well as its effects. It is in this context that we consider the role of anti-racist and minority group organisations in Liverpool and Wolverhampton.

We have already seen that one strain of the left-wing response to race has entailed a refusal to acknowledge the need for any specific race relations initiatives. A second strain is to be found within the anti-Fascist Committee in Wolverhampton (WARC) which has developed forms of organisation and strategies which can best be termed 'crisis reactivism'. Cases in themselves can of course provide excellent opportunities for anti-racist groups to mobilise support around parti- cular issues. The disturbances outside The George public house in early 1978 provided one such opportunity which at least initially was effectively exploited by WARC. This apart, the Committee's success has rested on its ability to draw attention to such issues as police/ black relations, education, immigration and the National Front. Where it has been less successful is in terms of the incorporation of these issues into longer-term broad-based campaigns. Cases or instances of police harrassment, in the case of The George disturbances, form the basis of an independent panel of inquiry, but the considerable efforts expended on defence campaigns have not been used to contri- bute to wider campaigns on police powers or specific areas of legis- lation, e.g. the campaign against the 'Sus' or 1834 vagrancy law. Local organisations have a vital role to play in building up support at that level for national campaigns. The same can be said of the organisation's campaign on immigration which has combined a concern with individual cases alongside a sporadic campaign to oppose racist immigration laws. The recent review of nationality legislation provided an opportunity for local groups to move away from defensive tactics to make a more constructive detailed contribution at the con- sultative stage of the Bill's passage. Although the re-endorsement of the 1971 discriminatory immigration act was always a likely con- sequence of any changes, few have denied the need for legislative reform in this area. This was an opportunity then to mobilise support for a non-racist Nationality Act which emphasised individual and group rights rather than an alternative device in the government's armoury for restricting black immigration. The failure to do so leaves little option now but to once more oppose the proposed legislation.

One problem with the Anti-Racist Committee lies in the narrowness of its political base. The caucus of its most active membership is predominantly white and from the local International Marxist Group.

Its failure to broaden its active base has had implications for
organisation in terms of its prevailing ideology, the nature of its
relationship with local organisations including black organisations,
the strategies pursued by the group and ultimately the impact of the
organisation. Popular anti-racist movements are not readily achiev-
able under the best of present circumstances. They do however require
the support and commitment of groups/individuals who do not take as
their starting point the inevitably racist character of the State at
national and local levels; who do not see access to, or working for,
or negotiating with the State as inevitably capitaulating to its
needs and logic; who do not see open 'on the street' confrontation
as the only form of authentic anti-racist activity. The organisation
also requires support from wide sections of the black community, if
they are to make any sort of contribution to the formation and development of independent black organisations. The Wolverhampton Committee
does have the support of the Indian Workers' Association (GB) and thus
the considerable mobilising potential of the latter e.g. for demonstrations. Apart from this, support from black organisations/indi-
viduals is minimal.
    In the absence of the above there is little payoff either for the
handful of highly committed individuals comprising the backbone of
the organisation or the wider struggle against racism. Prevailing
ideologies thus preempt any detailed consideration of the 1976 Act
or any active collaboration with statutory and semi-statutory bodies
responsible for its implementation. The legislative reform in question most certainly has its limits, but these must be partly considered in the context of the effectivity of such organisations as WARC.
It is certainly not the intention here to suggest that a direct
response to and exploitation of resources and provisions of the
legislation is the only authentic form of anti-racist activity.
Others have already been mentioned in the context of the erosion
of civil liberties. It is simply to identify what scope exists on
analysing the legislation on the one hand and local political conditions on the other. To bypass those agencies responsible for the
administration of the Act and to largely ignore the Act itself, as
WARC has largely done, might only serve in the long term to vindicate
the social control interpretation of welfare legislation.
    Some of the problems identified with respect to WARC are repro-
duced in the Merseyside Anti-Racialist Alliance, the equivalent
wholly voluntary and independent organisation in Liverpool, but
this group is rather broader-based than the Wolverhampton Committee.
Although a wide range of 'normal' protest activity has been organised by MARA over immigration controls, racism in the media, multi-
racial school closures, police racism etc., an increasingly important aspect of the work of the group has been the attempt to develop
specific working groups and initiatives in a number of areas (immigration, education, employment, media, health etc.) aiming to promote
wider campaigns and positive policies in those areas.
    Thus, for instance, in the field of employment, the organisation
has been instrumental in reactivating the dormant Trades Council
Race Relations Subcommittee, which includes key figures in ethnic
minority agencies, workers in relevant state departments, trade
unionists, researchers. The group has been working collectively

on a detailed argument for an Equal Opportunity Policy to be taken
into the trade union movement locally and into negotiation with the
local authority.

The Merseyside group, then, is attempting to develop constructive
interventions in those varied and multiple areas where racism operates, and has thus played a part in developing a more conscious and
cohesive set of political forces to act as a broadly-based and consistent pressure group operating within the local political formation. It
will shortly be taking part in a major joint local approach to the
local authority with a number of local black groups and race relations
agencies with respect to the implementation of Section 71 of the Race
Relations Act, for the development of a detailed Equal Opportunity
Policy, and the institutionalisation of some form of ongoing dialogue
and representation by minority groups.

The local state then affords an arena of struggle in which, despite
the constraints, greatly differing outcomes can be achieved, depending
in part on the ideologies, organisation and activities of the local
anti-racist organisations and the local left. In Wolverhampton there
has been a tendency by these forces to fail to identify the targets
that are in fact of most immediate relevance to the local ethnic
minority groups, namely local authority officers and elected members,
and where pressure is mounted it tends to be of a negative, oppositionist and over-general character. In Liverpool, on the other hand,
a more directed and constructive campaign is being developed by
sections of the Left and the anti-racist organisations in the face
of a generally unresponsive and indifferent local authority.

What is particularly interesting and significant to debates over
race and the state is the emergence in Liverpool of a number of state-
funded, para-professional black workers, drawn from the local black
population and dedicated to the promotion of its interests. They use
the resources and expertise at their disposal to promote black interests within the state machinery and simultaneously to promote autonomous and strong black organisations without. The serious struggle
for state reforms thus needs to complement the somewhat gestural
exposure of existing state malpractices. Together such strategies
might facilitate and ultimately require the creation of independent
organisations, part of whose role is to participate in and supervise
local state policy on race relations.

The group of black para-professionals is rapidly becoming the
hegemonic element which is forcing anti-racist and community organisations and the left in Liverpool to recognise the priority that
has to be given to securing the real immediate material advance of
black interests. Their forceful presence is now ensuring that the
dialogue and pressure on the local authority is not exercised in the
old paternalistic way, i.e. in the absence of those parties that are
most affected by racism. Thus it was this group who were instrumental in forcing the CRE to have some dialogue during their local
authority visit. And they are working to ensure that where local
authority initiatives are taken, these too are carried out in a way
which increases the involvement, resources and control of black groups.

In Wolverhampton, there does not appear to be an equivalent group
of black workers, developing a sustained and cohesive intervention
within the local authority. What black professionals there are work

mainly outside the official structures with CCR and the anti-racist
committee. Where the local authority has responded to its black
constituents, it has been as a response to spontaneous protest or
outbursts of violence between the police and black youth (as with
the Inner Area programmes' race initiatives).

The material discussed above in our view explodes many of the
false polarities thrown up by the radical critiques of the state's
role in race relations. It suggests that the self-help schemes,
urban aid programme, projects etc. often rejected as forms of
bribery which encourage rip-off entrepreneurship and token appointments, and as de-politicising and fragmenting enterprises may in
fact be weapons that can be used for the benefit of black interests
in terms of access to resources, a heightened political awareness
and cohesion, and may be used as a means of democratising the state
apparatuses by opening them up to black participation and control.

We are *not* suggesting that the specific mode of anti-racist
politics favoured here, with an emphasis on finding a way for the
autonomous black organisations to feed into local authority structures, is a *substitute* for more conventional forms of political action
or representation, through membership and organisation within political parties. We would, however, insist that such forms of politics
be seen as complementary and interdependent, and that a more
narrowly 'political' orientation has still to wrestle with problems
of direct participation, active representation, popular control,
etc. This is a concern frequently overlooked in the narrow
electoralism of the major political parties, and indeed in the
utopianism of the far Left too. (See *Red Bologna* for a concrete
discussion of these issues.)

This approach differs from forms of, on the one hand, pragmatic
reformism, in which statutory means, state agencies and apparatuses
are used to benefit the black community from above, and on the other
the ultimately insurrectionary approach which argues for the by-
passing or overthrow of the existing legitimate state machinery.
Our approach suggests a 'third way' in the relationship between
ethnic minorities and the state (just as in general we would argue
for a revolutionary political strategy which avoids the 'statism'
of both contemporary social democracy and orthodox Leninism).

The concept of an extended state introduced at the outset thus
embraces ethnic minority organisations as well as formally constituted agencies of the state. There clearly remain significant
differences in terms of location and role between such groups.
What is required therefore is the democratic transformation of
those structures which minorities inhabit or which in some ways
represent the minorities' interests. This means, in concrete terms,
developing ways of making the CRE and the local community relations
councils more representative and more accountable to the black
communities. It means developing mechanisms whereby politicians
and workers in local authorities are pressed into maintaining direct
consultations with members of ethnic minority organisations and
agencies on a regular basis. And it means the development of new
forms of devolution of power with respect to the decision-making
which affects ethnic minorities, as with the development of an
Ethnic Group Consortium, or Forum of Black Groups, which is formally

and permanently fed into local authority structures, an uncelebrated but very significant mechanism that is already developing in some local authorities.

It is important to note then that this strategy reflects the orientation of minority organisations in many parts of Britain. This is in direct contrast to various other theories which have been posited about the political outlook and organisation of black people. One of these argues that black youth are likely to orient themselves increasingly towards Third World revolutionary ideologies and ident- ities. Such ideologies are relatively insignificant in Liverpool, and even where they are more influential, as in Wolverhampton, they do not appear to estrange the black youth from local political struct- ures. One good example of this is the Wolverhampton Rastafarian Progressive Movement, which lost its premises (sited at the WCCR) as the result of the Authority's decision to relocate the WCCR. In defiance, the WRPM approached the Authority and demanded new premises to be provided immediately. In fact, the Authority has responded to pressure from this organisation and accommodation has been secured.

In Liverpool the dominant political ideology amongst black organ- isations is far closer to the strategy of 'radical pragmatism' (Mullard's 1980 misplaced polarity) or 'revolutionary reform' (Saunders, 1978) than to the philosophies of Rastafarianism or Pan- African Socialism, though there is also considerable sympathy for the promotion of an international black identity. Indeed the political outlook of the Liverpool Black Organisation seems to involve an amalgamation of all three of Miles and Phizacklea's (1977) perhaps wrongly categorised 'alternatives' i.e. 'ethnic organisation': the LBO's membership is overwhelmingly from one 'ethnic' group, the Liverpool-born blacks; 'black unity': the group advocates a broad black political identification, e.g. support for MARA's immigration campaigns; 'class unity': joint activities with white radical and labour movement organisations. Neither is the categorisation applic- able in the case of Wolverhampton, since black organisations do not seem to fall into any one of those alternatives provided. The form of organisation in fact depends on the context or the issue at stake, rather than on a single orientation.

It is also pertinent to note that the general struggle for black participation and control which can be seen perhaps as part of the black community's 'long march through the institutions' (Bowles and Gintis, 1976), is one which is supported in theory and in many of its publications by the CRE, and even in Government White Papers, e.g. 'Policy for the Inner City' (1977) which calls for active black participation in local decision-making. It also accords with current mainstream political ideology in Britain which pays lip-service to participation and democratic control of our institutions.

This is not to deny the formidable obstacles militating against the potential emergence of democratically-based race relations initi- atives at the level of the local state, and we might usefully conclude this section by reiterating some of them. In the first place there are the economic and social policies of the current Conservative Government (sadly only extending the Callaghan/Healey attacks on the Welfare State and the public sector). The effects of those are dis- proportionately felt in those areas of service provision directly

affecting the black population (as well as the wider working class)
and thus serve to impede new expenditure in the field of minority
group needs (e.g. the extension and improvement of Section 11 or the
Urban Programme). Such ideological predispositions as those underpinning present government policies in turn limit local effort, in
particular through a lack of any sustained and coherent programme to
eliminate racial disadvantage. It has already been suggested that
the Race Relations Act can only constitute one weapon in any government's armoury for combatting racism. An armoury which it must be
said is severely challenged from within the State's own ranks by the
legitimacy conferred on law and order agencies in their policing of
the black population. A major assumption on which our argument has
rested suggests that such obstacles as these must be identified and
taken into account in the context of developing effective anti-
racist strategies.

We have argued throughout this discussion that existing race
relations legislation and the statutory and semi-statutory mechanisms
and initiatives, though limited and in need of stronger powers, provide valuable room for manoeuvre and intervention by black groups,
the anti-racist movement and the left. This would, in effect, result
in the partial democratisation of the local state which can, in wider
strategic terms, be interpreted as an important step along the road
towards socialism in this country, where socialism is defined not in
terms simply of the economic relations of production nor of the
bureaucratic/paternalistic control of the monolithic state by the
social democratic or revolutionary Party 'representing' the people,
but in terms of the democratic extension and expansion of the state
to include real and varied forms of active representation of the
popular forces, in this case the racial minorities.

The struggle for racial equality and racial justics in other
words needs to be seen primarily as a popular democratic struggle
which, as with so many struggles, entails, in current conditions of
British parliamentary democracy, a complex, detailed and realistic
war of position to be waged by the ethnic minorities and anti-racist
organisations, involving the application of a consistent disposition
of forces to those key areas of the local state in which constructive
developments can be successfully fought for. In our view, research
can perform a useful political objective by assisting in the excava-
tion of those points of access to the local political system which
can be used and transformed to effect positive and democratically-
based political and policy changes to secure the elimination of
racial discrimination and disadvantage in this country.

Notes

1 An earlier draft of this paper was presented to the Brighton
   Polytechnic Conference on 'Race, Class and the State' (16 July
   1980).
2 In the discussion that follows we are less concerned with the
   precise nature of democratic control and accountability than we
   are with an acceptance of the principle. The constituencies involved in any extension of accountability would need to be
   negotiated between the CRE and black organisations.

3 Section 11 provides 75% grant for salaried local authority workers, mainly teachers, in areas of over 2% immigrant children. This is not available to Liverpool, through its small number of 'immigrants' despite its severe problems of *racial* discrimination and disadvantage. The outgoing Labour government was about to extend this legislation before it fell.

Acknowledgements

We should like to express our warm thanks to the following for their suggestions and comments on an earlier draft of this paper: Linda McCowen, John Solomos, Protasia Torkington, Rashid Mufti, and Julian Clarke; and to members of the LBO, MARA, MCRC, WARC, WCCR and CRE for the insights gained from discussions with them.

References

Barker, A. (1975), *Strategy and Style in Local Community Relations* (Runnymede Trust).

Ben-Tovim, G.S. (1978), 'The struggle against racism: theoretical and strategic perspectives', *Marxism Today*, July 1978.

Ben-Tovim, G.S. and Gabriel, J. (1979a), 'The Sociology of Race - Time to Change Course?' in *The Social Science Teacher*, Vol.8, No.4, April 1979 (special issue on 'Race and Education').

Ben-Tovim, G.S. and Gabriel, J. (1979b), 'The politics of race in Britain 1962-1979 - a review of the major trends and of the recent literature', *Race Relations Abstracts*, Vol.4, No.4, November 1979.

Bourne, J. (1980), 'Cheerleaders and Ombudsmen: the Sociology of race relations in Britain', *Race and Class*, XXI - 4, Spring 1980.

Bowles, S. and Gintis, H. (1976), *Schooling in Capitalist America* (Routledge).

Bridges, L. (1975), 'The Ministry of Internal Security', *Race and Class*, XVI - 4, April 1975.

Cockburn, C. (1977), *The Local State* (Pluto).

Coote, A. and Phillips, M. (1979), 'The Quango as Referee', *New Statesman*, 13 July 1979.

Corrigan, P. (1979), 'The Local State', *Marxism Today*, June 1979.

CRE Midland and Wales, *Plan '80*, unpublished document.

CRE Northern Interview, October 1979.

CRE (1980), *The Nature and Funding of Local Race Relations Work: Community Relations Councils*.

Demuth, C. (1978), *'SUS', a report on the Vagrancy Act 1824* Runnymede Trust).

Department of the Environment (1977), *Policy for the Inner Cities*, Cmnd.6845 (HMSO).

Dummett, A. (1973), *A Portrait of English Racism* (Penguin).

Dummett, M. and A. (1969), 'The role of government in Britain's racial crisis', in *Justice First*, ed. L. Donnelly (Sheed and Ward).

Gabriel, J. (1977), 'The concepts of Race and Racism: an analysis of classical and contemporary theories of race', Ph.D. thesis, University of Liverpool.

Gabriel, J.G. and Ben-Tovim, G.S. (1978), 'Marxism and the concept of racism', *Economy and Society*, Vol.7, No.2, May 1978.
Gabriel, J.G. and Ben-Tovim, G.S. (1979), 'The conceptualization of race relations in sociological theory', *Racial and Ethnic Studies*, Vol.2, No.2, April 1979.
Gramsci, A. (1971), *Prison Notebooks* (Lawrence and Wishart).
Hall, S. et al (1978), *Policing the Crisis* (Macmillan).
Hewitt, P. et al (1978), *A practical guide to the Race Relations Act* (NCCL)
Hill, M. and Issacheroff, M. (1971), *Community Action and Race Relations* (OUP).
Hindess, B. (1980), 'Marxism and Parliamentary Democracy', in Hunt, A. (ed.) (below).
Home Office Interview, October 1979.
Home Office (1974), *Equality for Women* - White Paper, Cmnd. 5724 (HMSO).
Home Office (1975), *Racial Discrimination* - White Paper, Cmnd.6234 (HMSO)
Home Office (1979), 'Some aspects of relations between the police and the public', *Evidence to Royal Commission on Criminal Procedure*, Memorandum No.10.
House of Commons, *Great Britain Parliamentary Debates*, Vol.906.
Hunt, A. (ed.) (1980), *Marxism and Democracy* (Lawrence and Wishart).
Jaggi, M., Muller, R. and Schmid, S. (1977), *Red Bologna* (Writers and Readers).
John, G. (1978), 'Black People', in *Social and Community Work in specific settings* (Open University) DE 206, 23.
Jones, P. (1980), 'Socialist Politics and the Conditions of Democratic Rule', in Hunt, A., op.cit.
Katznelson, I. (1971), *Black Men: White Cities* (OUP).
Labour Party (1978), *Race, Immigration and the Racialists*.
Laclau, E. (1977), *Politics and Ideology in Marxist Theory* (New Left Books).
Layton-Henry, Z. (1980), 'Commission in Crisis', in *The Political Quarterly*, Vol.51, No.4.
Lea, J. (1980), 'The Contradictions of the Sixties' Race Relations Legislation', in *Permissiveness and Control* (Macmillan).
MARA (1979), *Merseyside Against Racism – First Annual Report* (Merseyside Anti-Racialist Alliance).
Macdonald, I. (1977), *Race Relation – The New Law* (Butterworths).
McKay, D. and Cox, A. (1979), *The Politics of Urban Change* (Croom Helm).
Mercer, C. (1980), 'Revolutions, Reforms or Reformations?' in Hunt, A., op.cit.
Miles, R. and Phizacklea, A. (1977), 'Class, Race, Ethnicity and Political Action', *Political Studies*, XXV, No.4.
Miliband, R. (1978), *Marxism and Politics* (Oxford).
Mullard, C. (1973), *Black Britain* (George Allen and Unwin).
Mullard, C. (1980), 'The racial schools of Social Science', Paper to B.S.A. Conference, Lancaster University.
Poulantzas, N. (1980), *State, Power, Socialism* (Verso).
Prior, M. and Purdy, D. (1979), *Out of the Ghetto* (Spokesman).

Rendel, M. and Bindman, G. (1975), *The Sex Discrimination Bill, Race and the Law* (Runnymede Trust).

Rex, J. (1979a), 'Black militancy and class conflict', in Miles, R. and Phizacklea, A., op.cit.

Rex, J. (1979b), 'Race, Law and Politics', address to Annual Conference of B.S.A., Warwick, April 1979.

Rex, J. and Tomlinson, S. (1979), *Colonial Immigrants in a British City* (Routledge and Kegan Paul).

Rooney, B. (1980), 'Active Mistakes - a Grass Roots Report', *Multi-Racial Social Work*, No.1.

Rowbotham, S., Segal, L. and Wainwright, H. (1979), *Beyond the Fragments* (Merlin).

Runnymede Trust (1979), *A Review of the Race Relations Act 1976* (Runnymede Trust)

Sassoon, A.S. (1978), 'Hegemony and Political Intervention', in S. Hibbin (ed.), *Politics, Ideology and the State* (Lawrence and Wishart).

Saunders, P. (1979), *Urban Politics* (Hutchinson).

Select Committee on Race Relations and Immigration (1975), *Organisation of Race Relations Administration*, Vols.1-3 (HMSO).

Sivanandan, A. (1976), 'Race, Class and the State', *Race and Class, XVII*, Spring 1976.

Smith, D.J. (1974/5), 'Job discrimination and the function of the law', *New Community*, Vol.IV, No.1.

Smith, D.J. (1977), *Racial Disadvantage in Britain* (Penguin).

Sommerfeld, O. (1979), 'The Black Social Worker Project', in M. Marshall (ed.), *Social Work in Action* (B.A.S.W.).

People's History and Socialist Theory
Edited by Raphael Samuel

It is astonishing. It
has all the strengths, the excitements and the
inspiration of a Ruskin Workshop and it has its
shapelessness, too. After two splendid biblio-
graphical and methodological prefaces by Raphael
Samuel, we plunge into a kind of maelstrom. There
are fifty-two separate pieces (one good deed a
week?); some are long, some are short, some are
articles, some bibliographies, some merely notes;
some are recorded third hand, some carry reports
of ensuing debates. There is no index (it would
require a separate volume). The people's history,
genuinely so called, yields fairly rapidly to
essays of a theoretical intensity and sophistic-
ation which would stretch any Annalist (and which,
I understand, threatened to provoke a Second
Ruskin Strike).

What can you do with a book like this? Buy it,
that's what you can do. You won't regret it, even
if it carries you to the lip of lunacy. No one
interested in the practice and theory of popular
and socialist history, indeed in the very vitality
of history itself and in the rich and vigorous
historically informed culture which is surging up
in the people of this island now can afford to be
without it.' - Gwyn A. Williams, *The Guardian*

0 7100 0652 7 *Paperback £6.95 History Workshop Series*

Peter Hain
A Left Strategy for Labour

'What is the use of adopting socialist policies when the Party
leadership always ignores them and sells you out?' It was this cry
of frustration from Labour's constituency activists that demanded
the democratic reforms around which the struggle for power has raged
in the Labour Party since the mid-1970s. Escalating almost immediately into a battle between the left and the right wing establishment, this struggle has been vital and it will continue to be so.

Equally, however, the campaign - for mandatory re-selection, for
direct election of the leader and for democratic control of the
election manifesto contents- became so all-consuming that other arguably even more vital issues of political organisation and strategy
got neglected. Some on the Labour left have even advocated the
democracy reforms in terms which suggest that their achievement is
all that is necessary for Labour governments to implement socialist
programmes. Hold the leadership accountable and, hey presto, socialism will be ushered in. In this (perhaps unfairly caricatured) view,
the central problem for the Labour left is to replace the 'baddies'
with the 'goodies' in the commanding heights of the Party.

Such a view, of course, betrays little appreciation of the
obstacles which even the most well-intentioned Labour government
would face in confronting the capitalist class. Suffice to say that
it rests on a belief in 'parliamentary socialism'[1] of the most naive
kind. It is beyond the scope of this article to explore why this is
the case, so it will simply be asserted on the assumption that it is
common ground amongst serious socialists.

The more immediate and pressing problem with the Labour left's
emphasis on the Party *leadership* question is that too great a preoccupation with the consistent reneging by Labour leaders on the
Party's policies can obscure the real problems we face. Accountability of the leadership to the Party rank and file is a crucial precondition for socialist advance. But there is little point winning
internal democracy reforms in what may turn out to be an empty shell
in terms of its real working class base.

There is equally little point in pretending, as the right has
done, that the Party's problems have been primarily *organisational*.

They have not. They are *political*. Creating a mass party will not
be done by improving the agency system, restructuring the conference
or having a realistic subscription rate - whatever individual merit
there may be in such reforms.[2] It will only be done by re-casting
the Party's politics and strategy, and this article attempts to
suggest how that might be tackled. Moreover it will show that, if
carried through, the result would be not only to strengthen the
forces for socialism inside the Labour Party but to alter the whole
terrain on which the wider left operates.

CONTEXT

Before this is discussed however it is important that account is
taken of the political base of the left at present. In terms of
gut support we are collectively in a weak position. Without succumb-
ing to the myth that there was some 'golden age' of working class
support for socialism, the plain fact is that there is precious
little support now. Whereas as late as the 1960s socialism still
had strong appeal, both culturally and politically, this is no longer
the case. Socialist values have indeed received a sorry battering.
Discredited by the performance of Labour governments, tarnished with
the brush of statism,[3] and on the receiving end of a ferocious media
assault, it has become steadily more difficult to build up the kind
of reservoir of support for socialist ideas that is a prerequisite
for successful organisation. The abject failure of the Labour Party
and other left groups to secure their grass roots base has compounded
the problem. It is now also possible to see just how deep has been
the slippage within the trade union movement.
    These points are mentioned in passing in order to emphasise the
scale of task faced by the left. For, if the Labour left takes the
Party's working class backing complacently for granted, the far
left grossly exaggerates its own importance, and both display a
fatal tendency to *posture* rather than honestly get to grips with
immediate issues of tactics and strategy.
    There are however positive signs that this urgent need is being
recognised, reflected in various critiques of left orthodoxies.
From socialists in the women's movement has come an important attack
on the whole way the left conducts itself, both in terms of conventional Labour Party politics and the Leninist modes of organisation
of the far left.[4] Elements in the Communist Party have sought to
break 'Out of the Ghetto'.[5] Within the Labour Party a distinctive
'radical left' has emerged, primarily extra-parliamentary in orientation, yet insisting on a fusion with Parliamentary struggle.[6] There
has also been a significant move out of the far left and the
Communist Party, and into the Labour Party.
    Socialist politics is indeed in a state of flux, not to say
trauma, and yet there are real grounds for believing that a major
advance could now be made through the Labour Party if the Labour
left redirects its energies.

PROSPECTS FOR REVIVING THE LABOUR PARTY

There are many reasons why socialist activists have cause to be
sceptical of the Party's prospects, including of course the record
of recent governments. But, equally, there are a number of reasons
why revitalising the Party should be more possible now than at
probably any time since the War.

First, we have had since 3 May 1979 a right-wing rather than a
social democratic government in office, heralding an end to the post-
War consensus politics that have been practised whatever party was
in power. That consensus politics - whether the 'Butskellism' of
the 1950s, the technocratic 'Wilsonism' of the 1960s or the
'Corporatism' of the 1970s - stifled the possibility of radical
socialist measures. It had a debilitating effect on politics,
draining it of the sense of ideological purpose without which activists (especially on the left) can see little point to their involvement. Moreover, social democracy's permanent stranglehold on post-
War government has not delivered the economic goods as its apostles
- whether Anthony Crosland from the left or Harold MacMillan from
the right - had claimed it would. The option of giving British
capitalism a human face and managing it 'better' has now been demol-
ished, not so much in the eyes of socialists for whom it always was
fraudulent, but by its own intrinsic failures. Radical socialism is
now on the agenda partly because of these failures and partly
because of the Conservatives' own break with middle way politics and
their lurch into right-wing monetarism. It may take a little while
for the implications of the stark choice between monetarism and
socialism to seep through; and a lurch into coalition politics is a
serious possibility, as the ruling class looks for a more palatable
tools to manage the crisis and as ordinary voters plump for the
apparent security of the centre. In addition we ought to guard
against the 'fatalism'[7] which permeates the whole left - from
Trotskyites to Tribunites - under which capitalism seems always to
be approaching its final crisis. To analyse the downward trend of
contemporary British capitalism is not the same thing as providing
the means for mobilising the working class behind a socialist movement. Capitalism furthermore is a pretty resourceful animal, as
British history has shown. Nevertheless, as recession bites deeper,
there is the real possibility of winning mass support for socialist
policies again. The only question is whether the Labour Party will
be equipped to take full advantage of this. And part of the answer
must lie in defeating the Party's Right. For the Labour Right's
prescription, when it is not breathlessly haranguing those in the
Party who have the temerity to want genuinely socialist policies,
really amounts to a call for a social democratic party, possibly
drawing in others on the centre-right.[8] In short, it wants not only
an abandonment of the Party's socialist *raison d'être* but a reliance
upon precisely the kind of consensus politics which has dominated
all post-War British governments and has so abjectly failed. Those
are the policies which have presided over Britain's economic decline
and paved the way for Thatcherism. And if it is accepted that the
Party itself has suffered over the last two decades, then is it too
much to ask Labour's social democrats to acknowledge that they have

been in power whilst the demise which they now so eagerly seize upon occurred?

The *second*, advantageous factor is that the Tories' policies are exacerbating the more general economic recession and crisis of capitalism, and will increasingly provoke opposition from workers, regardless of what the Labour Party does. The tendency to see Thatcherism as an irrational lurch back to the 1930s is mistaken: Thatcherism is deliberately designed to attack working class living standards and to undermine working class power. As resistance on wages, jobs and cuts grows, so the opportunity for a political input to struggles that would otherwise remain 'economistic' will grow. The question is therefore likely to be less whether socialism will offer a rallying point, and more *which* socialists will have the credibility to assume the leadership of such struggles. Without doubt there will be an upsurge in political consciousness and participation, and the Labour Party is potentially best placed both to benefit from this and give it cohesion.

Third, a political vacuum has opened up within the trade union movement at the key level of rank-and-file activists. The shop stewards movement is much weaker now than in the 1960s and early 1970s, partly because of the anaesthetising effect of successive incomes policies - particularly the 1975-77 social contract - on rank-and-file activism. The decline of the Communist Party's industrial base has been important in encouraging a political vacuum and, although other groups (notably the SWP) are trying to provide leadership at this level, their role is largely peripheral and their effect minimal as compared with the period when the shop stewards' movement was at its height. Workplace activists have increasingly been looking for a radical socialist lead, both politically and organisationally, yet it should also be understood that the Labour Party will have to intervene in ways which have hitherto been avoided if it is to fill that vacuum (a point developed later).

Fourthly, there is a growing feeling amongst many of a progressive or radical persuasion who busied themselves in 'single-issue' politics in the 1960s and 1970s, that a broader political movement is necessary. Single-issue campaigns (e.g. CND, Vietnam, Stop the Seventy Tour, ecology, Anti-Apartheid, Anti Nazi League) have enjoyed a boom period during the past two decades, partly in response to the failures of parliamentary politics and the Labour Party in particular.[9] They have involved large numbers of people, and achieved important successes. Yet, at the end of the day, they have come up against power structures which it is simply not possible to combat within a 'single-issue' framework: a socialist response is needed.[10] Similarly, community action groups have been able to generate immense activity and enthusiasm for short periods - frequently putting local Labour Parties to shame - but have been unable to sustain their momentum.[11] Radical community activists, too, have started to look back to the Labour Movement.[12]

Fifth, the growth of the women's movement has opened up a vital extra dimension to socialist politics and enabled women to get involved in political action on *their* terms, pushing specifically women's issues onto the political agenda. Although groups to the left of the Labour Party have appeared to respond far more effectively

to the women's movement, their Leninist mode of organisation has now
come under strong attack from important layers in the women's movement. And, although that attack has also been directed at the
Labour Party, it is in a potentially better position to accommodate
their legitimate criticisms. The critique[13] made by socialist feminists of the vanguard party concept and of democratic centralism is
devastating and, whilst they are trenchant in their attack on
parliamentarianism and Labourism, the strength of their opposition
to the Labour Party would be mitigated if the Labour left demonstrated
serious signs of pursuing an extra-parliamentary strategy. The 1979-
80 campaign against the Corrie Bill showed how powerful a force could
be created on the basis of unity between the Labour left - inside
and outside Westminster - and the independent women's movement.
Indeed, without such a link between parliamentary and extra-parliamentary struggle, the campaign could not have been so successful.
It is likely also that the women's movement will increasingly run up
against the political and resource problems faced for example by
community action groups - something rather airily ignored in *Beyond
the Fragments*. Against this background, and with struggles escalating
over women's jobs, over nurseries and related 'bread and butter'
issues, the necessity for co-operation between the women's groups
and the Labour Party will grow.

Sixth, the far left is not enjoying the expansion that might have
been anticipated in the aftermath of the Wilson/Callaghan regimes and
under the threat of Thatcherism. We are in a markedly different
situation from Labour's last period in opposition, in 1970-74, when,
flowing through from the late 1960s and into the agitation of the
early 1970s, Trotskyite groups especially enjoyed a boom period.

Indeed the organised left outside the Labour Party is in crisis.
The Communist Party has been steadily dropping members. The International Marxist Group's membership has plummeted. The Socialist
Workers Party, although retaining its political position and consol-
idating its organisation, has notably failed to grow. Whilst the
rest of the left is a motley collection of splinter groups who revel
only in their sectarianism. The right-ward lurch of the student
movement into a political centrism (led by student Communists!) is
symptomatic of the present plight of left-wing politics. Yet the
left *inside* the Labour Party has increased its strength - a factor
which, coupled with the wider decline of the left, has encouraged
many socialists previously hostile to the Labour Party to join it.[14]

Seventh, youth politics - which in the late 1960s especially
developed its own distinctive momentum - is now in disarray. The
alternatives to the Labour Party look far less attractive than they
did in the days of the hippies and the student revolt. There is none
of that brash confidence amongst radical youth that inspired them to
feel they could take on the system by themselves only a few years ago.
Yet the huge mobilisation of (especially working class) youth
achieved by the Anti Nazi League in 1977-79 showed what could be
done. Given an open campaigning orientation, the Labour Party could
attract in tens of thousands of young people in a way that is prevented
by the present Labour Party Young Socialists: hamstrung by the
sterility of *Militant*'s politics, they appear incapable of grasping
the opportunity now before them.

This latter qualification aside, all these seven factors give
cause for encouragement in the task of rejuvenating the Labour Party.
But they also face Party activists with a moment of truth: in order
to create a *modern* mass party, a serious and quite fundamental change
of strategy is required. For there are also formidable obstacles
which can no longer be ducked.

THE MAIN PROBLEMS

Perhaps the most crippling problem is that the Party today is, and
historically has been, far too committed to parliamentarianism.
The dominant perspective has been that socialism could be achieved
through the ballot box alone. Such a perspective has not been confined to the Party establishment: the Left too have been guilty of
endorsing it. Whatever the attributes of Bevanism and however important is the role of *Tribune* today, both have suffered from too
unhealthy a preoccupation with Parliamentary politics. This is not
to argue against the primary importance of winning control at
Westminster or town hall level. It is simply to suggest that Party
activists have neglected the vital task of creating a mass movement
outside, capable of exerting sufficient power to make feasible
socialist changes through Parliament or the local Council.
    We have to be clear about where we think power really lies.
Those who travel the Parliamentary road alone presumably do so in
the belief that real power lies in Parliament: on that reasoning the
task logically becomes one of winning a majority in order to execute
that power. Yet surely our actual experience - quite apart from a
decent socialist analysis - tells us different? Effective power,
as opposed to the trappings of it, really lies in big business,
the multinationals and the private and public bureaucracies which
serve them. Power in short lies in the edifice of capitalism for
which the parliamentary system is a front.
    That being the case, the real priority must be to tackle the
sources of power at their roots. In opting for a largely electoralist strategy, the Labour Party has imposed a self-inflicted wound
which, besides restricting the possibilities for socialist advance,
has meant that the Party has been unable to involve its own membership and potential membership in active political campaigning.
There has been no conception of mass mobilisation or struggle.
    Part of the reason for this is the fact that the historical divi-
sion of the labour movement between the trade unions and the Party
was accompanied by a more or less strict demarcation between the
'industrial' and the 'political'. The trade unions set up the Party
to gain representation for the working class in *Parliament*; the
priority was not seen as being to build a mass political movement
based upon struggles outside. Another corollary was that the Party
only intervened on the shop floor through the unions - and usually
only through official channels. As a result the political links
between trade unionists and the Party have been steadily ossified,
weakening both wings of the labour movement. The demarcation has
bred economism amongst the trade unions. It has also meant that the
Party has not seen the need to create an extra-parliamentary movement
in the *community* to mirror that in the workplace.

CONTEMPORARY TRADE UNIONISM

A further problem about which especially the left in the Party is
misguided is the nature of contemporary trade unionism. There has
been too ready an assumption that the steady increase in trade union
strength (*viz*., better organisation and greater membership) *necessar-*
ily strengthens the forces for socialism. Of course, it goes without
saying that such advances are welcome and they strengthen the defensive capacity of working people. But too many on the left have a
totally romantic view of the trade union movement, which exposes
their lack of knowledge and involvement in it. It can be argued
that in the late 1970s the politicisation of the membership of public
sector unions (e.g. NUPE, CPSA, SCPS) over the cuts and wages has
been an important advance in a socialist sense. But that advance
must be set against two other trends to which insufficient acknowledgement is given and which are more significant.
     First, from the early 1960s onwards, the national trade union
leadership has been steadily absorbed into the power structure through
an increasingly corporatist mechanism of economic decision-making.
This mechanism has by-passed Parliament and traditional channels of
consensus building. And whilst it was largely jettisoned by the
Thatcher Government, the response of the TUC was highly revealing.
In the year that followed May 1979, there were repeated media reports
of TUC leaders 'not knowing what to do with themselves' now that they
had been pushed out of the corridors of power. Even allowing for a
predictable dose of media exaggeration, the fact is that trade union
leaders had become so used to operating within Whitehall that their
sudden ejection left them quite disorientated. Their co-option by
the state has been nowhere more stark than on pay. Incomes policy
has been the central cog of this corporatist mechanism which has
forced union leaders into the position of acting for government as
brokers between the interests of their membership and employers. As
a result, the political independence of the whole movement has been
weakened and rank and file activism smothered.
     The second worrying trend has been, contrary to media accusations
of increased trade union politicisation, an actual decrease in
serious political commitment by the membership at large. Because
their leaders have opted for the role of an institutionalised pressure
group, rather than a politically autonomous movement, there have not
been the conditions necessary for raising political consciousness.
     However, an equally important factor has been the kind of wage
militancy that has recently predominated. It has often reflected the
ethics of American-type trade unionism, narrowly self-interested and,
crucially, not linked to socialist struggle. This does not mean that
wage militancy is not essential - it is difficult to think of a
single recent major strike which should not have been supported to
the hilt. All that ought to be questioned is whether collective
bargaining as it is now conventionally carried out positively advances
the prospects for socialism. Now even to pose that question on the
left is to invite strident denunciation for 'selling out the working
class', for being in cahoots with the incomes policy lobby, etc. etc.
It therefore needs to be underlined that what is being challenged is
not the bargaining autonomy of the trade unions, still less the

necessity for rank and file independence and agitation. Something
quite different is at issue: the validity of the conventional wisdom
on 'free collective bargaining' which assumes that it will inherently
strengthen the substantive position of workers and conceivably (in
the case of the far left particularly), by increasing wage militancy,
escalate into confronting the whole capitalist system. It has to be
recognised that such a strategy has *not* altered the distribution of
wealth and income in Britain, which has remained roughly constant
this century. And why? Because it has not tackled the real power
relations in the economy. Screwing the system for all you can get
is not the same as changing the system. Unless the trade union movement orientates itself towards struggling for workers' control it
will remain trapped in the role of imitating capitalism rather than
replacing it. There is also the increasing problem of the trade
unions' relationship to the working class in its capacity as citizen
or consumer. Whether the left likes it or not - and chooses to
acknowledge it or not - the unity of working class people has been
injured by particular trade unions taking industrial action, especially in the public sector. This is a subject sensitively discussed
from a socialist standpoint by the authors of *In and Against the
State*.[15] At the very least it poses the need for a common bargaining
strategy by the whole of the trade union movement, not just over
wages, but jobs, hours, investment, prices, planning, and so on.
Again, to repeat, this is not to knock public sector workers' militancy - quite the reverse.

   We have the dichotomy of a national trade union movement which has
lost its way whilst at local level it has become far more assertive.
Even this should however be qualified, for the popular characterisation of a national leadership vs. rank and file conflict is today
less credible an interpretation than was the case certainly in the
1960s and most of the 1970s. The plain fact is that stop stewards
or militant Branch Secretaries have not always been able to carry
their troops with them. And that does not necessarily mean that the
troops are more militant: the sacking of Derek Robinson by Leyland
is testimony to that. For the left, the decline of the shop stewards
movement has been very serious, although this is not the place to
attempt an analysis of the factors involved.

THE LABOUR PARTY NOW

If we look now at the Party itself, far too much of what passes for
political activity is geared to 'declaratory politics' rather than
'activist politics'. Typically, discussion at CLP level is followed
by the passing of a motion which is sent elsewhere, thereby neatly
passing the buck and avoiding the pressing problem of implementation
or campaigning for such a policy at CLP level. In that way, not only
does much of a local Party's politics occur in a vacuum divorced
from the real world outside and from linking into working class
struggles, but it also fails to face up to the structure of power
that usually makes such 'resolutionary politics' irrelevant. The
left of the Party is no less guilty of this. Indeed, in some respects, it is *more* guilty, inclined to rest its laurels on ritual

denunciations and rhetoric, which produces a strong sense of self-satisfaction but again sidesteps a rather less comfortable reality. This is no less the case at national level. The National Executive Committee, despite its left composition in recent years and its important stands, appears not to conceive its role outside elections in *campaigning* terms. It is far too orientated to Parliament, to making demands on the Government (or Opposition, as the case may be). For instance, in the case of a national strike, the Party's function nationally ought to be to mobilise maximum support for picketting and so forth, not just by issuing appeal circulars, but by practical intervention. Similarly, it was noticeable that the Party's national campaign against racism, launched in 1977-78, was limited in effect to producing briefings, posters and leaflets. That compared with the huge momentum geared to *action* generated by the Anti-Nazi League during that same period.

The fact is that the Party has not considered strategy in sufficient depth. There is no clear view of how capitalism will be replaced by socialism, except by reliance upon securing electoral office which has to date been conspicuously unsuccessful.

From the standpoint of mass politics, the Party's *style* of politics is also a major problem. Particularly to outsiders, it is overly bureaucratic, cumbersome and organisationally conservative. It is actually very difficult to get actively involved in, which is ironic to say the least! By contrast, pressure groups or community groups offer a sense of immediacy and informality which is very attractive to new recruits wanting to do something positive but lacking in the confidence necessary to cope with relatively formal structures or responsibilities. The new member's first real contact with the Labour Party is usually at a Ward meeting, and that can be enough to put you off for life. You hear a recital of ECs, GMCs and LGCs, of minutes and motions. And invariably, when something needs to be done, a meeting is called to discuss doing something about it. You can happily spend every night of the week, pretty well the whole year through, going to meetings: meetings to decide how to call other meetings, meetings to discuss what to do after the meeting you have just called. It can be a comfy, boring little world of Labour Party meeting-goers talking to themselves rather than attempting to win support for socialism outside. Of course meetings can be crucial, and at least some are indispensable to a functioning democratic unit. But it is remarkable how the left - and not just inside the Labour Party - relies on meetings as a substitute for the admittedly difficult task of action.

Ward parties hold the key to a vigorous Party, yet they frequently appear to be 'all talk and no action'. People who join want to do something *political*, to feel involved in activity, and the Party will only be able to satisfy that unexceptionable desire by becoming a continuously campaigning movement rather than one which only really comes to life around elections.

There is also the crucial question about the organisational ideology of a Party professing to be socialist. This was raised sharply by the women's movement in the 1970s and is argued by the authors of that seminal work, *Beyond the Fragments*. They criticise male-dominated and essentially authoritarian left-wing groups, but also

focus on the more general problem of attempting to build socialism
within a Party structure that actually reproduces in itself many of
the worst features of hierarchy and elitism present under capitalism.
Labour must evolve a form of politics and of organisation that enables
members as far as is possible to live out their socialism in the
course of their Party activity.

STRATEGY

In order then to grasp the opportunities now before it, the Labour
Party will need to adopt an outward campaigning strategy. That of
course assumes acceptance of the principle that it is necessary to
create an extra-parliamentary dimension to its politics to complement
work within the Westminster and Town Hall systems. Indeed, it is
necessary to go further and give a priority to extra-parliamentary
action, even to the point of subordinating electoral politics to it.
For, unless activity is built from the bottom upwards, involving
ordinary people and Party activists in struggles for power over
their workplace, their neighbourhoods, schools, estates and so
forth, then we shall be unable to create an authentic form of
socialism rooted, not in hierarchical structures, but directly in
the people.

The mistake made by the Labour Party has been to assume that
socialism could be granted from above through governmental action
in a hostile capitalist environment. Equally, the defect of so-
called revolutionary left groups is their overriding preoccupation
with building a centralised Party structure which it is envisaged
will eventually amount a centralised coup against the capitalist
state. Both approaches seek to impose or introduce socialism from
the top down. Yet, unless people have actively been involved in the
process of themselves building socialism, the result will not be
socialism at all. It will be a mirror image of the present highly
centralised and increasingly authoritarian capitalist strcture.

That being accepted, the next question to be faced is whether
extra-parliamentary activity on its own is sufficient. For it is
one thing to point to the primary importance of such activity, but
quite another to reject entirely a role within the conventional
political system.

Traditionally, this question has been posed in terms of: reform
or revolution? Yet, as has been cogently argued by Geoff Hodgson,
one of the 'new left' in the Labour Party, it is false to pose the
choice for the left in that way.[16] He demonstrates first of all
that it is based upon a simplistic interpretation of Marxist theory.
Second, he shows how both a reformist and an insurrectionary
strategy are on their own inadequate and cannot succeed in an
advanced stage of capitalism such as exists in Britain. Socialist
reformism of the brand historically embraced even by the left of
the Labour Party assumes that it is possible to transform the
system from within, which is palpably not the case. Equally, however, an insurrectionary strategy fails on several grounds. It
does not connect into the contemporary institutions and culture of
the working class, nor does it acknowledge that Parliament is almost

universally seen as the legitimate democratic forum for change.
Moreover, the insurrectionary strategy of the far left has a fatal
flaw in its failure to provide a bridge between escalating agitation
and the conditions in which state power could be captured and socialist transformation begin. Whilst it emphasises struggle and confrontation, it does not offer a strategic perspective on how such activity
might make the massive leap forward to actually transforming society.
A huge cloud of rhetoric typically covers this major shortcoming.
And even when the far left falls back to a reliance upon what may be
termed rank-and-filism, serious problems remain. This switch has
been notable in recent years in the SWP for example. Whilst retaining its label as a 'revolutionary' Party, its popular appeal is actually made, not on a basis of the need for a revolutionary Party as
such, but on 'the need to go back and organise in the rank and
file'.[17] So the debate is not really between 'revolutionaries' and
'reformists', but between those who wish to work entirely outside the
system and those who see the need to keep a foot in both camps.
Furthermore, the latter are not actually reformists at all, for
reformism implies a belief in the parliamentary system being able
to deliver the goods necessary to implement socialism - a belief
clearly rejected by an increasing number on the Labour left.

Having, then, attempted to clear away the verbal undergrowth confusing the issue, it is evident that the record of the far left is
no better than that of the parliamentarians. Both have failed in
the sense that to date they have not achieved their objectives. Nor
is there any reason to suppose that they could succeed if they stick
to their respective strategies. In the case of the far left, they
suffer from problems of sustaining their activity rather in the
manner of single-issue campaigns and community groups. The SWP, for
instance, as the largest of the far left groups (excluding the
Communist Party), has a very high rate of turnover of membership.
And whilst their style of activism and their correct emphasis on
rank and file activity can win them recruits and support where there
is disillusionment with the Labour Party, the SWP too lacks a coherent
strategy for socialist change. A preoccupation with the 'here and
now' of politics may offer a sense of political immediacy that is
attractive to socialist activists and is often lacking in the labour
movement. But the prospects of socialism will only be seriously advanced by having a concrete programme for change that meshes into
contemporary political circumstances. (Of course, the Labour left
would be strongly at odds with much of the politics of far left
groups such as the SWP, the inherent authoritarianism of 'democratic
centralism', and their brand of Trotskyism, to name just two
examples.)

What is required is to press for parliamentary change as far as
the system will allow it, but from the base of extra-parliamentary
activism. Any other strategy in contemporary society is doomed,
either to absorption by the State (in the case of an exclusively
electoralist approach), or to frantic irrelevance at the margins of
society (in the case of fringe left groups). For example, the value
of the Alternative Economic Strategy, contained in Labour's programme
but espoused most vigorously by Labour's Left, is that it offers a
means of mobilising politically behind tangible policies which could

then be extended. In other words, it is not simply that the AES
policy package of increased public expenditure, planning, public
ownership and planned trade, offers a solution to the immediate
problems of unemployment and industrial decline, but that it could
become the focus for a political strategy, pressing such concrete
policies as far as is feasible within the present capitalist system
and thereby creating the opportunity to push further through and
beyond that system.[18] Too often, the left resorts to slogans for
'nationalisation' or for 'overthrowing the ruling class'. These,
whilst doubtless giving activists a sense of moral superiority in
posing 'correct' solutions in keeping with the pure milk of socialism, rely on abstract and rhetorical appeals. If the Labour left
are guilty of 'resolutionary' socialism, many in the rest of the
left can be indicted for 'rhetorical' socialism. However, this is
not to pretend that the AES as generally conceived is sufficient.
On the contrary, it is just the beginning of an assault on the whole
structure of power and ownership.

PROBLEMS OF FUSING PARLIAMENTARY WITH EXTRA-PARLIAMENTARY APPROACHES

The major failing of the British left has been its inability to fuse
parliamentary with extra-parliamentary strategies. That therefore
must become the overriding priority for the Labour left. But it is
as well to be clear from the outset about the problems inherent in
that task and what it entails at a practical level.

  It will not be easy, and it follows that it is no comfortable
panacea. To begin with, it requires a considerable break with tradition in the Labour Party. It must also be recognised that there
will remain a conflict between work within and work without. That
is unavoidable: it is in the nature of the power relations involved
that representatives holding office within the system will be subject to constraints and pressures that activists outside are not.
This will unquestionably cause tensions and will strain the relationship between the two. And so - whilst keeping a sense of
proportion - it should. Representatives of the labour movement
must expect to be placed under pressure from their own rank and file.
Indeed, they should encourage that pressure for it will strengthen
their hands in resisting the blandishments of bureaucrats or the
naked power of capitalists. If, for example, there had been mobil-
isations and threats of militancy by trade unionists whilst the
Labour Government was negotiating with the IMF, in 1976, the cuts
subsequently implemented may have been prevented. Or if the shop
floor had been actively demanding planning agreements in 1975, Tony
Benn's intentions whilst Industry Secretary may not have been
thwarted. Similarly, instead of seeing squatting as a threat to
their own political virility, Labour councillors should be prepared
to sanction squatting so as to make the best use of available empty
property (public and private) and to increase the pressure for decent
housing policies. At present all the leverage is exerted by the
system: we ought to reverse that by upping the ante at grass roots
level.

However, a totally different attitude is required from representatives. Instead of seeing themselves as repositories of wisdom, and
having some higher mandate in the Burkean sense, their role will be
as accountable delegates. Certainly, they should exercise their
judgement, experience and expertise, but they must also strive to
avoid slipping into the hitherto apparently irresistable position of
being packaged and stamped with official approval, and reciprocating
with fierce loyalty to the job. All too frequently Labour MPs and
councillors react to criticism and external pressure as if their own
pride is at stake when they should not allow themselves to be identified as apparatchiks of the system. Instead, they should see themselves as being aliens working temporarily within it, openly and
honestly explaining to all and sundry the constraints upon them.
But they should never allow themselves to get so caught up in the
game of apparently exerting power that they become tools of the very
system they ought to be infiltrating and undermining.

Expressed in this way, almost superhuman characteristics may be
expected of representatives. Certainly they will be expected to
display rather more loyalty to their working class base than usual,
and a different conception of the role of an MP or councillor is
necessary. But the real requirement is for a different political
strategy into which their roles as representatives will slot.

Even then, of course, progress is by no means guaranteed. Britain
is part of an international capitalist system, the ruling class may
ultimately resist the socialist movement with violence and in any
case will not relinquish power without bitter struggle. But to
acknowledge those facts of life should not relegate us to either a
strategy of impotence or to the fatalism so characteristic of many
on the left, waiting and hoping for the proverbial 'final crisis'
to turn up.[19]

Above all, the British left requires a *tangible* strategy for
bringing about socialist change. And it is this hitherto missing
dimension which can be found in the approach argued here. It is not
without problems or potential contradictions, but it does offer the
possibility of moving through a series of concrete stages towards
socialist transformation. That will however require the Labour Party
to be transformed itself.

REVITALISING THE LABOUR PARTY

The first and most pressing priority is politically to revitalise
constituency parties, beginning with several comparatively modest
changes. CLPs ought to be taking the lead in active campaigns, now
often initiated by community groups, trades councils, single-issue
groups etc., so that the local Party is seen as a natural focus for
radical change. The Labour Party needs to be viewed automatically as
the source of leadership and cohesion in local campaigns, not out of
any divine right, but by setting an example. Linked with this, CLP
headquarters should present an outward-looking image, becoming
'action centres' for the community, involving people not necessarily
in the Party and allowing them to use the Party's resources (e.g.
meeting room, duplicator). A sense of political excitement must be

built to replace the grey atmosphere of old canvass cards which pre-
dominates between elections in too many local Parties. Also crucial
to renewing the vigour of CLPs is to develop local newsletters,
ideally ward-based, delivered regularly door-to-door and written in
a style which is rather different from the Party's conventional
leaflets. There are lessons to be learned from community newspapers.
Basically, the style needs to eschew open Party propaganda which the
uncommitted view with total cynicism. Instead, parochial interests
and issues should be covered, based on a feedback from local people
and preferably containing news about the Party's plans to take up
the relevant matter. Once having gained sufficient interest locally,
a harder socialist message can be introduced, but only in a way which
avoids haranguing readers and which excludes inter-Party sloganeering.
In short, it is necessary to relate to immediate local concerns and
use those as a means of bridging the gap towards socialist ideas.
It would, of course, be easy to degenerate into mere populism, as
has been the case for the vast majority of the Liberals' 'community
politics' newsheets. Equally, it would be wrong to pretend that
there is any virtue in pouring out socialist or Tory-bashing slogans
when people are not listening. They have heard it all before and
Labour's record in office gives no cause for believing a new version
of the same old story. Still less are people interested in the
grating jargon of the far left.

Next, CLPs should help to set up or become closely involved in
tenants' associations and work with tenants organising for control
of their estates. The same principle could apply to residents'
associations or even street committees. The experience of the
community action movement - whatever its political limitations and
shortcomings referred to earlier - has shown that an enormous amount
of potentially socialist energy can be released if the correct
vehicle becomes available. The left has had its eyes too firmly
fixed at national state level. That may be understandable in terms
of analysing the exercise of power, but it neglects the problem of
mobilising working class *activity*. It is necessary now to create
ways of organising that enable people to become immediately involved
at levels they feel directly part of, and this has been a key in-
sight provided by community activists. If, moreover, a tri-partite
unity could be forged between independent community groups, trade
unions and the Labour Party, then the weaknesses existing at present
in each of the three could be repaired. We could then see the
development of a strategy intervening simultaneously at the point of
production (through unions), at the point of *reproduction* (in the
localities, through community groups) and in the *political* system.[20]
The role of some trades councils, the example set by Lucas Aerospace
workers and projects like the Coventry Workshops, are tentative
signs of moves in that direction. But the role of the Labour Party
is central to further progress along these lines.

It is also vital that local Labour Parties support and relate
to local women's movements and the various campaigns they initiate.
Working class women especially are often trapped at home and, in
their isolation, both lack the opportunities to fulfil themselves
personally and are vulnerable to media stereotyping of political
ideas. The Labour Party could assist them to organise, but only if

we learn from the women's movement and avoid paternalistic or bureaucratic modes of involvement and organisation. There could be considerable value in establishing renewed women's sections in CLPs, not
imitating the old, politically moribund, women's sections, but
reflecting the modern ethos of the struggles for women's rights and
equality. These could draw women into the Party whilst also providing them with the base to re-orientate the Party to their concerns.
In short, revived Women's Sections could become the vehicles for the
ideas of socialist feminism to be introduced into Labour Party
practice.

In a similar way it is important for the labour movement to provide for the input of minority concerns. In the 1970s we witnessed
an upsurge in confidence and willingness to organise on the part of
minority groups, such as gays and blacks for example. The decline
of traditional political parties has run alongside the emergence of
an interest-based form of group politics. Nationally this is
expressed in the high profile of the CBI and TUC, locally in community issue groups, and there is a kind of middle layer of sectional
interests which must be absorbed into the labour movement. In
particular, the problem of racism and the need to include black
people whilst also granting blacks autonomy for self-organisation,
must be given priority.

At national and local levels, the Labour Party should be involved
in single-issue campaigns such as the Anti-Nazi League and the
nuclear disarmament campaigns. This should be with a dual objective
of both mobilising the maximum impact on specific, important issues,
and building left unity where possible. Sectarianism is the cancer
of the left, inside and outside the Party. On the other hand, we
should not advance a model of left unity around a lowest-common-
denominator consensus, where a breadth of opinion is brought under
one banner only at the cost of politically anaesthetising any impact.
Such unity tends to give a priority to gathering respectable supporters and to a bureaucratic style of lobbying rather than to grass-
roots action, building up the base of support and involvement. We
should not fudge political differences or go for a minimal consensus
that means all things to all people. Instead, we should make a
careful selection of key issues within pressing problems around
which maximum activity can be generated. It is no accident that
successful recent campaigns such as the ANL have concentrated on
relatively narrow targets within problems (e.g. racism) which were
clearly much bigger. Above all, we want *unity in action* rather than
pursuing futile exercises in crossing t's and dotting i's to try and
arrive at a mutually agreeable *unity in theory*.

There are, however, two methods for specific issue campaigns.
The first (usually favoured by the present LPYS and some groups on
the far left such as the WRP) is to organise on the basis of a
campaign run and controlled by the sponsoring group, and invariably
requiring acceptance of a particular narrow socialist programme as a
pre-condition for involvement. Such an approach does not involve
large numbers of people and is often merely a recruiting front for
the organisation concerned. The second model is to involve the
maximum support possible on the basis of agreeing to a programme of
action. The latter approach has been found to be more successful,

provided it is led on the basis of clear though not doctrinaire
socialist instincts and a commitment to organising at grass-roots
level, rather than to passing resolutions in smoke-filled rooms.

For it is locally that a mass party will be built. Party activists ought to be initiating local campaigns against the cuts. These
have the potential of winning to socialist ideas huge layers of
people not previously politically aware but forced into awareness by
cuts in their services or facilities. To do that, however, Labour
Party members will need to offer both clear socialist policies (the
last Labour Government, after all, started the cuts), and clear ideas
for action. So far as the latter is concerned, it is difficult to
visualise how the anti-cuts campaign can be successful without the
use of nationally orchestrated industrial action. For, without the
powerful leverage industrial action would exert, there is a great
danger that brave localised acts of resistance (like in Lambeth)
will be isolated and crushed. There is no possibility of successful
local anti-cuts campaigns in the present hostile economic environment
without a mass national response. But, again, that will not be
forthcoming by relying upon appeals to trade union executives; local
Party activists must be organising actively for it.

This brings us to the crucial area of workplace action. Having
rejected the argument that it is not legitimate for the Labour Party
as such to organise industrially, there are two main areas of priority for intervention. The first is to implement the Party's existing
commitment to set up workplace branches. These would carry a socialist message into factories and offices and provide Party activists
with a framework for recruitment and organisation, whilst integrating
workplace branches within local Parties through direct constitutional
links.[21] The second area is perhaps more controversial and concerns
the need for the Party officially to organise support for strikes,
resistance to closures, struggles for recognition etc. At one level
Party headquarters ought to have organisers co-ordinating activity
amongst CLPs so that support for workers is maximised. At present,
the Party's official response tends to be confined to the level of
the NEC passing a resolution or sending an appropriate delegation.
Welcome though that is, it is not sufficient. And in the case of
major confrontations like Grunwick or so-called secondary picketing,
an organised campaign of political support from the Party could
immeasurably strengthen trade union struggles. Such a course will
also have the advantage of making the Party directly relevant to
the action taken by workers, rather than a body which periodically
asks for their vote.

Already, there have been initiatives on the Labour left to
intervene directly at rank and file level in the trade unions.
The Labour Coordinating Committee convened a conference to discuss
such a strategy in November 1980 and the idea has gained increasing
support.[22] If successfully pursued it will give Labour activists a
concrete point of entry into the shop floor movement, *as Labour Party
members* rather than as individual trade unionists. But it will do
more than that. It could help to rebuild a coordinated rank and
file trade union movement. For the decline of the Communist Party's
Liaison Committee for the Defence of Trade Unions, from its peak of

influence in the late 1960s to early 1970s, has left a crippling gap
which the Labour left must seek to fill. Clearly, however, such a
strategy could provoke conflict with the very trade union leaders who
are the Labour Party's paymasters. But that is not something which
should block it. Indeed, the consequences, if difficult in the short
term, could be profoundly healthy in the long term by bringing into
sharp focus issues of accountability and democracy within the unions
as well.

A NEW TERRAIN FOR THE LEFT

In these various ways, not only could the Labour Party be reorientated,
but a new and more fruitful terrain could open up in which the wider
left could cooperate. We need independent pressure and agitation
from autonomous groups outside to be engaged with struggle inside
the Party. Furthermore, implicit in such a strategy is the need to
offer to the people a vision of socialism as a genuinely liberating
force, of a decentralised form of socialism, based upon workers'
control and neighbourhood self-management. Our task is not to manage
capitalism better. Neither is it to allow socialism to become synon-
ymous with the dead hand of the State and centralised control. Of
course, we will have to wrest power away at a national level. But
this can only be achieved through a fusion of parliamentary and
extra-parliamentary pressure built from the bottom upwards.
  It is not suggested that this strategy will be easy to pursue;
formidable obstacles to its implementation remain inside the Labour
Party. What is being argued is that it is the only realistic
possibility for a concrete progression to socialism.

Notes

*   This article draws heavily on my pamphlet, *Reviving the Labour
    Party*, published by the Institute for Workers Control in June 1980.

1   Ralph Miliband, *Parliamentary Socialism* (Merlin Press, 1972).
2   A useful discussion of Party organisation is Dianne Hayter, *The
    Labour Party: crisis and prospects* (Fabian Tract 451, 1977),
    although it suffers the political shortcomings referred to.
3   This has been well analysed by Hilary Wainwright in *Beyond the
    Fragments* (Merlin Press, 1980) and in *The Crisis and Future of
    the Left* (Pluto Press, 1980).
4   Sheila Rowbotham, Lynne Segal and Hilary Wainwright, *Beyond the
    Fragments*, op.cit.
5   Mike Prior and David Purdy, *Out of the Ghetto* (Nottingham,
    Spokesman, 1979).
6   Geoff Hodgson, *Socialism and Parliamentary Democracy* (Nottingham,
    Spokesman, 1978).
7   See Geoff Hodgson, *Trotsky and Fatalistic Marxism* (Nottingham,
    Spokesman, 1975).

8 See for example William Rodgers, 'Labour's Predicament', *The Political Quarterly* (October-December 1979) and David Marquand, 'Inquest on a Movement',

9 See my *Radical Regeneration* (Quartet, 1975).

10 This is discussed in Peter Hain and Simon Hebditch, *Radicals and Socialism* (Nottingham, Institute for Workers Control, 1978).

11 Reasons for this are discussed by John Dearlove, 'The Control of Change and the Regulation of Community Action', in D. Jones and M. Mayo, *Community Work One* (Routledge, 1974), pp.22-43; by Tim Young, 'The Industrial Connection', in Peter Hain (ed.), *Community Politics* (John Calder, 1976), pp.116-34; and my introduction to the latter volume.

12 See Cynthia Cockburn, *The Local State* (Pluto, 1977), Jan O'Malley, *The Politics of Community Action* (Spokesman, 1977), and *Community Action* magazine which in recent years has increasingly orientated itself towards the labour movement.

13 *Beyond the Fragments*, op.cit.

14 An interesting analysis of this is Martin Shaw, 'Moving In and Moving On', *Labour Leader* (January 1980).

15 London Edinburgh Weekend Return Group, *In and Against the State* (Publications Distribution Co-op, 1980, and Pluto, forthcoming).

16 Hodgson, 1978, op.cit.

17 See for example Paul Foot's contribution to the 'Debate of the Decade', *The Crisis and future of the Left* (Pluto Press, 1980), or most issues of *Socialist Worker*.

18 This is argued cogently by Geoff Hodgson, *Socialist Economic Strategy* (Independent Labour Publications, 1979).

19 An excellent indictment of this is Hodgson, 1975, op.cit.

20 See Peter Hain ,*Neighbourhood Participation* (Maurice Temple Smith, 1980), especially Chapter 8.

21 For a good discussion of the issues involved, see Tony Banks, 'Workplace Branches', *Workers Control*, No.1 (1980) and Labour Coordinating Committee, *Towards a Mass Party* (LCC, 1980), pp.8-9.

22 See for example the Labour Coordinating Committee, *Labour Activist*, Nos.9, 10 (1980).

Ben Pimlott
Does Labour Always Fail?

How fast can a Labour government move, given the obstacles inevitably
facing it? No question is more fundamental to the politics of the
Left in Britain. Nina Fishman tackles it head on in an interesting
and provocative article (*Politics & Power Two*). The main lines of
her attack on the classic 'Labour Left' critique of the Attlee
administration are irrefutable. However, she over-reaches herself,
making her case vulnerable to a counterblast.

The Labour Left argument (as she presents it, and as apparently
typified by the Eatwell book) can be simply stated: the post-war
Labour government missed a golden opportunity for socialist change
by parliamentary means. Attlee and his colleagues not only failed
to wrest economic control from the capitalists; they created a
public sector which was socialist in name only, made up of 'pragmatic' public corporations which contained no element of internal
democracy. The explanation, according to the Labour Left as interpreted by Fishman, lies in the 'ideological ambiguity' of the Labour
Party, and its lack of socialist commitment. Hence the moral:
socialist advance will only come if Labour recovers its ideals, and
creates a desire for socialism both among itw own members and leaders,
and among the working class.

Nina Fishman's reply to this is that the Labour Left view puts
too much stress on moral force, and not enough on practical means
or possibility. To suggest that Labour might have been different
in 1945 is to ignore the extraordinary achievement of winning enough
votes to do anything at all. True, a ruling party might have been
able to do more if there had been a revolutionary situation as in
Russia after 1917. But there was no revolutionary situation in
Britain at the end of the Second World War, no civil or military
collapse and no vacuum to be filled. Furthermore, while Russia had
a long tradition of reform through government coercion, in Britain
'civil society' had repeatedly been successful in blocking attempts
at centralised direction.

Labour would have found it hard to extend the public sector much
further than it did, because workers in such industries as engineering and textiles were opposed to nationalisation and would have

resisted any attempt at government takeover. Nor was there any
practical alternative to the 'public corporation' model for nationalised industries. Trade unions could not both manage workers and
represent them, without a dramatic and improbable change of heart on
the part of the workers themselves. Thus Nina Fishman accuses the
Labour Left of pinning its hopes on 'some kind of messianic conversion
to socialism' within the working class, and sees no reason to believe
that workers will abandon self-interest and start pursuing the
collective good.

She suggests that, in reality, the working class had 'stopped and
drawn breath' in the post-War period after centuries of deprivation
and poverty, and was understandably delighted by its relative afflu-
ence. Since the Labour Left maintains that socialism can only be
achieved if the working class is itself socialist, the Labour Left
call for more socialist policies involves a demand for 'moral terror'
against the working class - urging it to go faster than it wishes to
go. In fact, such a policy will not succeed because workers are not
Stakhanovites, and exhortation will not make them so. 'If socialism
is not hardly enough to cope with the world as it is, then it is hard
to see how it can ever be achieved, except by coercion of the working
class', she writes. Finally, she asks: 'Why shouldn't socialism be
what the working class make of it? Surely the essence of *democratic*
socialism must be that it is finally the people, and not the Socialist Party, not the socialist state, who will determine the direction
in which to move.' Advance, if it is to come, can only come from
the working class itself - in its own good time.

I hope that this is a fair summary. If it is, Nina Fishman seems
to have thrown the baby out with the bath-water in a very uncompromising way indeed. But before coming to the stages of the argument
that make me uneasy, it is worth considering her basic critique.

I agree entirely that the 'Labour Left' assault on the 1945
government is misplaced and anachronistic. The Attlee administration
did not destroy capitalism. However, in the conditions that pre-
vailed just after the War, any serious attempt to do so would have
brought such a dangerous economic crisis that the major social reforms
of the period - above all, social security and a free health service -
would have been jeopardised without any probable gain.

Nor would Labour's strategy have been very different if the government had been led by leaders with a reputation for being left-wing.
In the 1930s, the bitterest 'Labour Left' opposition to the Bevin-
Morrison-Dalton leadership came from Sir Stafford Cripps and Aneurin
Bevan, both expelled from the Labour Party in 1939 for Popular Front
activities. In 1945 these two became leading members of the Labour
Cabinet, and neither of them made any serious attempt to push it in
a more socialist direction. As Chancellor of the Exchequer from
1947 to 1950 Cripps was much more of a Treasury man, an enthusiastic
deflater, than his predecessor, Hugh Dalton. Until April 1951, when
Bevan, Wilson and Freeman resigned over health charges and inaugur-
ated a left-right conflict in the Labour Party which was to last a
decade, Labour Left criticism of the leadership was more concerned
with foreign and defence matters than with domestic policy. Unless
one writes off the Labour Party altogether (which the Labour Left
never does), it is not helpful politically or historically to blame

a government retrospectively for not doing what very few of its own
supporters or critics suggested at the time.

Though there was no frontal assault on the Cabinet for not
destroying capitalism, there were many controversies over its decisions. Should a powerful National Investment Board be set up?
Should the Chancellor have ensured a closer Treasury control of the
nationalised Bank of England? Were the onerous conditions of the
American Loan inescapable? Could the burden of Crippsian austerity
have been shouldered more by the rich and less by the poor? Sometimes criticisms came from disillusioned socialists; more often they
came from Keynesian economists and planners who despaired, not of the
government's failure to destroy the system, but of an apparent inability to operate it efficiently. Yet, thirty years on, the remarkable thing is surely that the 1945 government managed to achieve so
much: more in terms of social welfare and greater equality than any
other administration of the century. The argument that it might have
gone further still if there had been greater commitment is puzzling.
No Labour government - apart, perhaps, from the short-lived administration of 1924 - has ever come into office on a bigger wave of pro-
socialist feeling and enthusiasm. Ministers, MPs and party members
shared a sense of destiny, of inaugurating a period of dramatic
change, and the general public was more receptive to this mood than
at any other time. If the Labour Left is suggesting that Labour and
the working class were not socialist enough in 1945 for a truly
socialist advance, then it must clearly be prepared to wait a long
time before any advance can be made.

But is the Labour Left really so crude and simple? Nina Fishman
is surely wrong in equating the attitudes expressed in the Eatwell
book (if she interprets these correctly) with those of the Labour
Left as a whole. The exhortatory element certainly remains, and so
does the legacy of 19th-century ILP evangelism and utopianism. The
Labour Left still places too much emphasis on 'winning the Labour
Party for socialism', without thinking enough about how socialism is
going to be implemented once this has been achieved: there is a
dangerous naivity in believing that an increase in the number of
left-wing MPs, or a left-wing manifesto, will do much to increase the
chances of a Labour government carrying out radical policies in office.

However, this is not all that the Labour Left believes. Nina
Fishman ignores (for example) the economic programme of the Labour
Co-ordinating Committee, based on import controls and withdrawal from
the EEC. Though this programme might not work, it is certainly a
policy that is not dependent on Labour Party or working-class
enthusiasm to enable a Labour government to carry it out. Perhaps
she takes the rhetorical fourishes of the Labour Left too much at
their face value. Much of the language of Labour Left evangelism is
empty. But there is some hard policy underneath.

It is the last part of Nina Fishman's article that creates most
problems. Her conclusion (socialist advance will not come until the
workers want it of their own volition) is a kind of *reductio ad
absurdum* of determinism. But thit is not quite as hard to take as
her definition of democratic socialism (what the workers want).
Socialism is a word which can mean many things. But to equate it
with the lowest common denominator of popular demand is to remove

from it all moral value, and abandon all the principles usually
associated with it. However much the working class may, on occasion,
reject the pursuit of greater equality, sexual liberation, collective
effort, workers' control or social ownership, most people who regard
themselves as socialists will continue to regard these as socialist
aims, and it makes little sense to say that they are wrong.

Nor is it necessary to believe that a Labour government can only
act in a positive way with working-class support. Labour has been
ahead of public opinion in the past - for example on capital punishment or homosexual law reform - and there is no reason why, in other
fields, Labour in power should not lead the working class rather
than merely follow it. It is not clear why, as Nina Fishman suggests,
it should be impossible to extend the public sector without 'coercion'
or 'force' in industries where the workers have been persuaded to
oppose nationalisation. Penal reform, liberal immigration laws, or
higher taxation to allow social welfare improvements, are policies
which the working class probably does not favour - but they are
perfectly feasible and could be carried out by a popularly elected
government.

Indeed, the view that policy must wait on the working class and
can go no faster than the working class is prepared to go disregards
the role of political leadership. It is true that in a relatively
affluent and stable society it may be hard to persuade the working
class of the need for drastic change. It is certainly impossible
to impose instant workers' control on an apathetic workforce. But
governments can tax wealth and high incomes, increase educational
equality or reallocate spending while the working class remains
indifferent or unaware of what is happening. So much attention has
been paid to the administrative obstacles to action in Britain that
the central truth of the British constitution is also forgotten: a
parliamentary majority remains legally sovereign, and the British
executive is among the most powerful and efficient in the world.

In this respect, the 1945 Labour government offers an excellent
model. The achievements of the Attlee administration were not
created by mass radicalism or grass-roots socialism, but by a
civil service machine trained by the necessities of war in the
methods of planning and control, and by experienced ministers with
a clear view of their own objectives. Both the evangelical optimism of the classic 'Labour Left', believing in socialism through
conversion, and Nina Fishman's deterministic pessimism, waiting un-
hopefully for the maturity of the working class, disregard the
scope for using the apparatus of the state to good advantage now.

David Fernbach
The Impasse Facing CND

The case against nuclear weapons in general needs no argument. They bring humanity to the brink of self-destruction in a way that is so far unique. Yet even so, the service of these weapons as a deterrent to conventional attack has blocked all attempts at a process of multi-lateral[1] nuclear disarmament.

This was already the position when the unilateralist movement was launched in Britain a quarter of a century ago. Where diplomacy failed to work, CND took its stand on a moral appeal. For sure, like every broad-based movement it contained different, even contrary tendencies. It had its military strategists as well as its canons and deans; it even had its apologists for the Soviet 'workers' bomb'. Yet it was the moral argument that gave CND its backbone and held it together.

The moral case for unilateral nuclear disarmament, by Britain or any other state, is perhaps as strong as can be made for anything. It should not be undervalued, especially not in the name of 'scientific' socialism. Nuclear weapons stand in a class by themselves as weapons of mass destruction, i.e. destruction of the civilian population. To use nuclear weapons against an adversary, even to threaten their use in any circumstance, expresses a readiness to massacre untold numbers of innocent (even unborn) victims, who have had not the least opportunity, as a soldier ultimately does have, to refuse to fight for an unjust cause. Viewed in terms of any humanitarian morality, nuclear deterrence is a crime on the Auschwitz scale: Bertrand Russell drew the logical conclusion in condemning Kennedy and Macmillan as 'worse than Hitler'.[2]

Two corollaries follow from this position. First, if it is immoral for Britain to deploy weapons of mass destruction, then it is similarly immoral to remain in an alliance whose strategy is based on the deployment of such weapons, i.e. NATO. Second, though so-called tactical nuclear weapons are designed for use against military targets, the collateral damage they would wreak, the radioactive pollution of the biosphere and the common technological base that they share with their 'theatre' and 'strategic' big brothers, together add up to a formidable moral case against these weapons too, even in the context of an otherwise non-nuclear defence policy.

The great majority who read this article, socialists from moral
conviction rather than direct experience of class oppression, will
long have opposed British nuclear weapons and NATO for this reason
alone. Yet we have not always given this question the priority it
deserves. We have voted for parties uncommitted to unilateralism.
We have paid taxes (the avoidable as well as the unavoidable) to
governments that use the money for Polaris. There were few indeed
who kept the unilateralist campaign alive during its dog years; not
many more than those committed to absolute pacifism, despite the
great difference that most of us see between killing the soldiers of
an aggressor army and killing the civilian population whom those same
soldiers repress at home. For most of us, unilateral nuclear disarmament was one particular cause we believed in among so many
others. And for most of the 1960s and 1970s, a cause that held
less appeal than many, for a whole host of reasons.

THE WEAKNESS OF 'SURVIVAL'

At the present level of human consciousness, it would seem, the moral
argument for unilateralism has to be substantially reinforced by
other arguments. The first of these, which already marked the
original CND, is the argument of survival. In *Protest and Survive,*
the basic text of the new CND, the theme of survival is given equal
place with morality. This makes a powerful combination. For in the
interval since the first CND, both humanitarian morality and hedon-
istic individualism have advanced considerably; the two aren't
necessarily contrary. On both counts, CND hopes to speak to every
individual in Britain; exterminism is not a 'class issue', so
Edward Thompson argues in *New Left Review.*[3] Those unconvinced by
the immorality of nuclear weapons can be convinced that unilateralism will at least save their own skins.
   CND has always argued that United States bases in Britain make our
country a prime target in the event of hostilities between the superpowers. In the present conjuncture of weapons and tactics, the
intended stationing of Cruise missiles focusses new concern on this
issue, while more accurate targeting and the increasing range of
tactical nuclear weapons seems to make escalation from conventional
to nuclear warfare more likely.[4] (The Soviets, for their part, have
always viewed nuclear weapons in a warfighting rather than merely
deterrent role.)
   Yet survival, which is now pushed so strongly to the fore, is the
weak link in the CND argument, in several different ways.
   First, abandonment of nuclear weapons gives no guarantee against
nuclear attack. Apologists for deterrence make hay with the fact
that the only time such weapons have been used in anger was against
a non-nuclear power, Japan. The comparison may be somewhat odious,
but aren't they always? As Field Marshall Lord Carver puts it:
'You cannot put the nuclear imp back in the bottle':
      'If the conventional war were not quickly conclusive, both
      sides would soon be tempted to make use of nuclear weapons,
      the loser, because he despaired of saving his position by

concentrational means; the victor, impatient to finish the
war and clinch his advantage.'[5]
A non-nuclear Britain in a non-nuclear Europe could be threatened with
nuclear attack unless it remained neutral in a conflict between the
Soviet Union and West Germany. It could in the worst case be threatened with nuclear attack if it resisted the landing at Heathrow of a
'Revolutionary Government of Workers and Peasants', as its Soviet
masters liked to describe the Indra clique of collaborators they tried
to install in Prague in August 1968. The only guarantee against
nuclear attack is the recorded message ready in Copenhagen that
broadcasts: 'We surrender'. That is a different option, but one
CND does not care to discuss.

The second flaw in the survival argument is the implication that
abandonment of nuclear weapons is necessarily a step towards peace.
Edward Thompson and his colleagues insist that every effort for
peace and disarmament made in the West European nations will further
the cause of detente and democracy in Eastern Europe: 'to the degree
that the peace movement in the West can be seen to be effective, it
will afford support and protection to our allies in Eastern Europe
and the Soviet Union ... and will allow the pressures for democracy
and detente to assert themselves'.[6] There is indeed likely to be a
causal chain running in this direction. But it is not the only one,
and it also seems somewhat invidious that British security should
rest on the success of the workers of Gdansk, as Edward Thompson
seemed to imply when questioned by Brian Walden.[7] There is an in-
contestable grain of truth in the argument that nuclear deterrence
has kept the peace in Europe for thirty-five years, by making war
'unthinkable'. You cannot have it both ways. If we do succeed in
bringing European nuclear disarmament, then war does once again
become 'thinkable'. And if industrialised states will today be very
wary of getting entangled in a military conflict with one another,
the lesson of history is that such things can start without deliberate intention on either side. On this count, too, CND's promise of
survival is considerably less than watertight.

The third flaw in the survival argument may be still more
serious. It is all very well to reply to those who, like Bruce
Kent's bishop, would be 'better dead than red':[8] 'Fine, you kill
the Russians or get yourself killed, but don't involve those who
don't share your views'. Yet behind its facile appearance, 'better
dead than red' hides something more substantial: the militant determination to stand up for the survival of certain values, even at
the price of non-survival as an individual; whether these values
are defined as Christianity, democracy or the free market. Those
unconvinced by CND's moral appeal (and they apparently include
bishops) will not necessarily be convinced by its prudential appeal
either. They are willing to die for something they deeply believe
in, and feel the solidarity of right-minded people throughout
British society.

THE ABSENCE OF POLITICS[9]

Besides the arguments of morality and survival, a further strand is
needed in the unilateralist appeal, i.e. a political argument. For
since the only justification for NATO's nuclear weapons is as a
deterrent to Soviet aggression, unilateralism immediately raises
certain major and divisive political questions. These include, in
particular, the nature and policies of the Soviet Union; the relation
between Britain, its European neighbours and the United States; the
significance of democratic institutions. In so far as unilateralists
are united by moral protest and the desire to survive, these divisions
are secondary. But if unilateralism is to become a successful political campaign, then the movement cannot avoid having, if not a rigid
line, then at least a certain range of consensus on these questions.
If this narrows its political base somewhat, excluding those unable
to find a place in the consensus, it more than makes up for this by
linking the issue of nuclear disarmament into a broader political
movement that has a chance of acceding to power, i.e. a 'historic
bloc' in the Gramscian term.

The original nucleus of unilateralists in the mid-1950s was
fairly marginal to the Labour movement. Yet as CND developed into
a serious political force it not only succeeded in mobilising the
Labour left (and the initially hostile Communist Party); it came to
seek the achievement of its goals through the Labour ·Party, in a
two-step process of winning a majority for the left within the
Party, followed by a majority for Labour in the general election.
To those of us who were involved in CND from the left, this seemed
only natural; but it is worth while reflecting from today's remove
on the political assumptions that came to be associated with CND.
In those days, the left saw the Soviet Union as a state that might
be repressive, but was essentially socialist. It was axiomatic that
Soviet foreign policy was purely defensive against Western imperialism; and in so far as the Soviet Union sought the expansion of its
social system (Cuba, for instance), this was something we wholeheartedly welcomed. As regards democratic institutions, we did
appreciate - up to a point - the value of hard-won liberties; we
understood the difference between bourgeois democracy and fascism.
Yet this was something in the superstructure, a distinction ultimately between the lesser and the greater evil, when contrasted with
the prospective blossoming of socialist democracy.[10] Finally, NATO
was a union of the capitalist classes under American hegemony, with
a view to preventing the spread of socialism; and the EEC was
designed to bolster NATO with economic support.

This was the broad left ideology of twenty years ago, which CND
linked up with and which carried the movement forward. As it
happened, the left proved unable even to overthrow Gaitskell, let
alone to grasp the reins of government. This would have required a
mass movement for radical change, such as the Labour Party had indeed
represented against the misery of the inter-War era, but which was
unlikely to be repeated scarcely a decade after the great advances
of 1945-51. Yet there was no other way that CND could have come
even as close to its goal as it did at the turn of the 1960s.

Now to open the *Morning Star*, you might fancy that little has changed. Yet what used to be the centre of the spectrum has now shifted significantly to one end. Since the collapse of the first CND we have seen Khrushchev's promises of goulash-socialism give way to Brezhnev's cynical repression; we have seen the invasion of Czechoslovakia; we have seen the recurrent workers' struggles in Poland; we have seen the development in our own part of the world of an ecological critique of the present social order, and a further radical critique from the women's and gay movements - in each case bearing equally on 'socialist' society; most recently, we have seen the economic crisis of Western capitalism matched by a different but equally severe crisis of the Soviet economy, and finally the invasion of Afghanistan. The result of these and other events, on the key political questions with which nuclear weapons are linked, is that the broad mass of informed radical opinion in Britain sees the Soviet and Western systems as at least equally part of the problem in the world today, value civil and political liberty over any promises of economic well-being whatsoever; and show considerable support for the principle of West European unity. Only on the last point are these *Guardian* readers significantly different from their counterparts as opinion leaders among the working class.

It is impossible today, therefore, to answer the question 'what happens after unilateralism?' in the way that CND did in the early 1960s. If it is a mass political movement we are after, then there is no mileage in repeating the old responses. At first appearance, in fact, it would look as if the political base for nuclear weapons had actually spread further left, as our prospective constituency now shares the views traditionally associated with the right, i.e. that Western values should be defended, that the Soviet Union is offensive (in both senses), and that internationalism should make a start on our own doorstep.

Edward Thompson and his colleagues seem to ignore the political dimension of the nuclear disarmament campaign completely. True, they stress their staunch opposition to Soviet 'socialism'; they seek to defend and indeed expand the zone of democracy; and they do not take up an anti-EEC stance (though the Labour left tries to pull CND in this direction). Yet these political positions are only brought in negatively, i.e. to defend CND against a charge that was fairly accurately made against its ancestor of twenty years ago. No attempt is made to tackle the political questions raised by unilateralism in a positive way. Here I am not referring simply to the *Protest and Survive* volume, which understandably cannot cover too much ground, but to the CND framework of discussion in general.

I am not completely sure of the reasons for this, But Edward Thompson provides some clues. Firstly, though the events of the last twenty years have shifted all of us to a more anti-Soviet view, there are many, especially in the older age groups, who still feel slightly embarrassed at their preference for the 'capitalist' West over the 'socialist' East, and have not fully thought through its implications. Edward Thompson tells us that, as against the prevailing wisdom in his youth that socialist states could never go to war with one another: 'We now know better. States which call themselves "socialist" can go to war with each other, and do.'[11] Yet he is evidently unwilling to consider the possibility that a state which calls itself 'socialist', i.e. the Soviet Union, might equally commit aggression against a state which does not call itself 'socialist', i.e. Britain or Germany following unilateral disarmament.

A second reason for the apparent reluctance to develop the political implications of CND shows through in Edward Thompson's *New Left Review* article. Here he ascribes the failure of the original CND to its lack of appeal to the generation who came politically of age in 1960, took the Bomb for granted, and preferred to concentrate on anti-imperialist work. It had always seemed to me, when I came into CND in 1960, that the movement had a special appeal to my age group; surely the demise of CND was not the dying-off of its elderly supporters, but the political impasse that the movement had reached. If Edward Thompson takes the 'second generation' editors of *New Left Review* as representative, I feel he is rather out of touch with more widespread ideological currents among those of us who have grown up under the shadow of nuclear holocaust.

As might be expected, the shift in the consensus of radical opinion has been greatest among those whose political socialisation is most recent. The young radicals of today are certainly more firmly for political freedom, more anti-Soviet and more pro-European than my contemporaries were in the early 1960s. But they are so not from a right-wing position, as an ideology justifying capitalist profiteering, but precisely from a left-wing position, an opposition to 'all conditions in which man is a despised, enslaved, neglected and contemptible being',[12] i.e. a position inspired by the same love of humanity that made Edward Thompson's generation supporters of Soviet 'socialism' and made my intermediate generation sit uneasily on the fence as Khrushchev proposed a 'peaceful transition'.

I believe there is the shadowy outline of a new historic bloc, which the younger supporters of CND are objectively part of, and can become consciously part of if the right connections are made. Unilateralism fits together most evidently with the ecological movement, nuclear war being the supreme ecocide, and the two being linked even technically through the nuclear fuel cycle. It can also fit together with women's and gay liberation, in as much as these movements have developed a critique of militarism as the complement of masculine psychology. In both these cases unilateralism can be borne forward on a still ascending tide. But it is also necessary to tackle the key political questions that unilateralism raises, and this I believe can also be done, if in a way very different to that of twenty years ago.

THE SOVIET UNION, EUROPE AND DEMOCRACY

The first question is our relationship to the Soviet Union as the source of possible aggression. The Appeal for European Nuclear Disarmament states: 'We do not wish to apportion guilt between the political and military leaders of East and West... Both parties have adopted menacing postures and committed aggressive actions in different parts of the world.'[13] This is true as far as it goes. Both superpowers and their camp followers share the fundamental guilt of deploying nuclear weapons; and as Bruce Kent reminds us: 'If Afghanistan is a shocker, then so was the inhuman war in Vietnam.'[14] As so often in politics, however, it is what is left unsaid that is crucial. It is Europe the Appeal is particularly concerned with, and in Europe there is no such symmetry between East and West. Here, as far as the writ of the Kremlin holds sway there is brutal repression of all progressive movements, and any pretence of democracy is a fraud. In Western Europe, for all the undoubted evils in our society, the existence of democratic institutions both sets definite limits to injustice, and provides the means for steadily working to erode it. Wherever people have the chance to choose which of the two systems to live under, they vote massively with their feet, whether East German workers fleeing to West Germany, or Polish and Soviet Jews escaping to Israel and the United States. The very idea of a mass migration in the reverse direction is quite ridiculous.

Many of us in the West, if we take only a minute to imagine ourselves living under Brezhnev's 'international dictatorship of the proletariat', can immediately list a whole handful of reasons why life would be personally quite intolerable. In my own case: as someone who tries to work actively for communism, I would long since have ended up in a labour camp; as an intellectual, I would have been asphyxiated by the all-embracing censorship; as a gay man, I would have no possible semblance of a decent existence; and I would suffer persecution by official anti-Semitism on top of everything else.

In the course of the present century, those European countries able to determine their destiny have increasingly become a consolidated zone of democracy, with even Spain, Greece and Portugal finally drawn onto the path pioneered in the northern tier. We have learned, at considerable cost, how to handle conflicts of interest, both between and within nations, in ways that stop short of armed struggle. On our eastern border, however, and biting into Europe as far as the Elbe, there is this bestial system of repression emanating from Moscow, which can permit neither national independence nor democracy.

We might speculate endlessly on the mysteries of Soviet policy formation. But Western Europe very definitely does have something to defend, as much as the citizens of any democratic state might need to defend themselves against a threat of dictatorship generated within their own society. The peoples of Western Europe are generally quite aware of this fact, above all in West Germany, where they have experienced the comparison of social systems most intimately. It is hard to imagine, therefore, that any security policy which does not include maintaining a sufficient military defence can ever win a majority in Britain or any other West European country. Still less could this be the result if the free countries of Europe had to reach a joint decision.

It is quite possible to maintain Western defence without posing any threat of aggression to the Soviet Union, and unilateral nuclear disarmament in Western Europe is the main part of such a change of posture. This would also be the acid test for the professed Soviet desire for genuine detente. If the unilateralist movement could develop into a movement for an alternative defence against the Soviet Union, then it might have a real chance of success. If it does not manage this transition, I fear it will block its own prospects from the start.

I find it difficult today to understand how anyone who tries to support the interest of working people can reject the need for Western defence, and I can only ascribe this to the structures of pro-Soviet ideology, which die hard.[15] As long as we leave the exposure of the Soviet system to reactionaries, we hem ourselves into precisely that political ghetto from which it is imperative to escape. But because the present article will raise objections on this crucial point, I shall just call two witnesses, out of a possible larger number, who have had particular personal experience of the Soviet system from within, and whom it has given particular cause for reflection.

The first is Zdenek Mlynar, former secretary of the central committee of the Communist Party of Czechoslovakia. Mlynar relates how, when the leaders of his country were abducted to Moscow for 'negotiations' following the August 1968 invasion, Brezhnev told them that, had the West tried to intervene in support of Czechoslovak freedom, the Soviets would have resisted 'even at the cost of risking a new war'.[16] It will be said that this was in defence of their existing sphere of influence. But these spheres of influence are precisely an agreement between the Soviets and the Americans. After an American withdrawal from Europe, who is to say exactly where the Soviet sphere of influence ends? In Czechoslovakia, moreover, we know that Soviet tanks suppressed the resurgence of freedom in a country that had developed democratic institutions a full half century before, just like its western neighbours.

The second witness is Rudolf Bahro, formerly in a position of responsibility 'on the ideological front' in the German Democratic Republic. Bahro draws a sympathetic picture of how the 'non-capitalist road' pioneered by the Soviet Union was a natural historical development in many parts of the world; it is simply that it stands in the way once industrialisation is completed. Yet Bahro has this to say about the consciousness of the present Soviet leaders:

'Even in the Soviet Union, where the revolution is already so far in the past that the leaders of today have scarcely learned anything from it but Stalinist bureaucracy, the communist tradition still bequeathes a certain uncomfortable inheritance. If they publicly renounced the idea, they would immediately be swept away. Pursued by an inescapable legitimacy complex, they need a distorted Marxism as their daily bread, and they must even believe in it themselves, at least in certain honest moments, for the sake of their own psychological survival.'[17]

Should we simply laugh, then, when we are reminded from the right that Soviet ideology dictates a policy of expansionism? Not an adventurist one, of course, but that they seek to see their particular flag hoisted over an increasing number of countries as much as those of us who believe in democracy seek to see democracy spread. It is just that dictatorship and democracy have different ways of spreading.

Viewed from the Kremlin, the 'socialist camp' stretches into the very marches of western Europe, dwarfing this little peninsular already in terms of geography. This peninsular however is thickly populated, and populated with highly skilled industrial workers, technologists, managers and scientists. Just across from the GDR, where 17 million Germans contribute so much to the CMEA's industry,

there are nearly four times more Germans again, and with an even
higher per capita product. These diligent workers have been bribed
and befuddled for a long while by their ruling classes, who are subtle
and skilled in the ways of ruling (not like the Romanovs) and have
managed to prolong their death agony an unconscionable long time. But
now the post-War boom really is over and the crisis of capitalism in-
tensifying: just like the 1930s. There are bound to be new violent
conflicts, both internal class conflicts and actual wars. As the
Americans gradually lose interest in Europe, the European states will
fall out among themselves as they always have done - that's at least
one thing the European people ought to be thankful to us and the
Americans for, nearly forty years of peace! That'll show the Eurocommunists a thing or two, it'll be the parties who stay loyal to
Marxism-Leninism that will lead the revolutionary struggles. Now of
course we've no intention of invading Italy, France or even West
Germany - despite everything the Germans have done to us in the past
- but it would be very foolish not to keep a military potential for
intervening in Western Europe if our vital interests were involved.
That's the best way we can ensure they'll be more cooperative with us
once the Americans go, and have a genuine detente as the French at
least seem prepared for sometimes. They talk so much about democracy,
let's see them when a Communist party wins an election victory at
last: their armies would be a bit more careful of any counter-revolu-
tionary coup if they had to take us into account. And once they've
made a revolution, even through parliament, and are allied with us,
then it would be impermissible to let their socialist gains be
wrested away by the forces of capitalism, any more than in Czechoslovakia or Poland.[18]

AN ALTERNATIVE DEFENCE POLICY

Politics & Power shares a broad consensus that the advance to socialism (I'd rather say 'communism')[19] can only proceed by an expansion
of existing democracy, as against the Leninist model of violent overthrow. Many of its articles are specifically designed to explore
positive alternative policies in several fields that a future radical
government could pursue. I strongly believe that this principle needs
to be applied equally to the field of defence. This is not just for
the traditional (and still valid) reason that the more democratic
and civilian an army, the less it can be used for internal repression.
It is also for the specific reason, in the context of the unilateralist campaign, that this will be greatly strengthened by our ability
to oppose the present disastrous policy of nuclear Atlanticism with
an alternative way of providing for the security of the British people
and those democratic institutions on which the strategy of the left
must be based. In place of what calls itself 'defence' but is not,
we need a policy that is genuinely defensive, not rejecting armed
resistance to aggression, but certainly rejecting any policy that
involves massive retaliation against the population of the aggressor
state.
    The ground on which we should challenge the present political
consensus is not the nature or intentions of the Soviet Union, but

rather the appropriate response to this. Not to drop bombs on the
oppressed people of the Soviet cities, in the fine traditions of the
British ruling class. But to make our own country a 'tough piece of
meat',[20] difficult for a potential aggressor to digest. This is the
aim of all systems of territorial defence, such as Sweden, Switzerland
and Yugoslavia already possess in different variants. As an island,
our particular national defence does not require massive conventional
forces. And a small fraction of the money presently squandered on
Polaris and Trident could serve to develop and equip a militia system
that would supplement the regular army in the event of invasion.

This will still be opposed by the right. It is not likely to
bring any large number of Conservatives into the unilateralist movement. But it will strengthen the political case for unilateralism,
making this acceptable to a wider public, while at the same time
linking the campaign in a synergetic relationship of mutual support
with the various struggles that lead in the direction of communism
via an expansion of democracy. There is certainly no guarantee that
the nuclear disarmament movement would be successful if it took such
a route. But this is at least a political route, which is precisely
what CND needs.

Universal military service, at least for men, was a traditional
demand of democrats and socialists. It was voiced by the British
labour movement until about a century ago, but faded as the army
ceased to be perceived as a possible force of internal repression.
(Even if, in the heyday of imperialism, the conscript armies of
other European powers were readily used against the colonised
peoples.) Today, male military service is the norm in all European
countries except Britain, Ireland (another island) and Luxembourg
(indefensible). The mass intake from all points of the class
spectrum, in countries marked by political democracy and the welfare
state, has had an effect quite unlike the recruitment into the
British army of young men with mediocre education, who are promised
a career and given good pay and conditions, in return for not asking
any awkward questions. Reforms already adopted range from relaxed
dress rules in the Netherlands through to trade unionisation in
Norway and 'codetermination' between officers and men in Sweden.
(Here, soldiers' representatives are actually empowered to challenge
any order from an officer except in battle.)

This is however still conscription into a regular armed force.
Switzerland has gone one stage further. It has only 3,500 professional soldiers for a population of 6½ million, and compulsory
basic training lasts only 17 weeks, followed by 3 weeks refresher
training for 8 out of 12 subsequent years, and occasional reserve
duty for some time beyond. Yet the Swiss Army's strength on mobilisation is 625,000, and it has a fair reputation in military
circles.[21]

As part of a radical movement for Britain in the 1980s, we could
campaign for a militia system that is considerably more advanced
than the Swiss. It should reflect as far as possible the principle
that military training is not an obligation imposed on the citizen
by the state, but a right that every citizen has to learn the use
of arms. Provision for conscientious objection should therefore
be extremely broad. Just as important, military training should be

open to women as well as men, on an absolutely equal basis. Besides
giving support to women's struggle for liberation, this will be an
additional tie to bind the armed forces to their proper task of serving the people.[22] From this base in the militia, it would be easier
for women to demand integration into the regular forces. Related to
this, gay men should also be able to play a full part in the military,
without being in any way forced to conceal our identity.[23]

A militia system of this kind would undoubtedly have a very beneficial effect on British society, increasing the confidence of working
people and maybe even providing a framework of self-discipline against
the wave of violent assault against women (rape), old people (mugging)
and gays (queer-bashing) that is an everyday fact of life in so many
of our cities. (Maybe this is dimly grasped by those who say: 'they
should bring back national service'.) Though such a militia would be
quite unprecedented in our peacetime life, there is a point of reference in the Home Guard of 1940-45.[24]

Whether the regular army could be reduced to Swiss proportions
(i.e. about 30,000, allowing for our greater population), or would
have to remain somewhere in between this and its present level of
160,000 (excluding navy and air force), is essentially a function of
our relationship with our European neighbours.

The argument for defending democracy applies equally to all West
European nations. Why then should American withdrawal mean the end
of defence cooperation between our countries, which are already
allied in so many other ways?[25] Indeed, if the zone of democracy in
Europe is divided, it will scarcely be able to withstand a determined
Soviet push forward - in which the military card is never the only
one. West Germany is a nation of 62 million, while the Soviet Union
has 260 million, more than four times as many. If defence is defined
as the defence of democracy, then why shouldn't British democrats see
the defence of German democracy as inseparable from their own?
American withdrawal, it seems to me, only makes the presence of the
British Army on the Rhine more important, if this is the clear wish
of the West German people.

Britain's position in Europe is a special one: both because of our
outlying geography, and because of our relationship with the English-
speaking world overseas. Both may lead us to feel that the problems
of the Continent are not our problems: an attitude that led to disaster once before in this century. We have a degree of freedom that
West Germany does not have towards the Soviet Union, no more than
Czechoslovakia did towards Hitler, but the other side of this is a
greater responsibility.

France left the NATO military organisation in 1966. Britain
could scrap Polaris and leave NATO tomorrow (officially, at one
year's notice) without making any immediate difference to the European
situation. NATO will continue to exist as long as the Americans feel
committed enough to Germany, i.e. to the existing frontier between
the two social systems. With Britain out of NATO, however, the
balance will shift towards American withdrawal, and isn't this what
we all want? If the issue of Britain leaving NATO comes seriously
onto the political agenda, then the issue of European defence
cooperation will necessarily arise side by side. And if unilateralism is identified with an anti-European position in military

relations, as the Labour left has always been identified with an anti-European position in economic and political relations, then there will be very many who are unconvinced by its political argument, and remain in thrall to the NATO establishment. A campaign that actually championed European defence cooperation, on the other hand, as an alternative to NATO, would stand a far greater chance of achieving nuclear disarmament.

Finally, there is the question of civil defence. It was the present government's despicable handbook *Protect and Survive* that gave the immediate occasion for Edward Thompson's pamphlet. CND is on firm ground in attacking in the strongest terms the entire so-called civil defence policy followed in this country for the past thirty years. Though for the same reason I hardly think this can be described as a 'new twist in the spiral of the arms race',[26] even in a nuclear-weapon state such as ours.

As argued above, the abandonment of nuclear weapons provides no guarantee against nuclear attack. The problem of possible nuclear blackmail has to be faced one way or another. The Swiss state, accordingly, showing for all its faults a genuine concern for the survival of its people, has shelter facilities for 80 per cent of the country's population. Anyone who has inspected or even seen photographs of these will be as impressed as by the same type of thing in Yugoslavia or China. They bear no resemblance to William Whitelaw's mockery. But again, should the unilateralist movement not strengthen its case by demonstrating a positive alternative to the present civil defence farrago, if it wants to convince the majority?

I have tried in this article to criticise the orientation of CND from a position of fundamental solidarity with its aims. There is always a danger, with political movements basing themselves on a moral appeal, that in the eagerness to spread a universal message, key corners in the argument are cut. CND, I believe, has always fallen into this trap, and yet the political consensus that buoyed it up twenty years ago has now largely evaporated. CND cannot simply repeat its campaign of the early 1960s, starting from a stronger base in the Labour movement and with greater support in the opinion polls. Lord Carrington recently predicted that, should Michael Foot become Prime Ministers, the realities of the situation would lead him to maintain nuclear deterrence;[27] I would agree. The new CND castle is being built on sand, and will collapse if it ever has to show the colour of its metal. The only way to effect a radical change of policy is by offering a genuine alternative. This may look a steeper hill to climb, but any progress made in this direction is at least on firm ground. I have given reasons why I am far from pessimistic, and believe that nuclear disarmament can be borne forward as part of a new radical programme. But 'protest and survive' is not enough. CND has evidently struck a chord. It has not yet tapped the energies that can lead it to victory.

Footnotes

1 It was only the rise of CND that turned upholders of the status quo into 'multilateralists'; just as the rise of the gay movement made the straight majority define themselves as 'heterosexuals'.

2 From contemplating such horror, Edward Thompson very wisely says: 'The deformed human mind is the ultimate doomsday weapon'. (E.P. Thompson and Dan Smith (eds.), *Protest and Survive*, Penguin Special, 1980, p.52).

3 'Notes on Exterminism, the Last Stage of Civilisation', *New Left Review* 121, May-June 1980, p.29.

4 See in particular Alva Myrdal, 'The Superpowers' Gave Over Europe', (*Protest and Survive*, pp.77-109).

5 *New Statesman*, 15 August 1980.

6 'Protest and Survive' (*Protest and Survive*, p.59).

7 *Weekend World*, London Weekend Television, 16 November 1980.

8 'Notes from the Concrete Grass Roots' (*Protest and Survive*, p.252).

9 This article was ready to go to press when I saw advance proofs of Raymond Williams' reply to Edward Thompson's 'Exterminism' - 'The Politics of Nuclear Disarmament', *New Left Review* 124, Nov-Dec 1980. Here the same weakness in the CND argument is indicated, i.e. its lack of politics, but from a position a long way from mine. Raymond Williams does not share Edward Thompson's reservations at referring to the Soviet Union as a *socialist* state, distorted but without apostrophes, while he wants the disarmament proposals of the West European left to be 'integral with renewed efforts to advance *socialism* within our own countries' (p.17). If the CND case is weakened by Edward Thompson's deliberate lack of politics, it would have far less force of conviction encumbered by the politics of Raymond Williams.

10 As that wily old philosopher Georg Lukács put it: 'Better the worst socialist country than the best capitalist country.'

11 'Protest and Survive' (*Protest and Survive*, p.49).

12 Karl Marx, 'Critique of Hegel's Philosophy of Right, Introduction', *Early Writings*, Pelican Marx Library, 1975, p.251.

13 *Protest and Survive*, p.224.

14 op.cit., p.252.

15 See my article 'Die Soziale Basis prosowjetischer Ideologie', *Befreiung* 11, Berlin (West), 1977.

16 Zdenek Mlynar, *Nightfrost in Prague*, London, Hurst, 1980, p.241.

17 Rudolf Bahro, *The Alternative in Eastern Europe*, London, NLB, 1978, p.239.

18 Cf. article from Moscow *New Times* quoted in *The Times*, 18 Nov 1980.

19 See my article 'Eurocommunism and the Ethical Ideal', Mike Prior (ed.), *The Popular and the Political* (London, Routledge, 1980).

20 This expression is from the Chinese. The question of China is always a good test for survivals of pro-Soviet ideology. Bruce Kent, for example, shows the cloven hoof as follows: 'Once we realise that the West has effectively made a military alliance with the Chinese, who regularly talk about war with the Russians, we can understand that the Russians might well have reason for a certain amount of additional anxiety' (op.cit., p.252). Three readily verifiable facts will serve to refute this insidious percolation:

(1) Soviet reference to the 'yellow peril' at the highest level
(Khrushchev), dates from the early 1960s.
(2) The possibility of detente between the United States and
China was opened in August 1969, when Soviet diplomats sounded
out the likely Western attitude to a Soviet 'first strike'
against Chinese targets.
(3) The Soviet Union, besides its strategic nuclear forces
targeted on China, maintains 46 highly mechanised divisions on
its (and 'Mongolia's') border with China, scarcely 300 miles
of grassland from Beijing. There is absolutely no way China
could present an equivalent threat to Soviet security, however
it tried.
Which side, then, should be anxious about a possible war?

21 See General Frank Seethaler, 'The Tactics of Dissuasion', *New
    Statesman*, 7 November 1980.

22 The only armies able to recruit large numbers of women for a
    combat role have been genuinely defensive ones. In Britain in
    1940, there were many women who wanted to bear arms; an 'Amazon
    Defence League' was formed, and Dr Edith Summerskill unsuccess-
    fully demanded that women should be allowed to join the Home
    Guard on equal terms with men. Tom Wintringham, the left's
    leading military spokesperson at the time, strongly supported
    this demand, explaining that 'whenever a people has been
    fighting for its life, the women have joined in' (*Picture Post*,
    15 June 1940).

23 Homosexuality in the British armed forces is still a criminal
    offence punishable by imprisonment, as well as grounds for
    discharge. In August 1980 the press reported yet again a
    further type of 'discharge': the bullying of a gay soldier by
    his comrades until he committed suicide. This is becoming an
    important issue for the gay movement.

24 See my articles 'A New Look at Dad's Army', *New Statesman*, 24
    October 1980; and 'Tom Wintringham: Britain's Forgotten Marxist',
    History Workshop 11, Spring 1981.

25 Dan Smith, in his contribution to the *Protest and Survive* volume
    ('The European Nuclear Theatre'), commends the European nuclear
    disarmament movement 'precisely because it does challenge NATO's
    unity' (p.123). But his argument, like all others in CND,
    sidesteps the crucial issue of whether the West European
    nations have a common defence need that is quite distinct from
    any American interest.

26 'Notes from the Concrete Grass Roots', loc.cit., p.247.

27 *Weekend World*, London Weekend Television, 16 November 1980.

D. Sassoon
The Silences of *New Left Review*

'... and what we cannot talk about we must pass over in
silence...' - Wittgenstein

1   INTRODUCTION

Just over twenty years ago *New Left Review* emerged as a result of the
fusion of *The New Reasoner* and *Universities and Left Review*. Two
years later political differences had paralyzed the board. The
vacuum was filled by Perry Anderson, Tom Nairn and Robin Blackburn.
Anderson's version of the 'take-over' can be found in *Arguments
Within English Marxism* (henceforth AWEM), pp.136-39. Its exact
history need not detain us further, nor do we have any reason to
doubt the veracity of Anderson's account. The small group which
began to edit the review in 1962, soon to be joined by other members,
succeeded in maintaining a substantial cohesion. The present editorial board has changed little in the past fifteen years. All this
represents a remarkable achievement. Journals have appeared and
disappeared in the fragmented world of British left-wing politics.
New Left Review (henceforth NLF) not only survived the difficult
early years, but quickly succeeded in establishing itself as the
major Marxist journal in this country and one of the foremost, if
not *the* foremost, in the English-speaking world. It expanded its
readership and the spectrum and numbers of its contributors. It
developed a publishing house which has been instrumental in the
diffusion of major foreign texts in a country notoriously proud of
its cultural self-sufficiency. Its individual members have contributed in general to the expansion of a socialist culture in this
country making their marks in diverse fields of study, from Japanese
capitalism to the Middle East and Iran, from Cuba to Scottish
Nationalism, from literary criticism to the study of Ancient and
Absolutist societies, from feminism to political economy, from
social history to psychoanalysis.

The revival of Marxist studies which has paralleled the growth of
the review cannot be disassociated from the diffusion of the works of
Antonio Gramsci and Louis Althusser. It was a former member of the
editorial board who was responsible for the translation of Althusser's
works. It was New Left Books which published them in conjunction with
those of his foremost pupils Etienne Balibar and Nicos Poulantzas.
It was another member of the Review who translated and edited parts
of Gramsci's works.

For the generation which grew up politically in the 1960s and 1970s
NLR has always been a fundamental point of reference. That this has
been the case even when the bulk of this generation has not adopted
the political position of the Review is a sign of its openness, of its
refusal to publish only those texts whose political position it could
share wholeheartedly. Yet this also signifies that the role of the
Review has been mainly a cultural one, that its task has been essentially one of *presenting texts*, offering theoretical frameworks, providing information. It is not a negative role. But this is not what
the Review was about or intended to be about.

Political 'intellectual' journals have, explicitly or implicitly,
an obvious ambition: to become a terrain of ideological unification
for intellectual groups. The potential 'market' NLR was facing was
one whose central terrain of mobilization was the Campaign for Nuclear
Disarmament. CND had achieved something unique: it had coalesced
large groups of people which had, as social groups, practically no
tradition of popular mobilization. In a sense CND was the harbinger
of future 'middle-class' single-issue pressure groups which would
become a feature of political life in the 1960s and 1970s. But CND,
in the eyes of the young editors of the Review, was doomed to failure
because of its pragmatism and moralism. It represented all the
limitations of the British radical tradition. The Review, once
the new board had 'taken over', had to set itself the task of presenting broad strategic guidelines to the remnants of this movement.
Not only did it fail to do so, but it also failed to offer a serious
strategic perspective which could be a rallying point for the
intellectual forces which have been politicized in the 1960s and
1970s. This is its central failure. What follows is a re-examination of the cultural production of NLR over these past twenty years
with a special emphasis on the post-1968 period. The criticisms
which result from the analysis of the contents should not detract
from the very real achievements which are outlined above.

The analysis of the contents, in any case, is not an exhaustive
one. Certain areas of study which have been often debated in the
review are not mentioned (e.g. the debates on literary criticism or
the coverage of the 'socialist' countries). Space and time prevent
a wider and deeper treatment. It is in any case unlikely that
further examination of the contents would substantially modify the
direction of the criticisms. The anniversary date which is used as
the excuse for this assessment is, of course, misleading. NLR is not
twenty years old except in the most banal chronological sense. The
story of the present NLR does not begin in 1960. It begins later,
when, after a period of adjustment, it starts to delineate its central
project. The starting-point of the analysis can only be the writings
on British history with which Tom Nairn and Perry Anderson announced

the theoretical break with the tradition of British Marxism represented by E.P. Thompson.

The continuation of this *querelle* after so many years, Thompson's
attack on Althusser, the reprinting of his 1965 polemic against the
new board of NLR ('The Peculiarities of the British' in *The Socialist
Register*), the 250-page book by Anderson against Thompson (AWEM) may
suggest that this article is an intervention in *that* debate. This is
not the case. Although a partisan stand is taken, particularly in
the concluding remarks, it is not in favour of either Anderson or
Thompson. Even the two contestants would admit that the world is
not divisible between Andersonians and Thompsonians. It is, however,
true that in the specific situation facing NLR in the early 1960s
those two positions exemplified the two most likely roads the Review
could in fact take. If that was really the case, there is very
little doubt that the left as a whole should be pleased that Anderson
'won' the contest. It is, of course, highly unlikely that Thompson
would have carried out the work of publishing the review. Anderson's
own account clearly indicates that the young editors of the review
'inherited' a journal no-one was prepared to edit.

One can, of course, speculate as to what a Thompsonian direction
of the review would have produced. The chances are that we would
have had twenty years of British labour and social history increasingly refreshed by periodical bouts of controlled hysteria of the kind
amply illustrated in the final pages of *The Poverty of Theory*.

Let us start, then, by the real beginning: the Nairn-Anderson
theses.

2   THE NAIRN-ANDERSON THESES

The series of essays which came to be known as the Nairn-Anderson
theses were both an attempt to map out the future project of the
journal and the beginning of a discussion. They amounted in fact to
the editorial programme of the review.

Looking back at the endogenous product of the editorial board since
then, one can immediately see how path-breaking and important the
theses were. They sought, to quote Anderson (AWEM, 138): '... to
provide a systematic historical explanation of the configuration of
class forces in English society and the nature of the present crisis
of British capitalism.' The polemic on these texts is well known.
The historical accuracy of the Nairn-Anderson theses has been examined
elsewhere and in any case does not concern us here. It may, however,
be useful to recall the central elements of these theses:
    'The distinctive facets of English class structure, as it has
    evolved over three centuries, can thus be summed up as follows.
    After a bitter, cathartic revolution, which transformed the
    structure but not the superstructures of English society, a
    landed aristocracy, underpinned by a powerful mercantile
    affinal group, became the first dominant capitalist class in
    Britain. This dynamic agrarian capitalism expelled the English
    peasantry from history. Its success was economically the
    'floor' and sociologically the 'ceiling' of the rise of the
    industrial bourgeoisie. Undisturbed by a feudal state,

terrified of the French Revolution and its own proletariat,
mesmerized by the prestige and authority of the landed class,
the bourgeoisie won two modest victories, lost its nerve and
ended up by losing its identity. The late Victorian era and
the high noon of imperialism welded aristocracy and bourgeoisie
in a single social bloc. The working class fought passionately
and unaided against the advent of industrial capitalism; its
extreme exhaustion after successive defeats was the measure of
its efforts. Henceforward it evolved, separate but subordinate,
within the apparently unshakable structure of British capitalism, unable, despite its great numerical superiority, to
transform the fundamental nature of British society.'
(Anderson, NLR 23, pp.38-39).

Thus the bourgeois revolution in Britain was not a revolution at all.
It was a compromise, a real 'historic' compromise in the strong sense,
not a mere tactical deal: 'Inside this permanent, organic "compromise" the landlords kept control of the State and its main organs,
as a government elite trusted (on the whole) by the bourgeoisie'
(Nairn, NLR 23, p.20). The central concepts of these studies came
from Nairn's and Anderson's interpretation of Gramsci, then
completely unknown in this country. Thompson's embarrassing attempt
to refute Anderson's reading of Gramsci was nearly entirely based
on an article written in 1960 by Gwyn Williams.

It is in a sense significant that the first attempt by the young
editors of the review to give a historical explanation of the configuration of class forces in English society had to rely on, so to
speak, 'imported Marxism' even though the chosen field was history
and when, by all accounts, history was, with economics, the privileged
terrain of development of British marxism. The necessity of importation was demonstrated by the text itself. The 'historic compromise'
mapped out by Nairn and Anderson had created a situation in which
'the working class could not distance itself aggressively from
society and constitute its own autonomous movement towards social
hegemony. The cutting instrument needed for this task was lacking.
That is, an intellectual stratum torn adrift from the social consensus with sufficient force and capable of functioning as catalyst to
the new force striving for expression against the consensus' (Nairn,
NLR 28, p.49).

The British working class did not produce its own stratum of
organic intellectuals. It did not produce its Rosa Luxemburg, its
Lenin, its Gramsci. Anderson now makes amends for having 'forgotten'
William Morris, and underestimated Maurice Dobb's contribution (AWEM,
p.139). These two names, of course, do not amount to a stratum, but
Anderson interprets the Gramscian proposition 'intellectual stratum'
as meaning a group of 'great intellectuals'. These reorganize
cultural relations and contribute to the formation of a new 'common
sense' of the masses. Now it is true that Gramsci uses the expression intellectuals also as meaning 'great intellectuals'. But his
true originality resides elsewhere. The originality lies in a novel
definition of the State as the 'ensemble' of activities which organize and render homogeneous the masses, establish the relations of
representation of the 'led' by the 'leaders', and involve the masses
in the State itself. The activities of the State construct the

integration of the led within the State. The led are integrated, *qua*
led, into the ensemble of state activities. The State then is the
organisation of the relation between leaders and led and intellectuals are precisely the group of people which organise such relations.
They cannot be reduced to the 'great intellectuals'.

Now when Nairn says that the working class could not become hegemonic because it did not possess an intellectual stratum sufficiently
independent from society which would 'function as a catalyst' he
gives an order of (relative) priority: the intellectual stratum must
be created in order to break up (or, at least, begin to break up) the
relation of subordination. The order of causality is such that it is
the non-hegemonic nature of bourgeois culture itself which pre-empts
the rise of a powerful intellectual group of the working class.

But before turning to examine the failures of the British
bourgeoisie let us return to a particular problem. In the passage
quoted above, Nairn stated that because of the 'historic compromise'
between landed interests and the bourgeoisie the working class could
not distance itself from society. This implies that it was integrated.
Yet Anderson argued that what blocked the emergence of a 'universal
ideology' in the British working class was its very separatedness:
'A combination of structural and conjunctional factors in the 19th
century produced a proletariat distinguished by an immovable corporate
class-consciousness and almost no hegemonic ideology... The English
working class has since the mid-19th century been essentially characterised by an extreme disjunction between an intense consciousness of
separate identity and a permanent failure to set and impose goals for
society as a whole' (Anderson, NLR 23, pp.41-42). But there is only
an apparent contradiction between Nairn's view that the working class
has not been able to separate itself from society and Anderson's view
that the problem is that it is enclosed in its own ghetto. The
mechanism of subordination of the led by the leaders operated precisely in this way. It integrated the working class as a separate
'ghettoised' working class. The existence of a revolutionary
intellectual stratum would have, for Anderson, challenged that
mechanism.

Here we face the most famous of the Nairn-Anderson theses: 'In
England, a supine bourgeoisie produced a subordinate proletariat.
It handed on no impulse of liberation, no revolutionary values, no
universal language' (Anderson, NLR 23, p.43). In other words 'no
Rousseau'. In his reply to Thompson Anderson explained that it was
not his intention to say that the English bourgeoisie had no cultural
achievements to its credit; 'What we said was that it produced no
major *political philosophy* that became hegemonic in the society.'

No major political philosophy indeed! Hobbes destroyed the ideological foundations of feudal society by removing at a stroke all
theology from politics and mapping out an independent field of
politics structured by its own autonomous rules. Locke, before Kant,
tackled the problem of reconciling formal equality with real inequality establishing the ideological foundation for the separation
between politics and economics. And then there appear the colossal
figures of Smith and Ricardo. But what is said of Smith and Ricardo
in Anderson? With Smith, he says, we have the 'hidden hand' replacing the 'general will'; 'political economy ... was a hypnotic,

monocular account of the economic system'; 'political economy was not
a comprehensive social thought - a *total theory of man and society*'
(Anderson, NLR 35, p.24 - my emphasis). Here we face what is an
obvious shift in argument, a 'slippage' we might say, from the quest
for a hegemonic major political philosophy to a 'total theory of man
and society'. But we have yet another 'slippage' which clearly
emerges in the next sentence when the double failure of the British
bourgeoisie *and* proletariat is that of not having produced '... either
a Marxism or a *Classical Sociology* of any serious kind.... It is
unique among major European nations. Britain alone has produced
neither a Lenin, a Lukacs, a Gramsci - nor a Weber, a Durkheim, a
Pareto' (Anderson, NLR 35, p.24 - my emphasis). Thus a 'total theory
of man and society' = 'a major political philosophy' = 'Classical
Sociology'. And 'Classical sociology' is a 'synthetic social thought'
which supersedes discrete 'political theory', 'economics' and 'history'.

Our purpose is not to refute the theoretical underpinnings of the
above. The pride of place given to Classical Sociology could be
questioned. The reduction of Smith's discovery to the axiom of the
'hidden hand' is ludicrous. It is very probable that Anderson would
not wish, after all, to defend every line; even though, after over
fifteen years, he seems to regret only the violence of his polemic
(AWEM, p.139). What does not function in Anderson's presentation is
that we move from the domain of an analysis which seeks to establish
the lack of a hegemonic form of bourgeois culture to one which seeks
to establish that British bourgeois culture is somehow 'inferior' to
that produced by the Continental bourgeoisie. But what is the criterion of 'inferiority'? It is clearly not a political one; i.e. one
which would seek to examine the effectiveness of bourgeois cultural
hegemony.

In fact the bourgeoisie is so hegemonic that it has operated in
such a way as to prevent the possibility of the development of a
hegemonic working class. Its failure to develop a Classical Sociology
is said to be one of the chief causes in the prevention of the rise
of a British Gramsci, Lenin, Lukacs. All in all, one should simply
take a couple of steps back and stare in admiration at this political
masterpiece. Of all the sins of the British bourgeoisie we could
enumerate we certainly could not include that of being 'politically'
more ineffectual than its European counterparts. What does Anderson
then mean by 'inferiority'? The test he seems to have proposed was
that of political cultural hegemony. Silently this test is abandoned
and another one seems to appear: 'intellectual standards'. This is
evident in the discussion on utilitarianism, the one candidate for
the role of 'major political philosophy'. Alas, 'Utilitarianism was
too crude and one-dimensional to triumph over society at large'
(Anderson, NLR 35, p.19). Anderson's profound distaste (not an
unjustifiable one) for utilitarianism had been violently evidenced
in his 'Origins of the present crisis'. The Utilitarians, the
positivistic ideologues of the mid-19th century, and their successors, the Fabians, are guilty of 'complacent confusion of influence
with power, bovine admiration for bureaucracy, ill-concealed contempt
for equality, bottomless philistinism ...' (NLR 23, p.39). And,
'Even in its original form as an ideology of the bourgeoisie, the

limitations of utilitarianism prevented it from becoming a hegemonic force'.

So, having forgotten Hobbes and Locke, dismissed Smith and Ricardo, Anderson has proceeded to exclude on grounds of 'quality' the Bentham-Webb axis. Yet is it not this axis which has operated over the last hundred years as the authentic ideological pillar of the British State? Is it not the notion of the separability of reforms (social engineering) whose tasks of identification and implementations will have to be the domain of a stratum of intellectuals and functionaries 'separated' from society, which is the authentic 'glue' which has managed to keep British society together, the leaders and the led, over two major crises, two major wars, the dissolution of an empire, and all that without any serious challenge to the order of society itself? Is it not this tradition from whence came the ideas of the two great reforming administrations this country has had: the 1906 Liberal government and the 1945 Labour government? Is it not abundantly clear that precisely because this tradition has also permeated Labourism that it is a truly hegemonic one? And not only in this country. It was again this tradition which in its Keynes-Beveridge form provided the framework for the post-War consensus of welfare statism, that very welfare statism which is now under challenge (but from the Right not from the Left).

In a recent issue of the Review Michael Rustin wrote that: 'The intellectual thrust of much Marxist writing, for example in the social sciences and in *New Left Review*, has been specifically directed against Fabianism, centrism and reformism, as if they were the principal obstruction to progress' (NLR 121, p.71). Indirectly yes, that indeed has been the direction of the subsequent work of NLR. But only indirectly. Anderson's strictures against the British tradition of philosophic radicalism and its Fabian-welfare statist inheritors remained, after 1968, undeveloped.

NLR has over the last fifteen years published critiques of Rousseau (Della Volpe NLR 59, Gerratana NLR 111), Freud (Althusser NLR 55, Lacan NLR 51, Timpanaro NLR 91 and NLR 95, Rycroft NLR 118, Middleton NLR 113-4), Leopardi (Timpanaro NLR 116), Hegel (Plant NLR 103 and 104), Heidegger (Gerratana NLR 107), Darwin (Gerratana NLR 82), Nietzsche (Gerratana NLR 111), but it has failed to publish a single critique of Hobbes, Locke, Hume, Classical political economy, the Utilitarians, the Fabians, the British school of analytic philosophy. And it is not only non-Marxist British culture which has received scant attention in its pages. Non-Marxist *European* culture, as can be seen from the list above, has been investigated only to a very limited extent. Particularly remarkable is the total absence of any articles on those masters of 'Classical Sociology' which Anderson has specifically indicated as being the authentic pillar of hegemonic bourgeois culture' there has been nothing at all on Weber, nothing on Durkheim, nothing on Pareto.

In his counter-attack against Thompson's criticisms, Anderson pointed out that the Nairn-Anderson theses were not to be considered the conclusion of a research but only temporary theses, the beginning of a discussion. This was certainly the way they had been presented. Why was the work not carried on? What is the motive for this

inexplicable silence? That that work needed to be carried on was and
is unquestionable. In what constitutes the second stage of Nairn and
Anderson's investigations, i.e. Perry Anderson's 'The Components of a
National Culture', he wrote:

'A political science capable of guiding the working class
movement to final victory will only be born within a general
intellectual matrix which challenges bourgeois ideology in
every sector of thought and represents a decisive, hegemonic
alternative to the cultural status quo. It is enough to say
this, to be reminded that in Britain, at present, there is
virtually no organized combat of any kind, anywhere along the
front. Worse than this, we do not have even an elementary
cartography of the terrain that must be disputed. The most
influential socialist work of the past decade was called
Culture and Society. Yet the British Left has few analyses
of its own society: it has none of its culture.'
(NLR 50, pp.4-5)

'Components of the National Culture' was a remarkable intellectual
tour de force, whatever its limits. Yet, after that, after what
Anderson himself described as being no more than a 'preliminary inventory', there has been next to nothing at all (that is apart from
a few articles on Literary Criticism and British Anthropology). Let
us then examine this 'preliminary inventory' for it may contain the
key with which to decipher the successive silence of the *New Left
Review*. 'Components' is in direct succession to the 'Origins of the
Present Crisis'. It opens by reiterating the accusation concerning
the lack of a Classical Sociology, what it now calls the 'absent
centre', in the UK, and the parallel failure to develop an indigenous
Marxism. To the absence of a native Classical Sociology Anderson
counterposes what he called a special feature of British cultural
life after the First World War: the dominance of conservative
'White' emigrés who in a relatively short period of time colonize
British culture. The names of these *maîtres d'école*? Here is
Anderson's list (p.17):

Ludwig Wittgenstein: Philosophy
Bronislaw Malinowski: Anthropology
Lewis Namier: History
Karl Popper: Social Theory
Ernst Gombrich: Aesthetics
H-J Eysenck: Psychology
Melanie Klein: Psychoanalysis

All in all four Austrians, one German, one Russian and two Poles.
The only two British names admitted in the Pantheon are Leavis
(Literary Criticism) and Keynes (Economics). It would be tedious
to start a long examination of the relative claims to the status of
maître d'école. Anderson himself recognizes that the achievements
of the 'white emigrés' are varied. To the brilliance and originality
of Wittgenstein it would be fruitless to counterpose the ideological
tenuousness of Berlin or the superficiality of Eysenck. Similarly
there is no point in attempting to find British names to counterpose
to Anderson's own choice (e.g. why not Oakeshott instead of Berlin,
Russell instead of Wittgenstein, why not mention that Eysenck's
work is not a German invention which has arrived on these shores

when Eysenck himself stepped out of the boat but the development and
continuation of the British school of psychometrics of Sir Francis
Galton, Karl Pearson, Charles Spearman and, last but not least,
Cyril 'Fraud' Burt). Suffice it to say that Anderson makes no
attempt to justify the claims he makes for the names on his list.
This is not a criticism which should be made only of this particular article. As we shall see, time and time again NLR presents
to its English readers various European Marxist texts selected with
criteria which are never made explicit.

The point we wish to make here then is not one of simple disagreement with the names on the list, or with their intellectual contribution. It is not in fact a question of the intellectual excellence of
Anderson's 'Modern Masters', intellectual excellence on which Anderson
himself has its doubts, or the fact that the demolition job on, for
instance, Wittgenstein is rather crude and entirely based on Gellner's
Words and Things. The question, surely, is whether the intellectuals
listed can be said to have really contributed in a determinant manner
to the consolidation and/or reorganization of the hegemony of the
dominant classes. For Anderson these are the distinctive contribution of the 'white emigrés' (p.19):
1 Having chosen Britain as a refuge from the tempestuous conflicts
  which were devastating Europe they 'flattered and enlarged every
  insular reflex and prejudice'.
2 They rejuvenated the traditional social science disciplines
  which, in Britain, having missed both of the 'great synthetic
  revolutions' (i.e. Marxism and Classical Sociology), were dying
  of 'inanition'.
3 They codified the slovenly empiricism of the past, and thereby
  hardened and narrowed it.
But if the main contribution of the 'white emigrés' has been simply
to ensure the rejuvenation of disciplines taught in university
departments by codifying something which already existed (the
slovenly empiricism of the past), then the effort is simply not
warranted. The point of the whole of the Nairn-Anderson theses
centres on the necessity to map out the central categories and concepts which have permitted the transformations of the British state
over the last hundred years, which have imbued the Labour movement
in such a way as to prevent the formation of a 'national class with
national aspirations', which have enabled intellectual forces to
become a mass without the upheavals registered in France or Italy,
etc. This is surely what was needed, not only according to the
present writer, but, according to the principal editors of the NLR
in the mid-1960s, that is in the crucial period which immediately
precedes the rise of the student movement, the development of massive
mobilizations around Vietnam, the growth of new political subjects
such as the women's movement and the diffusion of popular forms of
culture. The point of examining the achievements of great intellectual figures is surely not the mere academic exercise of distributing
diplomas of excellence, but that of ascertaining the extent to which
the central ideas of these intellectuals have become 'common sense',
have imbued society, constituting the ideological framework for a
remapping of social relations, of the relations between leaders and
led, of the relations between civil society and the State.

That central task was performed in Britain and it was performed by British intellectuals, whose talent, ability, lucidity, political acumen and - why not? - genius ensured that their ideas would travel outside these narrow shores and pervade other political systems. A talent, lucidity, ability, political acumen and genius, let me add, which is demonstrated not by any reference to criteria of excellence, but to criteria of political and social effectivity.

There have been (and here I schematize enormously) three broad developments of the modern State in the period demarcated by three central events, namely, the First World War, the Great Crash and the Second World War. These three broad developments were:

1 The development of a centrally planned economy under the direction of the Party-State (USSR and, after 1945, other countries);

2 An authoritarian form of capitalist state under the direction of a party-state which oversees a new form of State intervention in the economy under the sign of the mobilization from above not only of masses of people but of a new form of intellectual, the intellectual-functionary of a new social order, a figure unknown to classical liberalism (the case of Fascist Italy and Nazi Germany);

3 The Welfare State which, while maintaining and developing the legitimacy of political institutions which it inherits from a previous period, also develops and enlarges the political system by establishing new relationships of compromise with trades unions, employers associations, etc., and takes it upon itself to socialise some costs of production (e.g. transport, energy, etc.) and some of the cost of reproduction (expansion of education, health schemes, pension schemes) and, finally, to ensure successfully (at least until the late 1960s) economic expansion, low unemployment, rising welfare.

It is with this third development that we are concerned. There are three outstanding examples of this:

(a) Weimar Republic
(b) The American New Deal
(c) The British Welfare State.

The first resulted in a failure. The second never raised itself above the level of the most naked empiricism (but then it never needed to). The third, the British example, is undoubtedly the most outstanding not only in its practical implementation (viz. the long social-democratic consensus which has maintained its hegemony at least until 1979-80, but the war is not over yet) but also in its theoretical and cultural form. The achievements of John Maynard Keynes are so outstanding and unquestionable that they need not detain us. Keynes is acknowledged to be a *maître d'école* by Anderson himself, even though he reduces him to a mere theorist of the short-term (not a bad thing either, what the Left has always most visibly lacked was any idea of what to do in the short run, but *passim*). In Anderson's list we find no-one else who made the slightest contribution to the construction of the modern British political system. Berlin, indicated as the *'maître d'école'* of Political Theory, has done little more than restating the case for classical liberalism. As for Popper, the only possible candidate, it can hardly be said that his pronouncements in favour of piecemeal 'social engineering' are any advance on the British tradition of Utilitarian and Fabian radicalism.

To be sure, if we start using the category of 'Great Intellectual' to attempt to find the other 'theorists of the Welfare State', we would be in an embarrassing situation. Beveridge's achievements are certainly remarkable. Not very many other intellectuals have seen their ideas and proposals become so 'hegemonic' in society. But Beveridge was obviously no Weber. The 'great theorist' of the Welfare State was a 'collective intellectual' made up of a veritable mass of politicians, academics, chairmen of Royal Commission, pamphleteers, functionaries, broadcasters, journalists and government advisers. The individuals making up this collective intellectual may have had different formal political allegiances, but these always remained relatively irrelevant because they were never the cadres of any single political party: they were the functionaries of the new 'State', the organizers of a new consensus which imprisoned in one way or the other the two principal political parties of the British political system.

This collective theorist has obviously not produced a 'total theory of man', nor a 'classical sociology'. It produced something better: political hegemony. It acted according to Gramsci's particular notion of the intellectuals:

> 'By "intellectuals" must be understood not those strata commonly described by this term, but in general the entire social stratum which exercises an organisational function in the wide sense - whether in the field of production, or in that of culture, or in that of political administration. They correspond to the NCOs and junior officers in the army, and also partly to the higher officers who have risen from the ranks.'
>
> (*Selections from the Prison Notebooks*, p.97)

Anderson's transformation of Gramscian concepts and their transposition in the UK context had been done too mechanically. Gramsci's polemic against Croce cannot simply be reproduced as a polemic against 'great intellectuals' in terms of their alleged influence within specific academic disciplines. Gramsci had chosen Croce as the adversary whom it was necessary to confront because Croce, not only in his philosophical work, but also in his organizational and historiographical one, had reorganized the Italian petty bourgeois intelligentsia by reaffirming its separatedness from the peasantry and the labour movement and stressing its cosmopolitanism and non-national mentality. Croceanism is treated therefore as a political force and as the most articulate exponent of the underlying unity of Italian intellectual strata. There is no parallel unity among the great intellectuals identified by Anderson. They all represent the separatedness of academic disciplines. They do not form a collective ideological cement. They are not the 'collective' British Croce.

The 'slippage' from Gramsci leads Anderson away from a correct identification of the 'real target' and hence into the silence which will characterize the review's relations with British culture. But the silence is not coterminous with the boundaries of the UK. That very Classical Sociology which is held in such importance in the

determination of hegemonic positions on the Continent remains, as we
have seen, totally unexamined. Of the programme delineated in the
'Theses', only one element will be carried out: the importation of
European marxism. It is to this aspect that we must now turn.

3 THE IMPORTATION OF EUROPEAN MARXISM

The Review has often been accused of eclecticism, of being fascinated
by whatever brand of Marxism appeared on the other side of the Channel
and of presenting it to its British readers in tones of uncritical
adulation and appreciation. This last criticism is not devoid of
truth, although the ecstatic presentations are usually moderated by
a problematical 'perhaps':
    Louis Althusser's 'Freud and Lacan' (NLR 55) is 'perhaps the best
Marxist theorization of psychoanalysis that has ever been written'
(p.2). Poulantzas's book *Le politique et la lutte des classe* is
'perhaps the first systematic work of Marxist theory since the war'
(NLR 43, p.56). Lucio Magri's book on the May events' remains two
years later one of the very few systematic Marxist analyses of the
entire course of the French crisis - perhaps indeed the only one'
(NLR 60, p.93) perhaps supplanting André Glucksmann's 'Strategy and
Revolution in France 1968' (NLR 52) which was '... the fundamental
theoretical document of the younger generation of students and
intellectuals who launched the movement of May. Its analysis of
the key political and strategic problems of revolutionary struggle
is a signal guide to action, not only in France but in Britain and
in every other capitalist country' (p.8). And, but we had better
stop here, 'This issue of the review starts with one of the most
original philosophical essays to have been written in the last
decade: Sebastiano Timpanaro's "Considerations on Materialism"'
(NLR 85, p.1).
    The eclecticism of the Review is only apparent. The importation
of European Marxism had been filtered by a very definite grid and
the Review has also provided critiques of the authors it presented.
    Here is the list of the representatives of 'European Marxism'
presented in NLR with the number of the issue following after the
author's name:

'Western Marxists'	*Critiques/Assessments*
Adorno 46 47 81/7	
Althusser 41 55 64 -----------------	Geras 71, A. Glucksmann 72, Vilar 80, Gerratana 101/2
Bahro 106 ------------------------	Williams 120
Balibar 107	
Benjamin 48 62 77 108 123 ----------	Brecht 84, Bloch 116
Bettelheim ------------------------	Miliband 91
Colletti 56 61 65 86 93	
Claudin 106	
Della Volpe 59 113/4 --------------	Gerratana 111, Forgacs 117
Garegnani 112	
Gerratana 82 101/2 103 106 111	
Godelier	

'Western Marxists'	Critiques/Assessments
Goldman 92 ------------------------	Williams 67, M. Glucksmann 56
Gorz 37 52	
Gramcsi 32 51 ---------------------	Debray 59, Colletti 65,
	Anderson 100
Habermas 115 ----------------------	Therborn 67
Korsch ---------------------------	H. Korsch 76
Lukacs 39 60 68 -------------------	Lowy 91, Steadman-Jones 70
Luxemburg -------------------------	Geras 82 89, Lowy 101-2
Marcuse 30 45 56 74 ---------------	Cohen 57
Magri 60	
Poulantzas 43 58 78 95 109 --------	S. Hall 119, Miliband 82
Sartre 41 58 97 100	
Timpanaro 91 95 116 ---------------	Williams 109, Rycroft 118

This is undoubtedly a most impressive list. A list, I should add,
which is, if anything, an under-estimation in so far as it does not
attempt to include a number of articles which, though they are not
direct assessments of the authors in question, do touch on the issues
raised by these and other Western Marxists. Furthermore this list
should be integrated with the wide range of translations which the
NLR team has made available through its publishing company. Whatever
reservations one might have about some of the names on the list,
there is no doubt that the list taken as a whole constitutes a formidable range. Let us, however, concentrate on the main thinkers
only. In *Considerations on Western Marxism* (henceforth COWM) Perry
Anderson himself provides a critique of the various schools which
the review itself had presented over the previous fifteen years.
Here are the indictments against 'Western Marxism' as a whole:

1   Divorce from political practice (except Gramsci and, to a lesser
    extent, Lukacs and Korsch) (p.29).
2   Silence on 'the economic laws of motion of capitalism as a mode
    of production', no 'analysis of the political machinery of the
    bourgeois state' and no 'strategy of the class struggle necess-
    ary to overthrow (the bourgeois state)' (except, again, Gramsci)
    (pp.44-45).
3   Excessive concentration on philosophical problems (p.49).
4   '... the extreme difficulty of language characteristic of much
    of Western Marxism in the Twentieth Century was never controlled
    by the tension of a direct relationship to a proletarian
    audience' (p.54).
5   Constant presence and influence of European idealism (p.56).
6   Failure of the various schools within Western Marxism to engage
    theoretically with each other (p.69).
7   The surviving members of the Western Marxist tradition 'have
    so far proved unable to respond to the new conjuncture created
    since the May upheaval in France, with any notable development
    of their theory. For the most part, their intellectual course
    has probably already been run' (p.101).

It is difficult to refrain from picturing in one's mind the
sniggering faces of some of the NLR's most vociferous critics and

the irresistible chorus of 'I told you so' which rises in the air as
Anderson concludes by remarking that 'In England, especially, the
working class has remained industrially one of the most powerful in
the world, and the calibre of Marxist *historiography* has probably
been superior to that of any other country. The relative modesty
to date of Marxist culture in a wider sense in this region may itself be subject to surprisingly swift changes. For the law of uneven development governs the tempo and distribution of theory too:
it can transform laggard into leading countries, benefiting from the
advantages of latecomers, in a comparatively short period' (p.102).
But the satisfaction of the critics is ill-founded. It is an elementary rule of intellectual discourse that criticism, in order to
have any foundation, must be informed criticism.

So 'Western Marxism' too has been a failure, although, let me
hasten to add, it is the 'Western Marxism' which had been imported
by NLR. There have been, after all, important exclusions. But,
before turning to these, let us examine one of the reasons which
Anderson himself seems to indicate as contributing to the divorce
between theory and practice, namely the social origin of the Masters
of Marxism themselves. It is difficult to escape from the conclusion
that Anderson is obsessed with this problem. It is true that the
statement '... in the long run, the future of Marxist theory will
lie with intellectuals organically produced by the industrial working
classes of the imperialist world themselves, as they steadily gain in
cultural skill and self-confidence' (COWM, p.105) can be read in a
variety of ways. But what can we make of these words inserted in a
footnote: 'Perhaps (sic) the most distinguished socialist thinker to
have so far come from the ranks of the Western working class itself
has been a Briton, Raymond Williams' (p.105)? The inescapable conclusion is that the sentence 'intellectuals organically produced by
the industrial working classes' must be read as entailing biological
production, i.e. only intellectuals born and raised in a proletarian
milieu will develop Marxist theory. In the era of mass education,
mass communication, standardization of culture and of cultural models,
one would have thought that such sociological reductionism was dubious not only on theoretical grounds but on sheer empirical ones.
Anderson's obsession with the social origins of great intellectuals
is further evidenced by the fact that he brings to our attention the
interesting but quite irrelevant information that Lukacs was the son
of a banker, Benjamin an art dealer, Adorno of a wine merchant,
Sartre of a naval officer, Althusser of a bank manager while Colletti
(of course) only that of a bank clerk (COWM, p.26n).

Let us now turn to an examination of the screening mechanism which
has guided *New Left Review*'s importation of Western Marxism. A
cursory glance at the Review's own list will show that, roughly
speaking, Western Marxism can be divided into a humanist-hegelian
trend (e.g. Classical Frankfurt and Lukacs) and a challenge to this
trend (Althusser, Della Volpe/Colletti, Timpanaro). But Western
Marxism has not been confined to these schools nor to this debate.
The Review failed to tackle, challenge, examine and debate many
other trends and currents. Here are some of them:

1 Capital Logic School (Germany)
2 Second generation Lukacsian (A. Heller)
3 Polish Political Economy (from M. Kalecki to Oscar Lange and
   W. Bruns)
4 'Tuscan' Communist Philosophy (C. Luporini and N. Badaloni)
5 Italian Marxist-Positivist (Geymonat)
6 Southern Italian Gramscian-Togliattian School (G. Vacca,
   B. De Giovanni)
7 Italian 'Ouvrierist' School (M. Tronti, A. Asor Rosa and
   M. Cacciari)
8 Soviet Planning Economists (from G.A. Fel'dman to L.V.
   Kantorovich)
9 Second Generation Frankfurt (Habermas, O. Negt and A. Schmidt).
   However, an interview with Habermas has been published in NLR,
   and NLB has published Schmidt's *Marx's Theory of Nature*. But
   there has been nothing on 'third generation' Frankfurt, e.g.
   K. Offe.

The mechanism of exclusion has taken two forms. Either the schools
have never been mentioned or only attacks on them have been published,
at times without even explaining against whom the attack has been
published. An example will illustrate this last point. The only
living Italian Communist philosophy who has been published with great
regularity in NLR has been Valentino Gerratana. Of the five pieces
published, we have had one article on the relation between Marx and
Darwin (mainly of historical interest) (NLR 82), one on the relation
between Leninism and Stalinism (NLR 103) and then one attack on
Althusser (NLR 101-2).
    The two other pieces are apparently attacks on the European tradi-
tion of 'negative thought' (Nietzsche and Heidegger). The political
background of Gerratana's piece on Heidegger is particularly interesting. When Heidegger died (in 1976) Massimo Cacciari, one of the most
controversial Communist intellectuals in Italy, published in the Party
weekly, *Rinascita* (No.27, 1976) an article in which he asserted that
it was quite time that Marxism tackled some of the questions which
'negative thought' had posed. Cacciari had already dealt with these
questions at some length in his book *Krisis. Saggio sulla crisi del
pensiero negativo da Nietzsche a Wittgenstein* (Milan, 1976, which
New Left Books will never translate) in which he maintained that
'negative thought' has had a positive function in the crisis of
classical philosophy. Critics within the party (and some outside it)
have asserted that the consequence of Cacciari's attempt was that of
creating an unbridgeable gulf between philosophy and theory on the
one hand and politics on the other in order to reconstitute politics
on a pragmatic level divorced from the traditional embrace (in
Marxism) with philosophy. This was tantamount to a call to take
stock of the 'crisis of Marxism' and go beyond it, presumably in the
direction of reconstituting the Communist Party outside the framework
of a socialist project, and to abandon the concept of transition
'from' capitalism 'to' socialism. The result of all this could well
be a return via a rather devious route (Nietzsche, Heidegger *and*
Wittgenstein) to Popper's piecemeal social engineering.

In this context it is clear that Gerratana's piece was a direct
attack on Cacciari under the guise of a critique of Heidegger.
Cacciari's position could perhaps have been tolerated as long as
his remarks were confined to an exceedingly difficult book. But
Rinascita is read by over 100,000 people. Cacciari has a certain
following not only among young intellectual cadres, but also among
some of the Party leaders. Gerratana's article was a piece of
internal debate. None of this was made clear by the editors of NLR
(who knew very well who was the real target, for it was theirs as
well). The Italian readers of *Rinascita* were provided with a fuller
debate. Cacciari's response appeared in the following issue. The
readers of NLR were simply told that Gerratana's article was 'a
pungent commentary on current efforts - probably most frequent in
Italy or the USA - to reconcile the philosophy of Martin Heidegger
with that of Marx' (NLR 106, p.2).
One would have thought that Britain is adequately vaccinated
from Nietzsche and Heidegger (but vaccinated by British analytical
philosophy) to be able to examine serenely Cacciari's attempt. But
this inexplicable anti-Cacciari neurosis took an even more dramatic
turn when NLR published in No.112 a dossier of texts on Piero Sraffa
which had been compiled for *Rinascita*. This dossier was said to
represent 'an accomplished example of PCI cultural policy', and,
even though too ecumenical, 'the range and depth of treatment adds
materially to our knowledge' (p.2). If we compare the original
dossier with what NLR presents we come to the conclusion that
Rinascita's range of treatment is too wide for NLR to stomach.
Rinascita presented eight texts, NLR translated seven. Who is the
author of the missing text? Massimo Cacciari! (who would be
flattered to learn that he is considered to be such a serious
threat to the 'proper' development of British Marxism).
No doubt good explanations can be provided for the similar exclusion of the other schools of 'Western Marxism'. We shall have to
wait for a more informed explanation from the editors of the Review
themselves. It should be added that the publication of Luporini
and Badaloni as well as of G. Vacca and B. De Giovanni would have
gone some way towards presenting a brand of Marxism less divorced
from political practice than the theoreticians presented by NLR.
Most of the Italian 'schools' presented in my list not only coexist (and argue) from within the ranks of the PCI, not only have
they access to Party publications but are given direct political
tasks: Nicola Badaloni has been mayor of Leghorn for many years,
Luporini a Senator and a Councillor in Florence, De Giovanni is on
the Party committee for his region, Vacca is on the board of the RAI,
all of them are on the Central Committee, Asor Rosa and Cacciari are
MPs. To introduce these thinkers in Britain would have entailed a
more complex presentation of the Italian Communist Party and its
policies than has been the case. Instead it was decided to stop at
Lucio Colletti and present him as the surviving representative of
'Italian Marxism' with Timpanaro, whose work on Freud and materialism
has had but little influence in Italy, as the necessary counterpart.
It seems that one of the conditions established by the review to be
part of 'Western Marxism' is to be either an 'isolated intellectual'
(whatever that is) or, if member of a political party, to be
emarginated from its political life and in dispute with it.

Let us now turn to another exclusion of which NLR has, however, made amends: Jürgen Habermas. For a line of Habermas one has had to wait until 1979 when an interview (originally published in *Rinascita*, again!) appeared in No.115. Before that the only mention of Habermas had been in the form of an article by Göran Therborn in No.67. In it Habermas is criticised for a 'departure from Marxism ... far more radical than that of his forebears' (i.e. Horkheimer and Adorno) (p.75), for breaking with the student movement of 1968 on the issue of violence with warnings of 'left fascism' (which in the era of Baader-Meinhoff and Red Brigades is something one can begin to take stock of), for declaring that Marx's theory was 'vulnerable' to the refutations of the labour theory of value, the theory of the class struggle and the theory of base and superstructure. Ten years later it is not only Therborn which has changed position, as a cursory look at his books published by NLB would show, but Anderson himself. In the crucial 'Afterword' penned to the *Considerations on Western Marxism* Anderson admits it is time to stop the endless re-interpretation of the canonical texts and 'to proceed instead to scrutinize the credentials of the texts of classical Marxism themselves, without any prior assumption of their necessary coherence or correctness' (p.113). Marx's central weaknesses are (pp.114-15):

1 No analysis of the political structures of bourgeois class power.
2 Theoretical silence on the character of nations and nationalism.
3 Problems with the theory of value and the theorem of the falling rate of profit.

But, as we stated, NLR made amends for its exclusion of Habermas: 'The interview with Habermas which we publish here suggests that he has not been caught up in the rightwards movement of much of the left intelligentsia in Europe in recent years' (NLR 115, p.72), he 'displays intellectual integrity' and 'has something of value to offer to socialists who seek to understand the novel features of capitalist crisis today'. But does this 'something of value' depend on the fact that Habermas's explicit political position is on the Left? One would have thought that there is something of value in many authors who have a centrist or rightist position. Has not Anderson himself used a mass of material from non-socialist historians when writing his two volumes on the development of the State from Antiquity to Absolutism (and how right he was, he would not have got very far on Marxist historians alone!)? The grudging admission that there is 'something of value' (and the same thing could probably be said of all the other 'excluded') is immediately tempered by a puzzling statement: 'Taken as a whole Habermas's analysis is still quite distant from that which revolutionary socialists would make.' And what are 'revolutionary socialists'? The permutations, debates, controversies, etc., on the word 'revolution' have been such as to render its use extremely problematical, not to speak of the word 'socialist'. While it is possible to agree that - say - Harold Wilson can be safely left outside the frontiers of 'revolutionary socialism' (by his own admission, although some of us would maintain that the problem with Wilson is not his lack of revolutionism but his lack of socialism), what shall we do about the range

which includes everything from the Red Brigades to Ernest Mandel,
from Che Guevara to Georges Marchais - all of whom would claim the
term as applicable to themselves? But let us not be unduly naive.
When NLR talks about 'revolutionary socialism' it means a position
which is akin to theirs, a position which is spelt out with remarkable clarity by Anderson himself in the final pages of *Arguments
within English Marxism*. We shall want to return to those pages at
a later stage. Here it will suffice to remind the reader that for
Anderson the socialist revolution is a process which follows this
invariant sequence: fundamental economic crisis; bourgeois repression; revolutionary organs of proletarian democracy (dual power);
transitional demands; 'the ensuing social upheaval must rapidly and
fatally pit revolution and counter-revolution against each other in
a violent convulsion' (pp.194-95).

This is, of course, a position which is akin to the 'transitional
programme' of the 4th International (*The Death Agony of Capitalism
and the Tasks of the 4th International*, 1938). Not a surprising
result considering that the chief political allegiance of many of
the members of the editorial board of the Review is to the Trotskyist tradition. Given this commitment it is not surprising that *New
Left Review* should be disappointed with the actual political position of the European Marxists it has imported over the years. The
case of Gramsci is typical. Gramsci had been presented as a revolutionary thinker whose achievements had been taken over by the
Italian Communist Party and whose thought had been reinterpreted
in a reformist mould. In NLR 65 (1971), Colletti's review of Fiori's
biography of Gramsci was published and presented as a 'repudiation
of attempts to portray Gramsci as some kind of precursor of the
Popular Fronts and hence to establish a continuity between him and
the current policies of the Italian Communist Party' (p.2). By 1977
the situation had changed. In what has been the only thorough assessment of Gramsci to date in the NLR, Perry Anderson came to the conclusion that Gramsci in prison produced a 'non-unitary, fragmentary
theory, which inherently allowed discrepancies and incoherencies in
it' (NLR 100, p.72). Furthermore, and this is more serious, there
is not only a formal but a substantive analogy between key Kautskyist
and Gramscian concepts, and particularly between Kautsky's 'war of
attrition' and Gramsci's 'war of position' (p.62). To tackle Gramsci's
thought in an explicit way had become, for the NLR, an urgent task.
By 1977, when Anderson's critique was published, the 'Gramsci industry'
was blossoming, not only in Italy, but also in France, Britain and
the USA. In the introductory pages of his article Anderson justifies
the need for a critique precisely with reference to both Eurocommunism
and the British Left (p.6). An imported Marxist had taken some roots
in the culture of the British left. The NLR was the first to use
Gramscian concepts. The 'latecomers' to the scene used them to
produce analyses - to use a cliché - 'still quite distinct from that
which a revolutionary socialist would make'. The other imported
Marxists either suffered the same fate, i.e. entered the culture of
the British left but were interpreted in a 'non-revolutionary socialist' perspective (e.g. Althusser), or they themselves took a different
road from that advocated by the review. The editors of the review,

of course, could not be entirely surprised by this. Most of the chief representatives of imported Marxism had not been imported because the immediate political consequence of their theoretical position was a revolutionary one, but because their concepts, or, at least, the intellectual challenge which their concepts entailed, could help the development of revolutionary analyses. Thus no-one was in doubt as to the political position of the various members of the Frankfurt School, or of Della Volpe, or of Althusser. But the other, younger theoreticians, too, have not ended up in the political framework of the review. Nicos Poulantzas adopted an explicitly 'left Euro-communist' position, and so did Göran Therborn, Lucio Magri and, to some extent, F. Claudin. André Glucksmann is now 'born again' as the leading Nouveau Philosophe in Giscard's France. Lucio Colletti has written little of any importance since, having discovered that the labour theory of value is invalid, he has renounced Marx in favour of De Tocqueville and has come to the conclusion that what is wrong with Italy is due to the student movement of 1968 and the militancy of the trade unions. Regis Debray is in the French Socialist Party. This has not meant, in most cases, their exclusion from the pages of the *New Left Review* for the review has never been and has not become the house journal of a Trotskyist sect, and its latent 'sectarianism' has never eschewed the challenge of political positions opposed to its own.

4 THE UNITED KINGDOM

We can now turn to an examination of the contribution NLR has given to the 'concrete analysis of the concrete situation' (to coin a phrase) of the United Kingdom. That such analysis of the UK was an integral part of the programme of the NLR was never in doubt. The Anderson-Nairn theses clearly originated with this project in mind. Nairn and Anderson themselves, in 1964 and 1965, did not limit themselves to a reconstruction of the foundation of bourgeois hegemony in Britain and to a historical analysis of the nature of British intellectuals and of the British state. They also offered their readers the beginning of a concrete analysis of the incoming Labour administration. If we count the theses themselves as part of the review's 'corpus' on the UK, we see that in 1964 alone seven articles were written by Nairn and Anderson, two in 1965, and one (Anderson's reply to Thompson's attack) in 1966. In 1967 we had only one article (Blackburn on inequality in the UK in No.42). From 1968 to 1979 we have had about twenty articles on the UK. An issue of the review usually has about four major features, the review is published six times a year. Roughly 288 major articles have been published between 1968 and 1979. Twenty articles represent 7 per cent of total production. This is not to be taken too literally. I am not attempting an exact quantitative study; some issues of the review have been double issues, and one had been entirely dedicated to a major issue of British politics, the EEC (Nairn in NLR 75). But I think that the point is valid. There has been a chronic lack of interest in current UK issues in the review. One possible line of explanation would probably be unacceptable (and rightly so) to the editors of the

journal, namely that the primary task was to 'import' Marxism and
only when the culture of the British left was adequately reinvigorated
by a powerful injection of concepts and categories of analysis from
abroad, could this Left produce serious analyses. Such theoretical
'menshevism' could not be more alien to the review which has never
ceased to offer 'concrete analyses' of the 'real world'. No-one can
accuse the review of being simply a theoreticist journal.

A line of explanation could probably be found in the simple fact
that the review could not but reflect the weakness of the New Left in
general when it came to examining the problems of the UK. The New
Left had, after all, arisen with a strong internationalist element,
an internationalism which often became a simple cosmopolitanism.
Those who were active in the 1960s and in the early 1970s will
recollect that struggles abroad were usually seen to be more interesting and 'dramatic' than British developments. We knew more about
Cuba and Vietnam than about Britain. The events at the London School
of Economics in 1968 looked (and were) mere trifle when compared with
the Tet Offensive, the May events in Paris, the Prague Spring. We
over-reacted against the provincialism of the Old Left. I think
most of those who were active at the time would agree with this.
Furthermore we enclosed ourselves very quickly in an 'international
ghetto'. We were better informed and more interested in those small
groups with which the British New Left bore some resemblance than
with the wider social forces. What was interesting about the French
presidential elections of 1969 was the number of votes obtained by
the New Left leader Krivine, the interest in Italy was centre on the
small Manifesto group, in Germany it was the SDS not the SDP. A
parallel mentality developed in Britain: as the Labour Party was
considered to be incurably reformist it was more interesting to discuss the positions of the International Socialists, of the International Marxist Group or, even, the Socialist Labour League.

NLR was not able to break through this ghetto as it should have
done. On the contrary it reinforced it. The failure to provide
regular and concrete examinations of UK problems is its most significant failure. I have mentioned above that in twelve years there
were about twenty articles on the UK. If we look more closely at
these we would find that even that is an overestimate. Of these
twenty, two are interviews which are of value as documents, but not
as analyses: the interview with the Chief of Staff of the Official
Irish Republican Army (C. Goulding in NLR 64) and the interview with
A. Scargill (NLR 92). Another three are continuations of the Nairn-
Anderson theses on the formation of British intellectuals and the
historical foundations of the modern British state (Anderson NLR 50,
Nairn NLR 60, Nairn NLR 101-2). There have been three articles
specifically on Scottish nationalism (Nairn NLR 49, Nairn NLR 83,
Kiernan NLR 93) and one attack on Nairn's theses on nationalism
(Hobsbawm NLR 105). There is one article (*only* one) on Northern
Ireland (Peter Gibbon NLR 55, 1969). One of the twenty is a critique of the programme of the British Communist Party ('The British
Road to Socialism') written in 1970 by Bill Warren (NLR 63). There
have been thus *no* examination of developments in Northern Ireland
for the whole effective duration of the 'troubles' and *no* effective
examination of the programme of the British Labour Party, with the

exception of two pages written by Glyn and Sutcliffe in 1972 (NLR 76).
There has been an article on Enoch Powell by the prolific Nairn
(author of eight out of the twenty articles considered here) in No.
61 (1970) of the review, but no examination whatsoever of race relations and immigration. With the solitary exception of Nairn's piece
(not a very 'concrete' piece, but never mind) in 1979 (NLR 113-14),
there has been no analysis of the British crisis since Barnett's
piece on the Heath Government and the Unions in 1973 (NLR 77) and
Yaffe's critique of the Glyn-Sutcliffe theses (NLR 80). In fact if
we were to adopt a strict, if possibly narrow, view of what constitutes
a 'concrete analysis', i.e. a mapping out of the relation of forces
in the UK state, its economic, political and social problems and the
strategies adopted by the leading protagonists, we would be left with
very little. This very little is sometimes of a very high standard.
Tom Nairn's two articles on the Left and the EEC (NLR 69 and 75),
particularly his trenchant 120-page long sustained and controversial
piece is a clear example of such standards. That was also an example
of intellectual courage, taking on, as it did and in one fell swoop,
a great number of the *idées reçus* of the British left, not only its
traditional left, but also the various groups which wave so often the
flag of internationalism only to fall back, when the going gets tough,
in the tranquil pond of Little Englandism. But after this what are
we left with?

1 Andrew Glyn and Bob Sutcliffe, 'The Critical Condition of British
   Capital', NLR 66, 1971.
2 Robin Blackburn, 'The Heath Government: A New Course for British
   Capitalism', NLR 70, 1971.
3 Andrew Glyn and Bob Sutcliffe, 'Labour's Record', NLR 76, 1972.
4 Anthony Barnett, 'Class Struggle and the Heath Government', NLR
   77, 1973.
5 David Yaffe, 'The Crisis of Profitability: a Critique of the
   Glyn-Sutcliffe Thesis', NLR 80, 1973.

The first Glyn and Sutcliffe article was an attempt (later expanded
in a book published by Penguin and widely read and commented upon)
to demonstrate that the economic struggle of the working class had
been such as to cause a sharp decline in the level of profits of
British firms and that, consequently, the working class had advanced
its economic position. It concluded by remarking that 'A struggle
about wages, when it is successful in squeezing profits, cannot remain
a struggle about wages', it must develop politically. Whatever one
might think about the technical and theoretical plausibility of the
article (and Yaffe's critique is well-argued, though not convincing
and politically naive), one thing is certain: the question of the
trade unions' role in the determination of prices and profits and,
more generally, the role of the practice of the working class in the
crisis of British capitalism has been since the 1960s at the centre
of political debates in the country. Glyn and Sutcliffe's article
has thus the undoubted merit to direct itself to one of the central
issues. But, with the exception of Yaffe's piece, the debate was
not carried on in the pages of NLR. The matter was dropped. Nor
was it a little brick: it would have entailed a whole analysis

(economic and political) of the experience of the Social Contract.
But on this crucial experiment the review remained silent, once more.
    This was, of course, a matter of deliberate policy. Articles
which attempted to confront the problem of incomes policy were submitted, only to be rejected, as in the case of Bill Warren and Mike
Prior's 'Advanced Capitalism and Backward Socialism' which later
found its way into print thanks to the publishing house of the
Bertrand Russell Foundation, Spokesman Books.
    The electoral victory of the Labour Party in 1964 seemed to
herald a turning point in British politics. The review sought to
analyse this experience. Perry Anderson, writing in 1964, said that
'Perhaps for the first time in its history, the Labour Party now
possesses a coherent analysis of British society today, a long-term
assessment of its future, and an aggressive political strategy based
on both' (NLR 27, p.4). Wilson is seen as possessing a 'relatively
acute structural perception of British society' (p.5), a perception
which enables him to pose the question of detaching from the conservative bloc the 'technical intelligentsia', to embrace the banner of
modernism and efficiency by denouncing 'incompetent and amateur
sections of industry' as well as 'speculative and parasitical ones'
(p.6). 'For the first time in its history, the Labour Party is now
led by a man who by any standards is a consummately adroit and
aggressive politician. The long reign of mediocrity is now over....
The Labour Party has at last, after fifty years of failing, produced
a dynamic and capable leader' (pp.21-2). With hindsight it is easy
to be smug about these characterizations of Labour's worst Prime
Minister (to date). But Anderson's article is no mere paean of
praise. There is an acute perception of the ideological components
of Wilsonism and an attempt to individuate their problems. He
indicated that, with Wilson, the Left could have some room for
manoeuvre: 'Under his (Wilson's) leadership the whole Labour programme has become open-ended. It is not at any point socialist;
but nor is it, unlike its predecessor, inherently incapable of
debouching onto socialism. It is thus neither a barrier nor a
trampolin forthe Left: it is simply a political space in which it
can work' (p.21).
    What happened, after these pronouncements, to the Wilson administ-
ration of 1964-70 is well known. But the review did not follow this
analysis. It neither sought to rectify it, when political events
demonstrated its fallacies, nor did it seek to expand it, when its
insights should have been developed. The answer to six years
Labour government under the leadership of its 'dynamic and capable'
leader was utter silence. Finally, in 1972, we are given six
pages written by Glyn and Sutcliffe which in turn are no more
than a review of two assessments of the Labour government's record
edited respectively by W. Beckermann and by P. Townsend and
N. Bosanquet plus a couple of pages on the Labour Programme of
1972. That is all there was to say about 1964-70. In 1964 Perry
Anderson had taken the following stand on incomes policy:
    'Does this mean that the unions should a priori refuse any
    discussion of incomes policy? By no means.... What it does
    mean is that they should demand as a priority, not greater
    wage increases, but measures of workers' control. *For workers'*

control is the only negotiable exchange for an incomes policy:
it alone offers a genuine counterpart - powers and not pence.
The sacrifice of Trade Union autonomy to the State which is
involved in an incomes policy could *only* be compensated by
the gain in return of decisively increased autonomy and control
for the workers in the plant' (NLR 27, p.25 - his emphasis).
And after that? After that no discussion on workers' control. No
discussion on workers' control throughout the period of the 1964-70
Labour administration. Ditto for the period 1974-79. The Bullock
Report might never have been written. Incomes policies came and
went, but for NLR they did not exist, because during the entire
period 1974-79 there was not a single, solitary examination of current
Labour policies. The entire experience of the Social Contract did
not warrant a single line of analysis. There was neither an assessment of the fall of the 1970-74 Conservative administration nor a
contribution on the fall of the Labour one.

This is why the two articles by Blackburn in 1971 (NLR 70) and
Barnett in 1973 (NLR 77) stand out so much. Whatever their faults
they represented at least a serious attempt to analyse the direction
of conservative policies.

Blackburn's article sought to analyse the new course of the Heath
government and to relate its home and foreign policies. Blackburn
was writing before the famous U-turn and hence before the wave of
industrial militancy which would eventually lead to the confrontation between the National Union of Mineworkers and the Government and
to the 1974 General Elections. Heath's new course (modernisation of
British industry, control of trade union power, entry into Europe,
greater independence from the 'special relationship' etc.) was given
a strange welcome by the editors on the ground that 'it will disrupt
political patterns that have long been an obstacle to the spread of
revolutionary politics in Britain' (p.1) and 'If only British Marxists can abandon their traditional mythologies, then they will
discover that Heath is preparing the ground for the birth, or rebirth,
of revolutionary politics within the working class' (p.26). Re-reading this article now after nearly ten years it is difficult not to
see that Heath's attempt was, to a large extent, a dress-rehearsal
for Thatcherism. Yet one would doubt that NLR would now declare
Thatcherism to be a necessary stage prior to the development of
revolutionary politics in Britain. Blackburn's article suffered from
the over-assurance which is characteristic of the review's style.
Limited evidence is produced to make sweeping statements which are
often, shortly afterwards, contradicted by new developments. E.g.:

'Heath shows none of his predecessors' inclination to overestimate the political strength of the trade unions. His
approach to the electricity and postal strikes showed that
he knows how to gauge accurately the strength of solidarity
between the trade-union bureaucrats when it comes to a real
struggle with capital' (p.19).

'There is also considerable realism in [Heath's] abandonment
of attempts to secure trade-union support for an incomes
policy. Such attempts are quite redundant and out of place
in the context of the government's present political assault
on organized labour - though no doubt the time will come when

a suitably chastened TUC will be glad to endorse some new
variant of wage restraint, in return for a seat at the
negotiating table' (p.19).
Two years and a U-turn later, Anthony Barnett wrote a sequel to
Blackburn's: a reconsideration of Heathism. Here too we find the
same sweeping statements (e.g. the assumptions that tripartite state
boards armed with greater powers than Labour's Prices and Incomes
Board will 'become permanent features of bourgeois states', p.39)
and the same misplaced optimism: 'By 1973, when a new epoch opened
for Britain with entry into the Common Market, the working class had
said goodbye to a past of defeat in a way that raises new hope for
the future' (p.41). Nevertheless these two articles constitute the
sort of work NLR was duty-bound to engage in and produce frequently.
In the context of an on-going programme of research and study on the
political and economic developments of the UK, sharply defined theses
and provocative generalizations have a useful role to play. But this
is so only if they are part and parcel of a proficuous dialogue, not
if their rare appearances give them the status of papal pronouncements. After the Blackburn and Barnett pieces NLR has fallen into
a strange silence on everything which is connected to the British
political system. Yet the issues and questions raised by Blackburn
and Barnett have not disappeared.

5   WOMEN

In 1966 NLR published an important and lengthy article by Juliet
Mitchell on the structure of women's oppression: 'Women: The Longest
Revolution" (NLR 40). It was one of the very first articles on this
subject anywhere in the UK. It pre-dated the formation and development of the women's movement and hence, for a number of years,
constituted one of the few texts available on the question. As it
is known, Juliet Mitchell went on writing on feminism: *Woman's Estate*
was published in 1971 and *Psychoanalysis and Feminism* in 1974. But
NLR, though far from disregarding the issue, did not continue the
discussion adequately.
    Feminism, that is, contemporary feminism, appeared relatively late
on the scene, that is after the explosion of 'black power' and
'student power'. Even in the libertarian and semi-anarchical joy
of May 1968 in Paris, the voice of women remained muffled. Yet
today 'student power' is a dead slogan whilst the language of women's
liberation has pervaded large sections of the population, and of the
mass media, though at times and perhaps inevitably it has been
partially coopted or corrupted. Seen from this perspective Mitchell's
article constitutes an example of what the work of the review should
have consistently been: to intervene in a timely manner in the
initial stages of new developments and then to continue vigorously
the investigation and the debate.
    Mitchell's article generated an immediate reply. A brief and
harsh four-page comment by one of the editors of the review (Quintin
Hoare) appeared in the following issue. Mitchell's article was
lambasted as 'an unwitting proof that it is impossible to achieve

a global analysis of the position of women *outside* the premises of
classical Marxist discussion' (NLR 41, p.79), 'the result is not only
non-Marxist (that is, non-social, ahistorical), it is also sterile'
(p.80). The accusation of 'sterility' is particularly telling because
behind Hoare's criticism was the preoccupation that Mitchell's
article did not result in an understanding that the importance of
the struggle for emancipation of women resided in the contribution
it could make to the class struggle: 'The history which could provide
an analysis of the position of women and a context for their emancipation (politicization) is not some Hegelian concept - it is a concrete history which still largely remains to be written and made.
And this history can only become concrete if its basis is the class
struggle, *subsuming feminism and at the same time transcending it*'
(p.81, my emphasis). The harsh language used is all the more surprising when we consider that it is unusual for two members of the editorial board (as Hoare and Mitchell were and are) to clash so polemically.

Several years would elapse before the issue was taken up again.
In the interval a solitary, moving and beautiful document is produced:
in the series 'Work', where people are asked to write an autobiograph-
ical piece on their own work experiences, there appeared an article,
'The Housewife', signed S.G. There, in ten terrible yet quiet pages,
the reader could find a vivid expression of the anxieties, the guilt,
the depression and the desolution which are produced not by the well-
documented heights of horrors which humanity has engendered such as
famine, war, torture, concentration camps etc., but by the banalities
of everyday life: 'The mornings are always my worst time - the day
stretches ahead in dreary sameness, with no possibility of anything
unexpected' (NLR 43, p.51). Not far beneath the half-resigned tone
and the forced optimism that things would eventually improve there
could easily be detected a formidable anger ready to challenge the
whole world.

By 1970 the women's movement was large enough. Six hundred women
took part in a weekend conference at Oxford in the spring of that year.
NLR devoted three pages to it. The author of the piece, Branka Magas
(NLR 61) wrote that the Women's Liberation Movement had become 'a
force to which the Left in Britain will have to pay serious attention'
(p.31), and called for 'serious theoretical work' as well as for
'militant political action'. In subsequent years (1971-79) NLR published eight lengthy articles (i.e. of more than ten pages) on the
woman question. Of these eight, six were on the Domestic Labour
Debate, one was a critique of Alexandra Kollontai (J. Heinen, NLR
110) and one a lengthy review of books by K. Millet, E. Figes and
G. Greer (B. Magas, NLR 66). In this last piece B. Magas, for all
her insistence on the desirability not to break with orthodox Marxism,
wrote that Marxism had failed to develop a 'fully worked out theory
of the role of the family in advanced capitalism, or of the specificity of women's oppression' (p.91). She had also written, however,
that the central weakness of the three books reviewed consisted in
their 'failure to link sexual with class politics' (p.69). This
preoccupation with the connection between class and sex (evident also
in Q. Hoare's polemic) may be a partial explanation of why NLR has
concentrated, in its coverage of the Woman Question, nearly entirely
on the Domestic Labour Debate. The weight subsequently given to this

debate (to the virtual exclusion of anything else) since then may be,
in part, a reflection of the preoccupation of 'fitting' feminism into
Marxism, of establishing the 'credentials' of the housewife's labour
from the point of view of the capitalist mode of production and,
sometimes but not always, attempting to deduce the *potentiality* of
the housewife's contribution to the development of socialism from
her relation to the capitalist mode. Thus, in a sense, the chief
preoccupation of NLR, when faced with the emergence of the Woman
Question, was that of trying to examine it from the point of view of
orthodoxy. While this is the unmistakable impression one derives
from the paucity of the treatment of this question in the pages of
the review, some of the editors tried to push for a different
approach. David Fernbach (then a member of the editorial board),
basing himself not on theoretical deductionism, but on the evidence
of the political struggle in the USA, declared, in a review of Reimut
Reiche's *Sexuality and Class Struggle* (NLB, 1970), that 'After the
black movement, the women's liberation is at present the strongest
force in the American revolutionary movement' (NLR 64, p.95). But
the most provocative and refreshing comments published in the review
came from the pen of another member of the editorial board whose hands
were duly slapped by Robin Blackburn and Branka Magas in a subsequent
brief comment in NLR 67 (pp.110-12). In a rejoinder to Branka Magas's
review of Millett, Figes and Greer, back in distant 1971, Lucien Rey
stated that the real problem was not that a Marxist theory of feminism had not appeared, but that Marxism itself was incomplete, i.e.
that it does not possess the concepts which would enable one to produce such a theory or even to criticize Millett, Greer and Figes.
And he added further: 'The process of Marxizing feminism can only
take place *pari passu* with the process of feminizing Marxism' (NLR
66, p.96). The political consequences of this were that 'It could
be correct not only for women to organize themselves here and now,
but also to do so if and when there was a revolutionary party (the
famous Leninist party), even to the extent of forming their own
party, if the alternative was a male-dominated party - as it probably would be: all revolutionary parties so far have been male-
dominated. This means of course rejecting the idea of associated
or auxiliary (i.e. subordinate) women's movements. This is always
attacked as being divisive but then to perpetuate oppression, even
the forms of oppression, in the revolutionary party itself is
divisive too....' (p.96).

  Could not the reality of a growing independent women's movement
(which, contrary to Rey's expectation, did not and could not organize itself in the form of a political party) be examined and studied?
Could not its impact on the British political system be a proper
object of analysis? Could not the experience (both theoretical
and practical) of the movement in other countries be made available
to the readers of the review? Towards the end of her 1966 article,
Juliet Mitchell advocated four reforms (which Hoare dubbed as banal,
unexceptionable 'which anybody from the Liberal Party leftwards
should support' NLR 41, p.78): equal education, free state provision
of oral contraception, legalization of homosexuality and the abolition of illegitimacy. Some of these demands have since then been

(partially) implemented. New demands have emerged. But on all that, once again, the review has remained silent.

6 OTHER COUNTRIES

'"We Englishmen are Very Proud of our Constitution, Sir," Mr.
Podsnap explained with a sense of meritorious proprietorship,
"It was Bestowed Upon Us By Providence. No Other Country is
so Favoured as This Country..."
"And *other* countries," said the foreign gentleman, "They do
how?"
"They do, Sir," returned Mr. Podsnap, gravely shaking his head;
"they do - I am sorry to be obliged to say it -   they do."'
But now the roles are reversed. Mr. Podsnap is being arraigned in
his turn.
'"And *other* countries," said Mr. Podsnap remorsefully. "They
do how?"
"They do", returned Messrs. Anderson and Nairn severely. "They
do - we are sorry to be obliged to say it - in Every Respect
Better. Their Bourgeois Revolutions have been Mature. Their
Class Struggles have been Sanguinary and Unequivocal. Their
Intelligentsia has been Autonomous and Integrated Vertically.
Their Morphology has been Typologically Concrete. Their
Proletariat has been Hegemonic."'
(E.P. Thompson, 'The Peculiarities of the English', *Socialist
Register*, 1965, p.312)
As a matter of fact 'other countries', particularly other European
countries, don't do very well in *New Left Review*. The chief problem
seems to be that in practically all cases the working classes of
these countries continue to owe their allegiances to working class
parties which do not hold the review's political positions. Thus
the chief preoccupation of the review has been that of confronting
the Communist tradition in Western Europe. We have had articles
on the Italian Communist Party (though not a real analysis of the
'Historic Compromise') in NLR 50 (J. Halliday) and NLR 66 (L. Magri).
We have also had an interview with Giorgio Amendola (NLR 106) taken
from a book of interviews (*Parti communiste italien: aux sources
de l'eurocommunisme*, edited by H. Weber, Paris, 1977) which also
included interviews with P. Ingrao, A. Reichlin and B. Trentin (all
members of the left of the PCI). Typically it was Amendola, recognized leader of the right-wing tendency, who was selected by the
review. On the French Communist Party, apart from the special
issue on the May events (NLR 52), we have had Althusser's attacks
(104 and 109) and that's that. In NLR 58 Therborn dealt with the
Swedish Communist Party while the Finnish Communists got two articles
(Hynynen, NLR 57 and Haapakoski, NLR 86). The 'split' in the
Spanish CP was tackled by Claudin in NLR 70. Apart from these
articles which dealt specifically with communism,   Western Europe
since 1968 (before that date there was hardly anything on it) was
covered thus: Greece (3 articles), Turkey (1), Italy (2), Spain (2),
Portugal (1), France (3), Germany (2), Switzerland (1), Cyprus (1),
Iceland (1), Austria (1).

As can be seen, no major countries are excluded, although the
lopsidedness between the treatment of Germany and that of Greece
is remarkable, particularly if one considers that one of the two
articles on Germany is a highly literary piece by Hans-Magnus
Enzenberger pretentiously called 'An address on German Democracy
to the Citizens of New York' (NLR 118). The explanation is obvious (and I think it can be generalized): the post-War history of
Greece has been more 'exciting' than that of Germany, the 'class
struggle' has been more overt, so much so that it called for a
military reaction. The articles on Greece (all very interesting)
deal with the Colonels' junta and its aftermath. Yet the review
had started (see the Nairn-Anderson theses) with the intention to
measure itself against the 'foundations' of bourgeous hegemony.
In the context of this programme it would have been necessary to
examine closely and repeatedly the central political phenomenon
which has emerged in Europe: the German Federal Republic. What is
the nature of German Christian Democracy and of the SPD? the foundation of its 'economic success'? its system of industrial relations?
Ostpolitik? the particular role of German banks in Germany and in
the rest of Europe? Germany is now the dominant political power in
Europe, the saying 'an economic giant and a political dwarf' holds
no longer. In 1979-80 the particular role played in international
affairs by the Chancellor has been highly significant and must be
related to the problems afflicting American international hegemony.
Moreover the SPD has also been instrumental in propping up social-
democratic parties in the Iberian peninsula. If the British Left
must attempt to acquire a 'European dimension' as - rightly - demanded by T. Nairn in his EEC articles, then why disregard that pillar
of strength, the Federal Republic of Germany?

And what of the other two major European nations: France and
Italy? Here too NLR cannot be satisfied with its coverage. While
we have not had a satisfactory examination of the Italian Communist
Party since 1971 (Magri's piece in NLR 66), i.e. of the most power-
ful communist party in the West and the authentic founder of
'Eurocommunism', nor one of the central party of the Italian political system, i.e. the Christian Democratic Party, we have at least
been given an economic analysis (Salvati, NLR 76) and a political
one (a fairly ludicrous one, but never mind) in NLR 96. As for
France there seems to be only May '68 and the PCF. De Gaulle,
Giscard d'Estaing and Mitterand might as well never have existed.
Here is the country which has expressed more than any other its
determination to be an independent force, nay, more which has
repeatedly and with a relative success managed *to adopt* an independent policy (independent, that is, from the USA) while developing a
new brand of conservatism and this country, or, rather, its dominant
political forces, remain unanalysed.

The sheer weight given by NLR to analysing what the Marxist
Left does in Europe may lead one to a conclusion: namely that what
dominates NLR's European search is not the desire to achieve some
sort of understanding of the European political system, but the
need to confront itself with other 'models' of socialist strategy:
i.e. we can only learn from the Left, a position which, in the
realm of theory, fortunately does not hold any longer: for now the

Left reads and learns from non-Marxist thinkers such as Freud, De
Saussure, Foucault, etc.

There is still one more criticism. The Western European coverage
as well as that much wider and comprehensive of the Third World has
little or no comparative dimension. The analysis is in virtually all
cases a purely national one. The question of the specificity of
Germany, Italy or France from the point of view of the European
political system is never seriously tackled. The claim, to be found
in Anderson's *Arguments within English Marxism*, that 'Rather than
national independence, global interdependence was the tacit starting
point for assessing the contemporary conjuncture in Britain. Hence
not only the strongly (if not always accurately) comparative cast of
the review's work on England itself, but also the serial studies of
other societies - advanced capitalist, underdeveloped or communist -
which formed the staple categories of NLR coverage at the same time'
(p.150) - this claim is unfounded.

For something approaching a comparative problematic one must turn
to the frequent articles on the international economy, although even
here we are often faced with too high a level of theorization and
too little empirical evidence and comparative analysis. There are,
of course, outstanding exceptions to this, such as Bill Warren's
article 'Capitalist Planning and the State' (NLR 72, 1972) which is
truly comparative. But in general the not unjustifiable concentration
on economic trends cannot be an adequate substitute for a comparative
analysis of political tendencies. Even at the level of the international economy, NLR has consistently overlooked many of 'the great
issues' of the day, or more precisely, of the decade(s): the oil
crisis, the energy crisis, the introduction of new technology, the
international monetary crisis, the questions raised by the North-
South dialogue, the growth of the 'new industrialized countries' of
Asia (South Korea, Taiwan, Hong Kong, etc.), nuclear energy, etc.
Even in its treatment of the Third World NLR has not achieved a
truly comparative perspective. There is, of course, the odd exception, e.g. Therborn's article on 'The Travail of Latin American
Democracy' (NLR 113-14), but, on the whole, the coverage has been
extremely monographic. Of course, the treatment has been massive.
Since 1962 (when the present board 'took over'), there have been
over fifty articles on the Third World, a salutary corrective to
Eurocentrism. But the logic of coverage should not be the simple
academic one of discussing topics because they have been overlooked
by others. The logic should have some political foundation not un-
related to the centrality of certain countries to the international
system. It is difficult to see why Ceylon, with three articles (NLR
64, 69, 84), should be better covered than Germany. Behind this
extensive treatment there is the Third Worldism of the New Left in
general. But even accepting the fact that the limits of the NLR are,
to some extent, the limits of the New Left as a whole, it is difficult to understand why there has been nothing on Vietnam since 1968.
In this context one cannot but be faintly puzzled by Anderson's
self-congratulatory remarks: '... the international resistance to
the American aggression in Vietnam was the most successful anti-
imperialist campaign in the history of capitalism.... *New Left Review*

provided what arguably remains to this day the best synthesis of the
historical meaning of this signal moment in Gบิ้ran Therborn's text,
written during the Tet Offensive, "From Petrograd to Saigon"' (NLR 48,
48, 1968) (AWEM, p.152).

The list of silences of the review seems to be constantly expanding. Yet the editors of the review would not disagree with some of
the criticisms made so far. The whole of Anderson's dissatisfaction
with the results hitherto achieved are evident in *Considerations on
Western Marxism*. The self-criticisms are seldom explicit, but nevertheless evident: '... it can be said with some confidence that
it has mastered the terrain of the United States and England - respectively the lands of the wealthiest imperialist class and of the oldest
working class in the world - Marxism will not have measured itself
against the full reach of the problems with which the civilization of
capital confronts it, in the second half of the twentieth century'
(pp.102-03). We have seen the scant treatment granted to the UK.
It is, if anything, better than that accorded to the USA: since the
Nicolaus-Mandel debate (1969-70), there have been only three pieces
on modern America (J. Petras and R. Rhodes NLR 97, M. Aglietta NLR
110, and Mike Davis NLR 123).

7 INSTEAD OF A CONCLUSION

The brunt of the criticisms which emerge from this rapid overview of
the contributions which have appeared in the review over the years
have all centred on a single aspect: the missing elements. We have
seen that there has been little or no examination of the British
situation, a selective and discriminatory definition of what constitutes 'Western Marxism', a lack of comparativeness in assessing the
problems of the Third World, a refusal to tackle decisively and
systematically the crisis of American international hegemony and
its ensuing internal political crisis, a disregard for the concrete
realities of the women's movement, an inability to deal with the
leading social democratic and conservative forces in Britain and in
Europe. Further examination of the coverage of *New Left Review*
would only confirm these absences.

There is, of course, one obvious line of defence: 'No one writer,
or group of writers, can hope to encompass all the facets needed
for a living socialist culture' (Anderson in AWEM, p.206). It is
not an unreasonable defence, although, if it is adopted, it would
lead NLR to admit that it has not done what it had declared to be
its central task: to contribute to if not to produce the broad
guidelines for a revolutionary strategy in modern Britain. That
this was the central project is left in no doubt in the Nairn-
Anderson theses and it is significant that *Arguments within English
Marxism* ends with an examination of the differences between Thompson's
concept of gradual revolutionary transition (shared, as it is
correctly stated, by a broad spectrum that now stretches from Eurocommunism to left Social Democracy) and the review's own insurrec-
tionist stance. But NLR's conception of revolution has not always
been this. It has changed significantly from the early 1960s to

1968 and again from 1968 to the present. In between these watersheds
(which we will examine shortly) the actual production of the review
bears very little relation to the strategic changes. In other words
there has not been an explicit link between what appeared in the
review and its strategy. The link, of course, existed, but in a
hidden form. It was kept hidden by the failure to examine and criticize alternative strategies.

When the May Day Manifesto group was formed in response to the end
of the transient alliance between the Labour Party and the CND
intellectuals, NLB ignored it. When the Labour Left used the period
of the 1970-74 Conservative government to present a series of proposals embodied in the Labour Programme of 1973 (the 'alternative
economic strategy') which, for all its faults, represented a coherent
strategic formulation, NLR ignored it. When, as a partial result of
the introduction into British marxism of the works of Louis Althusser
(an achievement which owes a great deal to the review), there developed a blossoming of Marxist literature and interesting attempts to
use althusserian concepts (e.g. the reviews *Theoretical Practice* and
Economy and Society) NLR ignored them. It was only when the rise of
Eurocommunism, its impact among young and not so young intellectual
cadres in the Communist Party, and the spread of Gramscian thought
threatened to ensnare what was left of the 1968 movement into the
quagmire of reformism that NLR answered. And the answer was
characteristic:

1   Indirect attacks (e.g. Anderson on Gramsci, Loew's critique of
    Austro-Marxism considered to be a harbinger of Eurocommunism in
    NLR 118).
2   Direct attacks (Weber's article on Eurocommunism in NLR 110 and
    Mandel's book, a classic piece of sectariana, dubbed by Anderson
    'the most effective critique' of Eurocommunism).
3   Silence on Eurocommunist works on Gramsci (e.g. Buci-Glucksmann's
    book which appeared in France in 1975, or the now numerous texts
    by Italian communists). Silence on the policies, proposals and
    intellectual contributions of the Eurocommunist parties.

What was missing, evidently, was a discussion on the NLR's alternative strategic guidelines. That these were insurrectionary has been
obvious to any reader of the review. But this obviousness relied on
speculation and supposition, on the underlying problematic of the
majority (but not all) of the contributors. To *see* the insurrectionary alternative stated black on white in the final pages of *Arguments
within English Marxism* presented in the clearest of terms as being
the position of the review, of the entire review, of every one of its
members (but is that really so? No doubt some denials will be forthcoming) is, in a very real sense, a revelation. And it is a revelation which is introduced with these words: 'It would not be appropriate to reiterate in detail here the strategic conceptions of the
transition to socialism for which the present NLR has stood.' As
if these details and these strategic conceptions had been discussed,
examined, defended, upheld, refined, etc., before. The insurrectionary conception is something which had been hovering in the background
to be used as the unwritten text against which to pit the experiences

of the left-wing movements which had been analysed in the review in
the last twenty years. It is a conception which only at times
emerges dramatically and with great rhetorical effect as in this
passage used against Gramsci's war of position: 'For a Marxist
strategy within advanced capitalism to settle on a war of position
and an ethos of command to achieve the final emancipation of labour
is to ensure its own defeat. When the hour of reckoning in the class
struggle arrives, proletarian liberty and insurgency go together.
It is their combination and no other, that can constitute a true
social war of movement capable of overthrowing capital in its
strongest bastions' (NLR 100, p.71).

In *Arguments within English Marxism* Anderson recalls William
Morris's scenario of the 'English Revolution of 1952-54' in *News
from Nowhere*. Re-written in a masterly fashion and in modern terms
by Anderson, but faithful to the spirit and the letter of the
original, the process is the following:
   - Partial reforms of workers' condition lead to economic crisis.
   - Trade union demands complete socialization.
   - Government responds with force.
   - Workers create their own organs of sovereignty.
   - Government mass repression.
   - Intermediate classes waver and eventually join the workers.
   - Workers' representatives withdraw from Parliament and form
     their own Committee of Public Safety (situation of dual power).
   - Attempted negotiations between Government and Revolutionary
     Committee fail.
   - Bloody revolution with widespread desertion from rank and file
     soldiers.
   - The Forces of Socialism triumph.

Ninety years have elapsed since Morris 'imagined' with remarkable
intuition *the* revolution. Now, ninety years later, Anderson warns us
not to forget 'the necessarily sudden and volcanic character of revolutionary situations, which by the nature of these social formations
can never be stabilized for long and therefore need the utmost speed
and mobility of attack if the opportunity to conquer power is not to
be missed. Insurrection, Marx and Engels always emphasized, depends
on the art of audacity' (NLR 100, p.75) and, a page later, he adds
'This coercive state machine is the ultimate barrier to a workers'
revolution, and can only be broken by pre-emptive counter-coercion'.

That's it then. It will be sudden and it will be bloody. Time
will come when all will be clear and straightforward for it will be
(finally!) Labour versus Capital, Socialism versus Capitalism. The
pattern for this has been set once and for all in those fateful 'ten
days that shook the world'. From this Big Bang conception of revolution everything else follows, for if the hallowed model of the October
Revolution offers the unchangeable broad outline of the passage from
capitalism to socialism, then it obviously follows that it is this
conception which must be defended at all costs against subsequent
attempts to offer anything different. It must be defended against
Eurocommunists and social democrats, against Austro-Marxists and
their followers, against stalinists and bureaucrats, against the
wayward children of Gramsci (and Althusser).

But this is the spirit of Ernest Mandel and the Fourth International. It is not that of NLR. NLR is *not* a purist journal. However much it seems committed to an insurrectional strategy, it knows at some more or less conscious level that it is committed to such a strategy only because it remains unimpressed with alternative attempts. It is open to change. It wants debate and dialogue. Its latent sectarianism is tempered by tolerance. But it has also reached a dead-end. Any analysis of British political life and political struggles would force it to confront the problem of articulating plans and projects which must be rooted in contemporary reality, and would inevitably lead it to the necessity of beginning at the beginning, at the level of the existing struggles, the existing movements, the existing organisations, the existing framework of reference of ongoing politics. It would lead it towards the domain of politics, which is the domain of compromises, historic or temporary, and of alliances. It may, of course, choose to remain silent as the deeply pessimistic conclusion of *Arguments within English Marxism* seems to indicate: in evaluating Thompson and his own contribution, Anderson writes that so far all the two of them have done is to restate the works of others, Morris and Caudwell in the case of Thompson, and Luxemburg and Gramsci in his own case. They have not produced 'innovative advance into unknown territory. The reasons for that are not hard to seek: the absence of a truly mass and truly revolutionary movement in England, as elsewhere in the West, has fixed the perimeter of all possible thought in this period' (p.207). But then the example of Morris ('who did not exactly live at a high tide in the history of the British working class') 'shows how much can still be done in what appears to be adverse conditions'. And Thompson is then invited to forget the past and to explore new problems 'together'. The logic is implacable. The absence of a 'truly revolutionary and truly mass' movement in the West delineates the arena of the thinkable. The thinkable can only be reformist. Unless, by a sheer effort of the will, one is able to extricate oneself from it and then ... then what? 'Much can still be done'. One is at a loss to understand this sibylline pronouncement. One fears that after it there can only be silence or the definitive retreat into the study of the past.

It is not unfair to speak of a 'definitive retreat' into the study of history. History has been in fact the chief preoccupation of the editor of NLR. It is not only his masterly synthesis of the development of the State from Antiquity to Absolutism which can be brought forward as evidence. In 'Origins of the Present Crisis' Anderson wrote

'... until our view of Britain today is grounded in some vision of its full, effective past ... we will continue to lack the basis for an understanding of the dialectical movement of our society, and hence - necessarily - of the contradictory possibilities within it which alone can yield a strategy for socialism' (NLR 23, p.27).

Years later Anderson's silent study of history has yielded its verdict:

'The real terrain of arbitration between the two opposing conceptions which confront each other today (i.e. left social democracy and eurocommunism versus revolutionary socialism,

D.S.) is *historical* - not speculation on an unknowable future,
but examination of a known past. It is on that ground, the
firm earth of the historian, on which every Marxist should
keep their feet, that evidence points to the greater cogency
and realism of the tradition of Lenin and Trotsky' (AWEM, p.197).
Yet this verdict was not a foregone conclusion. The strategic perspective delineated in the conclusion of *Arguments within English
Marxism* has not been held throughout these last twenty years.

As we have recalled before, Anderson's initial exploration of the
possibilities opened to the left by the return of a Labour administration in 1964 did not preclude a long-term strategy of advance
towards socialism. The integral publication of the Central Committee
meeting of the Italian Communist Party held in November 1961 to discuss Khruschev's further revelations of Stalin's crime is preceded
by a ten-page introduction by Perry Anderson. The tone is positive,
at times even approving. The realism of the PCI is praised, its
policy of 'presence' in the institutions and in the economy is
commended.

This 'reformist' period is short-lived. The transition to a new
strategy is not prepared by a careful reappraisal of its earlier
position. The review confronts the student movement of 1968 and
produces a second strategic position: the Red Bases. The Red Bases
strategy was quickly forgotten. Re-reading not the main texts where
it was presented it is easy to understand why. The idea that students
could 'take over' the universities and turn them against the capitalist state using them 'sociologically' as a red base much as Mao took
over Yenan and used it militarily and politically will, undoubtedly,
sound fairly far-fetched, although it did not at the time, as it
was one of the major slogans of the student movement. But the Red
Base strategy also contained some insights (which were not further
developed). Its main proponent in NLR was 'James Wilcox', author
of the most important exposition. Writing in a style which is not
a million miles away from that of Robin Blackburn, 'Wilcox' asked
'whether the complex structures of late capitalism do not contain
areas, sociologically inaccessible to the repressive forces of the
ruling class, which can become growing points of revolutionary
power' (NLR 53, p.26). The Red Base was defined as an 'intermediary
institution of popular power' and hence as a real gain which could be
effectively politically defended. 'Wilcox' establishes his lines of
demarcation fairly strictly. He castigates those who 'portray the
revolution as 'a Last Trump that will transform social relations once
and for all' because it 'leads to an indefinite postponement of the
decision actually to start looking for ways to make the revolution
rather than wait for its immaculate conception in the womb of capitalism's general crisis' (p.26). It then condemns the strategy of
intermediary objectives. This strategy which, for Wilcox, does not
reflect Trotsky's transitional programme (and which he, mistakenly,
identifies with some sections of the Italian Communist Party) is
fairly familiar: the enlightened revolutionary elite poses demands
which the masses think justified but which are actually unacceptable
(in the strong sense) to the capitalist system. They are therefore
rejected. The masses then realize that what appear to be justified
and reasonable demands in fact cannot be conceded by capitalism.

Their consciousness is raised sky-high and they become convinced that socialism is the thing. The crucial point here is that NLR, through Wilcox, demarcated itself from this Big Bang theory of revolution and from the mindless search for reasonable but unacceptable (i.e. 'unreasonable') demands. It postulated a strategy towards socialism which would seek to isolate the weak links of the existing social order and at the same time create a space for the self-organisation of groups of people (here students, but the analogy can come to include other terrains). This view, however crudely expressed then, has the distinct advantage that it necessitates, if adopted in its essential terms, a careful assessment of the concrete situation, of the strength and weaknesses of the contending parties. It poses also a fundamental question, namely that of exercising a form of political power, that is a form of collective control. The 'occupants' of the 'Red Base' (but this phraseology is simply too picturesque to be of much further use) must learn to run it and therefore cannot allow themselves to be enclosed in pure rhetoric or in semi-anarchic joy. They still coexist within a socio-economic system which cannot but dominate and constrain the spaces conquered so far. Thus the theory of the Red Bases, once it loses its geographical obsession (i.e. the actual physical holding of a set of buildings, or the occupation of a territory, a sort of no-go area of socialism) could still provide a terrain for a fruitful debate between 'reformists' and 'revolutionaries' on questions of strategy.

This terrain, however, must disappear, when NLR takes its final Andersonian step into the whole-scale adoption of the October model. Let me not be misunderstood. The debate can continue and must continue on questions of theory and history, and, more specifically, on the kind of questions which contributors to NLR have raised and will go on raising on the ongoing processes of the international economy, on the struggles in the Third World, on developments in Europe, on British literary criticism and so on. But there cannot be a dialogue on questions of strategy.

How can there be a fruitful dialogue and debate when the answer to whatever question emanating from the Eurocommunist/social-democratic/'reformist' spectrum is the simple reiteration that 'when the hour of reckoning in the class struggle arrives, proletarian liberty and insurgency go together'? An example will illustrate this point. Thompson in an article entitled 'Revolution' (NLR 3, 1960) envisaged not a revolutionary culmination but a lengthy process in the course of which certain changes would have to occur. He cited as examples:

1   The breaking up of certain institutions (e.g. the House of Lords, Sandhurst).
2   Transformation of others such as the House of Commons and the nationalized boards.
3   New functions to institutions such as town councils, stop stewards committees, trades council etc.

Now these demands can be criticized on a number of counts, their vagueness is manifest. The text itself makes these changes dependent on the 'will' of the people without any hints that structural constraints may exist. But it is not Thompson's programme which is of

interest here. It is Anderson's answer (twenty years later!).
His answer is designed to stop any further dialogue: '... virtually
all the measures enumerated (by Thompson, D.S.) are compatible with
the maintenance of capitalist relations of production and the preservation of the bourgeois state' (AWEM, p.191).

But concrete proposals of reforms designed with *this British*
State in mind cannot be set against 'capitalism' in general or the
'Bourgeois State' in general. They must be set against this specific
state, this specific capitalism. And if this is done, then the
effective consensus which can be mobilized around these proposals
must be calculated as well as the probable outcome.

The silences of NLR which have been partially brought to light
by the examination of the actual contents of the review must surely
result from the logical impossibility of giving strategic 'concrete'
answers to the strategic 'concrete' questions of the 'reformist'
(to use the classical expression). That this is undeniable is
evident in Anderson's remark '... the absence of a truly mass and
truly revolutionary movement ... has fixed the perimeter of all
possible thought in this period.' (AWEM, p.207).

It seems to me, *on the contrary*, that for too long 'all possible
thought' has been given to the impossible and to the undesirable.
In the increasingly dangerous and difficult times we are entering
it is more important than ever to begin thinking anew - all of us,
including *New Left Review*.

David Cobham
The Socialist Economic Review Project: progress in the economics of the left

In what may turn out to have been the most important development in
the economics of the British left for many years, the first *Socialist
Economic Review* (SER) conference was held in London in September
1980; by the time this article appears its proceedings will have
been published in what is intended to be the first of an annual
series of *Socialist Economic Reviews*. This article sets out to
evaluate the SER project: it looks first at the context in which the
SER arose; secondly at the origins, objectives and potentialities of
the SER; thirdly at the first SER conference itself; and finally at
one area which is crucial for the left's economics, that of the
Alternative Economic Strategy (AES) and the various positions adopted on the left towards it (both those which were and those which
were not represented at the conference), in order to illustrate
some of the points argued in the earlier sections, and identify the
main areas of debate at the conference.

THE CONTEXT

Over the last twenty years there has been an enormous growth in the
number of left-wing economists in Britain: from the days when
Maurice Dobb and Ronald Meek were almost the only left-wing academic
economists, Marxists and socialists can now be found (albeit in small
numbers) in probably a majority of universities and polytechnics and
in most areas of academic economics. However, the output of economic
work of a specifically left-wing nature has remained relatively small
and the work that has been done is often poor in quality. Many left
economists write little or nothing for the left, and little or nothing
of direct political significance, while much of the 'economic' work
produced on the left is obviously written by non-economists. In
particular there has been a striking absence of good quality empirical
and policy-oriented analysis of the British economy from a socialist
viewpoint.
     In many ways the main forum for left economists ought to be the
Conference of Socialist Economists (CSE).[1] Founded in 1970, the CSE

has developed a substantial domestic and overseas membership, and it
sponsors a considerable range of working groups and conferences, a
regular journal and its own book club. However, its early years
were dominated by virulent and sectarian debates about the Labour
Theory of Value, and to a lesser extent about inflation and the
crisis of the British economy, which alienated many of the economists
who were initially involved in the CSE and many more who might otherwise have become involved. These debates have now subsided somewhat
but they have left the CSE dominated by sociologists rather than
economists and with a strong streak of self-conscious Marxist dog-
matism. Thus, although it is in many ways a vigorous organisation,
the CSE probably does not provide a forum for the majority of Marxist
economists, let alone for non-Marxist economists on the left. The
CSE is also outside the institutions and political culture of the
organised labour movement (there has even been a tendency among its
membership to see the CSE as an alternative to the existing political
parties); thus, although some work has been done within the CSE on
the AES,[2] many of the members are strongly opposed to it.

The only other organisations which provide any kind of focus for
left economists are the political parties themselves, in particular
the Labour and Communist parties. I am not in a position to discuss
the situation within the former, except to say that to the outsider
relatively little solid economic work seems to have come out of the
Labour Party as a whole, and even less from its left.[3] I am better
able to talk about the Communist Party (CP), which I suspect exemp-
lifies in a particular form a number of the problems of left economists and the left's economics. The CP includes among its membership
a considerable number of left economists (including representatives
of virtually every theoretical tendency), and it has an Economic
Advisory Committee which publishes its own *Economic Bulletin* and
holds an annual weekend seminar. However, the committee has been
hamstrung not only by disagreements about key issues such as inflation, incomes policy and the role of trade unions, but also by disagreements about its constitutional role within the CP, with views
ranging from those who think the committee should act as a trade
union research department, providing specific services as required
by the party leadership, to those who claim for the committee the
right to examine and criticise where appropriate the economic
implications of existing CP policy. The attitude of the CP leadership to the committee has generally been one of (not necessarily
benign) neglect, with the exception of some brief periods when the
leadership has appeared to accept the committee's plea for a more
constructive role and others when the relationship has degenerated
into outright abuse and stimatisation. Thus the committee has had
virtually no impact on the CP's economic policies, which have in
effect been determined by the political leadership on the basis of
political criteria and analyses. On the other hand the committee
has provided a useful, if somewhat introverted, forum and meeting
place for the left economists concerned, in which they have been
able to develop their ideas to some extent even if those ideas were
prevented from making an impact outside it.

While the organisations of left economists have been unsuccessful either in generating solid economic analysis on relevant issues

or in encompassing even a majority of the professional economists on
the left, the economic publications of the left have also been relatively few and uncomprehensive. *Capital and Class*, the CSE journal,
suffers like its sponsor from a paucity of economic material and
a tendency to Marxist dogma. The *Cambridge Journal of Economics*,
on the other hand, is academic and mainly theoretical; it also
suffers from the sectarian traditions (both towards orthodox economics and between the various factions of the left) characteristic
of what is defined at Cambridge as the left. *Labour Research* and
the relatively new *Labour Party Economic Review* provide useful
services to different sections of the labour movement but, because
of their size and their positions within that movement, are not
designed to carry serious analytical discussion. Finally the CP's
Economic Bulletin publishes some articles directed towards important issues but it has a very restricted circulation; it is also
probably trying to fulfil too many roles at once within a limited
format.

One particular characteristic of economic debates on the left
has been the tendency to settle economic issues of a factual
nature, concerning the relationships between variables such as
prices, income, public expenditure and investment, by appeal to
political arguments derived from particular views of socialism and
of revolution and from loyalty to some conception of the spirit
(and sometimes also of the letter) of Marx or to some 'basic
socialist principles'. This deplorable practice has of course had
a long tradition amongst Marxisn economists. For example
Hilferding's reply to Böhm-Bawerk's critique of Marx's value
theory contained no effective answer at the economic level but
rested heavily on an appeal to the alleged political and philosophical aspects of the Labour Theory of Value; in so doing it
set a pattern which was accepted even by those Marxian economists
who uncovered and made use of Bortkiewicz's solution to the 'transformation problem' (e.g. Sweezy, Dobb and Meek) and which, particularly in the hands of lesser practitioners, removed the Labour
Theory of Value from the sphere of rational argument. It is only
in the 1970s, some 70 years after Hilferding's work, that economists working from within the Marxian tradition such as Steedman,
Hodgson and Garegnani have come to reject the primacy of the
political over the economic asserted by Hilferding. This whole
debate remains one of considerable importance within the CSE
although the fury provoked by Steedman's original arguments for
the rejection of Marxian value theory has abated to some extent.

Other examples of this tendency to appeal to political arguments
over economic ones can be found in the debates on inflation and
the role of trade unions in Britain's economic performance within
and around the CP's Economic Committee. On the former the most
coherent position has been that expounded by Devine[4] which amounts
to a sophisticated left-wing version of costpush inflation theory,
while Purdy[5] has gone to some lengths to establish the inadequacy
of conventional left-wing explanations of Britain's relatively
poor post-War growth record and the need to include the nature of
the trade union movement and its interaction with other social
groups and economic forces in a full analysis of the question.

However, both positions have been consistently rejected by the CP
leadership, mainly on the basis of political arguments which can be
reduced to 'the working class is not responsible for anything under
capitalism' or 'it would be politically disastrous to admit that the
working class has any responsibility for inflation or low growth',
rather than on the basis of an alternative economic analysis such as
a monetarist theory of inflation or a serious examination of the role
of overseas investment.[6]

This assertion of the primacy of the political over the economic
has been a substantial obstacle to the development of an analysis
which *integrates* political and economic factors. There can also be
little doubt that it has contributed to the decision of large numbers
of left economists virtually to opt out of the few economic fora of
the left in favour of academic work whose direct political relevance
is at least muted. At the same time it has stimulated efforts by
some left economists to move out of the economic sphere in order to
confront the political arguments on their own level: Prior and Purdy's
Out of the Ghetto, for example, can be seen in this light. On the
other hand a significant number of left economists have remained
within the economic fora of the left, despite the hard work and
personal frustrations involved.

In the absence of a solid back-up the economic policies and
analyses put forward by the left have been characterised by eclecticism if not outright opportunism. Thus calls from the National
Institute for Economic and Social Research (the leading Keynesian
forecasting and research institute) for greater public expenditure
can be sure of a sympathetic reception in the *Morning Star* while
the incomes policy which the NIESR advocates receives much less
attention. The 'New Cambridge' views of the Cambridge Economic
Policy Group and the forecasts in their annual *Economic Policy
Review* have achieved considerable recognition among the left, yet
there must be a strong suspicion that this has more to do with their
policies of reflation and import controls than with the analysis on
which those policies are based. At the present time many voices on
the left are calling for a lower sterling exchange rate - exactly
the same voices in some cases as those which attacked the 1967
devaluation and the 1972-73 depreciation as causing inflation and
lowering real wages - but there is apparently no analysis of the
price level and real wage implications of depreciation in the present
situation. Finally the analysis of the potential employment effects
of introducing a shorter working week put forward by John Hughes
and the Trade Union Research Unit, with its apparent implication
that this institutional change would reduce unemployment substantially and at a stroke, has been widely accepted on the left, although
the analysis suffers from crucial weaknesses regarding real wages
and profitability.

THE SER PROJECT

It was against this background of the considerable but under-
utilised talent of socialist economists and the lack of an adequate
framework for left economic work that the SER project was conceived.

It was argued that left economists needed to do far more than before
to analyse developments in the UK economy, and related developments at
the international level, with a conscious orientation towards issues
of policy and intervention in current policy debates, and at a level
capable of commanding academic respect, but at the same time accessible to non-academics and non-socialists; that in recent years there
had emerged a body of left-wing economists working both in academic
institutions and elsewhere who could make at least a substantial
contribution to meeting this need; and that the appropriate framework would be an annual conference whose proceedings (including the
comments of discussants) would be published in a *Socialist Economic
Review* which would fill a gap in the existing array of left-wing
economic publications.

Two meetings of left economists were held in London in December
1979 and February 1980; the second decided definitely to go ahead
with the project, with the following statement of aims:
'The objective of the *Review* is to produce an up-to-date and
comprehensive analysis of significant developments in the
British (and, to a lesser degree, world) economy on an annual
basis. It will therefore be empirically oriented, though
theoretically informed, and will relate directly to current
policy issues from a socialist standpoint. It will be
broadly based, and will therefore necessarily incorporate,
express and perhaps resolve, differences of position on the
left.'
Two editors, a business manager and a working group were nominated,
to prepare the first conference for September 1980 and arrange publication of its proceedings.

The proposals before the original meeting (December 1979) had
suggested that all contributors to the SER might
'be expected to (1) take orthodox economics seriously,
(2) hold a non-conspiracy and non-reductionist view of the
capitalist state, (3) be prepared to enter serious discussions
of economic policy with non-socialists, (4) take a positive
and constructive attitude to the implementation of socialist
policies within advanced capitalist society, and (5) recognise
that the failure of the British left since the War to make
significant political gains is a reflection of its own inadequacies as much as of any difficulties external to the left.'
However, these points, which had not been intended to define a political line, turned out to be highly controversial, and they were therefore dropped in order to involve the broadest possible grouping of
people. There is thus no explicit political line incorporated into
the project, although the policy orientation of the SER implies a
concern with practical questions of economic policy that is likely
to be unattractive to some socialists.

There are a number of features of the SER as agreed upon at the
founding meeting in February 1980 to which special attention should
be drawn. Firstly, as already mentioned, the SER was intended to
have a strong orientation towards policy questions. The original
proposals in fact included the idea of a regular key article on
macroeconomic developments which would discuss the previous year's
experience and the prospects for the next few years. This particular

proposal was modified on the grounds that attaching extraordinary
importance to an article would immediately create a potential area of
disagreement. However, the thinking behind the proposal was generally accepted. Secondly the meeting agreed on the importance of
maintaining high intellectual standards. In the past, left economists
have produced theoretical work of a high calibre, e.g. in the
Cambridge capital theory controversy, in certain areas of macro-
economic policy and in industrial economics, but as argued above
policy discussions have often been written by non-economists on a
somewhat eclectic basis and to a much lower standard. Thirdly the
SER has a strong commitment against sectarianism, which is evident
in the rejection of any political line, in the procedure of publishing comments on papers by conference discussants and in the acceptance at the February meeting of the need to maintain reasonable
balance in the working group
    'between (a) political organisations, (b) Marxists and non-
    Marxists, (c) different academic disciplines, (d) academics
    and non-academics, and (e) men and women'.[8]
Fourthly the SER was conceived as providing a service to labour
movement activists, on the one hand, and as constituting a forum for
the development of new ideas on economic policy, on the other. In
the current situation of the British left there might appear to be
some contradiction between these two aims, since all too often
activists, particularly in the trade unions, want a straightforward
presentation of 'the truth' on economic matters where no agreed
version of the truth exists. However, the incorporation of such
aims implies a refusal to accept the concept of debate as a matter
for experts alone.
    Thus the SER project constituted a major initiative in the left's
economics. It contained the potential for a substantial increase
in the amount of good quality empirical and policy-oriented work
done by socialist economists, a greater cross-fertilisation of ideas
between different trends (including particularly non-Marxists and
economists from the left of the Labour Party who had never participated in fora such as the CSE), and ultimately for a major shift
in the level and nature of economic analysis among the left as a
whole.

THE FIRST CONFERENCE

The first SER conference was held in London in September 1980. It
included a session of review papers on the UK economy, the international economy and the Third World; a session on socialist policy
responses dealing mainly with the AES and import controls; a session
on macroeconomic policy including papers on monetarism and public
expenditure cuts; a session on government-trade union relations
and inflation policy; a session on taxation, incentives and unemployment; a session on industry with papers on the nationalised industries and on energy; and a final session on a paper on the principles
of democratic planning.
    It is clear that the SER conference stimulated a considerable
amount of work - many of the papers would not have been written if

it had not been for the SER - and much of this work was of a higher quality than conventional left economic discussion. The SER also stimulated debate on some important policy issues: for example, Paul Ormerod, in a provocative paper that was perhaps even more oriented towards immediate policy issues than most of the participants at the conference had expected (but was none the worse for that), discussed what 'the next Labour government' should do about inflation; David Purdy discussed more long-term aspects of government-trade union relations in terms of a new radical social contract; Pat Devine produced one of the first serious analyses from the British left of the problems involved and the many factors to be taken into account in drawing up a democratic system of economic planning; and Mike Prior analysed the options for the 1980s in one particular British industry, that of energy.

The conference also went some way towards the intention of bringing together the different trends of thought on the left. The contributors and participants at the conference included representatives of various tendencies of Marxists and non-Marxists and of various political organisations; the *Review* will also include a paper on import controls by Terry Ward of the Cambridge Economic Policy Group who was unfortunately unable to present it at the conference. And the general level of debate at the conference was refreshingly constructive and non-sectarian.

On the other hand the conference and the project as a whole have not yet won the degree of support from within the trade union movement that had been hoped for. The conference participants included a number of people from trade union research departments, but there must be many more such people who could have been attracted. Similarly two particular tendencies among left economists were somewhat under-represented, those of fundamentalist Marxism and of the non-Marxist left within the Labour Party. And although some of the papers dealt with issues of policy it was noticeable that other papers did not begin to confront such questions: for example, Ken Knight analysed trends in the composition of unemployment but had nothing beyond a rather maximalist conclusion to say regarding left policy towards unemployment; and Malcolm Sawyer's paper, which disposed very effectively of various right-wing arguments on taxation, social security benefits and incentives, had little to say on the (admittedly very difficult) questions of policy involved here. There is no need for every paper to treat policy issues, but subsequent conferences should have a higher proportion of papers doing so, and the tendency to spend too much time and effort criticising the right - which has always been easier, both economically and politically - and too little developing coherent and practicable alternatives must be resisted.

Many problems remain, in particular the need for wider involvement and closer contact with the labour movement and the need to develop further the high level policy discussion which is a large part of the raison d'etre of the SER. Nevertheless the project has made a good start and the first conference must be considered a success. The second SER conference, to be held in September 1981, will face a somewhat different task: on the one hand there will be no place for (and therefore no diversion of resources towards) the rather general surveys which opened the first conference; on the other hand the

proposed session on feminist issues will require substantial re-thinking
of some conventional left attitudes to economic policy.

ATTITUDES TO THE AES

One of the main plenary sessions of the conference was devoted specifically to the AES and a number of papers touched on it at various points.
In this section we shall first set out in a fairly stylised form the
four main attitudes held on the left towards the AES, and then relate
them to the papers at the conference and to the discussion of earlier
sections of this article.
    One important position on the left is that of outright hostility to
the AES. There are two different strands in this position, one arguing
that the AES is (objectively or subjectively!) a scheme for the revival
of British capitalism (which is assumed to be undesirable),[9] the other
arguing that as a strategy of advance towards socialism the AES will not
work.[10] The first strand relies almost entirely on political analysis
in which the principal role is played either by the ulterior motives of
Tony Benn or by the 'objective necessity' of wage restraint (and therefore attacks on trade unions, etc.) for economic growth in what remains
a capitalist economy. The second strand contains important elements of
economic analysis - e.g. the arguments that import controls would raise
the price of consumer goods, that shortening the working week is likely
to lower real wages, and that expected profitability rather than access
to finance is the crucial determinant of capitalist investment - as
well as political analysis of the opposition of capital to the AES, but
it rests primarily on political arguments which are merely reinforced
by a crude economic determinism.
    The other three main positions taken on the left towards the AES are
positions of strong support for different formulations of the AES. It
has long been obvious, though not always clearly articulated, that
there are many different versions of the strategy; here we shall differentiate between three such versions (referred to as AES1, AES2 and
AES3) on the basis of a political criterion - what concept of advanced
capitalist society underlies the strategy? - and an economic criterion
- what role do resource constraints and market forces play in the concept of a capitalist economy underlying the strategy? This contrasts
with other discussions of different versions of the AES which have
tended to focus on the differences in the economic policies included
in the strategy.[11] All classifications involve some simplification;
the justification for the differentiation and classification made
here is the hope that by posing certain key issues in stark terms it
will stimulate thought and help the debate to progress.
    The first version we shall consider, AES1, is a stylisation of
the kind of AES which dominates the thinking of many political figures
and groups on the left, including some in the Labour Party (in Parliament, in the constituencies and in the trade unions) and the official
leadership of the CP. The concept of capitalist society in this
version is one of relatively monolithic social groups (*the* working
class and *the* capitalist class), of a superstructure determined
fairly directly by the base, of a state which is essentially the
instrument or appendage of the capitalist class, and of a popular

consciousness which is determined principally by the mass media on the
one hand and by day to day economic conditions on the other. As
regards the underlying economic theory, resource constraints exist
only under capitalism and market forces are little more than a capitalist plot; the economy is viewed as a collection of entirely separate
compartments and the economic forces which might be supposed to
connect them do not exist: all marginal rates of substitution are zero
and profits have no economic function.
   AES1 is therefore a fairly straightforward collection of policies
in which direct controls play a large (and costless) part: a rapid
return to full employment is envisaged, achieved by increases in all
elements of final expenditure (mainly consumption - via increases in
wages, pensions and social security benefits - and private and public
sector investment), with problems of inflation and balance of payments
deficits being blocked off by price, import and exchange controls; at
the same time collective bargaining remains free because of the crucial
importance for political mobilisation ascribed to wages struggles; and
in the longer run the economic growth rate is expected to rise in
response to higher levels of investment directed via nationalisation
by the central government. There are of course many problems with
the purely economic aspects of AES1 which it would not be appropriate
to spell out in detail here.[12] Essentially AES1 is all but economically illiterate, and the primary reason for this illiteracy is the
subservience of the economic analysis to political judgments. For
example, AES1 does not consider the effects of wages struggles on
prices/profitability or on public expenditure and monetary growth
because free collective bargaining is sacrosanct on (simplistic and
reductionist) political grounds; nor does it consider shortages of
skilled labour and industrial capacity as constraints on inflation
because the rapid restoration of full employment is considered a
political necessity.
   However, some of the economic weaknesses in AES1 are made irrelevant by the rapid and costless transition to socialism which appears
to be implied by many expositions: it is assumed that implementation
of the strategy (almost as a substitute for the tendency for the rate
of profit to fall) induces a crisis which in turn brings about a
process of mass radicalisation that enables the government to move
rapidly forward with more explicitly socialist policies. Once
'socialism' is reached AES1 considers the 'planning' of incomes acceptable, so that the problems associated with free collective bargaining,
for instance, are eliminated. Finally it should be noted that,
although the theoretical underpinnings of AES1 show little or no advance on the left's traditional thinking, the very concept of an
alternative economic strategy marks a significant break with the
solidly oppositionist policies which have dominated the history of
the British left.
   The second version, AES2, represents the opposite end of the
spectrum in terms of both political and economic criteria. 'Revision-
ist' economists such as Warren, Prior and Purdy have developed a
critique of AES1 and by implication argued for a reformulation of the
strategy.[13] This work has advanced further on the political level
but in my view it needs to be complemented at the economic level by
an analysis that not only takes account of the economic problems in

AES1 referred to above but draws explicitly on the best elements in
orthodox economics, including those of (a narrow definition of)
monetarism; and AES2 as discussed here reflects this view.

Monetarism can be and is defined in a number of ways. In my view
it can best be seen as a spectrum, at one end of which are the 'soft'
or 'wet' monetarists, people who think money is extremely important
- for output in the short term, for inflation and for the exchange
rate; who think the self-equilibrating mechanisms in a capitalist
market economy are relatively weak; who think that the labour market
is different from other markets because labour is essentially different from other commodities rather than because of the existence of
trade unions; and who think that state intervention does have some
role at the macro level (in the form of coarse tuning) and that its
potential benefits at the micro level (particularly in the form of
the welfare state) far outweigh any economic costs involved. At
the other end of the spectrum are the hard-liners, the Thatcherites
and their (relatively few) academic supporters - people who think
that money is all-important for inflation and the nominal exchange
rate, that the self-equilibrating mechanisms in a capitalist market
economy are strong enough to make coarse tuning superfluous, that
the labour market would function like other markets if only there
were no unions, and that all state intervention is politically undesirable and economically harmful. It should be noted that the
empirical evidence tends to favour many of the propositions of the
'soft' or 'narrow' definition of monetarism; and that - unlike 'hard'
monetarism which is clearly permeated by right-wing ideological
elements - 'soft' monetarism can be formulated in purely technical
terms as an analysis of how a capitalist market economy works in
the short to medium run at the macro level.[14]

The concept of advanced capitalist society underlying AES2 is
one which emphasises the complexities and subdivisions within the
major social groups, denies even the 'last instance' determination
of the superstructure by the base, rejects reductionist and instrumentalist views of the state, and stresses the many facets of bourgeois culture and the autonomous hegemony of bourgeois ideology. At
the economic level resource constraints are recognised as potentially
important in socialist as well as capitalist societies and market
forces are seen as reflecting experiences and expectations (e.g.
of future income or future inflation) as well as immediate resource
constraints; the capitalist economy is viewed as a collection of
markets which are more or less closely connected and in which
important but not all-powerful equilibrating mechanisms therefore
exist. AES2 is not a package of (central) government policies like
AES1, but a strategy in which the central government operates a
relatively orthodox macroeconomic policy in recognition of the
unavailability of short run economic benefits from reflation and
of the low cost-effectiveness of direct controls, while - as its
side of a radical social contract - encouraging and providing a
framework for local, occupational and other groups - particularly
groups of workers at the point of production - to take their own
initiatives to improve economic and social arrangements of all kinds
and therefore the quality of life.

   Thus AES2 is a gradualist strategy in both political and economic
terms, and one in which the extension of democracy is a basic component and perhaps even the main driving force. Whereas a suitable slogan for AES1 might be 'Reflation, direct controls and wages struggles',
a suitable slogan for AES2 would be 'Tight monetary policy and joint
production committees' - the former designed to avert a financial
crisis and the latter a reference to the joint worker/management/civil
servant committees set up at all levels of industry during the Second
World War in an attempt to increase the production of munitions and
other supplies essential for winning the war against fascism. There
appear to be enormous political risks in AES2 insofar as some of the
workers' initiatives envisaged would apparently involve important concessions for no contractually agreed gain, since a major part of the
expected gain is that of a progressive political development which is
necessarily not subject to any contract (and is in any case revers-
ible). There were similar political risks in the wartime joint production committees (JPCs), where accusations of class collaboration
were often made against the CP and the left in general who put their
weight firmly behind the JPCs. However, it is arguable that the JPC
period is the only period in which the British left has moved decisively out of its normal oppositionist stance into a strong positive
position and that the strategy contributed substantially to the
massive political and social shift that took place during the war.
Furthermore any serious analysis of the risks involved in other strategies will reveal that they also are considerable: the main risks of
AES1, for example, are on the one hand that the left remains purely
marginal because its policies lack credibility and on the other than
a left government elected on the rebound from Thatcher (though in my
view this is extremely unlikely) and attempting to implement AES1
creates an economic and political crisis that sets the cause of
socialism back by several decades. By contrast AES2 at least holds
out, like the JPCs, the possibility of a major advance.
   While AES1 and AES2 represent opposing extremes in their political
and economic analysis, we can also define an intermediate position
AES3, which commands perhaps majority support among left economists.
The political analysis of AES3 goes at least some way towards that of
AES2 by recognising the complexity of the social structure of advanced
capitalist society, the relative autonomy of the superstructure, the
shortcomings of crude views of the capitalist state and the weakness
and indirectness of the relationship between mass media or economic
conditions and popular consciousness. At the economic level AES3
recognises the importance of resource constraints for the foreseeable
future and the existence of at least some weak self-equilibrating
mechanisms in a capitalist market economy. It has a less optimistic
view than AES1 of the potential short run economic benefits of reflation accompanied by price, importand exchange controls and accepts the
need for some sort of incomes policy to hold down inflation and facilitate planning in the (growing) public sector. AES3 remains essentially central government oriented in its approach to economic policy
and concepts of extending democracy are additions to the strategy
on the political level rather than basic components of it. As
regards the political scenario envisaged AES3 has a concept of
revolution as an extended period (a decade or so?) punctuated by

political and economic crises rather than a cataclysmic event (as in AES1) or an ongoing process (as in AES2).

The foregoing attempt to set out stylised versions of the four main distinct positions held on the left towards the AES has some bearing on the earlier discussion. In particular, it should be clear that only AES2 and AES3 contain the actuality or the possibility of developing an analysis of socialist strategy which integrates political and economic factors. The position of opposition to the AES discussed first contains at least in one strand some useful economic points but the opposition is ultimately the outcome of a political analysis. AES1 is based on a similar subservience of economic analysis to political arguments, and in this respect both of these positions follow squarely in the worst traditions of left-wing thought. By contrast AES2 as set out above represents the elaboration of a gradualist strategy at both the political and the economic level, a strategy in which economic and political analysis is therefore in principle integrated, while in AES3 the political analysis is in general at least sufficiently relaxed to allow economic questions to be decided on economic rather than political grounds and therefore to permit serious economic analysis.

The SER conference was refreshing and positive precisely because of the virtual absence of both AES1 and the standard 'anti-AES' position; and the main subjects of debate, explicitly or implicitly, in one form or another, were the issues that divide AES2 and AES3. Three of the papers given at the conference could be classified as within or near AES3 - the UK review paper by David Currie and Ron Smith, Adam Sharples' excellent survey of existing economic work on the AES, and Paul Ormerod's discussion of inflation policy - while David Purdy's paper on government-trade union relations and Pat Devine's paper on the principles of democratic planning are more obviously AES2. It is probable that the balance of opinion at the conference was weighted towards AES3. What is important, however, is that the common acceptance of the need for high level economic work and for economic issues to be decided on economic criteria, together with a minimum of shared political attitudes, constituted the basis for a generally very constructive discussion. If the SER can continue to provide the space for such discussion it will turn out to have been a very valuable and fruitful development in the economics of the left.

ACKNOWLEDGEMENTS

* The author is grateful to David Currie, Mike Prior and David Purdy for comments on an earlier draft. However, the views expressed in the article are his own, and in particular do not necessarily reflect those of the Socialist Economic Review Working Group or the Communist Party Economic Advisory Committee, of both of which he is a member.

NOTES

1   This paragraph is not intended to assess the overall contribution
    of the CSE, it is concerned only with its potential as a forum for
    left economists.
2   The latest and most important product of this work is the CSE
    London Working Group's *The Alternative Economic Strategy*,
    published (October 1980) jointly by CSE Books and the Labour
    Co-ordinating Committee.
3   Various groups within the Labour Party (as opposed to the Party
    itself) have published books and pamphlets - for example the
    Institute for Workers' Control and the Fabian Society - but this
    work has been of variable quality and has not been designed to
    contribute to debate amongst left (or any other) economists.
    Similar comments apply to the increasing number of economic reviews
    published in recent years by individual trade unions such as
    ASTMS and by the TUC itself.
4   Pat Devine, 'Inflation and Marxist Theory', *Marxism Today*,
    February 1974.
5   David Purdy, 'British Capitalism since the War', *Marxism Today*,
    September and October 1976.
6   The debate on inflation within the CP is surveyed in James Harvey,
    'Theories of Inflation', *Marxism Today*, January 1977.
7   These weaknesses are examined in David Cobham, 'Unemployment and
    the Shorter Working Week', *Economic Bulletin* (CP) No.5, 1979.
8   A 'reasonable balance' seems to have been achieved in practice
    along all except the last of these dimensions, where the unduly
    small number of women economists has been the major source of
    difficulty. The proposal to have a session at the next conference
    dealing specifically with feminist issues is an attempt to over-
    come this problem.
9   See for example Jonathan Bearman, 'Anatomy of the Bennite Left',
    International Socialism, series 2, No.6, 1979.
10 See for example Andrew Glyn and John Harrison, *The British Econo-
    mic Disaster*, Pluto Press, 1980, Ch.5, which draws heavily on
    Glyn's *Capitalist Crisis: Tribune's 'Alternative Strategy' or
    Socialist Plan*, Militant, 1979.
11 See for example Adam Sharples' paper at the SER conference; or
    Glyn's distinction, op.cit., between Tribunite and CP formulations.
12 See John Grahl, 'Problems in the Alternative Economic Strategy',
    Economic Bulletin (CP), No.4, 1979; David Purdy, 'The Left's
    Alternative Economic Strategy', *Politics & Power One*, 1980; David
    Cobham, 'Recent Writing on the Alternative Economic Strategy',
    Economic Bulletin (CP) No.6, 1980.
13 Bill Warren and Mike Prior, *Advanced Capitalism and Backward
    Socialism*, Spokesman, 1975; Mike Prior and David Purdy, *Out of
    the Ghetto*, Spokesman, 1979; David Purdy, 'The Left's Alternative
    Economic Strategy', op.cit.

Grahame Thompson
Public Expenditure and Budgetary Policy

INTRODUCTION

For one reason or another public expenditure has been propelled into
the foreground as the 'culprit' of Britain's economic problems. The
scramble to reduce public expenditure and 'balance the budget' has
been well under way for some five years now with varying degrees of
success. This is backed up by a sometimes 'hysterical' attack on
public spending and its supposed inefficiencies which has been conducted in the popular (and not so popular) press. The present attitudes towards public spending as a problem (as *the* problem) of the
economy stem largely from the events of 1974-76. In this article I
shall look at some fo the trends in public spending over the last
decade or so and try to analyse why it is that from the mid-1970s
public spending became a particular problem and focus of attention,
and discuss the situation in 1980 together with some of the likely
short-run developments. In the final section I shall briefly raise
alternative conceptualisations, policy suggestions and consequences.

THE 'CRISIS' OF 1974-76

Public expenditure as a percentage of Gross National Product (GNP)
had been held stable at about 40% during the 1950s and 1960s in
Britain[1] and the public sector borrowing requirement (PSBR - this
measures central and local government and nationalised industry's
net borrowing) was neither high in relation to GNP nor controversial.
In terms of budgetary policy it has been argued[2] that throughout
this period, and even into the early 1970s, a surplus on the current
account largely offset the deficits on the capital account so that
only small borrowing requirements were generated.[3] Because there
had been no necessity to generate any large current account deficits,
'Keynesian' demand management policies, as traditionally conceived,
had never really been pursued.[4] There was even a negative borrowing
requirement in 1969 and 1970.

It was only in the mid to late 1970s that all this got severely
disrupted. The ratio of public expenditure to GNP rose to about 60%
and this heralded a political outcry from a wide spectrum of opinion
that Britain's 'freedom and democracy' were at stake. Now, it is
notoriously difficult to put a definitive figure on either GNP or
the public sector expenditure proportion of it. In another paper I
have discussed this at some length and point out that actually such
a ratio could quite legitimately vary anywhere between 60% and just
over 30% in 1976. Commentators can choose the ratio that best suits
their purpose.[5] This point is recognised by those who are very much
against present levels of public expenditure[6] and I shall not repeat
the argument here since, in a sense, it does not affect the actual
constraints that were facing the government at the time when it
was trying to finance its expenditure. The focus below is not upon
this proportion as such but upon what the government has to finance
- the PSBR, which is the subject of so much attention in the
financial markets.

It is impossible to talk about public expenditure in isolation
from public revenue, particularly taxation. Britain is one of the
few countries where the budget, in terms of expenditures and receipts,
is not planned together, but rather where expenditure is planned
first and then revenues to meet this are 'planned' afterwards.
The 'planning' of revenues deserves inverted commas because such
revenue-raising is not really planned at all. Traditionally it
has been the yearly Budget (and more recently the twice yearly
Budget) which has set levels of anticipated revenues from taxation.
It is revenues, not expenditure, which have been used as an instrument for short-term management of aggregate economic demand, reacting to changes in economic circumstance in an attempt to regulate
the position of the economy. When revenues from taxation and user
charges for government services (though the latter comprise a very
small proportion of revenues) have not been adequate to finance the
planned expenditure, the shortfall has been met by borrowing.

This separation of revenue-raising and expenditure-planning
largely results from the (non) relationship between the traditional
Parliamentary way of organising the Supply Estimates and the graft-
ing on to this of an essentially *ad hoc* series of expenditure
planning mechanisms. At present the Public Expenditure Survey
Committee (discussed more fully below) plans public expenditure
over a four to five year rolling period, whereas the Budget is
addressed to very particular short-term contingent problems.

In March 1980, it so happened that the White Paper on public
expenditure[7] was published on the same day as the Budget was presented to Parliament,[8] but this did not mean that they had in any
real sense been planned together.[9] It occurred because of the
interim nature of the Conservative Government's previous White Paper
on government expenditure[10] which was published according to the
usual time-table in November 1979, but after only a few months of
Conservative administration.

The bulk of government revenue comes from taxation. Some 80%
has traditionally originated from this source though recently, and
particularly from 1975/6, borrowing has increased in relative importance as taxation revenue sources have slipped away. To a large

extent, this 'slippage' of tax revenues has been a result of deliberate government policy (though this has combined with the effects of
inflation). Two things are important here: in the first place nominal rates of tax had been kept down because of the attempts to generate and maintain an incomes policy in various forms; and secondly,
there had been a relative shift away from indirect taxation and
towards direct taxation during the 1960s and 70s.[11] What were the
reasons for this?

Let us take indirect taxes to start with. Any increase in nominal
rates on these immediately appears as an increase in the Retail Prices
Index (RPI). In this country wage negotiations are closely related
to changes in the RPI so when governments are at pains to get trade
union cooperation to restrain wage increases there are considerable
incentives not to increase the RPI 'unnecessarily'. The policy of
the Heath government over 'threshold agreements', which allowed wages
to increase automatically with increases in the cost of living,
largely accounts for the wages explosion in the 1973/74 'boom'.
The close relationship between wage bargaining and the RPI also
accounts for the attempted replacement of the RPI by the Conservatives'
'Taxes and Prices Index' first published in 1979. This took account
of the tax reductions in the June 1979 Budget. So far the attempted
removal of the RPI from its central position does not seem to have
succeeded. Even the introduction of VAT and subsequent increases in
its nominal rate have not as yet really prevented the relative decline
of indirect taxes. VAT is levied on a small range of goods and
services and its impact has therefore been limited.

The last two Conservative Government Budgets have, however, attempted to introduce a definite reversal of the trends in indirect and
direct taxation. The intention is to shift the tax burden very much
away from direct taxes and on to indirect taxes - in the name of incentives for the individual. In addition, Petroleum Revenue Tax is
likely to become more important in the next five to ten years, which
will alter some of these patterns even further.

Over the last two decades, direct taxation has increased in importance as a source of revenue, though it has not been fully adjusted
to keep abreast with higher expenditures. There has been no significant change in standard tax rates and obvious gaps in the mechanisms
for paying direct taxes have not been plugged. However, as personal
incomes increase with inflation, the tax net tends to be widened:
those with lower incomes become eligible for income tax, while those
with higher incomes are drawn into progressively higher tax brackets.
The effects at the lower end of the spectrum are more important.
Revenue from taxation increases relatively here. Low-income earners
are progressively drawn from non-taxed into taxed brackets (the so-
called 'poverty trap') while upper income earners can usually avoid
the highest marginal rates. When a marginal tax rate of 98 per cent
was in force for the highest earners, nobody need have paid more than
a 50 to 60 per cent rate because of the success of tax avoidance for
which the system created massive incentives.[12] The widening of the
tax net as a result of inflation has led to widespread opposition to
increases in direct taxation and much sympathy for reducing income
tax.

Despite this built-in resistance to the erosion of revenues from direct taxation by inflation, the overall tax burden remained pretty static during the 1960s and 1970s. This is because the effect of the wider tax net has been balanced by increased unemployment reducing revenue from direct taxes together with the fall in revenue from indirect taxation. In fact, between 1970 and 1975, tax revenues as a proportion of GNP declined.[13] Moreover, the ratio of tax revenues to GNP is lower in Britain than in most other European OECD countries and has tended to decline relative to these countries in the past two decades. Britain is not a relatively highly taxed country. Similar comments apply to the ratio of public spending to GNP where Britain is again unexceptional.

In relation to public expenditures it is worth tracing the development of the recent system of public expenditure and 'control'. In this case, 'control' deserves inverted commas since there does not seem to have been much of it, certainly not until 1976.

Since 1961 a system mentioned above and known as the Public Expenditure Survey Committee cycle (PESC) has been in operation.[14] This is an elaborate year-long round procedure of departmental examination of expenditure. It is based upon the statutory obligations of government apparatuses and any policy directives from the government.

A number of points can be made about this. It is a planning process that estimates expenditure on the basis of real resource use, that is, in *volume* terms. The burden of the process is to estimate the number of buildings, extent of equipment, numbers to be employed, etc. Such physical estimates are then converted into money total within the PESC process.

It is the job of the Treasury to reconcile these forecasts and bids. It does this on the basis of the *resource table*. This is based upon macro-economic forecasts and predicts the total amount of such resources likely to be available in the economy. From this total a series of deductions are made: that necessary to cater for the balance of payments constraint; that necessary for private corporate and non-corporate investment. The residual, when all these prior claims have been met, can then be distributed between private consumption and public expenditure. Whilst this is described in general terms here, it largely characterises the actual process. What this implies is that the planning of expenditure is done in relation to the estimation of GNP, and not in relation to the estimation of government revenues, while public expenditure is conceived as a 'residual' and is seen to 'compete' with private consumption.

The question of control over public expenditure arose very acutely in the mid-1970s. The PESC system traditionally planned in volume terms at *constant prices*. This was modified in the early 1970s to include some adjustment of the constant prices for the *relative price effect* (rpe). The rpe expresses the tendency for there to be different rates of inflation in the private and the public sectors.[15] This was built into the process to try to show the overall (money) demand in the future. But things began to go very wrong in 1974/5. Wynne Godley of Cambridge University pointed out that the expenditure in that year was some £5 billions higher than had been estimated and the Select Committee on Public Expenditure (SCPE) called the Treasury to account for this.[16] The Treasury replied that the discrepancy was more like £5½ billions. Some £2½ billions was as a result of declared policy changes on the part of the government, while the other £3 billions was the result of underestimating the rpe, because of inflation (largely in land prices) and unexpected increases in interest rate charges on Government debt.

The general point about this scrutiny by the SCPE was that it showed that public expenditure was for all intents and purposes out of control and that there was no proper accounting for it.

At about the same time the government was facing two further acute economic problems. Continued balance-of-payments deficits during the early 1970s had led to heavy borrowing from abroad and in 1976 there was a strong run on the pound which even persistent Bank of England intervention to bolster Sterling could not stop. The reserves were all but exhausted in the attempt to halt the run but this did not 'bottom out' until after the value of the pound had almost halved against the dollar. This led the government to call on the IMF for a £5¼ billion loan which was secured at the end of 1976.

This period also saw the culmination of the rapid increase in the PSBR. The immediate cause of the increase was the forces of inflation, debt repayment and rpe, but behind these were some important demographic and social policy changes. There had been a secular decline in the proportion of the population that was economically active, which increased the number of dependents.[17] In addition, social policies of subsidization and income maintenance had been secured by the trade unions in return for cooperation with incomes policies. The recession in the economy was leading to increased unemployment. All these and other reasons led to a sharp increase in public expenditure just at a time when revenues were being depressed because of the lack of adjustments in taxation policy. This led to a rapid build up of pressure on the PSBR, which reached the historically high level of £10 billion in 1976. At one stage the financial markets were not prepared to accept any further long-term government debt. The Bank of England was forced to raise the Minimum Lending Rate to 15 per cent and seek more easily obtainable short-term loans. Thus on the first occasion on which the government did try to institute a large deficit in the current account its efforts were severely thwarted and constrained by the financial markets.

All this led to the rapid institution of 'cash limits' on public expenditure and attempts to cut back the growth and even absolute levels of public expenditure. Whilst the imposition of cash limits has been largely attributed by the left to the intervention of IMF, it is clear that these were first proposed by the Treasury as a way of gaining control over public expenditure in a period of rapid inflation. Expenditure and the PSBR have to be financed in money terms - this was the constraint facing the Treasury and it is rather difficult to see what else it could have done at the time. Also, whilst the IMF did initially insist on cuts in public expenditure of between £3 billion and £4 billion these were largely forgotten or reinstated in the subsequent years when pressure on the exchange rate lifted. However, domestic political pressures to cut back on

public expenditure are a continuing legacy of this period, as are
the historically high level of the PSBR and interest rates.

Cash limits have been retained and extended. These now comprise
the main instrument of public expenditure control. They cover some
80 per cent of government expenditure. The areas not affected are
'demand determined' expenditures like social security benefits, unemployment relief and investment allowances of various sorts. The
actual levels of these cannot be easily fixed in advance. Cash limits
mean that it would not now be possible to 'fine-tune' the economy in
terms of varying expenditures even if the government wanted to do so.
Cash limits comprise three main elements: that part designed to cover
the planned real volume of expenditure; that part to cover expected
inflation; and that part designed to account for the rpe. Given
that the assumptions embodied in the provision of the latter two
elements are not made public by the government, there is no way of
knowing how much actual real expenditure is planned for or undertaken. Departments and spending units are just given a global total
within which they must work. In fact, since spending units are
reluctant to over-reach their expenditure limits, they have tended
to err on the side of caution (at least in the early years) and as
a result there has been considerable underspending, particularly in
the years 1976-1978. This underspending accounted for much of the
cutback in actual expenditure during those years.

THE ATTACK ON THE PSBR AND ON PUBLIC EXPENDITURE

Largely as a result of what has now been said above, the PSBR became
propelled into the foreground of political debate. At a time of
increasing public expenditure, with taxation policy and revenues
constrained, the result was a rapid increase in the PSBR. It has
remained at between £8 billion and £12 billion over the four years
since 1976 and the difficulty of cutting back on expenditure has
made it difficult to cut back on this figure. In addition the
Conservative Government is committed to reducing taxes, so it has
even less room for manoeuvre in trying to cut the PSBR down. Re-
financing such a high PSBR has meant keeping interest rates high,
but this in turn results in a growing government burden of interest
payment which, at £8,819 million in 1979, comprised *three-quarters*
of the total PSBR in that year.

Public expenditure has come to be seen as the scapegoat for most
of the ills of the economy. While this has been caused by a number
of factors, one of the most important of these, at least politically,
is the argument that such expenditure represents an unproductive
burden on the economy. Indeed, this is the Prime Minister's stated
position:

'First, if our objective is to have a prosperous and expanding
economy, we must recognize that high public spending, as a
proportion of GNP, very quickly kills growth... We have to
remember that governments have no money at all. Every penny
they take is taken from the productive sector of the economy
in order to transfer it to the unproductive part of it. That
is one of the great causes of our problems, because this

government have increased the unproductive sector and diminished
the productive sector, so that during the lifetime of this government we have had virtually no growth at all.'[18]
The echoes of this distinction can also be found in the Bacon and
Eltis thesis, though they make a more sophisticated distinction
between what is marketable and what is non-marketable.[19]

To explain fully why the 'government sector' is conceived to be
unproductive would take us deeply into political ideology. One of
the more obvious 'economic' aspects of such an explanation is that
it results from the idea that this sector does not do anything for
its income ' it 'gets something for nothing'. If one's ideology is
firmly based on the conception of the economy as a kind of family
budget writ large - a family budget where income from *work done*
constrains expenditure and where prudence and restraint are regarded
as highly virtuous - then to have a sector of the economy which is
not ultimately constrained in this way is highly disturbing. The
'government sector' has the power to tax and 'create debt' which
is not 'earned', or for which it does not have to exchange a service
or commodity, so it is not constrained in the same way as a family
budget is. This is not, of course, to suggest that the government
does not face constraints itself. The major constraint on the actual
level of the 'non-balanced budget' in the second half of the 1970s
was the estimation by financial institutions of what were the
correct and prudent level of government debt-holdings and the
resulting conditions they imposed in financing its deficit.[20]

However, in terms of political ideology, what seems to inform the
conception that government expenditure is unproductive is the concern
that the government's income or money, and hence its purchasing
power (which is what gives it command over economic resources) is not
subject to any 'automatic' market constraint. This takes the form of
a preoccupation with the sources of income of different economic
agents. How and from where do they generate their income? For
Bacon and Eltis, if it is marketed it is all right but if it is
non-marketed it is not.[21] For Mrs Thatcher, on the other hand, it
should be spent there as well and not transferred to be spent by the
non-productive sector.[22]

In addition to this, the whole area of budgetary policy is be-
deviled by conceiving of economic relations in terms of yearly
accounting identities. Such yearly accounting identities express
aggregated macro-economic variables. This gives rise to the idea that
there is some fixed quantum of resources which can be divided up in
various ways, and where a little more of one leads to a little less
of the other. All the major schools of economic analysis have their
own particular 'basic' equation of this character.

Some of the effects of this are quite pernicious. For instance,
it gives rise to one of the major contemporary ideological attacks
on public expenditure. This is that such expenditure 'crowds-out'
either private consumption or private investment. Now this is a
complicated area, since it is clear that, under rather special and
short-term conditions, forms of crowding-out do occur. What I shall
challenge here are what might be called 'theoretical crowding-out'
theses - that is theories of government expenditure which are

constructed around conceptions that centrally imply a crowding-out
type analysis. There are two main ways in which crowding-out is
employed in this manner: resource crowding-out, and financial
crowding-out.

The conception of resource crowding-out can perhaps be best illustrated by taking the case of employment. It is often argued that
the growth of employment in the public sector, particularly within
local authorities, has 'crowded-out' the growth of production in the
private sector. It is argued that labour has been 'syphoned-off'
from one sector to the other, largely because the public sector has
been able to offer better conditions of employment. This is attributed to the absence of real control over the expenditure of the
public sector - bureaucratisation has been mushrooming in the form
of increases in administrative personnel and so on.

In fact, two points can be made against this view. In the first
place, much of the increased employment in the public sector can be
accounted for by labour which was just not available in the private
sector before, notably women workers. There has been a significant
growth of women workers (particularly married women workers) who
have entered the labour market in the last ten years and they have
tended to do so via the public sector. In addition these women have
tended to be employed in part-time occupations, something again which
the private sector had not given them the opportunity to do. In this
way the public sector tapped a large new source of potential employees. (This is not to deny that these positions involved very low
pay on occasions, nor that women might have entered the labour market
because of the necessities dictated by a decreasing real family
budget with inflation and growing male unemployment, etc.) In the
second place, the private sector has been 'shedding labour' of
various sorts, particularly the non-skilled. Hence there was a
pool of labour available for the public sector to tap which no
longer entered into the private sector calculations.

The conception of financial crowding-out is a more serious one.
It revolves around the argument that investment has been delayed,
or not undertaken at all, in the private sector because of the
difficulty that the private sector has had in raising credit for
such investment. The argument involved the assertion that the
public sector, through the PSBR, had been 'absorbing' all the credit
that the financial markets were able to offer. In addition, since
the public sector needed to finance so much economic activity it,
in effect, forced up interest rates to encourage the private financial institutions to provide loans. In so doing it also encouraged
any private firms with spare investable money capital to invest in
government debt as well, and forgo other potentially profitable
'productive' investment in their own activity. Investing in government debt secured for such firms a 'riskless' high return on their
money capital which they were unlikely to find in the other forms
of manufacturing or employment creating investment that they were
alternatively considering.

Clearly, there could be some pertinence to this argument particularly in the rather special but short-lived circumstances of 1975/6.
But fundamentally it rests upon a theoretical argument that cannot
be rigorously sustained. In the first place it attributes 'blame'

for rises in interest rates to the public sector alone. However,
it could be equally argued that it is the terms and conditions under
which the private financial institutions will hold government debt
which 'determines' the interest rate. The government is forced to
increase the rate to satisfy the institutions themselves. Secondly,
it rests upon a conception that some given amount of credit is
available which is distributed between the two sectors - as more
of the credit goes to the public sector, so less is available for the
private sector. This fails to appreciate that under the present
arrangements of the financial system it is precisely the existence
of government debt which is a *condition for* private sector lending
by financial institutions. Such debt acts as a reserve base on
which the system can develop credit creation and lending. What is
important is the competitive conditions under which credit is made
available to different economic agents and in different forms (over-
drafts, shares, bonds, etc.), but there is little evidence to suggest
that the *binding constraint* upon undertaking investment in the private
sector is the 'cost of capital' registered by interest rates.[23] The
'crowding-out' thesis does not penetrate to the real reasons why the
private sector has become uncompetitive and is reluctant to undertake
'physical' investment, nor why the public sector should be in a position to require a significant (but temporary) unbalanced budget.
Such problems cannot be attributed to a single cause or solved by
a single simple remedy.

One other general point that helps to sustain the 'theoretical
crowding-out' argument is the idea that the constraint on the amount
of investment in the economy is the amount of saving undertaken in
the economy. There is a complicated relationship between savings and
investment because these are not homogeneous macroaggregates. For
instance, investment by agents can be of a number of different types.
What constrains the ability of agents to undertake investment of
varying kinds is the ability of the system to create credit for them
in various forms, not 'savings' as such.

In fact the savings which have any economic pertinence and effectivity in an economy like that of the UK appear as financial flows in
one or other of the financial institutions within the system - this
is what savings comprise - and these are mobilised into that system
of credit-creation by such institutions. Thus the notion of savings
is always problematical and not given in the form of a simple macro-
economic aggregate. The institutions (Commercial Banks, Pensions
Funds, Building Societies, etc.) are not mere intermediaries between
lenders and borrowers; they deploy their investments according to
particular criteria and within narrowly defined and specialised areas.
Their own policies and ways of working determine which agents will
be granted credit and under what conditions. Even if there is a
'demand' for credit from some agents, there is no guarantee that
credit will be advanced, and even if such credit is actually available
there is no reason why it should be advanced or taken up. In this
way these institutions can circumvent any simple effects of 'savings',
either by creating more credit under particular conditions, or by
'delaying' and holding up the creation of credit, or by channelling
investment into particular areas. The effects of such practices and
investments are not all on a par with each other.

These considerations also apply to industrial and commercial firms themselves with respect to their decisions about investments and other financial activity. Without analysing these practices and mechanisms, and how they were operating under particular conditions, little can be said about whether there was a real inability to supply credit in various forms to those agents who were demanding it.

The crowding-out argument holds that the PSBR forces out private manufacturing investment, but this assumes that particular investment projects were anticipated and would have been undertaken in the absence of a high PSBR. It also assumes that the relevant institutions and economic agents were willing to advance loans for these projects, but could not because of the PSBR. There is little evidence to support either assumption.[24]

On the contrary, it is clear that the PSBR as such has not constrained investment in the private sector. A look at the PSBR in relation to the savings-ratio in the economy as a whole makes two things apparent. Firstly, the ratio of savings to GNP has been increasing while the ratio of public debt to GNP has been falling; in fact, the latter ratio is at one of its lowest levels since 1900.[25] Secondly, the PSBR is much lower in real terms than it appears in normal terms, because in times of inflation borrowers gain at the expense of lenders and the government is a net borrower in nominal terms. Taylor and Threadgold estimate that, after adjusting for inflation, the PSBR averaged about £1,500 a year from 1975 to 1978, compared to an annual average of £8,000 million in nominal terms; they go on to suggest that the government was actually a *net saver* in real terms before 1974, and only became a substantial net borrower in 1978.[26]

The high savings-ratio combined with reluctance in the private sector to support 'physical' investment projects, together with the low real burden of public debt and the PSBR imply that the PSBR's present level can quite easily be sustained. In fact, for the flows of money embodied in the savings ratio to be channelled somewhere, some financial asset must be created to support them. If the private sector wished to create such assets, this could be supported by the present level of savings and the creation of credit activities articulated around them without causing serious problems with respect to the PSBR. The fact is that no such pressures seem to be emerging from the private sector which makes it doubly necessary for the government to try to stimulate such investment itself. Nor, according to Taylor and Threadgold, need such an increased nominal PSBR necessarily lead to an increase in the money supply.[27]

THE EFFECTS OF THE CUTBACKS IN PUBLIC EXPENDITURE

We are now in a position to say something about the possible consequences of the attempts to cut back on public expenditure.

One preliminary point is whether at the aggregate level there has been such a cut-back. This is difficult to determine because the various White Papers on public expenditure tend to recalculate the figures for previous years. Table 1 shows the position as outlined in the latest White Paper.[28] It seems clear that the

TABLE 1
Public expenditure 1974/5 to 1979/80 and plans 1980/81 to 1983/84

Year	*Amount*	*% change on previous year*
1974/75	71 662	+8.5
1975/76	71 936	+0.4
1976/77	70 154	-2.5
1977/78	65 934	-6.0
1978/79	69 611	+5.6
1979/80	69 930	+0.4
1980/81	69 501	-0.6
1981/82	68 700	-1.2
1982/83	67 700	-2.0
1983/84	67 100	-0.3

Notes:
1 Actual figures shown in £ millions
2 These are all at constant 1979 survey prices hence they
   represent volume term changes

Source: Cmnd 7841, Table 1.1, HMSO 1980a.

---

institution of cash limits in 1975/76 had some effects in subsequent
years but public expenditure increased again in 1978/9 and 1979/80.
The Labour government's plans were for a modest growth in public
expenditure between 1979/80 and 1982/83 so the Conservatives are
attempting quite a reversal of those plans. They plan a 4 per cent
decrease over the period 1980/81 to 1983/84, which for 1982/83, say,
represents a £9 billion reduction (11½%) on the Labour government's
proposals for that year.
    These are the plans; their actual outcome is another matter. It
is notoriously difficult to prevent public expenditure increasing in
real terms let alone actually cut it back for a sustained period.
How successful the present government will be remains to be seen.
Signs of difficulties are already emerging with the threat to suspend
all local authority capital expenditure if plans for cut-backs are
not kept to in the second half of 1980. Perhaps, then, the significance of the 'cuts' is less than is commonly presumed. So far there
has been more a drying up in the growth of public expenditure.
    What has happened, however, is that there has been a significant
redistribution of expenditure between the various items of public
expenditure and additional redistributions are planned for the future.
Expenditure on 'Law and Order', Defence and Social Security and
personal services has increased and is to be increased, while that
on such items as Education, Transport and Housing has decreased.
Besides these changes the most notable planned changes are reductions
in subsidies to industry, energy, trade and employment programmes
and in the provisions for borrowing by nationalised industries.

The most obvious recent increases in public spending have been on
defence and 'law and order'. Reductions have fallen particularly
heavily on local authority expenditure - this where most of the cut-
backs in transport, education and housing have occurred and where
they will be felt most acutely. Spending by local authorities
increased particularly rapidly in the 1970s, and now accounts for
about 30 per cent of total public spending, but about 65 per cent
of this is financed from central government. This is the element
which will be cut back (by cutting the Rate Support Grant). The
response will vary between local authorities, with some accepting
the cuts while others try to compensate by increasing local rates.
The result is likely to be greater local unevenness in provision
of services and increased political conflict between local and
central apparatuses of government.

Where cuts have taken place, capital expenditure has been cut
most severely and is likely to continue to take the brunt of any
further cut-backs. Current expenditure is always more difficult
to cut. This is encouraged by the way the programmes of expenditure
are organized and controlled. Expenditure is allocated separately
for capital purposes and for current purposes even for obviously
related functional areas and items. Thus there is no incentive
for spending units to economise on one or other of these categories
since trade-offs between them are not allowed in most cases. A
simple reform of public expenditure planning and control would thus
be to allocate expenditure for specific but functional areas and
items.

One area of public expenditure which recently became a particular
focus of political debate in the UK was the net contribution to the
EEC budget. This had risen from zero in 1973 to over £1,300 million
in 1980. With the lack of positive policy with respect to the development of the EEC by the Conservative Government, focus of attention
was directed towards the UK's net contribution to the budget.
Whilst the government is still committed to a reduction of its contribution so that a broad balance of contributions and expenditures
results, it seems to have settled for a negotiated compromise of a
reduction to some 350 billions for 1980. Whilst the absolute amount
of these net contributions is only marginal with respect to overall
public expenditure, as long as the EEC budget is seen as a separate
item into which countries feed revenue and draw benefits, the UK's
net contribution is likely to continue to be a political issue. In
fact a lot of this net contribution represents only a transfer of
resources from domestic agricultural subsidisation to European agricultural subsidisation. However, the latter obviously has balance
of payments implications, though this is probably less important
now than its implications for the PSBR, given the strong state of
the pound internationally.

This mention of the balance-of-payments consequences of budgetary
policy can introduce what could be the most important 'bright-spot'
in relation to the future constraints on government expenditure and
budgetary programming. It is clear that it is North Sea oil that
is contributing to maintain the balance of payments at manageable
(if deficit) levels in the face of the dramatic collapse of the
current account balance with respect to manufacturing. In addition

the revenue from the Petroleum Revenue Tax (PRT) - which is going
to become increasingly important for government revenue during the
next five years or so[29] - could be employed to release pressure on
the attempt to cut public expenditure and the PSBR. All this if
the Government wanted it to be employed in this way.

The existence of PRT seems to suggest that despite a great deal
of ideological huff and puff with respect to public expenditure and
the PSBR, government finances themselves are not in too bad a state
at the present. This is not to deny that there will continue to be
increased political pressures to cut back public expenditure margin-
ally in many areas and a continued policy of widening the scope of
payment for public services (health charges, school meals, school
transport charges, etc.). But at present there need be no full
scale attack on current levels of public expenditure. It is
important to recognise that the Welfare State is not being dis-
mantled by the present government. In some areas, in fact, expenditure is to rise under the present plans, for example expenditure
on health and some personal services. There is even a small
planned increase in social security payments, though, clearly,
increased pressure will be put on this item because of the likely
growth in the number of claimants. In addition, the Social
Security Bill will link the indexing of benefits to rises in
prices, not earnings, and further legislation is promised to
reduce the earnings-related supplements and introduce measures
to tax a number of forms of benefit.

Although all this is certainly not to be supported, the measures
suggested do not as yet indicate a real determination to dismantle
the social security system. Under present conditions this seems
to be politically impossible. The PSBR is likely to be discussed
more in relation to the 'control of the money supply' than in
relation to public expenditure as such. Given the difficulty of
controlling the money supply through the usual means, however,
it may be thought necessary by the present government, at some
stage, to drastically attack the present level of the PSBR in an
attempt to 'mop up' spare liquidity that currently characterises
the financial system. This might be thought one way of re-gaining
control of the money supply in the economy.[30]

A SOCIALIST RESPONSE?

In this section I want to raise a number of issues concerning the
socialist response to the present political debate about public
expenditure. Already a number of these issues have been hinted at.
I do not intend to reduce the present situation to one conceived
in terms of a general crisis of capitalism, or as an expression
of the general tendencies of capitalism.[31] My aim is to come to
grips with contemporary conditions as they are at present, and not
as socialists might like them to be focussed. One thing the present government has done is to interrupt the steady development of
State intervention which has been proceeding apace for some thirty
years without any real attempt to take an overall look at its
direction and at its effects and consequences. This may be a

period which gives the opportunity to socialists to undertake such a reappraisal and to take stock of their own commitments to various aspects and forms of government expenditure.

One of the problems with the present conceptualizations of public expenditure is that they lead to an analysis couched in terms of macro-economic aggregated variables. One of the tasks of socialists should be to attempt to break down this aggregation in various ways. The problem with macro-aggregates is that they do not operate as agents in the economy. Rather, they are the *results* of the action of agents and agencies.

Under the heading of 'public expenditure' a diverse set of economic relationships are included, some of which are for all intents and purposes directly equivalent to 'private sector' activity, as it is traditionally conceived. One case in point is the nationalised industries. It is not necessary to support all aspects of their organisation and management to see that a number of them have been particularly successful when measured against the general plight of British industry. So it seems rather shortsighted to restrict their borrowing simply as a result of a general concern with the PSBR.

This highlights the need to isolate and analyse the mechanisms and practices of those agencies involved with different types of expenditure in their own right. Along with this could go a questioning of the present divisions of 'public' and 'private' (which, after all, is only a legal definition). That 'private' expenditure is treated differently from 'public' expenditure needs to be questioned, particularly where this means that the domains of public expenditure are limited and restricted. For instance, it is at present difficult for the public sector to initiate forms of economic activity which are not already established, but where there might be an obvious need for them. This is because public expenditure is circumscribed in terms of the areas and forms that it can take. In relation to productive activity it is circumscribed either to subsidise present activity in one way or another *or* nationalise it, but not to initiate it (the NEB being a case which tried to break with these limits). Of course, if this is true of the way the public sector is circumscribed, it is equally true of the way that 'private' activity is circumscribed. Thus, it may be pertinent to question whether a lot of what is at present 'public' expenditure, and the manner in which such activity is conceived to function as a result of such a designation, should not be considered as 'private' in the way it operates and functions and vice versa. There seems no reason, for instance, why local authorities should not operate small businesses, or provide the finance for them, on a much wider scale than they do at present.

This is one way of combating the notion that the increase in public expenditure equals an increase in socialism. There may be no necessary connection between the two. In fact, it may be easier to initiate democratic control over forms of expenditure that are at present conceived to be private in character than over those that are public in character (e.g. defence spending). The general point here is that the priority of socialists should be to open up areas, *any areas*, in which it is possible to insert different forms of democratic and accountable control. Such priorities might cut across the present duality of 'public' and 'private' in terms of expenditure decisions and controls.

This argument applies to discussion of the PSBR as well. Clearly, one of the things to try to displace here is the concentration on one particular aggregative variable which informs discussion of the levels and degree of public expenditure. I have already argued that the PSBR is not the constraint on 'private' investment and consumption that it is supposed to be. It was also pointed out that the Public Debt is, in relation to GNP, historically at one of its lowest levels. At a time of rapid inflation borrwers gain and lenders lose, so it 'pays' to borrow here - the 'government sector' should be encouraged to borrow since the real burden that this represents to the tax-payer decreases through time. An over-sensitive concentration on one aggregative total, the PSBR, to the exclusion of discussion about the diverse kinds of economic relationships that it supports, should be displaced. But this then means that socialists themselves must consider these disaggregated expenditures and forms of economic activity and have policies about what they want to see done at those levels.[32] This also means we need more thought about where democratisation might be initiated and under what forms it can take place.

In addition to all of this, it is important to look seriously at where it might be possible to reduce the present constraints (whether 'real' or ideological) on the flexible increase in public expenditure. The present burden of re-financing the Public Debt is very high. Could this be reduced? One possibility here could arise as a side effect of the recent relaxation of all outstanding exchange rate controls. This now means that the range of economic agents who might be prepared to purchase UK government debt is considerably broadened to include overseas buyers. Such potential buyers will bring quite a diverse range of economic and financial calculations to bear on their purchase decision. These in turn will be related to quite a different set of domestic considerations (in terms of alternatives) from those that characterise the main UK internal purchasers. This could enable the government to re-finance its debt, or to increase its debt, at lower cost.[33]

Finally, we should not forget taxation policy. Two points are worth quickly mentioning. In the first place a proper and comprehensive indexation of indirect taxes would seem to be in order, and secondly there would seem to be a space for widening the tax base. The UK is typified by a very narrow tax base compared to other advanced capitalist countries. One obvious area here is a comprehensive capital gains tax. The pernicious and inequitable effects of not instituting such a tax with respect to the rise in house prices has recently been pointed out.[34] Although this does not look like an area in which immediate advance is likely to be made, socialists should argue for changes in this direction in relation to the more general objective of a widely deployed capital gains tax.

Footnotes

1 Ward and Neild (1978), Chapter 4.
2 By Mathews (1968) and more recently by Tomlinson (1980.
3 Current account expenditure includes such items as day to day
  running expenses, labour costs, maintenance etc., whereas

capital account expenditure includes mainly investment expenditure.
4   Keynesian demand management implies running up a current account
    deficit in times of economic inactivity to stimulate aggregate
    demand and running up a current account surplus at times of high
    economic activity to dampen down such demand. The emphasis upon
    the current account here arises because of the simple Keynesian
    national income identity. This is expressed as $Y = C+G+I+(X-M)$
    where Y equals national income, C designates consumption, G
    designates government expenditure, I stands for investment, X
    designates exports and M imports. All investment, whether public
    or private, is normally included under I so only current govern-
    ment expenditure comes under G. For a further discussion of this
    see Tomlinson (1980).
5   See Thompson (1979a).
6   Brittan (1978).
7   Cmnd 7841, HMSO (1980a).
8   HCP500, HMSO (1980b).
9   There has recently been an Institute of Fiscal Studies Report
    looking at ways in which the two sides of the Budget might be
    meaningfully combined and the House of Commons Treasury and
    Civil Service Committee is to look into this matter in the
    Parliamentary Session beginning in the autumn of 1980.
10 Cmnd 7746, HMSO (1979).
11 Direct taxation refers mainly to the taxation of incomes whereas
    indirect taxation refers to the taxation on goods and services.
12 Kay and King (1978), Chapter 4.
13 Ward and Neild (1978), Table 4.10, p.69.
14 For a discussion of the history and working of this see Wright
    (1977) and Pollitt (1977).
15 See Rees and Thompson (1972).
16 Godley's memorandum and the Select Committee's scrutiny can be
    found in HMSO (1976).
17 See Thompson (1979b), Table 5.
18 Mrs M. Thatcher, MP, *Hansard*, 25 July 1978, col.1400.
19 Bacon and Eltis (1976).
20 Tomlinson (1980).
21 Of course, the Bacon and Eltis thesis amounts to more than just
    this and neither is the thesis unambiguous in its form and impli-
    cations. For instance, it is clear that in terms of the balance
    of payments the distinction marketed/non-marketed has some
    pertinence. Goods and services must be *sold* overseas to meet
    any necessary constraint with respect to imports, which are also
    marketed.
22 Apart from some limited but necessary expenditure on the part
    of government which should be kept to an absolute minimum.
23 For an argument developed around this point see Thompson (1980).
24 Midland Bank Review (1980) and Wilson Committee (1980).
25 Reed (1977). There is no reason to believe that this has changed
    significantly since the publication of this article.
26 Taylor and Threadgold (1979).
27 See Taylor and Threadgold (1979), p.30.
28 Cmnd 7841, HMSO, 1980a.

29 Slightly conflicting impressions on this are given in HM Treasury (1980) and Forsyth and Kay (1980).
30 I discuss this at greater length in Thompson (1980).
31 As is done in CSE (1979).
32 One such attempt is made in Blake and Ormerod (1980).
33 There could obviously be some undesirable effects of this exchange control relaxation as well.
34 Atkinson and King (1980).

References

Atkinson, A.B. and King, M. (1980), 'Housing Policy, Taxation and Reform', *Midland Bank Review*, Spring, pp.7-15.

Bacon, R. and Eltis, W. (1976), *Britain's Economic Problem: Too Few Producers*, Macmillan, London.

Blake, D. and Ormerod, P. (1980), *Economics and Prosperity*, Grant Macintyre, London.

Brittan, S. (1978), 'How British is the British Sickness?', *Journal of Law and Economics*, Vol.21, No.2, October.

C.S.E. (1979), *Struggle over the State*, Conference of Socialist Economists State Group, C.S.E. Books, London.

Forsyth, P.J. and Kay, J.A. (1980), 'The Economic Implications of North Sea Oil Revenues', *Fiscal Studies*, Vol.1, No.3, July, pp.1-18.

HMSO (1976), *1st Report from the Expenditure Committee: The Financing of Public Expenditure*, HCP 69-11 1975/76.

HMSO (1979), *The Government's Expenditure Plans 1980-81*, Cmnd 7746, November, London.

HMSO (1980a), *The Government's Expenditure Plans 1980-81 to 1983-84*, Cmnd 7841, March 1980.

HMSO (1980b), *Financial Statement and Budget Report 1980-81*, HPC 500, 26 March 1980, London.

Kay, J.A. and King, M.A. (1978), *The British Tax System*, Oxford University Press, Oxford.

Mathews, R. (1968), 'Why has Britain had full employment since the War?', *Economic Journal*, Vol.LXXVIII, May.

Midland Bank Review (1980), *New Issues Stagnate in 1979*, Spring, pp.16-20.

Pollitt, C. (1977), 'The Public Expenditure Survey 1961-1972), *Public Administration*, Vol.55, Summer.

Read, D.J. (1977), 'Public Sector Debt',

Rees, P.M. and Thompson, F.P. (1972), 'The Relative Price Effect in Public Expenditure: Its Nature and Method of Calculation', Central Statistical Office *Statistical News*, 18 August, HMSO, London.

Taylor, C.T. and Threadgold, A.R. (1979), 'Real National Savings and its Sectoral Composition', *Bank of England Discussion Paper No.6*, October.

Tomlinson, J. (1980), *The 'Economics of Politics' and Public Expenditure: A Critique*, CSE Conference Paper, July.

Thompson, G.F. (1979a), *The Conceptualization of Government Expenditure*, CSE Conference Paper, July.

Thompson, G.F. (1979b), 'The Growth of the Government Sector', Unit 3 of Open University Course *Political Economy and Taxation*, OU Press, Milton Keynes.

Thompson, G.F. (1980), *Monetarism and Economic Ideology*, CSE Conference
    Paper, July.
The Treasury (1980), 'North Sea Contributions to Revenue and GNP',
    Economic Progress Report, No.123, July.
Ward, T.S. and Neild, R.R. (1978), *The Measurement of Reform of Budget-
    ary Policy*, The Institute for Fiscal Studies and Heinemann Books,
    London.
Wilson Committee (1980), *Report of Committee of Inquiry into the
    Financial Institutions*, Chairman Sir Harold Wilson, Cmnd 7937,
    June.
Wright, M. (1977), 'Public Expenditure in Britain: The Crisis of
    Control', *Public Administration*, Vol.55, Summer.

Tony Lane
Industrial Strategy and Trade Union Politics

'If the government of this country want their citizens to act
reasonably their first object should be to create a mood, an
attitude in which people will be readily disposed towards
reason, towards responsibility and towards dignity... Do not
seek to impose upon them some conception of restraint which
is entirely your own, which is not related to their circumstances, which draws nothing from them, no response at all.
You must get at the roots, get at the things which move
people...'
(George Woodwock at the TUC, 1962[1])

INTRODUCTION

The next Labour government will inevitably have some form of industrial strategy as its centrepiece despite past failures in that area.
Equally inevitable will be an emphasis within that strategy on dramatic improvements in industrial efficiency. There will also be an
entirely justified recognition that, without the willing commitment
of the trade unions, the whole enterprise will be null and void
before the starter raises his pistol.

However, any future strategy and associated institutions will go
the largely ineffectual way of the last unless there is a widespread
understanding of internal trade union politics. Not so much the
politics of right and left, of 'ins and outs', but an understanding
of how power is distributed, organised and deployed. Unless there
is a dense and rich understanding of these processes and the social
attributes that inform them, then the trade unions will not be
mobilised and the strategy will quietly, but nonetheless ignominiously,
collapse in frustration and another near-fatal dose of disillusionment.

The recently published Joint Trades Council Inquiry into State
Intervention in Industry has convincingly demonstrated that locally
active trade unionists knew next to nothing of the last government's
industrial policies, and that trade union leaders' minds were concentrated on other issues.[2] This was not anyone's *fault*. It is less

a question of apportioning blame, and more one of recognising that
certain forms of political practice (again in the broad sense of
politics) guaranteed ignorance on the one hand, and low priority on
the other.

The political problem did not lie with the trade unions, at least
not directly. The trade unions, long ago in the mists of 20th-century
antiquity, labelled industrial policy as 'political' - which meant
assigning responsibility for it to the Labour Party. Naturally they
would expect to be consulted and taken seriously when offering amendments, but still the initiative lay elsewhere.

Now policy makers working within a parliamentary framework can
be forgiven for thinking primarily in parliamentary terms. And that,
in the end, comes down to legislation. Parliamentarians, furthermore, tend to draw a sharp distinction between legislating and
administering: the latter function being the job of civil servants
and quasi-independent bodies like National Enterprise Boards and
Urban Development Corporations.

There is nothing necessarily wrong with that as a general principle. But when it comes to matters of industrial efficiency in a
country distinguished by its lack of it, yet whose people still aspire
to live at levels requiring it, then something more daring is needed.

What is needed is a policy which requires the active participation
of millions of people in tens of thousands of workplaces, in thousands of towns. Such a policy cannot be produced either by legislation or by bodies like the National Economic Development Council.
It can only be implemented by drawing on the trade union movement
from top to bottom. But the trade unions cannot be drawn in unless
they are involved, at all levels, in devising policy and unless
those responsible for its ultimate direction have a thorough grasp
of the operating principles of trade union politics.[3]

INDUSTRIAL POLICY SINCE 1960

One of the more remarkable things about industrial policy and politics in the last twenty years is its continuity. Even the present
government has retained the National Economic Development Council
(NEDC) established by the Macmillan government in 1962. It has also
retained the Sector Working Parties (SWPs) which were set up as ad-
juncts to the NEDC during the Industrial Strategy programme of the
last Labour government. It is worth noting, too, that despite a
public commitment to a politics of mayhem, the Thatcher government
has been quietly pursuing a hedge-betting policy of industrial
interventionism.[4]

The setting up of the NEDC marked a recognition of the deficiencies of British industry as compared with West Germany and Japan.
These countries, now fully recovered from the war, were rapidly
eating into British export markets. Most significantly, the construction of NEDC tacitly acknowledges that the remedying of deficiencies could not safely be left to 'market forces'.

What was needed, thought the government of 1962, was a 'national
assembly' of industrialists and trade union leaders, backed up by a
secretariat of economists, which could hammer out a consensus of

what needed to be done, and then urge it downward through their respective organisations. There is little need to parade all the familiar
evidence which shows how unsuccessful that approach has been.[5]

Since different industries and sectors within them experienced
varying difficulties, it was of course naive to believe that the
national equivalent of a Joint Works Consultative Committee would be
able to deliver very much. The setting up of Sector Working Parties
belatedly recognised this by establishing 'Joint Works Consultative
Committees' on a sectoral basis. There are now about 30 of them in
industries ranging from petrochemicals to domestic electrical appliances.

D.K. Stout, Economic Director of the NEDC secretariat, has very
neatly put his finger on the problems facing the SWPs:[6] 'A sector
working party rarely represents enough of the producers and workers
concerned - and not at the level where changes have to be negotiated...' And in similar vein: 'Other (recommendations) are difficult
to organise because they presuppose an understanding of the options
and considerable trust at every level inside the place of work.'

The two typical SWP recommendations quoted below reinforce Stout's
view:

'Management and unions must co-operate in discussing and
implementing those improvements in productivity which are
essential for the long-term prosperity of the industry...
Manufacturers are urged to offer products incorporating the
latest micro-electronic technology, in order to secure market
leadership.'
(*Domestic Electrical Appliances SWP*, Progress Report for
1980, NEDC)

'The Economic Development Council has started to develop a
fresh and deliberately profound and wide-ranging analysis
of motivation and attitudes of both management and workforce.
It is thought that a change in such attitudes is vital to
the development of a constructive and purposeful approach
to the solution of individual productivity problems.'
(*Food and Drink EDC*, Progress Report for 1980, NEDC)

These and similar forms of words make such a regular appearance one
suspects that, like stories in *Womens Weekly*, SWP recommendations
are written to a formula.

Simply in terms of the people sitting on them, the SWPs were not
nearly representative enough. As the accompanying table shows, shop
steward representation was very low:

Representation on Sector Working Parties, 1980*

Representatives	*Number*
Full-time TU Officers	44
Shop Stewards	9
Company Representatives	88
Civil Servants	28

Source: *SWP Reports*, 1980

* This sample covers ten SWPs and
EDCs. In five there was no shop
steward representation.

There was an even more glaring deficiency on the company side: all of
their representatives without exception were senior executives.   In
none of the ten SWPs sampled was plant management represented.   The
absence of such people can only have meant that questions of efficiency
were dealt with in a *global* manner.   Hence the blandness of recommendations.   This very quality raised insuperable problems for that minority
of SWPs which organised report-back sessions to delegate conferences
of shop stewards and managers: there was nothing specific enough to
result in any action at plant level.   Shop stewards who took part in
the Tyres SWP conference found it 'informative but a talking shop'.
No doubt that was a typical response.

It is difficult to believe that so far as the companies were concerned there was not a deliberate policy of excluding plant managers.
It is not hard to see why.   Stout hints at the answer when he says
that since companies compete with each other, they are reluctant to
divulge any data on plant operation that could be of advantage to
others.

Senior executives may have felt, and one suspects accurately, that
technocratically-minded managers might have forgotten their 'loyalty'
to the company.   Whatever the reason, there can be no doubt that if
managers had been included it would have been impossible to exclude
shop stewards.

Adequate representation at plant level would surely have improved
matters.   Workplace participants could only have recognised that an
SWP structure which operated solely at national level was not up to
the task - and then pushed for tiered structure which went down to
regions and localities.   It scarcely needs saying, however, that this
would have mounted a bigger threat to companies' competition policy.

While it is clear that competition policy rendered the SWPs much
less effective than they might otherwise have been, somewhat vaguer
questions of political ideology have also played a part.

All governments of the last two decades or so have tacitly recognised the stalemate in industrial politics.   And all until the present one have sought to resolve it through various policies and institutions designed to engender collaboration between the 'parties' of
capital and labour.   Implicit in approaches like the NEDC is the
immediate belief that so long as leaders are present there is a good
chance that the troops will subsequently follow.   Buried even deeper
is the liberal academic view that when men and women of 'public
stature' are made aware of problems, they can be relied upon to
reach the 'right' conclusions and persuade their lower echelons
accordingly.   This ideology, pervasive in the great majority of the
Parliamentary Labour Party and amongst liberal Tories, notes the
existence of competing power centres but assumes an ultimate identity
of interests, as in Lord Robens' pipe-dream of Great Britain Ltd -
with himself as chairman of the board!

While the ideology of 'common interests' has done nothing to
resolve the stalemate in industry, the trade union insistence on
playing its traditional role of a permanently defensive party in
opposition has also left the impasse untouched.   Neither in local
precedent nor in official policy has the trade union movement sought
to shift the collective bargaining frontier in the direction of
seeking joint control over investment and forward planning.   The

unions, in some cases even in formal agreements, have continued to acknowledge 'management's right to manage'.

The following extract from an interview with a senior shop steward at the now-closed Dunlop tyre plant in Liverpool shows how, even in an exceptionally well-organised plant, shop stewards accepted the 'rights' of management.

First, to set the scene. I had sifted through Joint Works Council minutes over a ten-year period, and came across a case where a steward raised the same item at almost every monthly meeting for more than a year. The management were complaining of poor productivity on case-making machines, the last stage of production before a tyre goes into a mould to get its tread. The senior steward of the section always gave the same reply: 'There aren't enough rings and stands.' 'Rings and stands' are very simple pieces of equipment which ensure that the tyre case or cover keeps its shape. If the covers were simply piled up, they would lose their shape and would not fit into the moulds: they would be scrap.

New case-making machines had been introduced which had a much higher output than the old ones. But the rings and stands available were only sufficient to handle the old output levels. So, rather than produce for scrap, the men were stopped working when all the rings and stands were full:

Billy Smith: With these new 61½" NRM machines we could do 35 covers a shift - on the old machines we could do about 11. Now they don't have enough rings and stands for the new 61½" machines. Eventually we got 50 or so painted and that still wasn't enough. We'd come in on the morning shift and maybe find the moulders down. Instead of keeping us working they'd knock us off. This was ludicrous because the moulders were doing three times what we were doing in an eight hour shift. Just because we didn't have the rings and stands they had to knock us off. I was continually complaining about this on the shop floor and at the JWC but we never got anywhere with it. Whenever I said 'rings and stands', they said 'we'll look into it and order another fifty'. We never got them. We lost an awful lot of production because of that.
T.L.: Why not have a strike about rings and stands?
Billy Smith: We didn't feel it was necessary. It was the responsibility of the company and if the union side was pointing out they were losing production then we'd done our job. Once we'd reported it, it was up to management. If a machine is lying idle then it's up to them to get it back in production. There was nothing we could do about it.

There is no doubt that this little story could be repeated many many times over - and as often today as yesterday. There are just two points to make about it: that an adequate industrial strategy will need to address itself to that sort of question; that there is no chance of it happening until trade unionists have a *direct* interest in the plants in which they work.

It is fair to say that no initiatives can be expected either from this government or from companies. Thanks to the great upsurge of plant-based trade unionism in the last 30 years, democratic sentiments

now run too deep for a re-assertion of traditional authoritarianism
to be successful. And ever more elaborate consultative procedures
disguised as 'participation' will be no more effective than those
of yester-year. Inroads *have* to be made into 'managerial prerogatives' and only trade unionists can make them.

Arguably, little would be needed in the way of legislation. An
amendment to the Industry Act requiring companies to disclose whatever
information the trade unions requested would be sufficient to enable
them to bargain effectively over investment and forward planning.
However, for the unions to be able to act effectively on the basis
of information disclosed, their representatives would need to be
equipped with a wider range of industrial skills than most now have.
And in addition, the membership would have to be prepared to take
traditional forms of action over exceedingly *non*-traditional issues.

It is precisely for these reasons that devisers of industrial
policies need to have a keen awareness of formal and informal union
politics. Given that the initial burden of an industrial strategy
aimed at improving efficiency would fall on the trade unions, ways
have to be found of deploying the full machinery of trade union
government. They will not be found without a thorough prior
knowledge of how power in the unions is distributed.

UNION POLITICS

'Trade unionists,' I was recently assured by a prominent figure in
the Scottish labour movement, 'are like shopkeepers. They wait
around all day for people to come and get served, close the door at
5 o'clock, and then go home to forget all about it until it is time
to lift the blinds the following morning.'

George Woodcock once said - when safely in retirement - something
remarkably similar:[7]

'Trade unionism is as routine as peeling potatoes. I don't
know anyone in whom it has induced a mood of reflection. At
least not inside the trade union movement. The lads themselves
don't seem to reflect very much. They have a stock issue -
and they just pull a stock solution off the shelf...'

Anyone with more than a nodding acquaintance of the trade union movement will be able to summon many a mental image of men and women who
fit those descriptions. Yet the movement is far from homogeneous
and contains many a contradiction. So while admittedly less easy,
it is nevertheless possible to summon images of others who by no
means fit the stereotype.

It is instructive to spend time in working hours with those
trade unionists who are in the front-line in the localities: the
shop stewards and the full-time officers. Only then is it possible
to see the pressures that at once push them into shop-keeping and
pull them into politics.

The reasons for these pushes and pulls are pretty obvious.
Officers, whether lay or full-time, are there to resolve the problems of members. Many of these problems are routine enough to be
handled with 'stock solutions'. But there are other problems, like
redundancies and factory closures, which require political changes

before they can be subject to 'stock solutions'. This tension inevitably reflects itself in internal politics.

Firstly, a quick look at the formal side of things. It would take
far too much space to fully examine inter-union variations of formal
government. So the account which follows deals with the Transport
and General Workers Union. This union has the most elaborate structure of lay participation. Its main difference from other unions lies
not in the vertical distribution of power, for all have a similar
hierarchy from branch, through district or region, to the national.
What makes the T&G unique is that it has a dual hierarchy: one is a
system of constituencies based on geographical location, the other
an industry system of constituencies. This of course requires a
wider spread of lay participation and allows, as we shall see, for
a much greater control of full-time officers.

In terms of its constitution, the T&G enshrines two forms of
electoral procedure: there is the universal franchise wherein
branches are the constituencies, and there is an electoral college
consisting of district committees. The universal franchise invariably
applies to the election of representatives from each of the 12
geographical regions to the General Executive Council, to the
election of delegates to the Biennial Delegate Conference, the
ultimate policy-making assembly, the election of delegates to the
six-yearly Rules Revision Conference, and the election of delegates
to the district committees.

The district committee structure is unique to the T&G. Every
branch is allocated to a 'trade group' - automotive, docks and water-
ways, transport, power and engineering, chemicals, 'white collar'
and so on - and each trade group has a district committee. The size
of that committee will vary according to the number of branches it
embraces. The network of district committees is extremely extensive.
Each geographical region is usually divided into geographical divisions, and each division has its quota of trade group district
committees according to the range of industries in which the union
has a significant presence.

The district committees form electoral colleges for elections to
the regional committees: members of the regional committee are
elected by the district committees. These latter also form electoral
colleges for the national trade group committees. And then the
national trade group committees in turn act as electoral colleges
for the election of trade group representatives to the General
Executive Council. The GEC, therefore, consists of members elected
by branch ballot and others who have come through the electoral
colleges. The directly elected members outnumber those indirectly
elected by roughly three to one. This unusual constitution allows a
high degree of lay participation in government. It also contains a
built-in requirement for the representation of varying industrial
interests. It also has the advantage of being extremely flexible,
which explains why the T&G has been an attractive proposition for
smaller unions looking for a merger.

Apart from the general secretary, who is elected by branch ballot,
other full-time officers are appointed after an oral examination by
the GEC. Subordinate to the general secretary at national level are
executive officers - such as the deputy general secretary - who have

administrative briefs, and national officers who are mostly assigned
to the various trade groups. All regions and most divisions have a
permanent secretary with administrative duties, and below them are
the district officers who are typically assigned to a trade group.
   The structure of the other major unions is less extensive. The
GMWU and the AUEW, for example, have only a regional and national
structure. Indeed the AUEW's executive, though elected, consists of
full-time officers. The simpler structure of these and other unions
- like the EEPTU and ASTMS - allows power to be more highly concentrated and gives full-time officers more individual autonomy. GMWU
regional secretaries are well-known for their almost baronial powers.
T&G regional secretaries are also people to be reckoned with, but
such is the nature of the GMWU's constitution that it allows for
much more regional autonomy than is the case in the T&G.
   This much - on constitutional matters - merely describes the
formal framework. It says little about the distribution of power
in practice. The discussion of this question which follows is more
or less applicable to all the major unions.
   No matter where you turn, in no matter what union, the key to
identifying who has got the clout and how they came by it comes back
to the locality and the branch. This is not to underestimate the
element of sponsorship exercised by full-timers, a matter which will
be dealt with below. The branch *has* to be the point of entry because,
no matter how influential the informal structures of power may be,
they still rest on constitutional legality.
   Disproportionate power attaches to the large branch, chapel, lodge
etc. In any given area there are likely to be a small number of very
large constituencies and a large number of small ones - assuming, as
is generally the case with the exception of the AUEW and EEPTU, that
branches are based on workplaces and not on territory.
   Small branches are as likely as not to be inoperative since a
smaller population is almost by definition less likely to throw up
sufficient people to take on the administrative chores. The two
large general unions try to overcome this difficulty by aggregating
the membership in small workplaces into 'composite' branches which
are based on territory. As most branch business is workplace
related, it will be appreciated that this expedient is rarely a
thorough success. It can only be expected to work in an industry
like road haulage where all members are subject to identical local
and national agreements.
   And so the importance of the large branch is obvious. It alone,
or in concert with others, is in a strong position to determine who
shall be elected to the position in question. In practice, therefore, the outcome of elections is not nearly as unpredictable as it
might appear in principle. Prior negotiation between several
branches in advance of an election can determine the outcome.
   This does not necessarily mean that small branches are completely
squeezed out. A candidate from such a branch may even, for reasons
internal to a large branch, be preferred and strongly supported.
But, as a general rule, the large branches will naturally seek to
place their own candidates.
   In deciding candidature much hinges on the 'political' character
of leading branch members and the state of play on the industrial

relations front. As a rough and ready categorisation there are those
who are 'pure and simple' trade unionsts who are primarily concerned
with issues affecting their own workplace; and there are the 'activists' whose concern extends to the power and influence of the union
on political as well as on industrial matters. The 'activists' tend
to look for the best person regardless of branch, the others for the
best person to represent sectional interests. For the activists the
ideal candidate is the one who is both industrially and politically
competent.[8] If the choice comes down to choosing between someone who
is politically competent but indifferent industrially, and another
who is politically weak but industrially strong, then it is likely
that there will be no contest. Regardless of label, the industrial
candidate will get it. Since only a tiny minority of active trade
unionists are also active politically, it follows that lay committees
are overwhelmingly composed of people whose competence is primarily
industrial.

The categories offered above are evidently crude: which was why
the qualification referring to the 'state of play on the industrial
relations front' was introduced. The categories are not black and
white but shaded. And the shade that is selected will vary according
to whether the firm and the industry is stable, or going through a
phase of upheaval for one reason or another. In circumstances where
the shop-floor organisation is under attack from management, or under
pressure from the membership, the branch is going to look for someone
who can be relied upon to put the union machinery to good use. Such
a person is not always the same one who is more appropriate to a
quiet phase.

Although shop stewards are lay officers in most unions, there are
no constitutions which have a place for stewards committees. Shop
stewards, accordingly, try to place their own nominees in key branch
positions. While branch elections are often contested, shop stewards
or their close associates[9] can be confident of being returned. The
reasons are straightforward. Firstly, the shop stewards are the only
organised group and can therefore mobilise. Secondly, every shop
steward, because he/she has been elected, will have a base amongst
the rank and file. Only on those rare occasions where there is a
rank and file rebellion, extending across a number of shop-floor
sections, are shop stewards' nominees likely to be overturned. The
corollary of steward control of the branch is that the same people
can also determine who gets elected to the other lay committees of
the union, from the locality and region through to the national
executive.

Shop steward permeation of lay structures is a relatively recent
development. It reflects the take-off of shop floor organisations
which began in earnest in the Second World War and was consolidated
in the 1950s and 1960s. Throughout that period, internal union
politics was essentially a contest between full-time officers and
workplace representatives. It should, however, be remarked, because
it has too often gone unnoticed, that the stewards often had powerful
allies within the ranks of the full-timers.[10] As bargaining shifted
to the workplace, it became less and less easy for full-timers to
control the lay committees through patronage and sponsorship. Yet,
while the power of full-timers has been eroded and their role re-
defined, they remain influential.

Constitutionally, there is no ambiguity about the position of the full-time officer. Regardless of whether they are appointed or elected, they are subject in principle to the instructions of lay committees. In most unions where officers are appointed, the officer is a member of only one branch but may attend all those falling within his purview. Ex officio they may attend certain of the lay committees as of right: they can speak but not vote. Indeed, appointed full-timers usually have no voting rights whatsoever except as a branch member. This disqualification is of no significance.

Local officers have 'portfolios' of companies for which they are responsible. It is unusual for these portfolios to have any industrial rationale: one officer may service members in a range of firms straddling a number of industries.

The definition of 'servicing' is flexible. Quite apart from questions of commitment (a vague but important variable), officers experience periods of hyper-activity lasting perhaps months, followed by temporary lulls. As this rhythm is dictated by external exigencies and not by a predictable programme, it follows that servicing *has* to be ad hoc and inconsistent.

Put at its most general, servicing entails responsibility for any industrial relations question. And, more nebulously, the responsibility for advising lay members and officers on constitutional matters and on union policy as it develops, for ensuring that branches function, and for encouraging lay members to take advantage of educational provision.

Yet if the responsibilities are clear enough, their execution is problematic. Exigencies constantly intervene: a dispute blows up unexpectedly; the mail brings a redundancy notification; there are national negotiations in London; a deputation awaits in the corridor; there's a brief to prepare for an Industrial Tribunal; there's an irate steward/manager on the 'phone. And this is not the half of it. Pressure is constant and its source rarely predictable. So much business is unfinished, half-finished and not done at all. All of this merely describes the full-timer's daily round (and, incidentally, that of a convenor in a large workplace): what is left out is the part played in internal politics.

When it comes down to particular roles, then no-one is better placed than the full-timer to ensure that union democracy flourishes. His or her ability in this respect is a function of command over information not so readily available to others. The full-timer can open doors, close them, leave them ajar, provide signposts that point in all manner of directions. Several things provide this ability.

Few workplaces, including many large ones, have efficient shop-floor organisations. What there is is typically held together by a small number of people plus a larger number of others - but where the tail is longer than the dog. Conviction fluctuates with the season and so does the supply of volunteers. The 'tail' regularly turns over its personnel for reasons ranging from family pressure to promotion to foreman.

It is *possible* for full-timers to interrupt this merry-go-round, to push it sideways and set it turning on another axis. They can feed in information on what is happening in other firms in the same

industry and the informal talk that escapes the minutes of meetings.
They can encourage new stewards and branch officers to attend meetings,
enrol on courses, to run for lay office or an officer's job. In
brief, they can amend perspectives and broaden horizons. And they
can do all this because their regular contact with other plants,
other officers both local and national (in their own as well as other
unions), their receipt of circulars and documents, not to mention
thèir niche in the grapevine, necessarily extend *their* horizons way
beyond the factory gate. Since they may also choose to do none of
this or do it cursorily, their significance becomes obvious.

Shop stewards are primarily elected for their competency on their
own patch. And for most of them that patch is simply a *section* of
their workplace, never mind the industry of which their enterprise is
a part. Consider, too, that the educational system in no way equips
school-leavers of *any* age with even a rudimentary knowledge of industry and appropriate skills of analysis. Just about every social
pressure pushes people into localised and sectional attitudes. The
more active stewards in multi-plant companies begin to break out of
this other-imposed isolation and learn of a wider world. It is, to
put it briefly, this learning of others' experience that leads them
into union politics.

If senior stewards and convenors begin to 'out-distance' their
colleagues, they nevertheless spend most of their time in one plant.
The full-timers, by contrast, travel widely. While they rarely have
the opportunity to acquire more than a glancing knowledge of the
industries with which they have contact (unless they are responsible
for one specialised industry), their horizons necessarily get extended.
Their specific expertise is, of course, in knowing their way around
employment legislation, types of agreement and systems of bargaining,
the ploys and stratagems of industrial relations managers. (It is not
for nothing that many full-timers - not to mention convenors - have
found it easy to become industrial relations managers.) They also
develop another very special kind of knowledge: no one else in the
union has the same opportunity as the local full-timer to become as
knowledgeable about the condition of union organisation in the
branches and in the plants.

The full-timers, because they are situated in a system of government controlled by elected lay members, will take a keen interest in
the proceedings of those lay committees that impinge upon them.
Indeed, they are in a strong position to exert considerable influence
upon them. And not only in making decisions. Their superior knowledge of union structure, coupled with certain 'facts of life' like
a sectionalised membership, the turnover of lay officers, enables
them to influence the possibility of branches sending representatives
to lay committees, as well as to nurse those they regard as suitable
candidates.

A quirk of constitution facilitates this. With the exception of
the AUEW, which provides for quarterly meetings of shop stewards within its divisions, no other unions provide constitutional local or
regional forums in which all lay officers may participate. Such
meetings do take place from time to time, but they are not obligatory.
This *absence* makes it much easier for the full-timers who have the
inclination, to exercise something like control over their local

government. It was blatant practices of this sort that sparked off
the rank and file rebellions of the 1950s, 60s and 70s.

BEYOND THE LOCALITY

As in the Labour Party, delegate conferences are responsible for broad
policy and the revision of rules. Here the similarity ends. In virtually all unions, the implementation of policy and its sharper definition is in the first instance the job of the lay committees, and in
the second that of full-timers acting on instructions.

This, simultaneously, underlines the importance of the full-timer
and the branch. The full-timers because they are the main line of
communication between lay committees and the branches; the branch
because it is the only legitimate source of resolutions and elected
representatives. But although it is important, if unfashionable, to
insist on the absolutely key function of the branch and the local
full-timer, it is equally important to be clear about the role of
national executives, national officers and the supporting head office
machinery.

As a general rule, members of national executives will have served
lengthy apprenticeships on local and regional committees. It is
common, furthermore, for EC representatives to continue to serve on
lower tiers as a means of preserving their electoral base. To state
the case at its best, this brings to the EC a wealth of knowledge and
experience of internal politics. It also brings, since in most unions
EC representatives are also active on the shop floor, a good feel of
the pulse in the workplaces. And then their regular contact with
local, regional and national officers provides information on how
such people choose to exercise their influence.

All of this knowledge serves EC members very well in their handling
of internal affairs: they will know where blockages are likely to
occur and how to get round them. However, another aspect of organisation makes it extremely difficult for an EC to formulate *programmatic*
policy, i.e. 'programmatic' in the sense of targeting a series of
objectives in a medium or long-term programme.

In principle that is a major part of the EC's role: it is supposed
to fill out the broad resolutions passed at conference and devise
means of implementing them. In practice this is most unlikely to
occur with respect to such resolutions which call, for example, for
the reorganisation of a particular industry.

A regular 'runner' at GMWU, NUR, ASLEF, T&GWU and NUS conferences
is a call for an integrated transport policy. Yet none of these
unions has ever prepared such a policy in a form which could be
acted upon by a government. And for two reasons. Firstly, because
such a policy is seen as 'political' and thus the task of the Labour
Party. Secondly, because the unions simply do not have an organisational structure appropriate to the task.

The first of these requires little elaboration, though it bears
weightily on the second. The expertise of trade unionists lies in
doing deals with employers on matters of the price and conditions of
labour. On this familiar ground they are confident and competent.
Matters of industrial policy, however, take them too far beyond their

area of specialised knowledge. No blame attaches: they are negotiators,
not planners. While nowadays there are many trade unionists with a
far broader industrial knowledge than their predecessors ever had,
they are nevertheless rather thin in the ground. So the trade unionists tend to look to others within the labour movement's ranks - the
Labour Party's policy sub-committees - to supply what they cannot
provide.

The second point on organisational structure reflects the first.
The executive committee cannot, with the best will in the world, provide programmatic policies which go far beyond industrial relations
questions. Their existing skills do not lie in that direction; they
are 'part-timers'; they do not have the back-up facilities from
within the union machinery to provide them with the necessary information. This of course is to describe the situation as it exists. It
is not to say that it could not be otherwise. But for it to be otherwise, trade unions would need to broaden their approach and be ready
to undertake activities conventionally passed to the Labour Party.

Within the unions there is no directly functional equivalent of
the internal civil service that stands behind the board of directors
of an enterprise. All large unions have research departments, usually
under-manned. But their function is primarily to service national
officers on matters of everyday business, and not the ECs in policy-
making. So, for example, when an EC member receives his papers for
the next meeting he will not, as a matter of course, find amongst them
background papers prepared by the research department.

In most unions research workers have staff as distinct from officer
status. This means that they have no *direct* access to lay committees:
they cannot, as of right, attend ex officio. This underlines their
role as servicing agents. There are probably implicit 'political'
reasons for this: without careful constitutional definition it might
be possible for a research department to constitute a power base in
its own right.

Research departments do not normally prepare briefs for officers
and lay members who sit on various TUC committees and other bodies
such as NEDC and its SWPs, Royal Commissions etc. All of these have
their own secretariats whose job it is to provide briefs. On large
matters relating to government economic and industrial policy, it is
common for the unions to lean heavily on the TUC's research department.
This is the only union research organisation continuously involved in
programmatic research. In the general run of things, the most that an
individual union's research department will be called upon to do in
these areas is to provide digests of briefs produced elsewhere.

THE REVOLT FROM BELOW AND ITS EFFECTS

The combination of the everyday pursuit of a myriad of specific problems and constitutional legality ensures that all unions have a plur-
ality of power centres that is almost certainly greater than in any
other British institution. Yet it has not ever been thus. The first
half of this century saw a far greater concentration of power at the
centre than now obtains.

That period of autocracy was a product of particular historical circumstances, a period in which unions as mass organisations were new phenomena, and where techniques of forming and holding together large-scale voluntary organisations had to be learned from scratch. It was, too, a period in which parliamentary democracy based on universal adult suffrage was an innovation. In short, the centralist phase of development coincided with a more general political phase in which large numbers of people were learning about democratic practices. Such circumstances readily lent themselves to a form of autocracy, especially when, as was the case in the 1920s and 30s, very high levels of unemployment were a major threat to the very survival of the nascent modern unions.

The situation in the last twenty years has changed dramatically, notwithstanding the currently anachronistic EEPTU and the not al-together successful attempts being made in the AUEW to turn the clock back. General secretaries remain powerful individuals and will continue to be so in the foreseeable future. But for all that, there is simply no comparison between the GMWU, the T&GWU, the NUM and the NUR of the early 1950s and the same unions in 1980.

That now dead era of unprecedented full employment accomplished both less, and more, than observers have allowed. The movement toward an articulated system of collective bargaining, wherein plant-level deals 'topped-up' the round at national level, upset an awful lot of established internal political conventions. It took shop-floor representatives into national negotiations, and ratification of many an agreement back to the shop-floor members who met in 'popular assembly'. Concurrently and connectedly, formalised procedures for handling everyday shop-floor conflicts created a new role in the workplace: convenors and shop stewards effectively became full-time trade union officers who were paid by the company. These twin departures diminished the power and in-fluence of national and local officers, and taught lay officers the virtues of having a powerful voice in trade union government.

Out of all this has come a new generation of general secretaries who for the most part genuinely believe in government by consent. And the same applies to full-timers all the way down the line. They can no longer be the barons many of them once were, or aspired to be. Furthermore, there are now a large number of full-timers who were once themselves numbered amongst the rebellious. Many have not turned out to be poachers turned gamekeeper. All of this, needless to say, gives added confidence to the lay committees.

The immediately foregoing gives the progressive side of the picture. Words of caution are now in order. What has been said here has been generalised from practices emanating from the large multi-plant companies. These places have been, as it were, the market leaders. They have set the pace and others have followed at greatly varying speeds.

There remain many corners of industry where shop-floor trade unionists shake their heads disbelievingly when they hear of ad-vances made in large firms. There are also big differences as between large companies in different industries. The food industry, for example, could almost be on a different planet when compared with vehicles and engineering. The effect of all this, since 'laggard' industries contribute to the union's lay committees in the same way as the 'leaders', is a certain tension in internal politics. This is not only reflected in committee debates. It is reflected, too, in the influence of full-timers: they are much more powerful in the laggard industries.

One final word on this question of redistribution of power. The growth in trade union democracy has been both real and significant, but it has also had its limitations. General political developments over the last few years have made it painfully plain that the active trade unionists, who keep the whole show on the road, have forfeited some of their legitimacy as more and more industries either totter or verge on collapse. Of course this erosion of legitimacy cannot be divorced from the ideological bankruptcy of the Labour Party in particular, and the left in general. Neither can it be divorced from the fact that within the unions, power has only been redistributed in the sense that it has been spread around an enlarged layer of lay officers and committee members. This is not to say that democratic *sentiments* have not been greatly enlarged amongst the mass of the membership. Clearly they have, for otherwise the shop stewards would have had no power base. It must, however, be recognised that as yet those sentiments have not congealed into convictions.

Despite these qualifications, it is safe to say that there can be no going back to autocracy although, of course, occasional hiccups are to be expected. Workplace representatives have learned that they cannot do without a strong voice on the lay committees. Full-timers, for their part, know that without the independently formed consent of the workplace they are apt to be relatively powerless.

Over and above all this has been the extraordinary flowering of the now widespread belief in popular control that is no longer mainly confined to the working class. The growth of demands for democratisation in more and more areas in the 1960s and 70s, coupled both with a greater experience of shortcomings in this regard and a readiness to resort to direct action, has produced a welling of sentiment that cannot easily be turned back. The trade union movement can be justifiably proud of its role in the surge of this tide. Whether other activists were aware of it or not, many of the organisations of the 1960s and 70s were translating trade union organising principles into other forms of social action.

TRADE UNION POLITICS AND INDUSTRIAL POLICY

Sketchy though this account of trade union politics has been, it does show something of the complexity of the subject. The importance of the necessity of at least a basic understanding of the general principles requires few additional words.

One of the prior conditions for a successful industrial strategy is an actively committed trade union movement. Such commitment simply will not be forthcoming if the 'strategy' is devised in remote committee rooms and presented to the TUC General Council as a more-or-less finished document. If the trade unions, at all levels, are not themselves engaged in preliminary discussions, then the next strategy will go the way of the last.

What this would mean in practice is simple and practicable. The
Labour Party-TUC Liaison Committee would need to devise a series of
straightforward discussion documents appropriate to the various
layers of the unions. This would be as much a political task as an
administrative one. Unless the various power centres were clearly
identified and key individuals co-opted, the entire process would
take too long to find its way through 'due process'. The key people
have been identified as: the full-time officers and senior shop
stewards in the localities. The key organisations are the branches
and the local and regional lay committees. It could be safely
assumed that the support of national officers and national committees
would be won without difficulty. The problem would lie in activating
the lower levels.

Pronouncedly at the national level, and less distinctly at the
local, change is in the air in the trade union movement. With the
benefit of hindsight, it is evident that from the time of the TUC's
agreement to play a part in the NEDC, the unions have steadily been
drawing away from a purely defensive stance and paying closer attention to what can only be called 'alternative strategies'.

This has been the product of two decades of exposure to the
mounting evidence of the relative inefficiencies of British industry
and government dalliance with measures to combat it. Above all else,
the trade union presence on an ever-widening range of quasi-independent bodies has brought representatives into close contact with
industrialists, consultants and economists. No matter how they
related to these people and re-interpreted what they said, the fact
remains that this association has left them with a much more
detailed knowledge than they ever had before.

This expansion of command of information and skills of analysis
is reflected at shop floor level too. While, no doubt, shop stewards
have found Joint Consultative Committees frustrating gatherings, a
reading of their minutes shows that many managements have been sub-
jected to some pretty sharp cross-examination. This was fuelled and
extended by the rapid growth of educational provision for rank and
file members.

Trade union research departments have expanded in size and have
been typically embarrassed by the wealth of talent amongst job appli-
cants. In the late 1960s, helped by substantial grants from such
unions as the GMWU, the T&GWU and the NUM, research standards and
capabilities were significantly enlarged with the creation of the
Trade Union Research Unit at Ruskin College. The 1970s saw a mushrooming in many large cities of Trade Union Research Units, mostly
funded by charitable foundations and commissions from local trade
union bodies.

A largely unnoticed departure has been the *ad hoc* use of unpaid
consultancy work from academics. There are now few universities or
polytechnics in industrial areas which do not contain handfuls of
people providing some sort of research facility to trade unionists.
In very recent months, economists at the Universities of Cambridge
and Warwick have been influential in formulating ISTC opposition to
the plans of British Steel.

What has happened to date is that the unions' ability to generate
and absorb information has not been matched by tactics and strategy

designed to maximise its utility. The problem here is that, while
on any objective criterion the unions may win a particular argument,
the result of that debate is not decided by a vote on the quality of
the contending arguments. As one T&GWU full-timer said to me after
his involvement with a factory closure:
> 'Our research lads and those at the universities did a cracking
> job. They tore the company's arguments to ribbons and even
> management conceded the strength of our arguments. Any decent
> referee would have stopped the right in the first round. But,
> you see, as long as they owned the factory they could do what
> they liked. All this knowledge is fine, but without the power
> it's not a lot of use.'

This mis-match between knowledge and power will have to be resolved.
It should be the task of an industrial strategy to recognise the
gap, and in close collaboration with the unions, seek to close it.

It was argued earlier that the main legislative requirement would
relate to the full disclosure of information. This would create the
potentiality for closing the gap between knowledge and power since
it would provide opportunities for bargaining over investment and
strategic planning at enterprise level. It must however be repeated
that, at the moment, trade union organisation does not have an
infrastructure which is large enough to digest and process the
volumes of information that would become available.

It is therefore obvious that union research departments need to
be significantly expanded and qualitatively developed. On the one
hand, the present function of servicing everyday needs would have to
be expanded because what is advocated (with regard to disclosure)
would result in a re-definition of 'everyday needs'. And on the
other hand the implication of bargaining over strategic planning is
that unions would have to provide alternatives. Programmatic
policy-making, while not inseparable from servicing daily needs,
is nevertheless a qualitatively different task. It would need to
be recognised as a distinct function.

It would be foolish to ignore the possible consequences of this
expansion of research and back-up facility. There are 'political'
risks, namely those of creating an 'intellectual elite'. These
could be partly alleviated by retaining the common distinction
between staff and officer. But in practice this almost certainly
would not provide an adequate check. Several measures suggest themselves which can be justified on 'political' and efficiency grounds.
While central research facilities would have to be expanded, there
is much to be said for devolution to the regions and localities.
Politically this would be desirable, and for maximisation of effectiveness it would be essential. People need to be on the ground,
close to the source of demand, visible and accessible.

While organisational measures of this kind would minimise the
risks of creating a new power centre, they would not of themselves
accomplish much in the way of eroding distinctions between mental
and manual labour. And such an erosion has to be seen as crucial
to a successful industrial strategy. Workers can only be expected
to be 'responsible' to the extent to which they have responsibility.
There is no responsibility without power, and no constructive power
without knowledge. This clearly means that large numbers of workers

must be able to argue with managers on their own terms and in their own language. They can only acquire managerial skills by undergoing training courses, and by putting some of them into practice by doing basic research themselves. In aggregate, a fair amount of shop-floor do-it-yourself research is *already* done. The scope for developing it is enormous and has obvious very positive advantages. It would help to break down the division between mental and manual labour, hamper the development of a trade union intellectual elite, and provide a framework wherein it would be possible to extend an industrial strategy right down to the individual plant.

It is hard to envisage an industrial strategy which did not employ machinery comparable to the Sector Working Parties. The point being made here is that what exists is not up to the task, and that other tiers need to be added. By extending it down to the regions and localities, higher participation rates become possible. And to the extent that trade union collaboration is actively sought, and their internal politics sensitively understood, then the impact on short and long term efficiency could be considerable. It should go without saying that an extensive Sector Working Party apparatus would have to be designed in close association with localised trade union organisations *and* plant managements. Full information disclosure is a necessary condition for ensuring participation of trade unionists and managements. For the one it provides the opportunity to negotiate rather than simply talk. And where management is concerned, it is a means of freeing them from the demands of 'company loyalty'.

Efficiency benefits could also be expected to accrue from disclosure. It would enable detailed information on plant operations to become public knowledge. This in turn would make it possible to identify 'best practice' plants as a datum for emulation, and give a surer guide as to where the state could most usefully intervene and in what manner. Without a procedure of this sort, it would be extremely difficult to make any serious attempt at planning within and between sectors. To be sure, indicative planning is the best that could be expected from what is proposed here. But that would prove to be more effective than the incredibly naive proposals from some sections of the Labour left who are infatuated with nationalisation as a remedy for all ills.

CONCLUSION

All the theory of trade unionism, be it from Lenin on the left or Flanders and Perlman on the right, has it that trade unions are ideologically and organisationally geared up to responding to daily events, and therefore devoid of any politics that go beyond tepid reformism. Such theories are totally ahistorical and therefore empty of universal validity.

In the UK, where class antagonisms have been channelled into industry to an extent almost unknown anywhere else, trade unionism has now reached the point where long-term survival depends on pushing through political changes in industry. This is the only way to counter attempts from the right to break the stalemate in their favour. The necessary changes can, with total legitimacy, be

presented as in the interests of all but a tiny minority of the population. They can also be presented as rational and intelligent
responses to the difficulties of British industry. The same can
hardly be said of present government policies which rely on a crude
admixture of authoritarianism and the malign invisible hand of the
marketplace.

Industrial efficiency has never been a favourite slogan of either
trade unionists or socialists with libertarian leanings. For the
former it has smacked of exploitation, for the latter of a centralised and omni-competent state. These suspicions are healthy. On the
other hand, we do not live in that utopian state of a global co-
operative commonwealth - though we should do nothing to hinder its
development, and everything to encourage it. As things stand, our
functioning, though fragile and imperfect democracy, demands a
certain level of efficiency to meet existing demands and expectations.
If we continue to fail to meet them, though hopefully modifying them,
then we leave the way open to all those forces hostile to democracy
which are more and more evident.

Footnotes

1 Quoted in G. Goodman, *Awkward Warrior*, London, 1979, p.328.
2 See Trades Councils of Coventry, Liverpool, Newcastle-upon-Tyne
   and North Tyneside, *State Intervention in Industry*, Coventry, 1980.
3 There is no detailed account of trade union politics in the
   English language, though R. Taylor's *The Fifth Estate* (London,
   1977) makes a creditable attempt. Interestingly, the best atmos-
   pheric accounts are all of the T&GWU: J. Goldstein, *The Government
   of British Trade Unions*, London, 1952; A. Bullock, *The Life and
   Times of Ernest Bevin*, Vols.I and II, London 1960; G. Goodman's
   biography of Frank Cousins,
4 See John Elliot, 'The Government and the Banks Step In', *Financial
   Times*, 28 October 1980. At the time of writing the government was
   actively involved with a rescue operation concerning Massey Ferguson
   plants in the UK. Substantial aid was offered to Bowaters to save
   their newspring plant in Ellesmere Port - and refused. Dunlop's
   have had 6 millions for Fort Dunlop in Birmingham. Many small-
   scale selective aid schemes have been implemented. Inmos and
   British Leyland continue to get funding.
5 An excellent account of British industrial politics is in Keith
   Middlemas's *Politics in Industrial Society*, London, 1979.
6 D.K. Stout, 'De-Industrialisation and Industrial Policy', in
   F. Blackaby (ed.), *De-Industrialisation*, London, 1978, esp.
   pp.189-95.
7 Quoted in T. Lane, *The Union Makes Us Strong*, London, 1974, p.260.
8 'Political competence' is tacitly defined as a conscious grasp of
   the ideological import of various political tendencies; of how,
   and on what basis, alliances are formed within a particular union
   and within the labour movement generally. It also presupposes a
   readiness to intervene in these processes.
9 Behind most shop stewards in large workplaces stand one or more
   persons who act as 'shadow' stewards. Holding no office, they
   act as intermediaries between the steward and his constituents.

10 It is important to note the extent of sponsorship from the top
    in the T&GWU. Successive general secretaries from Frank Cousins
    in the mid-1950s to the early 1970s, Jack Jones in the 1970s, and
    now Moss Evans in the 1980s, have all actively contributed to the
    downward extension of power. The same has happened, though less
    markedly, in the GMWU after David Basnett's succession to Jack
    Cooper, who was arguably the last of the old-school autocrats in
    the general unions.

Barbara Bradby, Collette Cullen, Brian Farrell, Lorelei Harris,
Anne Marie Hourihand, Austen Morgan, Teresa Moriarty, Anne O'Donnell,
Julie Parsons, Gerry Sullivan, Brian Torode, Ruth Torode, James Wickham

An Open Letter to the British Left on Ireland

Dublin, October 1980

Dear Comrades, Sisters, and other fragments of the long-lost
British left,

We, who are trying to live and act in a politically responsible manner
in the Republic of Ireland, write to express our frustration and
annoyance at your continuing ignorance and apparent unwillingness to
learn some of the basic political facts of life in this country.

When the British left holds conferences that relate to Ireland,
or publishes issues of its journals on Ireland, the entity referred
to is not what geographers call the island of Ireland, nor is it the
state that calls itself 'Ireland'; it is Northern Ireland, that part
of the island where some people call themselves Irish, others call
themselves British, while a third group (on occasions including
elements from the first two) call themselves Ulster people. As the
currents in British politics which we refer to would all claim to be
against the partition of Ireland, the contradictions in their thinking are truly Hegelian. In denying any possible political right of
Northern Ireland to be part of Britain, such currents assert that
Northern Ireland *is* Ireland, thereby negating the existence of the
State into which they advocate the North should be absorbed.

The rest of Ireland becomes once again Britain's offshore island,
where the British left can retire to country cottages, away from the
bustle of political life in the metropolis, to consume brimming pints
and search for the authentic pre-revival folk music. Undeterred by
the fact that Guinness's was the first brewery in these islands to
completely convert to carbonized keg production, they fail to notice,
like good political tourists, that 'traditional music' in the west
of Ireland is largely sustained by German, American, Breton and other
sightseers, with the odd influx of Dublin lads down for the wet weekend. So, the British left comes to Ireland to fulfil its preconcep-
tions of Celtic tradition, and the local electronics factory has been
carefully sited so as not to spoil the view. In the words of James
Connolly in 1915: 'the fight in Ireland ... [becomes] ... one for the

soul of a race ... [for] her religion, her love of nationality, her
strict sexual morality, her natural affection for the weak, her
sympathy for suffering and distress'.

We believe there are very good reason why the British left continues to obliterate the Republic from its political map. If any serious
attempt were made to analyze this part of Ireland, gaping contradictions would emerge in the politics of support for the Provisional IRA,
whether that support be critical, conditional, unconditional, uncritical, uncritical but not unconditional, unconditional but not uncritical
or just plain confused. Would you be able to go on permutating and
combinating like this if you were living here?

As we write, socialist feminists in Britain are holding a conference on 'Imperialism'. One of the countries to be considered in the
metropolis is 'Ireland'. As far as we are aware, no one from the
Republic was invited to speak or even informed of the conference.
This we regard as cultural and political imperialism. Are the sisters
aware that, in the name of the same Catholicism they appear to support
with marian fervour in the North, the family planning clinics in the
south are under threat of closure by the state and contraception is
about to be restricted by law to married couples who can afford to
pay for it? Those of us who are involved in the 'women's right to
choose' campaign are trying to change a law of 1861 on abortion, the
Offences Against the Person Act, which carries a maximum penalty of
life imprisonment. Only a few weeks ago, the 'Council for Social
Concern' - an umbrella group for the Irish Family League, *Viatores
Christi*, STOP (Society to Outlaw Pornography), the Christian Political
Action Movement, the Concerned Doctor Group, and Youth Alert -
called publicly on the Minister for Justice to apply this law to all
those involved in abortion referral to Britain. If socialist feminists were aware of such facts, would they seriously be able to support
a struggle which, in effect, amounts to the Catholic and irredentist
south attempting to seize a united Ireland where the oppression of
women would reach new dimensions?

We have heard rumours of the enthusiastic support expressed at the
recent Beyond the Fragments conference in Leeds for the movement of
the Polish strikers against the Party. Whatever is thought of the
Polish struggle, we hope that the British left does more to inform
itself about Catholic nationalism in Poland than it does in the case
of Ireland. When we see the portrait of the Pope being hung outside
the factory gates, or enclosed in the large pen used to sign the
agreement on 'free' trade unions, we do not leap for joy. Ireland
at the time of the Pope's visit was the closest most of us have come
to living under a totalitarian regime. No opposition at all was
possible. There was complete self-censorship of the media. Yet the
main reaction from comrades in Britain was one of minor amusement.
When somebody recently daubed a feminist slogan at the base of the
huge concrete phallus which the Pope left behind him in Dublin's
Phoenix Park, the newspaper reported: 'Gardai are investigating'.
Would they have bothered to investigate if the slogan had been
'H Block'? It was no accident that a Polish Pope came to visit
Ireland as, in effect, an official state visitor. Nor is it insig-
nificant that the ceremonies throughout the state mixed the imagery
of the Ku Klux Klan with the organization of the Nuremburg rallies.

Poland is the other European country where nationalism has always been predominantly a *Catholic* nationalism. While not wishing to deny that there has been and still is an anti-clerical wing in the republican movement, no one could seriously argue that this tendency has ever been dominant. Until recently, elements of the republican movement which took an interest in working class politics remained within the framework of nationalism. But, since the 1960s, the sudden mushrooming of an Irish working class in the Republic has produced a political movement that has completely burst the bounds of traditional nationalism. It may be embarrassing to the British left, but Sinn Fein The Workers' Party has grown faster than any other political party here in the last few years, and was crucial in the organization of the tax marches which brought a quarter of a million people onto the streets.

These points are borne out by looking at recent issues of left journals in Britain devoted to Ireland. *Scarlet Woman* has just produced an issue on women in Northern Ireland, which apparently sees no contradiction in printing nationalist positions without any consideration of the nation Northern Ireland is expected to join. *Head and Hand*, the review of socialist books associated with the Conference of Socialist Economists, is about to produce an issue with a special section on Ireland, again heavily weighted towards the North and the national question. The current issue of *Spare Rib* contains an interesting debate on the question of feminism and nationalism in the North, which we welcome; but we do object to the article being entitled 'Irish Women Speak', when it was not thought relevant to ask any women south of the border to contribute. As it happens, there has been a heated public debate among feminists here recently on whether or not the issue of the women in Armagh Gaol is a feminist one. The editorial comment at the end of the article informed us that 'the relevance of Ireland for British feminism' would be discussed at the socialist feminist conference. What about the relevance of British feminism for Ireland, sisters?

The Connolly Association, the CPGB's Irish organization, publishes a paper in London, the *Irish Democrat*. The Irish CP supports the Provisionals, and the British Party tends to follow suit. But when the *Irish Democrat* carried the banner headline 'Sile de Valera: The Voice of Young Ireland', one wonders just how far right the CP's nationalism will stretch. The headline hailed Sile de Valera's role in the replacement of Lynch by Haughey in 1979. Many other British groups similarly saw the success of Fianna Fail's right-wing as some sort of progressive development. Do we really have to spell out that Haugheyism is the diversionary use of nationalism to deflect and defeat the incredible surges of working class and feminist consciousness which have manifested themselves in recent years?

In nationalist ideology, the 'poor old woman' is an important image for the Irish nation. Her sons find glory in fighting the foreigner. In inevitable death, they become reunited with the mother. In concrete terms this means supporting the farmers of rural Ireland against the urban working class. It means defending the Irish nation, 'her strict sexual morality', against the onslaught of foreign immorality. It means allying with people like Meena Cribbins, president of Mna na hEireann, who believes that 'this whole campaign was planned internationally, [that] money was poured in from abroad and [that] the family planning clinics are the main agents of it. Their first attack was on the Irish language, they had to get rid of the language because that's the basis of any country; then they set up a group to remove corporal punishment from schools, they had to rear a generation that would know no control; then they were ready; their next step was contraception'.

There are many queries in this letter. This is because we would like you seriously to work out your position on Ireland, North and south. We believe that the key to doing this is waking up to the Republic's existence, to the nature of the state here, to the enormous changes taking place in working class and feminist politics and, consequently, in conceptions of national identity. If this were done, then it might be possible to look sanely at what is happening in the North without losing face over the abandonment of previous positions.

We are not grousing about being ignored. On the contrary, we would rather be forgotten than be on the receiving end of the kind of intervention in Irish politics that you support. But it is not only us who are affected; it is all progressive elements in the working class and women's movements here.

Yours,